The Law of Duress and Necessity

The language of duress and necessity is found in crime, tort and contract. This book explores those pleas, in both case law and theory, across the subject boundaries, and across jurisdictions. In doing so, it seeks to identify the lessons which each area of law can learn from the others, and to tease out common themes while demarcating important differences. The overall outcome is a law more coherent and understood in sharper detail.

This book considers the law of England and Wales, Australia, New Zealand, Hong Kong and Canada, as well as the American tortious defence of necessity.

Nathan Tamblyn is Senior Lecturer at the University of Exeter Law School.

The Law of Duress and Necessity

Crime, Tort, Contract

Nathan Tamblyn

Routledge
Taylor & Francis Group
LONDON AND NEW YORK

First published 2018 by Routledge

2 Park Square, Milton Park, Abingdon, Oxfordshire OX14 4RN
52 Vanderbilt Avenue, New York, NY 10017

Routledge is an imprint of the Taylor & Francis Group, an informa business

First issued in paperback 2019

British Library Cataloguing in Publication Data
A catalogue record for this book is available from the British Library

Library of Congress Cataloging in Publication Data
Names: Tamblyn, Nathan, author.
Title: The law of duress and necessity : crime, tort, contract / Nathan Tamblyn.
Description: Abingdon, Oxon [UK] ; New York : Routledge, [2017] | Includes bibliographical references and index.
Identifiers: LCCN 2017019503 | ISBN 9781138297999 (hbk)
Subjects: LCSH: Duress (Law) | Coercion. | Necessity (Law) | Contracts. | Torts. | Criminal law.
Classification: LCC K579.D8 T36 2017 | DDC 345/.04—dc23
LC record available at https://lccn.loc.gov/2017019503

ISBN: 978-1-138-29799-9 (hbk)
ISBN: 978-0-367-89083-4 (pbk)

Typeset in ITC Galliard Std
by Swales & Willis Ltd, Exeter, Devon, UK

To Dr Milner

With thanks for comments and support: Anne Barlow, Christine Bicknell, Charlotte Bishop, Alastair Hudson, Timon Hughes-Davies, Richard Edwards, Andrea Lista and Severine Saintier.

Contents

Table of cases

England and Wales

America

Australia

Hong Kong

New Zealand

Singapore

Prologue

The language of duress and necessity is found in crime, tort and contract. This book explores those pleas, in both case law and theory, across the subject boundaries, and across jurisdictions. In doing so, it seeks to identify the lessons which each area of law can learn from the others, and to tease out common themes while demarcating important differences. The overall outcome is a law more coherent and understood in sharper detail.

Comparative law

We could take any two legal systems and compare them. But we might be comparing apples with oranges. Is it meaningful to ask which is better? If instead our aim is to make our apples better apples (to stretch the analogy), then we need apposite comparators.

I have chosen England and Wales, Australia, New Zealand, Hong Kong and Canada. This is because the case law from these jurisdictions is interwoven. For example, in contract law, English cases refer to Australian and New Zealand and Hong Kong cases; Australian law discusses English law; New Zealand law cites English and Australian law; Canadian law considers English and Australian law; and Hong Kong law discusses English and Australian law. A similar pattern can be found in tort and criminal law.

Because the case law in these jurisdictions is interwoven, to understand any one tends to require a consideration of the others. This also means that the doctrines found in each jurisdiction are sufficiently close as to make the differences between them a source of fruitful comparison.

There are two further preliminary notes.

First, Hong Kong law features strongly in the contract law chapters. There is very little Hong Kong tort or criminal law relating to duress and necessity, nothing which calls for more than a footnote.

Second, in tort law, although the case law tends not to refer to it, the academic commentary principally makes comparison to qualified privilege in American law. Because of that, and also because the comparison is interesting and informative, we will also consider American law in that context.

Methodology

The aim is to produce the best account of the law of duress and necessity in crime, tort and contract, in terms of theory, and consistency with the case law. My conclusions are set out at the end of each chapter. Before arriving at those conclusions, each chapter sets out the 'evidence', i.e. the principal cases and the academic theory or commentary. (The principal cases are those identified as such by subsequent cases and academic commentary.) In each sub-section, the cases are usually taken chronologically, so that we can consider them in context, and so identify which ideas are novel or isolated and which are enduring. Within each chapter, as the evidence proceeds, it is discussed, both case law and theory, and comparisons are made between subject areas and jurisdictions. Each conclusion draws together all the analysis in that chapter.

The overall lessons, from all the chapters, are extracted and woven together in the Epilogue.

Finally, a word on chapter order. Tort law divides itself in two: intimidation and duress, which correlates strongly with contract law; and necessity, which interleaves with criminal necessity, which in turn merges into criminal duress. So that is the order adopted here: tortious intimidation and duress (the only chapter purely on tort law), then contract law, then necessity in tort, with its criminal correlates, finishing up with criminal duress. This presents the topics as a progression of contiguous case law and philosophical concepts.

1 Tort

Intimidation and duress by threats

In tort law, duress by threats can take two forms: a cause of action called intimidation, and potentially a defence. We start by considering intimidation. We then turn to the defence.

The two-party tort of intimidation has not enjoyed full-bodied scrutiny. The tendency has been to obscure and confuse it with the three-party tort of causing loss by unlawful means. There are also a number of areas of controversy: which unlawful acts support the plea of intimidation; whether that includes threatened breach of contract, or even threats of lawful acts; and whether there might be a defence of justification. We address all these points in this chapter. But first we must discuss the case law to see if we can at least identify the general shape of the tort of intimidation, and mark it out from the three-party tort of causing loss by unlawful means.

1.1 Intimidation: English case law

In *Gilbert v Stone*,[1] the defendant stood accused of entering a close and taking a gelding. He said that he did this only because he was threatened life and limb by twelve armed men. It was held no defence to trespass that a defendant acts from fear or threats of another, because the victim (the owner of the gelding) cannot sue the duressor, whereas the defendant can.

While *Gilbert v Stone* is usually taken as authority for the proposition that duress is not a tortious defence, Murphy says it necessarily also recognises that two-party intimidation is a cause of action, in asserting that the defendant can sue the duressor.[2]

Little attention was given to intimidation until *Rookes v Barnard*,[3] which was a three-party case. Union members A threatened employer B that they would strike, in breach of contract, unless B dismissed non-union employee C, which B did, lawfully. C's claim against A was made out. Threatening breach of contract was held to be unlawful means sufficient to support a tortious cause of action.

1 (1647) Aleyn 35, 82 ER 902; Style 72, 82 ER 539.
2 Murphy, 'Understanding Intimidation' (2014) 77 MLR 33, 46.
3 [1964] AC 1129.

Lord Devlin approved the definition of intimidation given in *Salmond on the Law of Torts*. The two-party version was expressed as follows: 'it is an actionable wrong intentionally to compel a person, by means of a threat of an illegal act, to do some act whereby loss accrues to him'. Lord Devlin said that 'the essence of the offence is coercion'. Note too, what should be obvious, that threats can be implicit as well as explicit.[4]

Then in *Morgan v Fry*,[5] Lord Denning MR gave the following definition, which has been regularly quoted in subsequent cases:

> There must be a threat by one person to use unlawful means (such as violence or a tort or a breach of contract) so as to compel another to obey his wishes: and the person so threatened must comply with the demand rather than risk the threat being carried into execution. In such circumstance the person damnified by the compliance can sue for intimidation.

In *JT Statford & Son Ltd v Lindley*,[6] in the Court of Appeal, Lord Denning MR said that a bare threat is not intimidation (though it may, for example, be assault). He said that there must be a threat, coupled with a demand, intended to coerce the threatened party into doing something he was otherwise unwilling to do.[7] Salmon LJ said that the essence of intimidation is damage caused by a coercive threat to do some unlawful act.[8]

In *News Group Newspapers Ltd v SOGAT 82*,[9] the judge said that the tort is not complete unless the person threatened succumbs to the threat and damage is suffered.[10] He also said that the threats must be serious and taken seriously. But better language would be: the threats were coercive (rather than serious). The judge also said, quoting from *Clerk and Lindsell*, that the complainant must be the person whom the accused intended to injure. But, we might note, this requirement of an intention to injure was not mentioned in the previous cases. And an intention to injure, in two-party cases, seems less apposite than an intention to coerce. Also, identifying an intention to injure, in the cases themselves, is sometimes lacking, sometimes forced.

In *News Group v SOGAT* itself, the accused, who were employees on strike, were threatening, among others, a fellow employee. They engaged in acts which made her feel frightened and unsafe. The judge held that intimidation was made out.

4 *Rookes v Barnard* [1964] AC 1129, 1209 (Lord Devlin). See too: *Godwin v Uzoigwe* [1993] Fam Law 65 (Stuart-Smith LJ); *Berezovsky v Abramovitch* [2011] EWCA Civ 153.

5 [1968] 2 QB 710, 724.

6 [1965] AC 269.

7 [1965] AC 269, 283–284.

8 [1965] AC 269, 302. On appeal, the House of Lords expressly refused to consider the tort of intimidation or endorse what was said in the Court of Appeal.

9 [1986] IRLR 337.

10 That loss is an essential ingredient is confirmed again in *Miller v Steiner* [2015] EWHC 2796 (Ch), [87], [98].

He said that their coercive threats were designed to persuade her to cease working for their mutual employer. But, we might note, an intention to persuade her to cease working for their employer is not necessarily the same as an intention to cause her loss. (They might have been content for her to find immediate work, as long as it was elsewhere.)

In *Godwin v Uzoigwe*,[11] the complainant was treated as a 'household drudge and virtually a slave'.[12] She was beaten if she did anything which displeased the accused, and she was forbidden from leaving the house or making friends. Intimidation was made out, and she was awarded £20k.

Dillon LJ, though finding it unnecessary to give a definition of intimidation, did recite the approach of the trial judge: after quoting from *Morgan v Fry*, the trial judge described the tort as 'intentional unlawful coercion', and as requiring a threat of unlawful conduct with the intention of compelling the other person to obey the accused's wishes, with that other person in fact coerced so to act. Here the stress is on intention to coerce, not to injure.

Yet Steyn LJ said that the tort of intimidation required that the accused should have acted with the intention of injuring the complainant. He said that, in this case, the accused must have foreseen that their coercive behaviour would be injurious to the complainant, which therefore involved an intentional infliction of harm.

Note that the complainant suffered no out of pocket loss. To use the language of personal injury, she suffered no special damages, only general damages. Other causes of action in that case were assault and breach of contract (the accused had promised her an education). To the extent that intimidation supplemented the money recoverable, or explained it on an alternative basis, the real complaint is injury to her dignity and feelings, as a result of being coerced into a degrading role. It has been recognised in a subsequent case that injury to feelings can sound in intimidation,[13] and there is academic support for this position too.[14] This also provides the better explanation for *News Group v SOGAT*: yes, the strikers wanted their colleague to stop working for their employer, but to achieve that, they intended to frighten and torment her, and for that she might recover substantial damages.

Thus, an intention to cause loss, if it is required as an element of two-party intimidation, should be understood not as restricted to financial loss, but also in terms of injury to feelings or dignity. And we can go further still. The intention to coerce is an intention to erode the complainant's autonomy. This too is an intention to harm. At this point, a separate and additional ingredient of an

11 [1993] Fam Law 65.

12 For another allegation of drudgery, see: *Gumpo v Church of Scientology Religious Education College Inc* [2000] CP Rep 38.

13 *Mbasogo v Logo Ltd* [2007] QB 846, [97].

14 McBride and Bagshaw, *Tort Law*, 5th edn (Harlow: Pearson, 2015) 720; Carty, *An Analysis of the Economic Torts*, 2nd edn (Oxford: Oxford University Press, 2010) 115; Giliker, 'A "New" Head of Damages: Damages for Mental Distress in the English Law of Torts' (2000) 20 LS 19.

intention to harm is redundant, because it is necessarily contained within the idea of an intention to coerce.

In *D&C Builders v Rees*,[15] the accused threatened not to pay, in breach of contract, what it owed to the complainant, unless the complainant accepted lesser payment. This the complainant did, because its financial pressures meant it needed to accept any money rather than none at all. The purported settlement agreement was set aside for duress. Lord Denning MR said that intimidation was also made out. The complainant recovered the outstanding amount, seemingly either under the original contract, alternatively as damages for intimidation.

Similarly, in *Kolmar Group AG v Traxpo Enterprises Pvt Ltd*,[16] the accused threatened not to supply goods, in breach of contract, unless the complainant agreed to pay a higher price. The complainant recovered the additional payment, either in restitution, the variation having been set aside for economic duress, alternatively as damages for intimidation.

We come now to the three-party case of *OBG Ltd v Allan*.[17] This recognised a new tort, expressed by the majority as follows: where A uses unlawful means against B, i.e. means which are actionable by B,[18] or would be if B suffered loss, which interfere with B's freedom to deal with C, thereby causing loss to C, as A intended, then C can sue A.

As for intending C loss, this is satisfied when that is A's desired end, or the means by which A enriches himself, especially where A's gain must be C's loss, but not where it is merely a foreseeable consequence of A's actions.[19]

All judges couched the discussion in terms of interfering with C's economic or business interests. This in itself indicates that the three-party tort is different from intimidation, where non-economic interests can be the subject of the claim, as in *Godwin v Uzoigwe*.[20] Further, for the three-party tort, Lord Hoffmann acknowledged in *OBG v Allan* that it need not involve any threats.[21] This is obviously right: unlawful means is a broad concept, and not restricted to threats. But it reveals a yet further difference from intimidation, which is solely about threats.

15 [1966] 2 QB 617.

16 [2010] EWHC 113 (Comm).

17 [2007] UKHL 21.

18 The need for means to be unlawful 'as against' B finds expression in other cases too: *Rookes v Barnard* [1964] AC 1129, 1207 (Lord Devlin); *News Group Newspapers Ltd v SOGAT 82* [1986] IRLR 337, [104] (Stuart-Smith J); *Godwin v Uzoigwe* [1993] Fam Law 65 (Stuart-Smith LJ); *Dawson v Bell* [2016] EWCA Civ 96, at first instance (annexed to the appeal judgment) at [125].

19 [2007] UKHL 21, [62]–[64] (Lord Hoffmann), [164]–[167] (Lord Nicholls). See too: Deakin and Randall, 'Rethinking the Economic Torts' (2009) 72 MLR 519, 542; Sales and Stilitz, 'Intentional Infliction of Harm by Unlawful Means' (1999) 115 LQR 411, 428.

20 Some authors argue that the three-party tort should not be restricted to a business context: Sales and Stilitz, 'Intentional Infliction of Harm by Unlawful Means' (1999) 115 LQR 411, 431; Stevens, *Torts and Rights* (Oxford: Oxford University Press, 2007) 189. For example, from Peel and Goudkamp, *Winfield & Jolowicz, Tort*, 19th edn (London: Sweet & Maxwell, 2014) 586, what if neighbour A threatens away potential purchasers B from the private house which C is trying to sell?

21 [2007] UKHL 21, [7].

Otherwise, Lord Hoffmann said that two-party intimidation may raise different issues.[22] A similar reservation had previously been made by Lord Reid in *Stratford v Lindley*.[23]

This reservation was seized upon in the subsequent conspiracy case of *Revenue and Customs Commissioners v Total Network SL*,[24] where the clear message was that, in two-party cases, the unlawful means do not have to be independently actionable by the complainant.[25] This finds further support in *OBG v Allan*, where Lord Nicholls advanced a minority view that 'unlawful means' embraces all acts which a person is not permitted to do, whether by the civil or criminal law, without the act necessarily being actionable by the party threatened.[26] That position in turn finds academic support,[27] and earlier judicial support in *Rookes v Barnard*, where Lord Reid spoke in terms of threatening to do what a party had no legal right to do,[28] and Lord Pearce spoke of threatening to use any means to which the party was not entitled by law.[29]

For two-party intimidation, it should not be required that what is threatened be actionable if it were carried out.[30] For example, the accused might threaten to harm the complainant's wife,[31] or anyone with whom the complainant has a strong bond of affection.[32] This could certainly be coercive. Indeed, we might note that both criminal duress (see Chapter 5) and contractual duress (see Chapter 3) can be pleaded when threats are made against anyone for whom the person threatened reasonably feels responsible. It should be no hindrance to a claim in intimidation that the complainant themselves could not sue for harm threatened against their family.

Summary

Intimidation in English case law tends to be expressed in terms of intentionally coercing the complainant, in order to procure a change in the complainant's behaviour against their wishes, by threatening otherwise to commit an unlawful act. The better view is probably that the unlawful act need not be

22 [2007] UKHL 21, [61].

23 *JT Stratford & Son Ltd v Lindley* [1965] AC 269, 325 (Lord Reid).

24 [2008] UKHL 19.

25 [2008] UKHL 19, [43–44] (Lord Hope), [99] (Lord Walker agreeing with Lords Hope and Mance), [124] (Lord Mance), [223] (Lord Neuberger).

26 [2007] UKHL 21, [162].

27 Neyers, 'The Economic Torts as Corrective Justice' (2009) 17 Torts LJ 162; Sappideen and Vines (eds), *Fleming's The Law of Torts*, 10th edn (Pyrmont NSW: Thomson Reuters, 2011) 786; Carty, 'The Modern Functions of the Economic Torts' (2015) 74 Cambridge LJ 261, 281.

28 [1964] AC 1129, 1169.

29 [1964] AC 1129, 1234.

30 In the Canadian case of *AI Enterprises Ltd v Bram Enterprises Ltd* [2014] SCC 12, the court said that there is no reason why 'unlawful means' must be the same in two-party intimidation and in three-party cases. See too: Lee, 'The Unlawful Means Tort in Canada' (2014) 130 LQR 559, 563.

31 McBride and Bagshaw, *Tort Law*, 5th edn (Harlow: Pearson, 2015) 693 n 90.

32 Murphy, 'Understanding Intimidation' (2014) 77 MLR 33, 41, 44.

independently actionable. There is also clear authority for the proposition that a threatened breach of contract is unlawful so as to give rise to a plea of intimidation. Indeed, the complainant might have a choice between, on the one hand, contractual duress and rescission, perhaps followed by restitution, or on the other hand, tortious intimidation and compensatory damages. Also, the complainant must comply with the duressor's demand, and this must cause loss or harm, which can include injury to feelings.

There is some suggestion that the duressor must have an intention to injure the complainant. I have argued that intention to injure is subsumed within an intention to coerce, since coercion involves harm to the complainant's dignity. This will be explored more fully below, when considering the rationale for intimidation. Otherwise, a separate ingredient of intention to injure confuses two-party intimidation with the three-party tort of causing loss by unlawful means, as we shall shortly discuss. But first, we shall consider how foreign case law approaches the tort of intimidation.

1.2 New Zealand case law

The leading case of two-party intimidation is *Huljich v Hall.*[33] There the accused threatened to distrain the complainant's cattle. The court acknowledged two-party intimidation, quoting from *Salmond on Torts*, and *Morgan v Fry*. The judge said that an essential ingredient is the intention to compel another person to take a particular course of action. The threat must include a 'do this or else' element. Intimidation was not made out in this case because, although the complainant was threatened, there was no attempt to force upon her a particular course of action to which she succumbed.

Intimidation was made out in *Dandoroff v Rogozinoff*,[34] where the complainant entered an agreement under threats of physical violence. The agreement was set aside, and the price paid by the complainant was recoverable in restitution. In addition, the court said that, as a result of the intimidation, the complainant had suffered humiliation, embarrassment, indignity, distress and disruption. (He collapsed in the street, was hospitalised, and there diagnosed with severe psychological stress.) But this was said to constitute 'personal injury by accident', and so governed by statute to the exclusion of any common law remedy. Nevertheless, the analysis recognises that intimidation might sound in damages for injury to dignity.

A recent case is *Outtrim v Li*,[35] whose reasoning is to be criticised. The court said that threats of illegal action do not found the tort of intimidation, citing *Huljich v*

33 [1973] 2 NZLR 279. Following *Rookes v Barnard*, two-party intimidation was previously acknowledged in the three-party case of *Pete's Towing Services Ltd v Northern (except Gisborne) Road Transport and Motor and Horse Drivers and their Assistants Industrial Union of Workers* [1970] NZLR 32.

34 [1988] 2 NZLR 588.

35 [2010] NZAR 282.

Hall, which said no such thing,[36] and when threats of unlawful acts are indisputably the basis on which all other courts have applied the tort of intimidation.

1.3 Australian case law

Two-party intimidation was recognised in *Northern Territory v Mengel*.[37] Again the court quoted from *Salmond on Torts*. But intimidation was not made out, because there was no threat, and certainly no threat to do anything unlawful, and no indication that the complainant's behaviour had been induced by any threat.

Intimidation was made out in *AS v Murray*.[38] There the accused demanded that the complainant pay a sum of money, which the complainant did, in order to avoid disclosure to his wife that he had joined an online dating agency. The court held that the tort of intimidation had been made out, quoting from *Morgan v Fry*. The unlawful means were identified as the statutory crime of blackmail. The price paid by the complainant was recovered as damages for intimidation.[39] He was also awarded exemplary damages.

1.4 Canadian case law

In *Central Canada Potash Co Ltd v Saskatchewan*,[40] the accused threatened to revoke the complainant's mining license unless it reduced its production, to comply with regulations designed to support the potash mining industry. Those regulations were held to be *ultra vires*. Intimidation was not made out. The accused, a government minister, was said to have no intention of injuring the complainant; rather, he sought compliance with legislation, as was his duty. But, we might say, if an intention to injure is not a necessary part of the tort, the better explanation for the case is that the accused did not threaten to do anything unlawful.[41]

36 The court in *Huljich v Hall* merely noted that a threat to behave illegally which in fact caused loss was not actionable without an intention to coerce. We might similarly note that, while an illegal act which causes loss was, without more, thought actionable in the Australian case of *Beaudesert Shire Council v Smith* (1966) 120 CLR 145, that case was subsequently overruled in *Northern Territory v Mengel* (1995) 185 CLR 307.

37 (1995) 185 CLR 307. Three-party 'intimidation', as in *Rookes v Barnard*, was previously recognised in Australia in *Sid Ross Agency Ltd v Actors & Announcers Equity Association of Australia* [1971] 1 NSWLR 760, and endorsed in *Construction, Forestry, Mining and Energy Union v 321 Boral Resources (Vic) Pty Ltd* [2014] VSCA 348, without admission that the tort in *OBG v Allan* is part of Australian law. As to which, see too: *Sanders v Snell* (1998) 196 CLR 329.

38 [2013] NSWSC 733.

39 The complainant had pleaded that the agreement, under which he paid the price, was to be set aside for duress, and the price recovered in unjust enrichment. This surely could have been an alternative basis, consistently with the English decision *Kolmar v Traxpo*.

40 [1979] 1 SCR 42. For a similar case, see: *Cheticamp Fisheries Co-op Ltd v Canada* [1995] NSJ No 127.

41 Just because regulations are subsequently declared *ultra vires* does not mean that what was previously done to bring about compliance with those regulations was done using unlawful means. See also *Roman Corp v Hudson's Bay Oil & Gas Co Ltd* [1973] SCR 820, discussed below.

The court said that there is no intimidation in two scenarios:

First, where a party to a contract asserts what he reasonably considers to be his contractual right and the other party, rather than contesting, follows a course of conduct on the assumption that the assertion of right can be maintained.

However, it is not clear what the threat is in such a situation. Where is the 'do this or else' demand? If the accused is saying, you must do this, it is your contractual duty, otherwise you are in repudiatory breach and I will terminate, that might count as a 'do this or else' demand. But if the complainant capitulates because it assumes that the accused is correct, then it is not the threat which caused compliance, but the complainant's shared belief as to its duties under the contract.

Second, the court said that there is no intimidation where the course of conduct which the accused seeks to induce is that which the complainant is obligated to follow. But the better way of approaching this is to say that the complainant has not suffered any loss as a result of the threat, since it did what it had to do anyway. In other words, the 'loss' was caused by the pre-existing duty.

However, the court went further and agreed with *Winfield & Jolowicz* that, in a two-party case, if what the accused threatens is breach of contract, then the complainant can have remedies only in contract law, and the tort of intimidation is not available. This position was recently repeated without demur in *AI Enterprises Ltd v Bram Enterprises Ltd*,[42] a three-party case. This is out of keeping with the English position in cases like *Kolmar v Traxpo*. We consider in detail below the relationship between intimidation and threatened breach of contract.

In the meantime, there are a number of cases of two-party intimidation. Successful cases include the following. In *Boychuk v Northwest Territories Housing Corp*,[43] threat of violence forced the complainant to abandon a building contract. He was awarded damages consisting of his share of the uncompleted contract, and punitive damages. In *Mintuck v Valley River Band No 63A*,[44] which quoted from the New Zealand case of *Huljich v Hall*, a farmer was intimidated into abandoning his farmland, for which he received compensation.

Intimidation was not successful in *Roman Corp v Hudson's Bay Oil & Gas Co Ltd*.[45] There, Canadian owners of a uranium mine planned to sell a large share of the company to an American business. The Prime Minister declared concern, and said that legislation might be introduced to prevent the transaction. As a result, the sale fell through. Intimidation was not made out. It was held that a declaration made in good faith by a minister as to government policy sought to be implemented by legislation was not a threat to do anything unlawful.

Other unsuccessful cases of intimidation include *Tran v University of Western Ontario*,[46] where the complainant failed to identify any threat, and *Robin Hood Management Ltd v Gelmich*,[47] where the complainant never capitulated to the threat.

42 [2014] SCC 12.
43 [1985] NWTJ No 47.
44 [1977] MJ No 14.
45 [1973] SCR 820.
46 [2015] ONCA 295.
47 [2016] SJ No 481.

Does intimidation apply only in a business context? In *Kelleher v Langille-Westhaver*,[48] a neighbourly dispute over an alleged dog attack saw the complainant threatened with violence if he reported the matter. The court said that intimidation could plainly not succeed because the complainant suffered no economic loss; all this took place in a private context, and not in a business context. That approach seems unduly narrow, and would provide no remedy for a situation like *Godwin v Uzoigwe* or *AS v Murray*.

In contrast, in *McIlvenna v 1887401 Ontario Ltd*,[49] the court said that a business context was not an essential ingredient of the tort after all. In that case, a preliminary hearing, the complainants had been threatened with violence and ejected from a bar because of the way they smelled, as a result of which they claimed to suffer damage to their dignity. This was a sufficient pleading to allow the claim to progress.

1.5 Hong Kong case law

In *Lin Man Yuan v Kin Ming Holdings International Ltd*,[50] the complainant was threatened with violence so that he might settle a dispute. As a result of the threat, he moved his family to safety, and suffered mental distress. He was awarded aggravated and exemplary damages for intimidation.

The court also said that intimidation can be made out simply when unlawful threats are made, intending to cause harm, and actually causing harm. But this means that the tort is no longer about coercion. Indeed, as the court itself accepted, it becomes a tort of intentional infliction of injury.

The Hong Kong court was drawing on cases like *Chang Ming Fang Jacqueline v Zhang Zi Qiang*.[51] There the complainant was threatened with violence in an unsuccessful attempt to get her to lend money to the accused. Intimidation was made out. Similarly, said the court in *Lin Man Yuan*, it cannot be right that a debt-collector can be sued only in intimidation if he succeeded in collecting the debt. So now, not only is coercion abandoned, but so too is the requirement of capitulation.

However, in *Chang Ming Fang*, the complainant also sued in the torts of assault and harassment. A one-off threat of imminent violence is sufficient to give rise to assault. Two threatening incidents can give rise to harassment. The unsuccessful debt-collector is addressed adequately by these torts.

***

The case law in England, Australia, New Zealand and Canada frames the tort of intimidation in terms of the accused intentionally coercing the complainant.

48 [2016] NSSC 200.
49 [2015] ONCA 830.
50 [2015] HKCU 1223.
51 [2009] HKCU 1293. See too: *Wong Wai Hing v Hui Wei Lee* [2000] HKCU 164, on appeal at [2001] 2 HKC 19.

In England, there is a less dominant suggestion that an intention to injure is also required. In contrast, in Hong Kong, the tort of 'intimidation' seemingly centres upon an intention to injure to such an extent that coercion of the 'do this or else' sort is no longer needed, nor is there any requirement that the complainant capitulate to the threat. The tort in Hong Kong has become something of a hybrid between a tort of intentional harm, and harassment.

Intention to injure arises for discussion because of a confusion between two-party intimidation and the three-party tort of (intentionally) causing loss by unlawful means. The three-party tort is also primarily concerned with economic loss, as we saw above, which perhaps further explains the uncertainty, seen most clearly in Canadian law, about whether intimidation extends beyond the economic context. So we need to clarify the relationship between intimidation and the three-party tort.

1.6 Intimidation and three-party cases

There is no such thing (any more) as three-party intimidation. The idea of three-party intimidation was given high visibility by *Rookes v Barnard*. But since *OBG v Allan*, this has been re-characterised as a tort of causing economic loss by unlawful means. This three-party tort would cover the following scenarios:

- A could beat up B to prevent B going to work for C.
- A could steal B's tools to prevent B from finishing their work for C.
- A could refuse, in actual breach of contract, to supply B with products which they need in order to fulfil their obligations to C.
- A could threaten to beat up B unless B eschews any dealings with C.

This tort is not three-party intimidation any more than it is three-party battery or three-party theft or three-party breach of contract. Rather, it is a three-party tort of causing loss by unlawful means. Those unlawful means can include battery or theft or breach of contract or intimidation. But in each of those cases, it is two-party battery or theft or breach of contract or intimidation. The three-party tort asks if there has been a two-party unlawful means. If there has been, and it affects a third party, a separate third-party tort is made out. Intimidation exists only in a two-party form, even if a three-party tort can piggyback onto it.

To emphasise this last point: some authors say that two-party intimidation is a variety of the three-party tort,[52] or should be.[53] But that is not right.

52 Peel and Goudkamp, *Winfield & Jolowicz, Tort*, 19th edn (London: Sweet & Maxwell, 2014) 586; *Clerk & Lindsell on Torts*, 21st edn (London: Sweet & Maxwell, 2014) [24–60], [24–69]; Carty, *An Analysis of the Economic Torts*, 2Bnd edn (Oxford: Oxford University Press, 2010) 115; Sappideen and Vines (eds), *Fleming's The Law of Torts*, 10th edn (Pyrmont NSW: Thomson Reuters, 2011) 784; Burns, 'Tort Injury to Economic Interests: Some Facets of Legal Response' (1980) 58 Can Bar Rev 134, 135; Sales and Stilitz, 'Intentional Infliction of Harm by Unlawful Means' (1999) 115 LQR 411, 435; Thomson, 'Redrawing the Landscape of the Economic Wrongs' [2008] Edin LR 267, 270. See too the New Zealand case of *Outtrim v Li* [2010] NZAR 282.

53 Deakin and Randall, 'Rethinking the Economic Torts' (2009) 72 MLR 519, 548.

The three-party tort requires that A use unlawful means as against B in order to injure C. If what A does is threaten B, for that to constitute unlawful means, the threat itself must be actionable. An actionable threat is precisely the tort of intimidation. In other words, intimidation is not a variety of the three-party tort, but a separate tort which can fulfil the three-party tort.[54] This point was acknowledged by Lord Hoffmann in *OBG v Allan*.[55]

As the three-party tort is currently formulated, intention to cause C loss is an essential ingredient. That must be right. When A harms B, then usually A incurs liability to B. And no doubt, a familiar consequence of B being harmed is that it hampers B's ability to deal with C (and other third parties). This alone should not mean that C (and others) can also sue A for the harm to B, actual or threatened. That would extend A's liability so far as to be unrealistic or unworkable. Alternatively, we might say that A's liability to C is precluded through doctrines like proximity and remoteness. So if C is to have a cause of action against A, arising out of A's dealings with B, then we must overcome remoteness, and avoid an open-ended liability to third parties, by making C a proximate and foreseeable victim. An intention to cause C loss does just that.

So intention to cause loss is an essential ingredient in the three-party tort of causing loss by unlawful means. But it does not follow that it must also be an essential ingredient in two-party intimidation. On the contrary, it should not be an ingredient in intimidation, as discussed above in the context of *Godwin v Uzoigwe* and *News Group v SOGAT*. Further, it is notable that cases like *Rookes v Barnard* and *Morgan v Fry*, which set the template for the tort of intimidation, do not resort to an intention to cause injury. That appears to have crept in later, by an unreasoned acceptance of a definition given in *Clerk & Lindsell*, no doubt augmented by a confusion between the three-party tort, and two-party intimidation.

Let us also contrast intimidation with a person who merely declares that they will act in a certain way. That is not threatening. We might not want them to act that way, and them doing so might cause us grief in one form or another. But it is not a threat, in the legal context of intimidation, if their declaration contains no 'or else' element. Without providing the complainant with a choice of behaviour which could change the outcome, the accused is not seeking to coerce or railroad the complainant into acting non-autonomously.

Whereas, there is no intended coercion of C in the three-party tort. A is acting upon B in order to harm C. A is not making any threat to C. A is not trying to change C's behaviour. A is not giving C any alternative options. A is simply trying to inflict harm on C indirectly. If A was threatening C – 'do this or else I will inflict harm on you indirectly through B' – that would be a straightforward two-party intimidation.

In short, intimidation requires a demand, but not an intention to injure or cause loss; whereas the three-party tort involves no demand of the third party, but needs an intention to cause them loss. The two torts are different.

54 Murphy, 'Understanding Intimidation' (2014) 77 MLR 33, 43.

55 [2007] UKHL 21, [49].

1.7 The rationale for a tort of intimidation

Some say that the tort of intimidation is about maintaining the integrity of economic competition by setting limits to rivalrous behaviour.[56] But that fails to account for cases which involve no economic competition, like *Godwin v Uzoigwe* and *AS v Murray.*

Some say that the threat to commit unlawful acts is itself equated to, or coloured by, the unlawful acts themselves,[57] which explains why the threats are actionable. But that seems a sleight of hand: threatening to do something is not the same as doing it, and intimidation almost always involves the accused not doing what they threatened (because the complainant capitulated). And as Dietrich says, it is the threat to do something which forces the outcome, an outcome which would otherwise not have arisen had the duressor acted without threatening.[58]

Instead, the essence of intimidation is coercion, as Lord Devlin said in *Rookes v Barnard.* It involves compelling another to obey one's wishes, as Lord Denning said in *Morgan v Fry*, repeated in the New Zealand case of *Huljich v Hall* and the Australian case of *AS v Murray.* Similar supportive statements can be found in *Stratford v Lindley* and *Godwin v Uzoigwe.* Coercion needs policing because of its potential to interfere with autonomy.[59] Autonomy is something we tend to value, for the following reasons:

For a start, autonomy is central to Kant. Controversy remains about how precisely to read Kant in all his technical complexity. But the following general account arises from a combined reading of *The Metaphysics of Morals* and the *Groundwork*, and it has intuitive appeal.

Kant urges us to behave rationally, making choices free from the slavery of unthinking desires and inclinations. If we can identify a maxim or rule of behaviour which could be adopted by everyone without logical contradiction (the formula of universal law), then, he says, we can have confidence that such a rule is grounded in or cognised by reason rather than base or selfish desire.

Further, he says, humans have an inner dignity or innate worth, in particular because of the shared capacity for noble reason, which means that they are ends in themselves and not merely things to be used by others (the formula of humanity).

Or, to put it another way, if we value the ends we have chosen for ourselves, then we must esteem the capacity which has chosen those ends.[60] And, if we are behaving rationally, rather than from a blinkered selfishness, then, following the formula of universal law, if we esteem the capacity for rationality in ourselves, we must also esteem it in others. As O'Neill says, the intuitive appeal in any test

56 Deakin and Randall, 'Rethinking the Economic Torts' (2009) 72 MLR 519.

57 Carty, *An Analysis of the Economic Torts*, 2nd edn (Oxford: Oxford University Press, 2010) 121; Murphy, 'Understanding Intimidation' (2014) 77 MLR 33, 38.

58 Dietrich, 'Lawful Coercive Threats and the Infliction of Harm' (2000) 8 Torts LJ 187.

59 Murphy, 'Understanding Intimidation' (2014) 77 MLR 33.

60 Wood, 'Humanity as End in Itself', in Guyer (ed), *Kant's Groundwork of the Metaphysics of Morals: Critical Essays* (Lanham, MD: Rowman & Littlefield, 1998) 176. See also: Korsgaard, *Creating the Kingdom of Ends* (Cambridge: Cambridge University Press, 1996) 121–123.

of universality is that, if we are to act morally, we should not single ourselves out for special treatment.[61] Indeed, whatever our starting point, whether Kant or anything else, however we define our own self-identity, we ought to allow the same for everyone else.[62] It erodes the stability of what we value in ourselves if, inconsistently, we deny it to others. And once that inconsistency is noticed, it hangs as a persistent shadow, a reminder that we cannot have full confidence that our behaviour is morally without blemish.

To return to Kant, when we interact with other people, and our behaviour is inevitably circumscribed by rules, if those rules are grounded in reason, it means that those rules are free from selfish desires and personal viewpoints. They are universal rules each of us would have chosen using our own capacity for reason. In this way, though we are governed by rules, we still act with autonomy, because they are rules we prescribe for ourselves. They are not imposed upon us by others. All of which in turn creates an environment which mutually recognises that human inner worth.

Similar notions might be derived from a comparison with Rousseau and *The Social Contract*, said to have influenced Kant.[63] The idea of political autonomy might be expressed as follows: citizens, though bound by laws, might still be considered free when those laws are of their own making, rather than imposed upon them by other parties. So too with Kant: moral behaviour might be governed by maxims, but if they are universal and derived through reason, they are rules we would all choose for ourselves.

Mill was unpersuaded by the practical reality of so-called self-government. Instead, in a democracy, he feared the 'tyranny of the majority'. In *On Liberty*, he was concerned to carve out, for individuals, spheres of freedom from society's interference. Hence the harm principle: the only purpose for which power can be rightfully exercised over any member of a community against his will is to prevent harm to others. But the goal is again to protect individual autonomy.

Autonomy, he says, allows for experiments in living, that we might find better ways, or if not, affirm why our current ways are worth keeping. Autonomy also allows us to develop our individual capacities, rather than acting as mere automatons. Further:[64]

> It is not by wearing down into uniformity all that is individual in themselves, but by cultivating it and calling it forth … that human beings become a noble and beautiful object of contemplation; and as the works partake the character of those who do them, by the same process human life also becomes rich, diversified, and animating … strengthening the tie which binds every individual to the race, by making the race infinitely worth belonging to.

61 O'Neill, 'Consistency in Action', in Guyer (ed), *Kant's Groundwork of the Metaphysics of Morals: Critical Essays* (Lanham, MD: Rowman & Littlefield, 1998) 117.

62 See too: Dworkin, *The Theory and Practice of Autonomy* (New York: Cambridge University Press, 1988) 30–32.

63 Reath, 'Legislating the Moral Law' (1994) 28 Nous 435; Robert and Cureton, 'Kant's Moral Philosophy' (2016) *Stanford Encyclopedia of Philosophy*.

64 Mill, *On Liberty* (1859) ch III.

Thus, we can conclude as follows. Coercion is wrong to the extent that it forces a complainant to change their behaviour for the selfish reasons of the accused. This denies the complainant the freedom to choose their own goals. It also denies them the dignity of an equal status, because it fails to respect them as having the capacity to choose such goals. And it deprives them of the chance to use or develop that capacity, when doing so can entail personal fulfilment, perhaps social utility, even inspiration.

The tort of intimidation recognises that coercion is wrong. But we still need to identify the ingredients which mark out unlawful coercion from legitimate if forceful persuasion. This we will do over the following sections by considering: threats of unlawful acts in general; threats of breach of contract in particular; and threats of lawful acts.

1.8 Unlawful acts

Not all coercion should be legally actionable. Like it or not, we are all of us liable to be persuaded, by subtle or strong-arm tactics, to behave contrary to how we might otherwise have chosen, by teachers or politicians or corporations or doctors and so on. Sometimes we even come to be grateful.

Causing loss might be an intrinsic part of what makes a threat or action coercive. In other words, were it not for the loss, we might otherwise have been able to ignore the attempted coercion. Nevertheless, the fact that coercion foreseeably or intentionally causes us loss is not enough. For example, it might be only by threatening an end to pocket money that a parent convinces a child to do their homework. That should not be actionable. Nor should it be tortious for a customer to boycott a retailer whose products are tested on animals or made in sweatshops. We still need something more.

One bright line is where the duressor threatens to do something unlawful. So, if someone does an unlawful act, consequences follow, like criminal or tortious liability. If someone threatens an unlawful act, and for the purpose of being coercive, that engages the tort of intimidation. To this extent, the tort of intimidation polices coercive activity, by drawing a line consistent with the rest of the law: it outlaws the leveraging of activities which other areas of the law have already proscribed.

What counts as unlawful? In the three-party tort of causing loss by unlawful means, in *OBG v Allan*, it was held that what A does to B must be independently actionable by B. But that does not help. One of the independently actionable things which A can do to B is to commit the tort of intimidation. That does not tell us what the ingredients of intimidation are.

Nevertheless, we might say, by analogy, that for intimidation, what the accused must threaten is, not perhaps actionable, because after all the accused has not carried it out but only threatened to, but at least amenable to a *quia timet* injunction restraining the threatened conduct. I suggest that is too narrow. For example, the accused might threaten to harm the complainant's wife. Or the accused might threaten to harm himself. We know well that these circumstances can be deliberately coercive, because they have grounded the defence of duress in criminal law (see Chapter 5). But in neither case would the complainant be able to obtain an injunction. And while it might be possible for the wife (but not the husband) to obtain an injunction in the first scenario, still there could be no injunction restraining the accused's own self-harm in the second scenario.

Lord Devlin had this to say on remedies for intimidation.[65] If the complainant resists the threat, he might obtain an injunction. If the threat is carried out, he might sue for damages. But if he complies, then he cannot sue on the threatened wrong, because that wrong has not happened, nor can he obtain an injunction against the execution of a threat he has already avoided through submission.

And there is yet a further problem here. An injunction is anyway a discretionary remedy. It cannot be used as the foundation for a non-discretionary tort. In other words, there is a three-way difference between: first, a court saying that the facts have not been made out to support a tortious cause of action; second, a court saying that the facts have been made out, so the cause of action is fulfilled, but the claimant is to be restricted to the remedies available as of right, with the additional discretionary remedies denied in this case; third, a court saying that the facts have been made out, but exercising its discretion to deny that this amounts to a cause of action in this case. The first and second are standard fare. But the third is unprecedented and objectionable. Yet it would be the position if the tort of intimidation responded only to situations where a discretionary remedy would be granted. Imagine if a breach of contract gave a cause of action only according to the court's discretion. In effect there would be no rule of law in such a context, only the discretionary exercise of power.

So what counts as unlawful for the tort of intimidation should not be measured by whether it would be actionable by the complainant, or amenable to a *quia timet* injunction. Simply put, the accused should not be allowed to leverage any illegal activity in order to coerce the complainant.

Thus, if the accused threatens to commit a crime, it should not matter that the crime gives no private cause of action. (There is otherwise no academic consensus on this point.[66]) What is threatened is certainly unlawful, and, as I have argued above, what is threatened ought not to be independently actionable by the complainant anyway. Sales and Stilitz say that the intention to cause harm makes up any shortfall.[67] But I do not think that helps, since the essence of the tort is not intentional harm (despite Hong Kong case law), but rather coercion. Any illegality should suffice. This is also in keeping with contractual duress, which makes no mention of the need for what is done or threatened to be otherwise independently actionable (see Chapter 3).

65 *Rookes v Barnard* [1964] AC 1129, 1208.

66 No: Stevens, *Torts and Rights* (Oxford: Oxford University Press, 2007) 190. Yes: Carty, *An Analysis of the Economic Torts*, 2nd edn (Oxford: Oxford University Press, 2010) 113; Weir, 'Chaos or Cosmos? *Rookes*, *Stratford* and the Economic Torts' [1964] Cambridge LJ 225, 232.

67 Sales and Stilitz, 'Intentional Infliction of Harm by Unlawful Means' (1999) 115 LQR 411, 422.

However, incidental illegality can be irrelevant: to adapt Heydon, if one person threatens another in an illegally parked car, that illegality is irrelevant.[68] Elias and Ewing even plausibly suggest that, if the accused threatens to act in breach of contract, when he could have so acted without breach, that threatened illegality should again be irrelevant.[69] More generally, the tort of intimidation can take a lead here from contract law, which is familiar with the idea of overlooking any illegality which lacks centrality or gravity in the context of the claim.[70]

So at this point we might say that any threatened crime or tort ought to support a plea of intimidation – as long as what is threatened is intended to coerce, and does in fact coerce. There are two further topics. What about threatened breaches of contract? And what about threatened lawful acts? We shall take each of those in turn, below.

1.9 Threatened breach of contract

There are a wealth of contract cases which speculate on the relationship between contractual duress and tort.

In *The Universe Sentinel*,[71] Lord Diplock said that economic duress is not itself a tort, but the facts might equally give rise to a tort, in which case the complainant might have an alternative remedy in damages. Lord Scarman said that once duress was proved, not only does that render a contract voidable, but also it is actionable as a tort. In *The Evia Luck*,[72] Lord Goff alluded to the issue of whether duress was also tortious, without offering a final opinion. Dillon LJ referred to the 'tort of economic duress' in *Alec Lobb (Garages) Ltd v Total Oil (Great Britain) Ltd*,[73] as did Mance J in *Huyton SA v Peter Cremer GmbH & Co*,[74] while the court referred to the 'wrong of duress' in the Hong Kong case of *Lau Ying Wai v Emperor Regency International Ltd.*[75]

In *Banque Keyser Ullmann SA v Skandia (UK) Insurance Co Ltd*,[76] the court said that the remedy for duress was rescission, not damages. But the point was thought open in the later case of *Ruttle Plant Ltd v Secretary of State for the*

68 Heydon, 'The Defence of Justification in Cases of Intentionally Caused Economic Harm' (1970) 20 U Toronto LJ 139, 171.

69 Elias and Ewing, 'Economic Torts and Labour Law: Old Principles in New Liabilities' [1982] Cambridge LJ 321, 341.

70 *ParkingEye Ltd v Somerfield Stores Ltd* [2012] EWCA Civ 1338. For example, in *St John Shipping Corp v Joseph Rank Ltd* [1957] 1 QB 267, a ship owner who overloaded his ship contrary to statute could still sue for freight; and in *Shaw v Groom* [1970] 2 QB 504, a landlord who committed an offence by failing to give his tenant a rent book could still sue for rent. The latest case on illegality is *Patel v Mirza* [2016] UKSC 42, which gives a comprehensive review of the doctrine.

71 *Universe Tankships Inc of Monrovia v International Transport Workers Federation, The Universe Sentinel* [1983] 1 AC 366, 385, 400.

72 *Dimskal Shipping Co SA v International Transport Workers Federation, The Evia Luck* [1992] 2 AC 152, 165.

73 [1985] 1 WLR 173, 177.

74 [1999] 1 Lloyd's Rep 620, 638.

75 [2015] HKEC 53, [11].

76 [1990] 1 QB 665, 780, a point not made on appeal at [1991] 2 AC 249.

Environment and Rural Affairs.[77] In *Bank of India v Riat*,[78] the judge said that it was well settled that duress is not a tort, citing *The Universe Sentinel*, where of course Lord Scarman said the opposite. In *Kolmar v Traxpo*,[79] as we have seen, the judge awarded the same money remedy, either in restitution following rescission, or as damages for intimidation.

In Australia, in *Equiticorp Financial Services*,[80] the judge said that duress yielded remedies either of rescission, or damages 'where the economic duress is a tort', citing in support Lord Scarman in *The Universe Sentinel*. In *Electricity Generation Corp v Woodside Energy Ltd*,[81] McLure P left open the question whether economic duress was also part of tort law. Murphy JA said that economic duress was not itself a tort, but he acknowledged that intimidation was 'another tort'. In the New Zealand case of *Dandoroff v Rogozinoff*,[82] the guarantee was set aside for duress of the person. On the facts, the court also found a number of other torts, including battery and intimidation.

From a tort perspective, the relationship is much clearer.

Canadian case law doubts that threatened breach of contract can support a plea of intimidation. But English case law is certain that it can, ever since *Rookes v Barnard*. That was a three-party case, where A threatened B with breach of contract in order to harm C. We now know from *OBG v Allan* that this represents a separate three-party tort of causing loss by unlawful means. The unlawful means in *Rookes v Barnard* was a threat, and hence the tort of intimidation. What was threatened was a breach of contract, and C's claim was made out. In other words, although *Rookes v Barnard* was a three-party case, the facts reveal that threats to breach a contract support the unlawful means of two-party intimidation.

Some authors, though not all,[83] express concern that this produces a coincidence of actions in tort and contract. They say that a complainant, faced with a threatened breach of contract, should be restricted to contract remedies[84] and not avoid contract rules on remoteness which limit the extent of damages.[85] They say that, if threatened with violence, tortious remedies

77 [2007] EWHC 2870 (TCC), [85].

78 [2014] EWHC 1775 (Ch), [55].

79 [2010] EWHC 113.

80 *Equiticorp Financial Services (NSW) Ltd v Equiticorp Financial Services* (NZ) Ltd (1992) 29 NSWLR 260, (1992) 9 ACSR 199, 232.

81 [2013] WASCA 36, [23], [150–[151].

82 [1988] 2 NZLR 588.

83 Elias and Ewing, 'Economic Torts and Labour Law: Old Principles in New Liabilities' [1982] Cambridge LJ 321, 334; McKendrick, 'The Further Travails of Duress', in Burrows and Rodger (eds), *Mapping the Law: Essays in Memory of Peter Birks* (Oxford: Oxford University Press, 2006) 198; Sales and Stilitz, 'Intentional Infliction of Harm by Unlawful Means' (1999) 115 LQR 411, 424.

84 Carty, *An Analysis of the Economic Torts*, 2nd edn (Oxford: Oxford University Press, 2010) 119; Burns, 'Tort Injury to Economic Interests: Some Facets of Legal Response' (1980) 58 Can Bar Rev 134, 136.

85 Deakin et al., *Markesinis and Deakin's Tort Law*, 7th edn (Oxford: Oxford University Press, 2013).489; Sales and Stilitz, 'Intentional Infliction of Harm by Unlawful Means' (1999) 115 LQR 411, 423; Hoffmann, '*Rookes v Barnard*' (1965) 81 LQR 116, 127–128.

might not provide adequate protection,[86] but if threatened with breach of contract, contract remedies are sufficient.[87] But if a preventative injunction, or compensatory damages, are not adequate in the first scenario, why assume they will be adequate in the second?

Here are some examples of when contractual remedies might not be sufficient.

First, to adapt *D&C Builders v Rees*, if the complainant accepts a lesser sum rather than nothing, to stave off bankruptcy, but unsuccessfully because the lesser sum was insufficient after all, the true loss flowing from the bankruptcy is more than simply the unpaid balance of the contractual debt.[88]

Second, in *Halpern v Halpern*,[89] a Jewish family sought to settle an inheritance dispute by referring the matter to a Jewish arbitration. A settlement agreement was reached which included a term requiring all documents to be destroyed. The complainant later said that the settlement agreement was procured by duress. The court accepted that rescission of the agreement could be possible. But since the documents could not be reinstated, if they had been destroyed, that might further prejudice the complainant. In which case, said the court, a suitable remedy in equity or tort might be needed to do justice.

Third, more generally, the very existence of the doctrine of contractual duress is an admission that capitulating to the demand is sometimes necessary because other contract remedies, like damages for breach, would not prove sufficient. That is why contractual duress provides yet further remedies, like rescission, which in turn clears the way for a claim in unjust enrichment for restitution.

And yet, if a complainant capitulates to the demand, thereby avoiding any threatened breach, so that the original contract is performed after all, there is nothing to rescind. The remedy for any loss must be in tort.

Fourth, an accused might threaten breach of contract unless the complainant acts for the benefit of a third party, like joining a union or donating to charity. If the complainant does so, the contract with the accused goes through performed as originally agreed. There is nothing to set aside as regards the accused. The complainant might be able to set aside any contract, for example with the union, if the union had actual knowledge of the threat, in which case the complainant might also be able to recover their membership fees in restitution. But they will have no remedy if the union or charity had no such knowledge. In this case, the only remedy is against the accused, in intimidation, seeking compensation for any loss.

There is anyway no conflict between contract and tort when what is threatened is breach of contract, for the following reasons:

86 Peel and Goudkamp, *Winfield & Jolowicz, Tort*, 19th edn (London: Sweet & Maxwell, 2014) 587.
87 Carty, *An Analysis of the Economic Torts*, 2nd edn (Oxford: Oxford University Press, 2010) 119; Burns, 'Tort Injury to Economic Interests: Some Facets of Legal Response' (1980) 58 Can Bar Rev 134, 136.
88 Murphy, 'Understanding Intimidation' (2014) 77 MLR 33, 53.
89 [2007] EWCA Civ 291.

(1) In the three-party scenario, where A breaches their contract with B, even if C can sue for the three-party tort of causing loss by unlawful means, only B can sue on the contract. Thus A faces two actions, one in contract with B, for the breach of contract, and one in tort with C, for intentionally inflicting harm indirectly. There is no inconsistency here or overlay.

(2) In the three-party scenario, where A threatens to breach their contract with B, then B can sue in intimidation, and C can sue for the three-party tort of causing loss by unlawful means. A faces two sets of liability in two different torts. Again there is no inconsistency or overlay.

(3) In the two-party scenario, where the accused simply breaches their contract with the complainant, then the complainant can sue in contract – and only in contract, or at least, not in intimidation, because there has been no threat. Whether there is a two-party tort of intentionally causing loss, and whether such a tort can be grounded on actual breach of contract, and whether that would be objectionable for giving concurrent actions in both contract and tort arising out of a breach of contract, nevertheless that has nothing to do with the separate tort of intimidation, which requires a coercive threat.

(4) In the two-party scenario, if the accused threatens to breach their contract:

First, the threat of breach might itself be an actual breach, i.e. an anticipatory repudiatory breach (sometimes also known as a renunciation). The complainant could accept the repudiation, terminate the contract, and sue for breach. Or the complainant could affirm the contract, and sue for breach. But either way, the complainant has resisted the demands and sued upon an actual breach. If the complainant resists the demands, there is no tort of intimidation, because any threat had no causative effect (it did not induce submission by the complainant).

Second, and alternatively, the complainant, fearful of the breach being carried out, complies with the accused's demands. The breach never happens. The complainant can sue in the tort of intimidation.

Now it might also be, in this last instance, that the complainant has a contractual remedy as well. For example, if the accused threatens, in breach of contract, not to supply the complainant unless the price is raised, and the complainant accedes to the demand, this might constitute contractual duress. In this case, the variation can be set aside, and any overpayment subsequently recovered as restitution through an action in unjust enrichment. Note, however, that this is not suing upon any breach of contract. It is rescission and restitution, not compensatory damages. The only route here to compensatory damages is not through breach of contract, because the contract has been rescinded (so there is no contract to sue upon), but through the tort of intimidation, so once more there is still no inconsistency or overlay. Indeed, either route might lead to the same outcome, as cases like *Kolmar v Traxpo* demonstrate. Nor is this approach unprecedented. For example, with misrepresentation, a complainant might rescind, or sue under statute for a tortious measure of compensatory damages.

A final objection concerns affirmation.

In contract law, the complainant may be taken to have affirmed the contract, despite any initial duress, even simply by the passage of time since the duress wore off.[90] This should also preclude any claim in tort. The principal value of contracts is their reliability. If a contract is tainted by duress, and so voidable, its status needs to be confirmed in order to salvage any of the contract's value. This means that, once the complainant has regained their autonomy, they must elect whether to rescind – and if they do not, they are taken to have affirmed the contract. The contract must then be carried out. It would undermine the confirmed status of the contract if the duressee could breach it, saying that they were, after all, pressured into the affirmation, so that any damages they might have to pay for breach would anyway be recoverable by them in turn for the initial intimidation.[91]

But this result can easily be avoided. For a start, the complainant could be taken to have waived their right to claim in tort, in the sense of having chosen instead the inconsistent rights of an affirmed contract.[92] But more straightforward than that, it can be said that no claim in tort even arises: affirmation is deemed by law to be, by its nature, a free choice, even if sometimes an implicit choice. Which means that it was the complainant's free choice after all, and not the threats, which caused the affirmed validity of the contract.[93] If the threats have no causative effect, there is no tort of intimidation.

In short, intimidation can encompass threatened breach of contract. It produces no inconsistency or tension with contract law. And a threatened breach of contract is, after all, a threat to do something unlawful.

1.10 Threats of lawful action

Why should threats of lawful action be tortious? When they amount to an abuse of rights. This claim we consider in the first part of this section. Then we discuss some Victorian case law which appears to stand in the way.

Abuse of rights

We know from criminal law that a lawful threat might support a plea of duress: for example, when the duressor threatens to harm themselves unless the duressee complies. So might intimidation respond to threats of lawful acts when made for the purpose of being coercive? But again, as we have seen, coercion alone cannot

90 *North Ocean Shipping Co v Hyundai Construction Co (The Atlantic Baron)* [1979] QB 705.

91 Peel and Goudkamp, *Winfield & Jolowicz, Tort*, 19th edn (London: Sweet & Maxwell, 2014) 588 n 143; McBride and Bagshaw, *Tort Law*, 5th edn (Harlow: Pearson, 2015) 702; *Clerk & Lindsell on Torts*, 21st edn (London: Sweet & Maxwell, 2014) [24–70].

92 Giliker, *Tort*, 5th edn (London: Sweet & Maxwell, 2014) [16–042].

93 With torts other than intimidation, it is conceptually consistent, albeit factually unlikely, for a complainant who contracted under duress of the person or of goods, to affirm the contract but still want compensation for personal injury or detention of goods. Affirmation of the contract need not affect their ability to sue for battery or conversion.

be enough: a parent can threaten to withhold a child's allowance, or a customer to boycott a retailer. Something more is needed. Usually that something more is a threat to act unlawfully. If lawful act intimidation is also to be recognised, the best candidate for that something more is malice, in its natural meaning of spite or ill-will. This is because hiding behind the lawfulness of acts in order to act maliciously is an abuse of rights.

In *Rookes v Barnard*, Lord Reid said that a party can threaten to do what he has a legal right to do.[94] And in *OBG v Allan*, Lord Hoffmann was against the idea of looking at the accused's motive.[95] But more recently, the courts have been open to the idea that threats which are not unlawful might still be 'illegitimate',[96] no doubt echoing the same openness expressed in contractual duress cases (see Chapter 3).

Some authors see little possibility of tort liability for lawful act duress.[97] And for good reason, says Stevens: by relying on unlawfulness, the court does not have to stray into policy questions about whether a particular course of action, though lawful, is nevertheless illegitimate or unfair.[98] Weir says that restricting the tort to unlawful means results in clarity, when other criteria, like abuse of rights, are too vague to be an appropriate constraint on liberty of behaviour.[99]

However, there is no such uncertainty at this point. Rather, there is clarity: the accused cannot act maliciously. Abuse of rights is the explanation for why that might be. The courts do not have to decide whether the accused's behaviour is unfair or abusive, all things considered. All they have to do is make a factual finding of malice.

Other authors are more positive.[100] *Fleming* says that, just because unlawful conduct is not cured by good intentions, it does not follow that lawful conduct is unaffected by bad intentions.[101] Hoffmann says that we can ensure civilised behaviour by prohibiting unlawful means, or unlawful purposes.[102] Some say that the three-party tort is already best understood as an example of abuse of rights.[103]

94 *Rookes v Barnard* [1964] AC 1129, 1169.

95 *OBG Ltd v Allan* [2007] UKHL 21, [14] (Lord Hoffmann).

96 *Berezovsky v Abramovitch* [2011] EWCA Civ 153, [5]; *Dawson v Bell* [2016] EWCA Civ 96.

97 Peel and Goudkamp, *Winfield & Jolowicz, Tort*, 19th edn (London: Sweet & Maxwell, 2014) 588; Sappideen and Vines (eds), *Fleming's The Law of Torts*, 10th edn (Pyrmont NSW: Thomson Reuters, 2011) 786.

98 Stevens, *Torts and Rights* (Oxford: Oxford University Press, 2007) 189–190.

99 Weir, *Economic Torts* (Oxford: Clarendon Press, 1997) lecture 3.

100 Fridman, 'Malice in the Law of Torts' (1958) 21 MLR 484. Goodhart says that sooner or later English law will need to follow German law, and recognise that the exercise of a right which can have no useful purpose except the infliction of injury is unlawful: *Essays in Jurisprudence and the Common Law* (Cambridge: Cambridge University Press, 1931) 37.

101 Sappideen and Vines (eds), *Fleming's The Law of Torts*, 10th edn (Pyrmont NSW: Thomson Reuters, 2011) 783.

102 Hoffmann, '*Rookes v Barnard*' (1965) 81 LQR 116, 118.

103 Neyers, 'The Economic Torts as Corrective Justice' (2009) 17 Torts LJ 162; Dietrich, 'Lawful Coercive Threats and the Infliction of Harm' (2000) 8 Torts LJ 187.

I have made the same argument for lawful act conspiracy.[104] And Murphy says that in two-party intimidation, if what is threatened is lawful, that might also be an abuse of rights.[105]

So let us explore in more detail the notion of abuse of rights.

In English law, abuse of rights is best understood, not as a free-standing doctrine, but as an underlying rationale in various contexts.[106] It is a concept found in other jurisdictions, where, although its precise requirements vary, a common theme is that abuse of rights involves the malicious infliction of harm.[107]

Schauer questions whether it is appropriate to call it 'abuse' of rights.[108] If we were omniscient, he says, we could prescribe all rights in absolute terms, with a full list of their exceptions. But since we cannot predict the future, we need flexibility. So certain behaviour, he says, is presumptively lawful, until it is taken too far – at which point we call it an abuse of rights. But what we really mean, he says, is that there is no longer any right to behave that way.

Be that as it may, it still leaves the question: when is a right taken too far? For abuse of rights, the best answer seems to be when it involves the malicious infliction of harm.

No doubt there are economic arguments against the malicious infliction of harm. For example, say Liebermann and Syrquin, if money demanded as the price of not acting goes beyond the utility or income foregone of that action, then that extra price is waste.[109] Similarly, when what is threatened would not be done for its own sake, but is threatened only so that it will not be done for a price, that too is surely pure waste.

As a matter of principle, Weinrib explains it this way.[110] Rights are markers of freedom. I am free to pursue my own ends, subject only to your right to do likewise. But if I use my rights, not to pursue my own ends, but only to prevent you from achieving yours, then rights are no longer markers of freedom, but instruments of subordination. Similarly, Gutteridge says that a rule of law should not be transformed into an instrument for the gratification of private spite.[111]

Kant says that malice is the essence of vileness and wickedness. Humanity, he says, consists in sympathy and pity, whereas malice, to be pleased when others

104 Tamblyn, 'Lawful Act Conspiracy: Malice and Abuse of Rights' [2013] SJLS 158.

105 Murphy, 'Understanding Intimidation' (2014) 77 MLR 33, 42 n 43.

106 Other contexts might include misfeasance in public office, nuisance, and malicious prosecution: Neyers, 'Explaining the Inexplicable? Four Manifestations of Abuse of Rights in English Law' in Nolan and Robertson (eds), *Rights and Private Law* (Oxford: Hart, 2012).

107 Gutteridge, 'Abuse of Rights' (1933) 5 CLJ 22; Perillo, 'Abuse of Rights: A Pervasive Legal Concept' (1995) 27 Pacific LJ 37; Reid, 'The Doctrine of Abuse of Rights' (2004) Electronic Journal of Comparative Law; Lenaerts, 'The General Principle of the Prohibition of Abuse of Rights' (2010) 18 European Review of Private Law 1121.

108 Schauer, 'Can Rights Be Abused?' (1981) 31 Philosophical Quarterly 225.

109 Liebermann and Syrquin, 'The Use and Abuse of Rights' (1983) 4 Journal of Economic Behaviour and Organization 25.

110 Weinrib, 'Two Conceptions of Remedies' in Rickett (ed), *Justifying Private Law Remedies* (Oxford: Hart, 2008).

111 Gutteridge, 'Abuse of Rights' (1933) 5 Cambridge LJ 22, 23.

suffer, to bring about unhappiness wilfully, is cruel and inhuman.[112] Finnis offers another Kantian reason against malice: it is wrong to inflict suffering on another person for one's own gratification, because that treats the other person as a means and not also as an end in himself.[113] Butler, the nineteenth-century satirist, puts the same point colourfully: as men take pleasure in pursuing, entrapping and destroying all sorts of beasts and fowl, and call it sport, so would the malicious man do men.[114]

Thus someone who acts from malice reduces their victim from a person to an object of sport, or simply a tool for self-gratification. The malicious infliction of harm turns the exercise of lawful rights into an abuse of rights, and that warrants censure. It comprises a cynical misuse of the law, which the law itself need not tolerate.

There is a concern among some authors that malice ought not to be the touchstone of abuse of rights because, they say, motives are inscrutable.[115] This is baffling. The criminal law has long inquired into such subjective mental states as intention, recklessness, dishonesty and belief. How can we tell a person's motives? Ask them. And then consider the credibility of their answer against, among other things, the consistency of their testimony and the totality of the evidence. Determining the credibility of witnesses has forever been the courts' daily task. And while acting from malice might be rare – I should certainly hope so – the case law reveals that the courts are able and content to find it.[116]

Victorian case law

A clutch of cases from the end of the nineteenth century stand against the idea that malice converts a lawful act into something which warrants censure. But those cases provide no fatal obstacle here.

In *Chasemore v Richards*,[117] a Local Board of Health drained percolating water to supply a town, which reduced the flow of water to the complainant's mill. The court held that there was a right to drain water percolating on one's own land. The trial judge found explicitly that the Local Board of Health acted without malice.

112 Heath and Schneewind (eds), *Kant: Lectures on Ethics* (Cambridge: Cambridge University Press, 1997) 153, 197, 200, 420–421.

113 Finnis, 'Intention in Tort Law' in Owen (ed), *Philosophical Foundations of Tort Law* (Oxford: Clarendon Press, 1995) 244.

114 Butler, 'Varieties of Malice and Corruption' in Rorty (ed), *The Many Faces of Evil* (London: Routledge, 2001) 153.

115 Gutteridge, 'Abuse of Rights' (1933) 5 Cambridge LJ 22, 26.

116 For example, in nuisance: *Christie v Davey* [1893] 1 Ch 316; *Hollywood Silver Fox Farm Ltd v Emmett* [1936] 2 KB 468. And in lawful act conspiracy: *Quinn v Leathem* [1901] AC 495; *Huntley v Thornton* [1957] 1 All ER 234; *Gulf Oil (Great Britain) Ltd v Page* [1987] Ch 327; *Lonrho plc v Fayed (No 5)* [1994] 1 All ER 188. See also two Singaporean cases: *X Pte Ltd v CDE* [1992] 2 SLR(R) 575; *Lim Leong Huat v Chip Hup Hup Kee Construction Pte Ltd* [2011] 1 SLR 657.

117 (1859) 7 HLC 349, 11 ER 140.

Lord Wensleydale made reference to Roman law before concluding that the civil law, also adopted in Scotland, deems an act, otherwise lawful in itself, illegal if done with a malicious intent of injuring a neighbour. But he concluded that this principle found no place in English law.

In *Borough of Bradford v Pickles*,[118] the accused drained water which percolated through his land, thereby depriving the local town of its water supply. He did this to exert pressure on the town to buy his land at a high price. Unlike *Chasemore v Richards*, the trial judge did find malice. But on appeal, the court held that he had a right to extract percolating water, and that motive, even malice, did not preclude him from exercising that right.

Lord Watson said that, contrary to Lord Wensleydale, Scots law did not recognise abuse of rights. But Reid[119] and Taggart[120] say that this is wrong. Yes, it is a marginal doctrine, as abuse of rights is bound to be, but it is a viable principle, and was even then. More generally, the decision in *Bradford v Pickles* has drawn criticism.[121] And on similar facts, the French courts have declared such behaviour to be an abuse of rights.[122]

Then we come to *Allen v Flood*.[123] The head-note says that 'an act lawful in itself is not converted by a malicious or bad motive into an unlawful act so as to make the doer of the act liable to a civil action'. That is misleading.

First, the head-note does not reflect the multiplicity of approaches of the judgments in *Allen v Flood*.

The three dissenting judges said that a person has a right to carry out his trade. Any interference is actionable, unless done with just cause, but not if done from malice;[124] and this defendant had acted without just cause or with malice.[125] Thus there was unlawful interference from the outset; malice negatived any defence of just cause.

As for the assenting judges, some simply countered by denying that there was a right to carry on a trade without interference.[126] True, some said expressly that

118 [1895] AC 587.

119 Reid, 'The Doctrine of Abuse of Rights' (2004) Electronic Journal of Comparative Law.

120 Taggart, Private Property and Abuse of Rights in Victorian England (Oxford: Oxford University Press, 2002) 149.

121 Gutteridge, 'Abuse of Rights' (1933) 5 Cambridge LJ 22, 44; Allen, 'Legal Morality and the *Ius Abutendi*' (1924) 40 LQR 164. It was cited, but otherwise ignored, in *Hollywood Silver Fox Farm Ltd v Emmett* [1936] 2 KB 468, where malice was relevant to a finding of nuisance.

122 Gutteridge, 'Abuse of Rights' (1933) 5 Cambridge LJ 22, 33; Perillo, 'Abuse of Rights: A Pervasive Legal Concept' (1995) 27 Pacific LJ 37, 43–44; Taggart, *Private Property and Abuse of Rights in Victorian England* (Oxford: Oxford University Press, 2002) 146–147. On French law, see too: Walton, 'Motive as an Element in Torts in the Common and in the Civil Law' (1908) 22 Harv LR 501.

123 [1898] AC 1.

124 [1898] AC 1, 71, 84 (Lord Halsbury LC), 112, 114 (Lord Ashbourne), 115 (Lord Morris).

125 The first instance decision was based on the same principle: *Allen v Jackson* [1895] 2 QB 21, 28. That judgment was unanimously upheld by the Court of Appeal. It was also the basis in principle adopted by six of the eight judges summoned to give their opinion to the House of Lords. The extraordinary procedure of *Allen v Flood* is well recounted in Heuston, 'Judicial Prosopography' (1986) 102 LQR 90.

126 [1898] AC 1, 138 (Lord Herschell), 173 (Lord Davey). This was the opinion of the other two judges summoned to advise the House of Lords.

malice or a bad motive does not render a lawful act tortious,[127] but they also went on to state that there was no malice in the case anyway,[128] this being simply an instance of competition in labour,[129] with the defendant acting as a mouthpiece for his co-workers.[130]

Second, the head-note in *Allen v Flood* does not represent the law more generally. A number of judges, before, in and after *Allen v Flood*, have entertained the possibility that acting maliciously can be tortious.[131] In particular, malice can render otherwise reasonable behaviour a nuisance.[132] And malice is best viewed as an essential ingredient in the tort of lawful act conspiracy.[133] Indeed, it is notable that a plea of conspiracy was withdrawn from the jury in *Allen v Flood*,[134] as was a plea of intimidation.[135] Therefore, the role of malice in intimidation was simply not an issue in that case.

Some authors describe the decision in *Allen v Flood* as a hindrance,[136] and have suggested that it ought to be revisited.[137] But, Ames says[138] it has anyway 'been made harmless' by the subsequent decision in *Quinn v Leathem*.

In *Quinn v Leathem*,[139] the defendants were officials of a butchers' union, and they demanded that the claimant butcher sack his non-union employees. When the claimant refused, the defendants ensured others would not trade with the claimant. The claimant sued successfully in lawful means conspiracy. The House of Lords were unanimous; and malice was central to the decision.

127 [1898] AC 1, 92–93 (Lord Watson), 123–124 (Lord Herschell), 151 (Lord Macnaghten), 166–167 (Lord Shand), 171–172 (Lord Davey).

128 [1898] AC 1, 131 (Lord Herschell), 162, 167 (Lord Shand).

129 [1898] AC 1, 163–164 (Lord Shand).

130 [1898] AC 1, 148, 151 (Lord Macnaghten), 177 (Lord James).

131 *Mogul Steamship Co v McGregor Gow & Co* (1889) 23 QBD 598, 609–610 (Lord Esher MR), 626 (Fry LJ), on appeal at [1892] AC 25; *Allen v Flood* [1895] 2 QB 21, 38 (Lord Esher MR), [1898] AC 1, 156 (Lord Morris); *Quinn v Leathem* [1901] AC 495, 537–538 (Lord Lindley); *Giblan v National Amalgamated Labourers' Union of Great Britain and Ireland* [1903] 2 KB 600, 619–620 (Romer LJ), 623 (Stirling LJ); *Sorrell v Smith* [1925] AC 700, 713 (Viscount Cave LC); *Crofter Hand Woven Harris Tweed Co Ltd v Veitch* [1942] AC 435, 453 (Viscount Maugham), 468 (Lord Wright).

132 *Christie v Davey* [1893] 1 Ch 316; *Hollywood Silver Fox Farm Ltd v Emmett* [1936] 2 KB 468; *Hunter v Canary Wharf Ltd* [1997] AC 655, 721.

133 Tamblyn, 'Lawful Act Conspiracy: Malice and Abuse of Rights' [2013] SJLS 158.

134 [1895] 2 QB 21, 23, 26, 31 (Kennedy J); 41 (Lopes LJ); [1898] AC 1, 148 (Lord Macnaghten), 170 (Lord Davey).

135 [1898] AC 1, 99–100 (Lord Watson), 148 (Lord Macnaghten), 170 (Lord Davey).

136 Heydon, 'The Defence of Justification in Cases of Intentionally Caused Economic Harm' (1970) 20 U Toronto LJ 139, 177; Heydon, 'The Future of the Economic Torts' (1975) U Western Australia LR 1, 14; Burns, 'Tort Injury to Economic Interests: Some Facets of Legal Response' (1980) 58 Can Bar Rev 134, 149; Heuston and Buckley, *Salmond & Heuston, Law of Torts*, 21st edn (London: Sweet & Maxwell, 1996) 345–346. But in favour: Weir, *Economic Torts* (Oxford: Clarendon Press, 1997) 21.

137 Hoffmann, '*Rookes v Barnard*' (1965) 81 LQR 116, 138–141.

138 Ames, 'How far an act may be a tort because of the wrongful motive of the actor' (1905) 18 Harv LR 411.

139 [1901] AC 495.

The Earl of Halsbury LC said that the defendants had acted maliciously in order to injure the claimant.[140] Lord Macnaghten said that the defendants had acted to harm the claimant so as to wreak their vengeance.[141] Lord Shand noted that the defendants had acted with malice.[142] All three of those judges had sat in *Allen v Flood*.

Lord Shand, who was in the majority in *Allen v Flood*, distinguished the cases by saying that, in *Allen v Flood*, the defendant conspired but only to promote his own trade interests through competition in the labour market, whereas in *Quinn v Leathem*, the defendants were motivated by malice to injure the claimant.[143] This would suggest that the absence of malice was a deciding factor after all in *Allen v Flood*.

Lord Brampton also appears to have laid his decision on the grounds of the defendants' malevolence to injure the claimant.[144] And Lord Lindley noted that the defendants had been found by the jury to have acted from malice, and he himself described their conduct as reprehensible.[145] Subsequent cases have also described *Quinn v Leathem* as a clear case of malice.[146]

So *Allen v Flood* is not such a strong case as it is sometimes taken to be. Motive, and in particular malice, can be relevant in tort law – which is not to say that it is always relevant.[147] The proper role of malice in the tort of intimidation, when threatening lawful acts, can be explored through the following three situations:

(i) A decides not to contract with B out of malice. No doubt this is disappointing behaviour, but it would likely be very rare that the law would intervene, because it is usually lawful not to contract with people.[148] At any rate, the tort of intimidation would not apply because there have been no threats.
(ii) A threatens not to contract with B, in order to get B to do something they would not otherwise have done. This should not be tortious. For example, it should be lawful for A to say: that they will not buy B's products until

140 [1901] AC 495, 505–506.
141 [1901] AC 495, 511–512.
142 [1901] AC 495, 513.
143 [1901] AC 495, 512–515.
144 [1901] AC 495, 531.
145 [1901] AC 495, 535–536.
146 *Sorrell v Smith* [1925] AC 700, 735–736 (Lord Sumner), 744–746 (Lord Buckmaster); *Crofter Hand Woven Harris Tweed Co Ltd v Veitch* [1942] AC 435, 452–453 (Viscount Maugham), 473–474 (Lord Wright); but see *Ware and de Freville Ltd v Motor Trade Association* [1921] 3 KB 40, 67 (Scrutton LJ).
147 Ames, 'How Far an Act May Be a Tort Because of the Wrongful Motive of the Actor' (1905) 18 Harv LR 411; Fridman, 'Motive in the English law of Nuisance' (1954) 40 Virginia LR 583, 595.
148 A contrary example might be salvage, a service now almost universally rendered under contract (in the shape of Lloyd's Open Form). A ship is under a duty to assist another in distress, when it is safe to do so. Failure to assist is a crime: Merchant Shipping Act 1995 (UK) Sch 11 Art 10, as further elaborated in Pt II r 3. See too: *Temperton v Russell* [1893] 1 QB 715, 728 (on maliciously preventing a person from contracting).

B stops testing on animals; or that they will not perform in B's club if it excludes black musicians.[149] And harking back to Canadian law, it should be possible to threaten a company with consequences if it fails to comply with regulations,[150] or to threaten legislation to regulate corporate behaviour.[151] In these scenarios, there is no malice.

(iii) A threatens not to contract with B, out of malice, in order to coerce B to act differently. This could be covered by the tort of intimidation. For example, it should be tortious for A to threaten to reveal truthful information, lawfully but spitefully, simply to procure behaviour by which B demeans or ruins himself.[152] (Indeed, if A were to demand money instead, that could be blackmail.)

It is not malice alone which makes these actions tortious. The other elements of intimidation must also be made out, such as an intention to coerce. The tort of intimidation is about policing coercive behaviour. Where the threat leverages lawful acts, but is made maliciously, that is a cynical misuse of the law, an abuse of rights, which could be sufficient to support a plea of intimidation.

1.11 Defence of justification

Is there a defence of justification to intimidation? There is no academic consensus: some authors say that there is probably no such defence to the tort of intimidation,[153] while others are in favour of the idea.[154]

When might a justification defence be invoked? Judicial examples include the two following:

(1) Where A threatens, in breach of contract, to withhold delivery of goods from B, because B has, in breach of contract himself, not yet paid the first instalment.[155]

149 *Scala Ballroom (Wolverhampton) Ltd v Ratcliffe* [1958] 3 All ER 220.

150 *Central Canada Potash Co Ltd v Saskatchewan* [1979] 1 SCR 42.

151 *Roman Corp v Hudson's Bay Oil & Gas Co Ltd* [1973] SCR 820.

152 For similar liability, on such facts, in conspiracy, see: *Gulf Oil (Great Britain) Ltd v Page* [1987] Ch 327; *Lonrho plc v Fayed (No 5)* [1994] 1 All ER 188; *X Pte Ltd v CDE* [1992] 2 SLR(R) 575.

153 Fridman, *The Law of Torts in Canada* (Toronto: Carswell, 1990) 289; *Clerk & Lindsell on Torts*, 21st edn (London: Sweet & Maxwell, 2014) [24–71]; Carty, *An Analysis of the Economic Torts*, 2nd edn (Oxford: Oxford University Press, 2010) 101, 110; Sales and Stilitz, 'Intentional Infliction of Harm by Unlawful Means' (1999) 115 LQR 411, 418; Ong, 'Two Tripartite Economic Torts' [2008] JBL 723, 744; Heuston and Buckley, *Salmond & Heuston, Law of Torts*, 21st edn (London: Sweet & Maxwell, 1996) 363.

154 Burns, 'Tort Injury to Economic Interests: Some Facets of Legal Response' (1980) 58 Can Bar Rev 134, 136; Deakin and Randall, 'Rethinking the Economic Torts' (2009) 72 MLR 519, 551; Davies, *Accessory Liability* (Oxford: Hart, 2015) ch 6; Heydon, 'The Defence of Justification in Cases of Intentionally Caused Economic Harm' (1970) 20 U Toronto LJ 139, 171–182.

155 *Rookes v Barnard* [1964] AC 1129, 1209.

However, if B's breach is repudiatory, A can accept it and terminate the contract. Before doing that, A can spell out this likelihood in strong terms, and give B an opportunity to rectify their position. In this case, A is not threatening anything unlawful, or anything lawful maliciously. In short, the tort of intimidation is not made out anyway.

If B's breach is not repudiatory, then in the absence of any contractual entitlement to do so, A cannot withhold delivery in breach itself. There is no defence of 'tit for tat' breach.[156] Put another way, two wrongs do not make a right.

A similar conclusion can be drawn from the New Zealand case of *Dellabarca v Northern Storemen and Packers Union*.[157] There the possibility of a defence of justification seemed attractive to the court, although the point was not decided. But that case also held that contributory negligence is no defence to the intentional torts. By analogy, one party's prior breach of contract should be no defence to the other party resorting to tortious intimidation.

(2) Where a co-employee is a troublemaker who foments dissent, so that their colleagues threaten the employer that they will no longer work alongside him.[158]

Such a situation arose in the Australian case of *Latham v Singleton*.[159] Some of the defendants were held to have a defence of justification, because their predominant motive was to serve the purposes of their union. Other defendants had no such defence, because they acted out of spite against the co-employee.

But *Latham v Singleton* was a conspiracy case. It was also a three-party case. Further, the decision seems wrong. If the employees have concerns, certainly they can raise this with the employer. And if no satisfactory result ensues, they can seek alternative employment elsewhere. But, in the absence of some statutorily protected labour dispute, surely they cannot do wrong, and breach their contract, to force the employer to do what he does not wish or have to do, and thereby injure a co-employee. On such facts, the employees are surely guilty of the three-party tort, just like in *Rookes v Barnard*.

So neither judicial example of a justification defence is persuasive. Note too that both examples concern breach of contract. This is perhaps no coincidence: the tort of procuring breach of contract also purports to recognise a defence of justification. But that does not mean that the defence should extend into the tort of intimidation. For a start, there is a difference between, on the one hand, using persuasion to procure someone to breach their contract with a third party, and on the other hand, threatening to do something unlawful unless the duressee themselves capitulates to the demand. There is no reason to suppose, even conceptually, that a defence in a three-party tort of procuring breach

156 The same point has been made in a three-party context of inducing breach of contract: *Camden Nominees v Forcey* [1940] Ch 352; *Smithies v National Association of Operative Plasterers* [1909] 1 KB 310.

157 [1989] 2 NZLR 734.

158 *Morgan v Fry* [1968] 2 QB 710, 729 (Lord Denning MR); *Cory Lighterage v TGWU* [1973] ICR 339, 357 (Lord Denning MR).

159 [1981] 2 NSWLR 843.

ought to apply in a two-party tort of intimidation.[160] We should be even more concerned when the defence works so badly already in the tort of procuring breach, as we shall now explore.

Procuring breach of contract, and justification

The starting point is *Glamorgan Coal Co Ltd v South Wales Miners' Federation*.[161] In that case, miners abstained from working on certain days, as directed by their federation, but in breach of contract. Their purpose was to reduce production and so maintain the price of coal, upon which the amount of their wages depended. The federation had no defence of justification to inducing breach of contract.

Romer LJ, in a paragraph often cited and followed in subsequent cases, said that 'it would be extremely difficult, even if it were possible, to give a complete and satisfactory definition of what is sufficient justification, and most attempts to do so would probably be mischievous'. Similarly, authors say that what constitutes justification is vague and unclear,[162] or incapable of exact definition.[163]

This uncertainty does not bother Goudkamp, who says that, as long as the primary wrong is properly defined, defences can have more flexibility, since only the wrongs, not the defences, are meant to guide people's behaviour.[164] This is doubtful. Surely someone who acts in self-defence is reassured, even emboldened, by knowing that this is permissible. More generally, parties seeking legal advice want to know if what they plan to do is legal overall; they are not guided solely by that part relating to wrongs, and ignore the other part where the defence says the behaviour is permissible after all.

In *Glamorgan Coal*, Romer LJ then said, in effect, that the court had to look at all the circumstances and itself decide whether it felt that what the defendant did was 'justified', whatever that means, and seemingly only by reference to the judge's own internal and unaccountable moral compass.

Howarth is not concerned by this.[165] He says that justification should be a defence where it is not fair, just and reasonable to impose liability. But as a consequence he admits, for example, in the context of strike action, that the courts would have to decide on the 'substantive merits' of the strike, i.e. whether it was morally proper to strike. Surely that involves an array of considerations, not just moral but also political and social, which go beyond the constitutional role of the courts?

160 See too: Carty, *An Analysis of the Economic Torts*, 2nd edn (Oxford: Oxford University Press, 2010) 63.
161 [1903] 2 KB 545, upheld on appeal [1905] AC 239.
162 Carty, *An Analysis of the Economic Torts*, 2nd edn (Oxford: Oxford University Press, 2010) 63.
163 Peel and Goudkamp, *Winfield and Jolowicz on Tort*, 19th edn (London: Sweet & Maxwell, 2014) [19–016].
164 Goudkamp, *Tort Law Defences* (Oxford: Hart, 2013) 139.
165 Howarth, 'Against *Lumley v Gye*' (2005) 68 MLR 195, 225.

This raises problems which we shall consider again in the context of the would-be defence of lesser evil necessity (see Chapter 4), but they are relevant here too:

In *Monsanto plc v Tilly*,[166] the claimant was licensed to grow genetically modified crops. The defendants pulled up some of the crops in protest. The claimant sought an injunction. The defendants pleaded necessity, but unsuccessfully.

Stuart-Smith LJ said that the defendants were acting to draw publicity to their cause. They sought to change government policy, and that should have been by democratic means, or perhaps through judicial review. Mummery LJ said that the plea was not justiciable, because the issues strayed beyond the constitutional function, and indeed structural competence, of the court to decide. The potential risks and rewards of genetically modified crops were a matter of state policy and political judgement, which called for wide-ranging inquiry beyond the limited evidence and issues pleaded by adversarial parties in a private dispute.

Similar concerns can be felt behind the Court of Appeal's decision in *R v Jones*,[167] where the defendants unsuccessfully pleaded necessity to a charge of criminal damage, committed at a military airbase in protest at the war in Iraq. Framing the question in terms of justification: was the war in Iraq good or bad, and for whom, and over what period, and according to what set of values?

Asking judges to rule on such matters raises what Gardner calls the democracy problem:[168] unelected judges making political decisions about what activities or policies are best for society. Similarly, we saw earlier how Stevens counsels against the court straying into policy questions about whether a particular course of action is legitimate or fair.[169] He was arguing against lawful act intimidation, inaccurately I suggested – but his criticism is apposite here.

Weir suggests a different formulation, that there might be a defence of justification, in three-party cases, if the means used are not excessively wrongful, like a white lie or trivial breach of contract.[170] But trivial breaches are unlikely to be coercive.[171] And if they were trivial, presumably they would not cause loss. Yet if they did cause loss, and that was the intention all along, why should that be acceptable?[172]

In *Glamorgan Coal*, Romer LJ's only contribution towards a definition of justification was negative: he said that it was no justification that the federation acted in the best interests of its members, or without any malicious intent to harm the employer, a sentiment repeated in other cases.[173] Thus Deakin et al. say that the scope of the defence is so limited as to be practically meaningless, at least in labour disputes.[174]

166 [1999] All ER (D) 1321.
167 [2005] Crim LR 122, on appeal at [2006] UKHL 16.
168 Gardner, S, 'Necessity's Newest Inventions' (1991) 11 OJLS 125, 133.
169 Stevens, *Torts and Rights* (Oxford: Oxford University Press, 2007) 189–190.
170 Weir, 'Chaos or Cosmos? *Rookes, Stratford* and the Economic Torts' [1964] Cambridge LJ 225, 230.
171 Heydon, *Economic Torts* (London: Sweet & Maxwell, 1973) 55.
172 Sales and Stilitz, 'Intentional Infliction of Harm by Unlawful Means' (1999) 115 LQR 411, 418.
173 *Greig v Insole* [1978] 1 WLR 302; *Read v The Friendly Society of Operative Stonemasons of England, Ireland and Wales* [1902] 2 KB 88.
174 Deakin et al., *Markesinis and Deakin's Tort Law*, 7th edn (Oxford: Oxford University Press, 2013) 478.

When might a justification defence be successful? Let us consider three examples.

(1) As a rare example of justification succeeding, reference is often made to *Brimelow v Casson*.[175] There the defendants were held justified in their action, of persuading theatre managers to refuse their premises to the claimant's use, even in breach of contract, in a concerted effort to force the claimant to pay his chorus girls a living wage.

And yet it was no defence in *Glamorgan Coal* that the defendants were acting in good faith to improve wages.

The facts of *Brimelow* were described subsequently as being 'in the nature of a public scandal' and 'utterly disgraceful'.[176] In *Brimelow* itself, the judge stressed that the low wages were forcing the chorus girls into 'immorality'. What this meant was not spelled out, but did include one girl living unmarried to another member of the cast, 'a dwarf . . . an abnormal man . . . a terrible and revolting tragedy'. That moral outlook would surely gain no traction in the twenty-first century. The case has never been the basis of any subsequent decision.[177]

(2) A second potential justification mentioned by the courts is when A and B both contract with X, for example to buy the same property; neither A nor B would incur tortious liability in persuading X to uphold their contract (and so break the other).[178]

And yet, this seemingly sensible suggestion was rejected in the Australian case of *Zhu v Treasurer of New South Wales*,[179] which went further to hold that a defendant, to be justified, must protect only a superior (not an equal) right, and do no more than is reasonably necessary.

In that case, the court said, if X agrees to sell property to A, and that contract is specifically enforceable, then A gets an equitable interest. If X later agrees to sell the same property to B, such that B too might get an equitable interest, nevertheless equity principles prefer the equitable interest which arose first in time. Thus, said the court, it is not an example of competition between rights, but one in which A has a right, and B has no right at all.

But that is not true. B has a contractual right, and they can sue X upon it. Nor do the plain facts of the above example shield A from all possible tortious liability. For example, if B was about to sign with X tomorrow, as A well knew, and A managed to sign with X today, with the intention of procuring breach of B's contract, perhaps even out of spite, that may well incur tortious

175 [1924] 1 Ch 302.

176 *Pritchard v Briggs* [1980] Ch 338, 416.

177 Carty, *An Analysis of the Economic Torts*, 2nd edn (Oxford: Oxford University Press, 2010) 69. Nevertheless, Cane suggests that it might not be wrong to induce breach of a contract which itself is a vehicle of wrongdoing: '*Mens Rea* in Tort Law' (2000) 20 OJLS 533, 554. The better approach might simply be to say that such a contract is already illegal, so the court will not enforce or uphold it.

178 *Read v The Friendly Society of Operative Stonemasons of England, Ireland and Wales* [1902] 2 KB 88, 95; *Edwin Hill & Partners v First National Finance Corporation plc* [1989] 1 WLR 225, 230.

179 [2004] HCA 56.

liability – and the court would likely exercise its discretion not to specifically enforce A's contract after all.[180]

More generally, the court in *Zhu* characterised contract rights as quasi-proprietary, and then seemingly suggested that they must therefore be inferior to proprietary rights.[181] But that does not follow. Quasi-proprietary does not mean morally less important than proprietary. It simply indicates that something is not fully proprietary.

Consider the following: a piece of jewellery, which is half silver and half gold, is not worth less than another piece which is all silver, simply because the first piece has only half the amount of silver; the other half is gold, worth more than silver, making the total worth more as well.

Contract may be quasi-proprietary in nature, but it can also be characterised as a personal right. It does not follow, as a matter of logic, that it must be less morally important than a full proprietary right. That it is also a personal right has weight, perhaps even more weight. What is morally more important, my property interest in a pencil, or my contractual interest in a life-saving operation going ahead?

Further, let us assume that an otherwise tortious act of procuring breach of contract might be justified if the defendant acts to protect at least an equal right, or perhaps only a superior right. This means we need to know which rights are superior to contract rights – even accepting that contract rights might be equal to each other, which I do not think must obviously always be true. So we must come up with a ranking of all rights against each other, which seems utterly unrealistic. Are all rights commensurable? What is the order here: the right to privacy, the right to a fair trial, the right to education? And if the rankings are decided by judges, does this not simply restore the democracy problem?

(3) Justification was successfully invoked in *Edwin Hill & Partners v First National Finance Corporation plc*.[182] There the defendant held a first legal charge over property, as security for the debt of a developer, who was unable to repay the loan or raise finance for carrying out the development, for which the claimant had been appointed as architect. The defendant agreed to provide the necessary further finance on condition that the claimant was replaced. The claimant sought damages for procuring breach of contract. The defendant was held justified because he was acting to protect an equal or superior right.[183]

180 See too: *Temperton v Russell* [1893] 1 QB 715, 728 (on maliciously preventing a person from contracting).

181 Davies says that property rights are 'commonly thought' to be superior to personal contractual rights, without giving any reason or evidence to back that up: Davies, *Accessory Liability* (Oxford: Hart, 2015) 230.

182 [1989] 1 WLR 225.

183 This followed the decision in *Read v The Friendly Society of Operative Stonemasons of England, Ireland and Wales* [1902] 2 KB 88, order varied on appeal [1902] KB 732, where the court said that justification for interfering with another's contract rights required that the defendant was acting to protect an equal or superior right in himself, although the defence of justification was not successful in that case.

Despite that language, the effective reasoning was put upon a different basis, and went like this. The defendant, as a secured creditor, had the right, upon the developer's default, to sell the land or appoint a receiver. If that had happened, the architect contract would have come to an end by operation of law, without any liability. So surely, said the court, if the defendant avoided that drastic outcome, and instead reached an accommodation with the debtor, which nevertheless had the same result for the architect, still no liability should accrue. Of course, that does not follow logically: just because the law holds a party harmless for an outcome produced one way, it does not mean that the party is also held harmless for the same outcome produced other ways. But behind the court's decision seems to be a policy argument, that a contrary verdict would be an impediment to the desirability and perhaps commercial reality of financial restructuring which avoids insolvency.

In *Anstalt v Mir*,[184] a similar argument was made explicitly, that an administrator should be able to invoke the defence of justification when selling property when the sale thereby entailed a breach of contract. Otherwise, the submission went, the whole insolvency process would be unduly hindered. The court thought it a powerful argument, but declined to rule upon it in the context of a summary judgment application.

So it may be that there is a defence specific to insolvency law when it comes to procuring breach of contract. But that specialist context need not entail the recognition of a defence more generally.

In *Edwin Hill*, the court seems to suggest that property rights are superior to contract rights, on the basis of the following example. X carries on building operations on his land, that may, to the knowledge of X, interfere with a contract between A and B to carry out recording work on adjoining land occupied by A. But unless X's activity amounts to a nuisance, said that court, he is justified in doing what he did.[185]

But surely X does not need a defence of justification. Surely what X does is not even presumptively tortious. It cannot be that A and B might agree a contract which, just because X knows about it, renders presumptively tortious any use X makes of their own land lawfully (and without malice). There is otherwise something wrong with the ingredients of the tort of procuring breach of contract, if liability arises simply by being aware of causing a breach of another's contract. Instead, following *OBG v Allan*, if what is required is an intention to cause the breach, as an end in itself or as a means to an end, then, on the previous example, no liability would arise in the first place, where X's only intention is to use their own land.[186] In this case, without tortious liability, there is no need to resort to the defence of justification.[187]

184 [2011] EWHC 3310.

185 Similar examples can be found in the Australian case of *Independent Oil Industries Ltd v The Shell Co of Australia Ltd* (1937) 37 SR (NSW) 394, 415–416.

186 Similarly, in the criminal case of *R v Jogee* [2016] UKSC 8, it was said of the crime of aiding or procuring, under s 8 of the Accessories and Abettors Act 1861, that the defendant must intend the principal to commit the crime, and that mere assistance with foresight is not enough.

187 For a similar argument, see the Canadian case of *Sar Petroleum Inc v Peace Hills Trust Co* [2010] NBCA 22.

In similar vein, two more common examples of a would-be defence of justification might be similarly dispatched.

First, where a member is struck off by a regulatory body, to the extent that this inevitably and foreseeably interferes with any contracts that member might have previously agreed, surely it is not even presumptively tortious. The regulatory body seeks to act according to its remit. Any consequential breach of contract with third parties is not intended as the end in itself or a means to that end. Again there is no tort, and so no need to resort to any defence of justification.[188]

Second, a doctor might tell a patient to stop work for their health.[189] If the patient does stop work, but in breach of contract, surely the doctor's advice is not even presumptively tortious. For a start, they are fulfilling a duty to the patient.[190] More than that, any breach of contract is not intended as an end in itself or the means to an end. Put another way, the patient's good health is sought to be advanced, and that need not necessarily involve any breach of contract.

Heydon goes further. He says that if it is not actionable for a doctor to save a patient's life by telling them to break an employment contract, it should not be fraud for the doctor to lie, by telling the patient that he (the patient) has already been dismissed.[191] But that seems extraordinary. It is for the doctor to advise, not to deceive their patient and thereby rob the patient of autonomy. Surely the patient could sue the doctor. In contrast, other authors suggest that fraud and physical violence can never be justified,[192] nor any tort nor breach of fiduciary duty.[193]

Summary

There is no warrant for recognising a defence of justification to the tort of intimidation. No case has upheld such a defence in the two-party context. There are no persuasive examples of when it might even be applicable. Most discussion tends towards three-party cases and procuring breach of contract, where the defence

188 Which means the court's approach was wrong in *Posluns v Toronto Stock Exchange* [1964] OJ No 792, upheld on appeal [1968] SCR 330.

189 Davies, *Accessory Liability* (Oxford: Hart, 2015) 234; Heydon, 'The Defence of Justification in Cases of Intentionally Caused Economic Harm' (1970) 20 U Toronto LJ 139, 168.

190 See too: Stevens, 'Why Do Agents Drop Out?' [2005] LMCLQ 101, 107.

191 Heydon, 'The Defence of Justification in Cases of Intentionally Caused Economic Harm' (1970) 20 U Toronto LJ 139, 178, 181. Heydon also says that, while it is wrong to hit someone, it may yet be justified if the defendant acts in self-defence. Which is true, but that is not a broad-brush defence of justification, but a tailored defence of self-defence. And a defendant sued in intimidation could similarly plead any generally available tortious defence, like self-defence, or necessity. But otherwise, it is difficult to see why or when an accused should nevertheless be able to say that their threatened tortious or criminal behaviour was defence-less yet 'justified', whatever that might mean.

192 Sappideen and Vines (eds), *Fleming's The Law of Torts*, 10th edn (Pyrmont NSW: Thomson Reuters, 2011) 779.

193 Stevens, 'Why Do Agents Drop Out?' [2005] LMCLQ 101, 108.

of justification is highly problematic. It has no clear or workable definition, and it encourages an unpredictable and untrammelled discretion on the part of the courts to make unaccountable moral judgments. The defence of justification should not be adopted for the tort of intimidation.

1.12 Duress by threats as a tortious defence

We return to *Gilbert v Stone.*[194] To repeat, the defendant stood accused of entering a close and taking a gelding. He said that he did this only because he was threatened by twelve armed men. It was held no defence to trespass that a defendant acts from fear or threats of another,[195] because the victim (the owner of the gelding) cannot sue the duressor, whereas the defendant can.

But if a defendant is carried onto another's land, the carriers, not the defendant, are liable for trespass.[196] So too if a third party takes the hand of the defendant to strike the victim, or whips the horse upon which the defendant rides so that it runs over the victim.[197] A similar principle arises in *Scott v Shepherd.*[198] In that case, A threw a lit squib into a market. It landed on B's stall, who threw it away, landing on C's stall, who threw it away, whereupon it blew up in D's face. The majority held that A had trespassed against D, the necessary (we might say, instinctive or at least foreseeable) acts of B and C not breaking the chain of causation.

Beyond this very old strand of case law, most tort books make no mention of a defence of duress. Those which do tend to deny that the defence exists.[199] But the authors of *Fleming* are open to the possibility that duress in tort might develop along the same lines as criminal law.[200] And Edelman and Dyer argue for the recognition of a defence of duress, as follows.[201]

First, they say that the reasoning in *Gilbert v Stone* has been overtaken, because the victim might be able to sue the duressor by invoking the three-party tort of intentionally causing loss by unlawful means, following *OBG v Allan.*

But, we might respond, it does not follow, just because the victim can sue the duressor, that therefore the victim should not be able to sue the duressee

194 (1647) Aleyn 35, 82 ER 902; Style 72, 82 ER 539.

195 A point confirmed by Blackstone J in *Scott v Shepherd* (1773) 2 Black W 892, 96 ER 525.

196 *Smith v Stone* (1647) Style 65, 82 ER 533.

197 *Gibbons v Pepper* (1695) 1 Ld Ray 38, 91 ER 922.

198 (1773) 2 Black W 892, 96 ER 525.

199 Giliker, *Tort*, 5th edn (London: Sweet & Maxwell, 2014) 447 n 205; Peel and Goudkamp, *Winfield & Jolowicz, Tort*, 19th edn (London: Sweet & Maxwell, 2014) [26–107]; Witting, *Street on Torts*, 14th edn (Oxford: Oxford University Press, 2015) 339; *Clerk & Lindsell on Torts*, 21st edn (London: Sweet & Maxwell) [3–146]; Epstein, 'Defenses and Subsequent Pleas in a System of Strict Liability' (1974) 3 J Legal Stud 165, 169, 174; Goudkamp, *Tort Law Defences* (Oxford: Hart, 2013) 89; Fridman, *The Law of Torts in Canada* (Toronto: Carswell, 1990) 281.

200 Sappideen and Vines (eds), *Fleming's The Law of Torts*, 10th edn (Pyrmont NSW: Thomson Reuters, 2011) 112–113.

201 Edelman and Dyer, 'A Defence of Duress in the Law of Torts?', in Dyson et al. (eds), *Defences in Tort Law* (Oxford: Hart, 2015).

(the actual thief, on the facts of *Gilbert v Stone*). This is especially so when the duressee can sue the duressor in the two-party tort of intimidation, and presumably obtain an indemnity. We might frame the question this way: should it be the duressee or the victim who bears the risk of the duressor's insolvency?

Second, Edelman and Dyer say that the boundary between necessity and duress is paper-thin, so that there is no principled reason to recognise necessity / duress of circumstances, and not duress by threats. They say that duress in tort should align with developments in criminal law.

To evaluate this claim, we need a full understanding of the tortious defence of necessity, its relationship to the criminal defence of necessity, and the further relationship between criminal necessity and criminal duress. That analysis will come in Chapters 4 and 5. But we can summarise the conclusions here.

The defence of necessity comes in various forms.

Best interests intervention (in both tort and crime) enables a willing volunteer to provide necessary assistance to someone unable to consent to being helped. It is about advancing the victim's best interests. That is not applicable here, where, through a plea of duress, the defendant seeks to protect their own interests at the expense of the victim.

There is, potentially, a defence of lesser evil necessity (again in both tort and crime). In broad terms, it is where the defendant acts wrongfully to avoid something even worse. The precise test resorts to language which is somewhat archaic: it speaks of doing no more than reasonably necessary to avoid an inevitable and irreparable evil, as long as the evil inflicted is not disproportionate to the evil avoided. In Chapter 4, I argue that we should reject this defence. This is because its utilitarian calculus is capable of producing outcomes which are morally unacceptable, and it requires judges to take policy decisions beyond their constitutional competence. So let us put this defence to one side too.

Finally, in tort, there is a defence of private necessity. In brief outline, there must be an actual danger, of death or serious injury. The defendant's response to the danger must be reasonable, which includes the question of whether there were lawful alternative ways to respond. The need to act cannot be due to the defendant's prior negligence. The defence enables the defendant to act, without liability, upon another's property, but not upon another's person. The rationale for the defence can be found, as a matter of property theory, in the limits necessary to justify the institution of private property, or in the fact that property rights are derivative of, and so yield to, personality rights.

Let us compare this tortious defence of private necessity with criminal law.

Criminal law, across various jurisdictions, recognises some form of defence of duress by threats, and duress of circumstances (also called necessity or emergency). The general tendencies, for both types of criminal duress, are to require: a grave threat such as death or serious injury, which the defendant has not brought upon himself, when there is an absence of alternative responses or escape, and the defendant's response must conform to an objective standard of reasonable behaviour. As for criminal duress of circumstances, I argue that this too is justified by the same rationale as for the tortious defence of necessity.

In light of this, we might make the following argument. (i) In English criminal law, the defences of duress by threats and duress of circumstances are substantially similar. (ii) The ingredients of those defences, as just recounted, already align with the tortious defence of necessity (itself akin to duress of circumstances). (iii) Taking these two points together suggests that a tortious defence of duress by threats would be workable.

But what is the rationale for the criminal defence of duress by threats? Is that equally applicable to a tortious defence of duress by threats?

The criminal defence of duress by threats starts by noting the sympathetic position of the defendant: he has been coerced (which is wrong for the reasons we have already considered) by unlawful threats, usually of death or serious injury. That could also apply in tort law. But it is of central importance to the criminal defence that the defendant is also a victim of the duressor, no less than the third-party victim the defendant acts upon in turn. And the criminal law continues to proscribe what the duressor does, and holds the duressor accountable for the harm to the third party.

That same reasoning can be applied in tort law, as follows.

If the defendant needs to raise a defence of duress, it is because he has committed a tort against a third-party victim. There would be no need for a tortious defence if what he did was otherwise lawful. So the third-party victim suffers a tortious wrong. Yet even if the defendant is provided with a defence of duress, the wrong suffered by the third party remains tortiously proscribed. For example, the victim might sue the duressor for procuring the tort, a doctrine which characterises the duressor as a joint tortfeasor with the defendant.[202] Thus the victim is still able to sue, to vindicate his position, and obtain compensation.

Further, while the duressor has threatened the defendant with harm, this is done to procure the tort against the third-party victim. To that extent, both the defendant and the third party are victims of the duressor. The defendant is not transferring any risk of harm onto the victim. This is because the duressor is not threatening the defendant with harm, simply as an end in itself, but in order to galvanise the defendant into acting against the victim. If anything, the victim is the primary target, in which case, it may well ought to be the victim, rather than the defendant, who bears the risk of the duressor's insolvency.

Let us take stock.

The boundary between necessity and duress is not paper-thin, as Edelman and Dyer suggest. The criminal defences of duress by threats and duress of circumstances

202 The leading case is *CBS Songs Ltd v Amstrad Consumer Electronics Plc* [1988] AC 1013, 1058. See too: *Brooke v Bool* [1928] 2 KB 578; *Wah Tat Bank Ltd v Chan Cheng Kum* [1975] AC 507, 514; *Credit Lyonnais Bank Nederland NV v Export Credits Guarantee Department* [2000] 1 AC 486, 497–498. For academic confirmation, see: Deakin et al., Markesinis and Deakin's Tort Law, 7th edn (Oxford: Oxford University Press, 2013) 888; McBride and Bagshaw, Tort Law, 5th edn (Harlow: Pearson, 2015) 882; Davies, Accessory Liability (Oxford: Hart, 2015) 194–195; Carty, 'Joint Tortfeasance and Assistance Liability' (1999) 19 LS 489, 492; Dietrich, 'Accessorial Liability in the Law of Torts' (2011) 31 LS 231, 232; Sales, 'The Tort of Conspiracy and Civil Secondary Liability' [1990] Cambridge LJ 491, 502–507.

have different rationales. But those different rationales for the criminal defences apply equally to the tortious defences. So to the extent that criminal law has both forms of duress, and tort law already has one form (necessity / duress of circumstances), it could equally have the other (duress by threats). After all, both forms, despite different rationales, have substantively similar content.

It is not necessary for tort law to have these defences. It could be acceptable for tort law to take a stricter line, and deny a defence that is otherwise available in criminal law. But it does risk anomaly for tort to recognise one type of defence (necessity / duress of circumstances) and not the other (duress by threats) when: a threat from either source can be equally coercive; a sound explanation is available for why both types of threat might be recognised as defences; and criminal law, noting all this, otherwise applies substantially the same test to recognise both types of duress.

This is not to say that the duress defences in tort would be identical to those in crime. Once again, tort law can hold the defendant to a stricter standard. For example, criminal duress tends to allow the defendant to be reasonably mistaken in perceiving the threat, whereas in tort law, private necessity probably demands that the danger be real.

Further, the two duress defences in tort law need not be identical to each other. In criminal law, there is an important difference: with duress by threats, the defendant can act on another's person, but with duress of circumstances, he can act only upon another's property. For the same reasons, the same approach ought to follow in tort law. Further, in criminal law, for the time being at least, duress is no defence to murder. Consistency would require that any tortious defence of duress by threats similarly be no defence to intentional killing.

1.13 Conclusions

The rationale for the tort of intimidation is that it polices coercive behaviour. Coercion is wrong to the extent that it forces a complainant to change their behaviour for the selfish reasons of the accused. This denies the complainant the freedom to choose their own goals. It also denies them the dignity of an equal status, because it fails to respect them as having the capacity to choose such goals. And it deprives them of the chance to use or develop that capacity, when doing so is personally fulfilling and socially inspiring.

Intimidation is a two-party tort. Intimidation is where the accused threatens, explicitly or implicitly, that, unless the complainant does what the accused demands, the accused will do something unlawful. The threat must be intended to coerce the complainant, and it must in fact coerce the complainant, causing the complainant to comply with the demand.

The unlawful acts, if they were to be carried out, need not be independently actionable by the complainant. Any threatened crime or tort should suffice to ground the plea of intimidation.

Also, any threatened breach of contract should ground the plea. A careful analysis reveals that there is no inconsistency between remedies for intimidation and remedies in contract. Compensatory damages are available in the tort of intimidation when they are not available in contract, and also when there are no effective remedies in contract. Yes, in some cases, the complainant may have a choice between compensation in tort and rescission in contract, but those remedies are different, not inconsistent, and the choice works well in other areas of law, such as misrepresentation. The compatibility is so thorough that, for example, just as affirmation would preclude a plea of contractual duress, so too would it prevent a claim in intimidation (on the basis that the complainant's affirmative choice, not the threats, caused the subsequent transaction).

Thus, as regards threats to act unlawfully, the tort of intimidation polices coercion by drawing a line consistent with the rest of the law: it outlaws the leveraging of activities which other areas of the law have already proscribed, such as crime, tort and breach of contract.

It may also amount to intimidation to threaten to do something lawful out of malice, meaning spite or ill-will. The moral wrong here is that someone who acts from malice reduces their victim from a person to an object of sport, or simply a tool for self-gratification. Hiding behind the lawfulness of acts in order to act upon others maliciously is a cynical misuse of the law, an abuse of rights, which the law itself can rightly censure.

It should not be necessary that the accused intended to harm the complainant. Indeed, such an ingredient is redundant, since an intention to coerce is an intention to harm the complainant's autonomy. The possible need for an intention to harm seems to have arisen by confusion between the three-party tort of causing loss by unlawful means with two-party intimidation. Further, the tort of intimidation is not restricted to economic harm, and the complainant might also recover for injury to feelings.

There should be no defence of justification. The idea of justifying a threat to act unlawfully or abusively is challenging enough. Worse still, justification is a concept incapable of definition, which seems potentially to give the courts an unpredictable discretion to decide cases simply according to a judge's inherent and unaccountable sense of moral justice. There are no persuasive examples of when it might even be applicable, and no case has upheld such a defence in the two-party context.

Duress by threats is not currently recognised as a tortious defence. But it could be. Tort does recognise the defence of necessity. It is substantively aligned with the criminal defence of duress of circumstances. This in turn is largely similar to the criminal defence of duress by threats. This suggests that tort law too could also recognise a defence of duress by threats, in similar terms to its defence of necessity. And even though duress by threats and duress of circumstances have different rationales in criminal law, those different rationales apply equally to support the respective defences in tort law.

A tortious defence of duress by threats would be largely the same as the tortious defence of necessity. However, duress by threats might also allow a defendant to act on another's person, and not just their property. But consistency with criminal law would currently preclude the defence extending to intentional killing (until duress is recognised as a defence to murder).

2 Contract

Necessity and unconscionable bargain

There are three reasons to consider the doctrine of unconscionable bargain.

First, this is where necessity finds expression in contract law: a complainant's necessity, if exploited, might ground a plea of unconscionable bargain.

Second, there is a live debate as to whether contractual duress should incorporate a test of unconscionability. Contractual duress is considered in the next chapter. I shall argue against such incorporation, but an informed decision about that debate can be made only with a proper understanding of unconscionable bargain.

Third, there is a further question whether contract law should recognise the concept of lawful act duress. Again, that is discussed in the next chapter. I shall argue against such recognition, not least because unconscionable bargain already provides relevant coverage. So that coverage needs to be identified here.

This chapter begins with a detailed analysis of the case law. The challenge here is identifying precisely what is the legal test for unconscionable bargain after all. Then the theory is discussed, in light of the case law, to ascertain the doctrine's rationale. After that, the remaining controversies surrounding unconscionable bargain can be addressed. The conclusion draws it all together.

2.1 English case law

Early cases dealt with the troubles of expectant heirs. But it is clear from those cases that there was no distinct doctrine relating to expectant heirs. Rather, expectant heirs were simply a category of person who could bring themselves within unconscionable bargain.

In *Earl of Chesterfield v Jansen*, the complainant was a wealthy man aged 30 who had nevertheless incurred significant debts. To pay them off, he obtained a further loan of £5000, promising to repay £10,000 within a month after the death of the Duchess of Marlborough, from whom he hoped to inherit, in case he should survive her. That agreement was upheld.

In one report,[1] Lord Hardwicke LC explicitly identified five types of fraud.

1 (1750) 2 Ves Sen 125, 28 ER 82.

First, actual fraud – presumably, the tort of deceit.

Second, fraud which

> may be apparent from the intrinsic nature and subject of the bargain itself; such as no man in his senses and not under delusion would make on the one hand, and as no honest and fair man would accept on the other.

In other words, we might say, there is equitable fraud where the terms of the contract are inexplicably unfair.

Third, fraud which

> may be presumed from the circumstances and condition of the parties contracting ... to prevent taking surreptitious advantage of the weakness or necessity of another: which knowingly to do is equally against the conscience as to take advantage of his ignorance: a person is equally unable to judge for himself in one as the other.

In other words, there is equitable fraud where one party takes unconscionable advantage of the weakness or necessity or ignorance of another party unable to judge for himself.

Fourth, fraud which is a 'deceit on the other persons not parties to the fraudulent agreement'. An example given of this last type is where a debtor enters a deed of composition with his creditors, but, unknown to the others, promises a greater pay-out to one creditor to induce them to sign. The other creditors, who relied on an equal composition, are thereby deceived.

Fifth, fraud 'which infects catching bargains with heirs, reversioners, or expectants, in the life of the father'. This does not appear to be a separate category. Rather, Lord Hardwicke notes that these 'have generally been mixed cases, compounded of all or several species of fraud'. There is 'sometimes proof of actual fraud', i.e. type one. 'There has always been an appearance of fraud from the nature of the bargain', i.e. type two. 'There is always fraud presumed or inferred from the circumstances or conditions of the parties contracting: weakness on one side, usury on the other, or extortion or advantage taken of that weakness', i.e. type three. 'In most of these cases have concurred deceit and illusion on other persons', i.e. type four, and specifically, deceit of the ancestor who expects the heir to inherit, not the creditor.

A second report makes no specific mention of bargains with heirs at all.[2]

A third report again suggests that bargains with heirs are not a separate category: 'contracts with young heirs and reversioners are generally compounded of the topics of fraud presumed or implied'.[3]

2 1 Atk 301, 26 ER 191.
3 1 Wils KB 286, 95 ER 621.

The next case is *Earl of Aylesford v Morris.*[4] There Lord Selborne LC said that there is no older head of equity than that described by Lord Hardwicke in *Jansen* as relieving against the fraud which infects catching bargains with heirs. That is potentially misleading: the reports suggest, as we have seen, that *Jansen* viewed bargains with heirs not as a separate type of fraud, but as a circumstance in which equitable fraud might arise.[5]

Lord Selborne continued:

> [Lord Hardwicke] proceeded to note two characters always found in [catching bargains]. There is always fraud presumed or inferred from the circumstances or conditions of the parties contracting – weakness on one side, usury on the other, or extortion, or advantage taken of that weakness. There has been always an appearance of fraud from the nature of the bargain.

These 'two characters' correspond to type-two (inexplicable bargain) and type-three (taking unconscionable advantage) fraud. It is true, in the first report, that Lord Hardwicke says that both types of fraud were 'always' present in bargains with heirs. But this is not repeated in the other reports. And in none of them does Lord Hardwicke appear to suggest that both must necessarily be present before the court will intervene in bargains with heirs. Rather, the clear suggestion is that the court would intervene in any single type of fraud.

So to the extent that both types of fraud, i.e. inexplicable bargain and taking unconscionable advantage, must now be present before the court intervenes in bargains with heirs, that is a new development on the part of Lord Selborne.

Lord Selborne explained that fraud need not mean deceit, but an unconscientious use of power, given the circumstances. Further,

> when the relative position of the parties is such as prima facie to raise this presumption, the transaction cannot stand unless the person claiming the benefit of it is able to repel the presumption by contrary evidence, proving it to have been in point of fact fair, just, and reasonable.

This introduces another novelty: a presumption which transfers the burden of proof onto the accused to show that the bargain was fair, just and reasonable.

In *Morris*, the facts were as follows. A nobleman aged 22 was entitled to large property if he survived his father. The young man had debts, and to pay them off took out a loan at 60%. The court noted that the complainant had no competent advice, and no information as to his own means. This, the court said, constituted a 'state of circumstances', coupled with the terms of the bargain being 'prima facie oppressive and extortionate', which placed the burden on the accused to show the transaction was fair, just and reasonable. The accused failed to justify the transaction. The court ordered repayment of the principal with interest at 5%.

4 (1873) LR 8 Ch App 484.

5 Perhaps Lord Selborne acknowledges this when he himself describes catching bargains as 'generally mixed cases'.

(Modern pay-day loans, advertised on television, often charge interest as much as 1500%, and these to people not even expecting the imminent inheritance of a fortune. How are they not unconscionable bargains in light of *Morris*?)[6]

The case law is not confined to expectant heirs.[7] Reference is also made to the poor and ignorant.

In *Fry v Lane*,[8] Kay J said that fraud is presumed when there is weakness on one side and extortion on the other; whereupon the accused must prove the contract fair, just and reasonable. The judge did not say explicitly that the terms of the transaction must additionally be oppressive, but he did say that undervalue may be 'so gross as to amount of itself to evidence of fraud'.

Kay J said that the doctrine of unconscionable bargain is not restricted to bargains with heirs. 'Another analogous case is where the vendor is a poor man with imperfect education.' The judge considered a number of cases before concluding by way of general principle that a court might set aside a transaction 'where a purchase is made from a poor and ignorant man at a considerable undervalue, the vendor having no independent advice', unless, the judge said, the purchaser proves the transaction was fair, just and reasonable.

This 'poor and ignorant' jurisdiction is again not presented as a separate doctrine, but rather, alongside bargains with heirs, as an example of the type of cases where presumed fraud applies.[9]

As for the facts in *Fry v Lane*, the complainants, whom the judge did indeed describe as poor and ignorant men, 'in a humble position', the workman of a plumber, and a laundryman, were also expectant beneficiaries under a will. They sold their legacies, which would time take to arrange payment of, for immediate cash, at a considerable undervalue (around a quarter of its value). They were without proper advice; they received advice only from the accused's solicitor, who therefore acted for both sides, but with too much favour, the judge said, towards the accused. The judge went as far to say that an experienced solicitor,

6 In Hong Kong, under the Money Lenders Ordinance (Cap 163): making a loan with an interest rate which exceeds 60% is a criminal offence, and the loan is unenforceable (s 24); and a loan with an extortionate interest rate (a rate which exceeds 48% is presumed extortionate) can be rewritten by the court (s 25).

7 Discussions often suggest that salvage is a good example of unconscionable bargain: Burrows, *The Law of Restitution*, 3rd edn (Oxford: Oxford University Press, 2011) 307; Virgo, *The Principles of the Law of Restitution*, 3rd edn (Oxford: Oxford University Press, 2015) 284. But this is wrong. If a rescuer agrees a salvage contract, true enough such a contract can be set aside if it is unfair to the person imperilled: *The Medina* (1876) 1 PD 272. But the contract can also be set aside if it is unfair to the rescuer: *Akerblom v Price* (1885) 7 QBD 129; *The Phantom* (1866) LR 1 A & E 58. Not only that, but the court will then impose terms on both parties. Further, it is a criminal offence for the master of a passing ship not to rescue those in need, if it is safe for them to do so: Merchant Shipping Act 1995, Sch 11, Pt 2, s 3. And the person in peril cannot even refuse rescue: *The Auguste Legembre* [1902] P 123. And even if the parties do not enter any contract, still the rescuer is entitled to be paid under statute: Merchant Shipping Act 1995, sch 11: International Convention on Salvage 1989.

8 (1888) 40 Ch D 312.

9 Similarly, in *Mountford v Callaghan* (18 October 1999), the judge acknowledged, in light of *Fry v Lane*, that poor and ignorant was only 'one of a family of protections offered by the court to defeat oppressive conduct'.

'if he allows a sale at an undervalue, can hardly have duly performed his duty'. He also stressed that the parties to these transactions did not 'meet on equal terms'.

The transactions were set aside. However, the judge also found that there was no 'moral fraud' on the part of the accused, and so the complainants were not awarded costs. Presumably then there was no extortion or taking unconscionable advantage, despite *Jansen* and *Morris*, indeed *Fry v Lane* itself, requiring the contrary.

The judge in *Fry v Lane* averted to a former law which allowed the court to set aside transactions with reversioners at an undervalue, on that ground alone.[10] That law had already been repealed by the time of *Fry v Lane*. But perhaps its spectre confused the judge and explains why moral fraud was not thought necessary in *Fry v Lane*.

In *Creswell v Potter*,[11] Megarry J identified three requirements for unconscionable bargain: 'first, whether the plaintiff is poor and ignorant; second, whether the sale was at a considerable undervalue; and third, whether the vendor had independent advice'. There are three points to note.

First, this approach overstates the relevance of the complainant being poor and ignorant. As *Fry v Lane* made clear, that condition is only one set of circumstances, another being the condition of expectant heir, which might raise the presumption of fraud.

Second, there is no mention in *Creswell v Potter* of extortion or taking unconscionable advantage, contrary to *Jansen* and *Morris*.

Third, as to independent advice, certainly the judge put great store by the fact that the complainant in *Creswell v Potter* received none. But he later said 'I do not think that the requirement of independent advice should be regarded as absolute.' After all, not all advice gets followed. Perhaps the position is best summed when the judge said 'the more usual it is to have a solicitor, the more striking will be his absence, and the more closely will the courts scrutinise what was done'.

As for the facts of *Creswell v Potter*, the complainant gave up her share in the house, said to be at least £150, about 10% of the house value. In return she was released from the mortgage (which stood at £1200). The judge said that this transaction was at considerable undervalue. He then characterised the transaction as 'a gift' from the complainant to the husband. But, we might note, gifts are not properly amenable to the language of undervalue; they are necessarily given without legal expectation of anything in return.[12] If instead the transaction was a bargain, it seems doubtful to call it a considerable undervalue, to give up a small share in return for freedom from the demands of a large mortgage.

10 On that former law, see: Enonchong, *Duress, Undue Influence, and Unconscionable Dealing* (London: Sweet & Maxwell, 2012) [15–028].

11 [1978] 1 WLR 255.

12 In *Langton v Langton* [1995] 3 FCR 521, it was held that unconscionable bargain does not apply to gifts. The opposite conclusion was reached in *Evans v Lloyd* [2013] EWHC 1725 (Ch), consistently with the position in Australia in *Louth v Diprose* (1992) 67 ALJR 95, and in New Zealand in *Dark v Boock* [1991] 1 NZLR 496. If gifts are subject to the doctrine of unconscionable bargain, it must be on a basis other than undervalue. Indeed, in *Louth v Diprose*, in setting out the test for unconscionable bargain, no mention was made by Brennan J of any need for undervalue.

Megarry J preferred 'less highly educated' to ignorant, which anyway resonates with Kay J's 'imperfect education'. He also preferred 'member of a lower income group' to poor. But in that case, there was nothing to suggest a weaker position in the complainant relative to the accused. Quite the opposite – they had the same level of earnings: the complainant was a Post Office telephonist, and the accused, her husband, was a carpenter.

The dispute concerned the complainant giving up her share of the remaining equity in the marital home (after the substantial mortgage was accounted for) upon their divorce. Presumably they were both 'poor and ignorant'. What is notable about *Creswell v Potter* is how one-sided was the inquiry. There is no suggestion anywhere in the judgment that the husband had behaved in an unconscionable manner. Instead, the judge simply concluded that the husband had failed to prove that the transaction was fair, just and reasonable.

Subsequent cases have extended beyond expectant heirs, and the poor and ignorant, to talk in terms of general principle.

In *Alec Lobb (Garages) Ltd v Total Oil GB Ltd*, the complainant ran a garage and needed to refinance. It had previously borrowed from the accused petrol company, which had a charge over the premises and a covenant requiring the complainant to purchase petrol from it exclusively. The accused agreed a refinancing package which involved a lease-back arrangement which tied the garage into the relationship for a further 21 years, but with provision for mutual breaks after 7 and 14 years. Ten years into the arrangement, the complainant sought to have it set aside.

At first instance,[13] Peter Millett QC, sitting as a deputy high court judge, heard arguments on economic duress and unconscionable bargain. As for the latter, he said:[14]

> the court is concerned, not with the reality of the weaker party's consent, but with the conduct of the stronger; for the word 'unconscionable' seems to relate both to the terms of the bargain and to the behaviour of the stronger party. It is not enough to show that the bargain was a hard or unreasonable one.

He went on to say that the accused must have 'imposed the objectionable terms in a morally reprehensible manner, that is to say, in a way which affects his conscience'.[15] He also said that it was probably not possible to reconcile all the authorities. Although he did not refer to them in his judgment, we can see that *Morris* and *Fry v Lane* and *Creswell v Potter* were cited to the court.

13 [1983] 1 All ER 944, upheld on appeal [1985] 1 All ER 303.

14 [1983] 1 All ER 944, 961.

15 For this, the judge cited *Multiservice Bookbinding Ltd v Marden* [1978] 2 All ER 489. That case was concerned with the question whether a mortgage lender was entitled only to repayment of the principal debt and interest and costs, or additionally any collateral advantage. There was no discussion or citation of the case law on unconscionable bargain.

Millett QC said that three elements had almost invariably been present before the court intervened:[16]

> First, one party has been at a serious disadvantage to the other, whether through poverty, or ignorance, or lack of advice, or otherwise, so that circumstances existed of which unfair advantage could be taken ... Second, this weakness of the one party has been exploited by the other in some morally culpable manner ... And third, the resulting transaction has been, not merely hard or improvident, but overreaching and oppressive. Where there has been a sale at an undervalue, the undervalue has almost always been substantial, so that it calls for an explanation, and is in itself indicative of the presence of some fraud ... In short, there must, in my judgment, be some impropriety, both in the conduct of the stronger party and in the terms of the transaction itself (though the former may often be inferred from the latter in the absence of an innocent explanation) which in the traditional phrase 'shocks the conscience of the court'.

This restores the principle, from *Jansen* and *Morris*, that there must be exploitation or moral fraud on the part of the accused. It confirms Lord Selborne's innovation that there must be both exploitation of a serious weakness and oppressive terms.

As for the outcome, Millett QC agreed that the complainant was at a serious disadvantage because of its desperate financial position, coupled with a covenant that precluded recourse to other sources of finance. But there was no element of undervalue, the terms were not oppressive, and the judge could find 'nothing whatever for criticism in the defendant's conduct'.

As for the question of independent advice, Millett QC had noted that the complainant had its own solicitors and accountants, which seems to have been treated as a point in favour of the accused. But, he said, the complainant 'had not taken his advisers into his confidence, and had neither asked for nor received comprehensive legal and financial advice'.[17] In the Court of Appeal, Dillon LJ noted that the solicitors had advised against the transaction, but the complainant declined to accept that advice. He said that 'it would be unreal, in my judgment, to hold that if the transaction is otherwise tainted, it is cured merely because [the complainant] had independent advice'.[18] (A similar point is made in the Canadian case of *Downer v Pitcher*, discussed below.)

Next came two Privy Council decisions, which feature prominently in subsequent case law and commentary. They both confirm the need for moral impropriety on the part of the accused.

In *Hart v O'Connor*,[19] on appeal from New Zealand, the complainant sought to set aside the sale of farmland on the basis that the vendor was not of sound mind.

16 [1983] 1 All ER 944, 961.
17 [1983] 1 All ER 944, 962.
18 [1985] 1 All ER 303, 312.
19 [1985] AC 1000.

Unconscionable bargain was also canvassed, but it was something of a secondary argument, and so received only brief consideration. The court said that an unconscionable bargain was 'of an improvident character made by a poor and ignorant person acting without independent advice which cannot be shown to be a fair and reasonable transaction'. It cited *Morris* for the idea that equitable fraud involved the unconscientious use of power. The court then said that 'it is victimisation, which can consist either of the active exploitation of a benefit or the passive acceptance of a benefit in unconscionable circumstances'.

The sale was upheld. There was no evidence at all to suggest any impropriety on the part of the accused.

In *Boustany v Pigott*,[20] on appeal from the Caribbean, the complainant successfully sought to set aside a lease which had been negotiated on very unfavourable terms with a vulnerable old landlady. The court said that it was 'in general agreement' with the submissions of counsel for the accused. In the report there then follow five submissions, all of which focus on the need for unconscionable conduct or moral impropriety by the party impugned. Counsel then, predictably, submitted that the trial judge found no unconscionable behaviour on the part of his client. This the court rejected; there was clear evidence from which it could be inferred that the accused had behaved unconscionably.

Those five submissions should not, as they sometimes are, be treated as a restatement of the law of unconscionable bargain. The court did not accept them as such. They were submissions tailored, in the finest traditions of partisan advocacy, to the client's best argument. The court was prepared to announce its 'general' agreement, a rather non-committal phrase, not least because it was so sure that the outcome on the facts was against the accused even in light of counsel's submissions on the law. I urge this caution simply because the submissions all focus on one aspect of unconscionable bargain, namely conduct by the accused. In this regard, *Boustany v Pigott* does entrench the need for exploitation. But this is only one aspect of unconscionable conduct, and *Boustany v Pigott* did not address the other aspects explicitly.

As for independent advice, it is notable that in *Boustany v Pigott*, the vulnerable landlady did have 'forcibly' pointed out to her the disadvantages of the new lease by an independent barrister. But this was in the presence of the accused. And the landlady insisted on proceeding. It reinforces the point, made by Dillon LJ in *Alec Lobb*, that independent advice need not always cure an unconscionable bargain. Further, the barrister in *Boustany v Pigott* comes in for criticism. The court said that he 'should never have agreed to prepare the new lease, [and] appreciated that he had not done a good day's work if [the landlady] was his client'. This seems apiece with the dereliction of the solicitor's duty in *Fry v Lane*.

Subsequent decisions all ground the doctrine of unconscionable conduct in one or more of the above cases.

Three further cases return to the question of legal advice.

20 (1993) 42 WIR 175.

In *Credit Lyonnais Bank Nederland NV v Burch*,[21] the central issue was undue influence; unconscionable conduct was not pleaded, although the court did feel moved to comment on that doctrine. Millett LJ emphasised that it would not have made any difference to the outcome had the complainant entered the transaction after taking legal advice. 'Such advice is neither always necessary nor always sufficient. It is not a panacea.' The purpose of advice is not so much to protect the complainant against herself, he said, but against the accused:[22]

> The solicitor must not be content to satisfy himself that his client understands the transaction and wishes to carry it out. His duty is to satisfy himself that the transaction is one which his client could sensibly enter into if free from improper influence; and if he is not so satisfied to advise her not to enter into it, and to refuse to act further for her if she persists.

In *Portman Building Society v Dusangh*,[23] Ward LJ said that a transaction between the complainant and a third party can be set aside if the third party had actual or constructive notice that the transaction was the result of unconscionable conduct by the accused.[24] (But on the facts of the case, the transaction was upheld.) He also said that legal advice might not be 'so much an essential freestanding requirement, but rather a powerful factor confirming the suspicion of nefarious dealing'; but on the facts, this was not such a bad transaction that no reasonably competent solicitor could have permitted it.[25]

Finally, in *Jones v Morgan*,[26] Chadwick LJ said that the purpose of legal advice was to protect the interests of someone who might otherwise be 'naïve, trusting and unbusinesslike' so that the parties to the transaction are able to meet on equal terms after all. Indeed, he later said that the complainant who received proper advice would not be at a serious disadvantage vis-à-vis the accused. And while, the judge continued, an accused might not know what advice the complainant had in fact received, it sufficed that the transaction was one which a competent solicitor could advise in favour of.

Jones v Morgan talks in terms of the relative position of the parties. Yet in *Mountford v Callaghan*,[27] the judge said that there was no support in the case law 'for a judgment about the relative poverty and ignorance of the contracting parties'. That is out of line with *Morris*, where Lord Selborne spoke about 'the relative position of the parties'. And in *Alec Lobb*, Millett QC

21 [1997] 1 All ER 144.
22 [1997] 1 All ER 144, 156.
23 [2000] All ER (D) 582.
24 See too: *Qutb v Hussain* [2005] EWHC 157 (Ch).
25 The cases often use this double negative. It is clearer simply to say that this was a transaction which a reasonably competent solicitor could have advised in favour of.
26 [2002] 1 EGLR 125.
27 (18 October 1999).

spoke about 'the stronger party' and a 'serious disadvantage *to* the other', and Dillon LJ spoke of '*inequality* of the parties' (my emphasis). The other jurisdictions discussed below also stress the relative position of the parties.

Summary

To plead unconscionable bargain in English law:

First, there must be some weakness on the part of the complainant. This can include poverty or ignorance or necessity, or the moral naivety that comes from being a young expectant heir.

Second, the accused must have taken advantage of the complainant's weakness to procure the transaction, and the ascendant view is that the accused's conduct in doing so must be morally unconscionable. It is difficult to see how an accused can take advantage of a weakness in the complainant which they also share, at least in cases of circumstantial weakness (like necessity). And much of the discussion of morally reprehensible conduct is couched in terms of making unconscionable use of the power arising from the accused being in a stronger position. In this case, it is a weakness relative to the accused which matters.

Third, the terms of the transaction must be oppressive, rather than merely improvident or unreasonable. However, this seems to overlook the possibility, acknowledged in Australian and Canadian law, that the equitable fraud might lie in procuring the contract at all, rather than its terms. We return to this point below.

All three elements of unconscionable bargain are necessary to raise a presumption that the transaction amounts to an unconscionable bargain, at which point the burden moves to the accused to show it was fair, just and reasonable after all. Factually, however, these lines of inquiry blend together: the court has acknowledged, for example, that an oppressive bargain without explanation is itself evidence of exploitation. But it seems that the complainant's weakness at least must be separately identified and not merely inferred.

As for independent advice, the more consistent position appears to be as follows. Lack of independent advice is not a necessary ingredient to show unconscionable conduct; but it will cause the court to cast greater scrutiny over the transaction. If the complainant received independent advice, and the transaction was one which a competent solicitor could advise in favour of, then that counts in favour of the accused. Indeed, it might mean that the complainant stood in no position of relative weakness. This is because the purpose of independent advice should be to protect the complainant against exploitation, and to ensure that the parties meet on equal terms.

Mere receipt of advice does not cure what would otherwise be an unconscionable bargain, if no competent solicitor could advise in favour of the transaction. Also, the advice must be properly independent, meaning: that the adviser is independent of the accused or the other party to the transaction; and that the advice itself is given privately to the complainant, rather than in the presence of the accused. It seems that the court is less concerned with the actual advice given to the complainant, which may anyway be privileged.[28] Rather, the court seems more concerned with whether it reasonably appeared to the accused that the complainant received independent advice.[29] That perspective would certainly be consistent with the approach which asks whether the accused themselves has behaved unconscionably.

2.2 Australian case law

There are two principal decisions which loom large in Australian law.

The first is *Blomley v Ryan*.[30] (It was also cited with approval by Millett QC in the English case of *Alec Lobb*.)

In *Blomley v Ryan*, a sale of farmland was set aside. The vendor was an old man of failing intellect who was intoxicated at the time. The sale was said to be at a substantial undervalue (about 25% less), concluded with undue haste, and without adequate advice.

McTiernan J quoted from the English cases of *Jansen* and *Morris* before summarising that equitable fraud arose where 'advantage was taken of weakness, ignorance and other disabilities on the side of the [complainant] and the contract was derived from such behaviour and it is an unfair bargain'. He said that 'the essence of such weakness is that the party is unable to judge for himself'. The allegation could be then answered by showing that the bargain was not unfair to the weaker side. The judge also stressed the relative weakness of the complainant to the accused.

Fullager J said that equitable fraud was not so much about the assent of the complainant to the transaction, but the behaviour of the accused. He continued:[31]

> The circumstances adversely affecting a party, which may induce a court of equity either to refuse its aid or to set a transaction aside, are of great variety ... among them are poverty or need of any kind, sickness, age, sex, infirmity of body or mind, drunkenness, illiteracy or lack of education, lack of assistance or explanation where assistance or explanation is necessary.

He said that the common characteristic was that such weakness placed the complainant at a disadvantage vis-à-vis the accused. Again, this is a position of relative weakness.

28 And indeed privilege was invoked in *Jones v Morgan*.

29 In *Portman Building Society v Dusangh*, Ward LJ said: 'The appellant has also to face the further difficulty that, as the building society knew, he did receive independent advice. The society was entitled to assume it was advice directed towards saving him from himself.' In other words, from the perspective of the building society, the independent advice received by the complainant was well given.

30 (1956) 99 CLR 362.

31 (1956) 99 CLR 362, 405.

The judge continued that it did not appear essential that the complainant should suffer detriment by the bargain. That is consistent with my observation above that a fair contract might still be the result of exploitation if the complainant would never have entered it otherwise. Nevertheless, Fullager J said that, while inadequacy of consideration is never of itself a ground for relief, it was often important to support the inference that disadvantage existed and unfair use was made of it.

Both *Blomley v Ryan* and the earlier decision it mentions of *Cooke v Clayworth*[32] were cases of intoxication, and in both cases the judge made the following distinction.

On the one hand, merely being drunk affords no ground for relief. As Fullager J said, it would be dangerous to countenance the view that a person could escape the obligations of a contract simply by proving they were 'in liquor'. We might add, no one should be able to escape a contract simply by showing that they were poor, or an expectant heir.[33]

On the other hand, where the complainant was seriously affected by drink, to the knowledge of the accused, equity might refuse its aid; and where a disadvantageous contract was obtained by 'drawing him into drink', or there had been real unfairness in taking advantage of the complainant's condition, the transaction might be set aside.

Thus an important consideration is the knowledge of the accused. It is not simply that the complainant was intoxicated; what is relevant is that the accused knows that the complainant is, by reason of intoxication, under a serious disability. The accused who procures this state of affairs obviously has knowledge of it.

Fullager J also noted the inadequacy of the advice which the complainant received. The judge said that the solicitor was acting for both sides; had he been acting for the complainant alone, he would not have allowed the terms of the transaction. This is reminiscent of the criticism of lawyers in *Fry v Lane* and *Boustany v Pigott.*

Kitto J, dissenting on the facts, said that whether or not the complainant was intoxicated due to his own self-indulgence was irrelevant, because unconscionable bargain was not a doctrine 'which extends sympathetic benevolence to a victim of underserved misfortune; it is one which denies to those who act unconscientiously the fruits of their wrongdoing'. In other words, the complainant's prior fault does not justify exploitation.

He referred to the English case of *Fry v Lane* before saying: first, the complainant must be in such a debilitated state that there was not a reasonable degree of equality between the parties; second, this condition was sufficiently evident to the

32 (1811) Ves Jun 12, 34 ER 222.

33 Not just because the poor or heirs should be held to their contractual obligations. It is also in their interests that others contract with them, which will happen only if the contracts are known to be enforceable. Similarly, in the Hong Kong case of *Tong Kwok Cheong v Tong Wai Lin* [2014] 1 HKLRD 339, discussed below, the court said explicitly that there was no presumption that bargains involving expectant heirs were unconscionable.

accused as to make it unfair to accept the transaction. More generally, he said that unconscionable bargain applies:[34]

> whenever one party to a transaction is at a special disadvantage in dealing with the other party because illness, ignorance, inexperience, impaired faculties, financial need or other circumstances affect his ability to conserve his own interest, and the other party unconscientiously takes advantage of the opportunity.

The second principal case in Australian law is *Commercial Bank of Australia Ltd v Amadio.*[35] (In turn, *Amadio* was cited with approval by the Privy Council in *Boustany v Pigott*, and by the English Court of Appeal in *Portman Building Society v Dusangh.*)

In *Amadio*, elderly migrants with little English were asked by their son to execute a mortgage over their property to secure the overdraft of his company. The son told them, falsely, that the mortgage was limited in time and amount. The mortgage was set aside, a majority of the court relying on the ground of unconscionable bargain. The court fully endorsed the approach taken in *Blomley v Ryan*. We shall consider only what was added by the judgments.

Mason J emphasised that the complainant's disability must be 'special'. The doctrine does not apply, he said, whenever there is merely some difference in bargaining power. The disability must seriously affect the complainant's ability to make a judgement as to his own best interests, and when the accused knows or ought to know of the existence of that condition and of its effect on the complainant.

The judge also said that if the accused did not have actual knowledge, but was aware of the possibility of the complainant's condition, or was aware of facts which would raise that possibility in the mind of the reasonable person, the result will be the same.

In the English case of *Portman v Dusangh*, as we saw, the court also suggested that constructive knowledge might suffice. But *Blomley v Ryan* was couched in terms of actual knowledge.

Deane J (with whom Mason and Wilson JJ agreed) repeated that inadequacy of consideration was not essential. He gave the apt example of a guarantee:[36] the terms may be fair, but a third party gets the benefit, and the guarantor all the burden. If that guarantor was procured to act, unconscionably, then equity might intervene. A similar situation arose on the facts of the Canadian case of *Morrison*, discussed below. There, the complainant had entered into a mortgage. The terms were fair. But she should never have given the mortgage in the first place, and it was set aside.

34 (1956) 99 CLR 362, 415.
35 (1983) 57 ALJR 358.
36 The same example was adopted in the Hong Kong case of *Standard Chartered Bank v Shem Yin Fun* [2002] HKEC 582.

In *Amadio*, Deane J also said that the accused, through its solicitor, if it did not know of the complainant's weakness, nevertheless had no reasonable basis for believing that they had received proper advice, and at best closed its eyes to the complainant's vulnerability.

Blomley v Ryan and *Amadio* form the bedrock for subsequent Australian decisions.

In *Louth v Diprose*,[37] the weakness was emotional dependence.[38] A woman extracted, from a man infatuated with her, a gift of money to buy a house, playing upon his love for her by making suicide threats, and dishonestly manufacturing an atmosphere of crisis about her. It was held that the gift was procured by unconscionable conduct, and she was ordered to transfer the house to him.

Brennan J said that a gift could be set aside for unconscionable conduct ordinarily when three factors arise: first, a relationship between the parties which, to the knowledge of the accused, places the complainant at a special disadvantage relative to the accused; second, unconscientious exploitation of that disadvantage by the accused; third, overbearing of the complainant's will such that they are unable to make a worthwhile judgement as to their best interests.[39] There is, aptly in the context of gifts, no mention here of the need for 'undervalue'.

Deane J added that the inquiry concerned whether it was unconscionable for the accused to procure, accept or retain the benefit of the transaction. This is consistent with the notion of passive acceptance of an unconscionable transaction, as mentioned in the Privy Council decision of *Hart v O'Connor*.

Two final cases return to the issue of what is meant by 'special' weakness.

In *Australian Competition and Consumer Commission v C G Berbatis Holdings Pty Ltd*,[40] lessees of commercial premises were in litigation with the lessors. But the lessees also wanted to sell their business, which depended on obtaining a renewal of the lease, to which they had no contractual right. The lessors did renew the lease, but on the condition of discharging all current claims against them. This was held not to be unconscionable.

Gleeson CJ said that the lessees had no special disadvantage. They had two financial interests: their claims, and the sale of their business, and chose to prefer the latter. He said that the lessees suffered from no lack of ability to judge or protect or conserve their financial interests. What the lessees lacked, he said, was the commercial ability to pursue both interests at the same time.

It is important to emphasise that it is not simply a complainant's inability to judge their best interests which matters; the doctrine should also apply where the complainant, fully lucid of their situation, finds themselves unable to protect their interests. Hence Gleeson CJ was right to talk in terms of a lack of ability to

37 (1992) 67 ALJR 95.

38 Emotional dependence was similarly the disability in *Bridgewater v Leahy* (1998) 72 ALJR 1525.

39 This is a rare example, in unconscionable bargain, of talk of an 'overborne will'. It seems misplaced. We shall reject such an approach to contractual duress (Chapter 3) and criminal duress (Chapter 5).

40 (2003) 77 AJLR 926.

protect or conserve one's best interests. This finds support in the judgment of Kitto J in *Blomley v Ryan*, where he too talks about the complainant's inability to conserve his own interests.

Finally, in *Kakavas v Crown Melbourne Ltd*,[41] the complainant was a high-stakes gambler who alleged that a casino had exploited his inability, by reason of his pathological urge to gamble, to make decisions in his best interests. He sought to recover his gambling losses. The claim was dismissed.

The court said that equity does not relieve a complainant from the consequences of improvident transactions conducted in the ordinary and undistinguished course of a lawful business. A complainant who engages in risky business, said the court, cannot expect equity to relieve him of the coming home of those risks. There was no evidence that the complainant had a continuously operating compulsion; he was able to make decisions when to gamble and when not, even if, once engaged in gambling, he was then in the grip of excitement. In moral or social terms, the court said, a casino might be said to victimise gamblers who choose to frequent it, but in law there is nothing wrong with conducting lawful business which accommodates the desire of people to make use of it. And, we might note, that must be right – otherwise an off-licence cannot sell wine to someone who likes to drink, and a cake shop cannot sell pastry to someone who is overweight.

(In similar vein, in the Canadian case of *Downer v Pitcher*, below, the court said that 'special' vulnerability was outside the reasonably tolerable differences and risks which characterise normal human interaction.)

The court in *Kakavas* also considered the notion of constructive notice. It said that constructive notice was used in the context of property, to decide whether a subsequent legal interest had priority over an earlier equitable interest. But, said the court, constructive notice had no application to commercial transactions, and none to unconscionable bargain. Of course, this is seemingly contrary to what was said by Mason J in *Amadio*, but that judgment was reinterpreted: what was relevant, said the court in *Kakavas*, was knowledge or wilful ignorance. This was also consistent, the court continued, with Deane J's judgment in *Amadio*, where that judge spoke about turning a blind eye.

Summary

Whereas the position in English law explicitly requires three elements to be present to found a plea of unconscionable bargain, Australian case law suggests that only two are needed: a special disability on the part of the complainant relative to the accused, and that it would be unconscionable for the accused to procure or retain the benefit of the transaction. There is no third requirement that the transaction be at gross undervalue. After all, the consideration may be adequate, and yet the transaction itself is still unfair.

The Australian case law also confirms that it is the relative weakness of the complainant to the accused which matters. And it stresses, rightly, that the

41 (2013) 87 ALJR 708.

complainant's weakness must be special, not merely the ordinary incidence of a weaker bargaining position, nor the everyday urges which cause people to patronise lawful business (like a gambler to gamble). Again, like English case law, the idea arises that relief might be given to passive acceptance of an unconscionable bargain, although no case was decided on that basis.

As for constructive knowledge, the most recent pronouncement denies that constructive knowledge is enough: what matters, said the court in *Kakavas*, is the accused's actual knowledge or wilful ignorance.

The Australian case law has been open to acknowledging the very wide range of weakness which equity might protect – not just expectant heirs or the poor and ignorant. The range of weakness includes financial need, the need for assistance or explanation, indeed need of any kind. The lists given in the case law are explicitly not closed. What links all these weaknesses is the complainant's inability to judge or promote or conserve their best interests.

2.3 New Zealand case law

The principal case in New Zealand is *Nichols v Jessup*.[42] (It was cited with approval by the Privy Council in *Boustany v Pigott*.) It proceeded immediately after the earlier Privy Council decision in *Hart v O'Connor*, appealed from New Zealand. It represents a forthright response to that decision, a deliberate restatement of the New Zealand law on unconscionable bargain. In its turn, it also discusses the Australian cases of *Blomley v Ryan* and *Amadio*, and the English case of *Fry v Lane*.

The case itself concerned a complainant whose neighbour convinced her to enter a transaction granting mutual rights of access over their driveways, which increased the neighbour's property value significantly while diminishing the value of the complainant's property. The case was remitted to the trial judge, but before doing so, the Court of Appeal gave guidance on unconscionable bargain.

Cooke P noted that, while there was previously no need for moral fraud, as per *Fry v Lane*, now there was, following *Hart v O'Connor*. But he also said that in this case, although the accused did not set out intentionally to exploit the complainant, he must have realised, or ought to have realised, the imbalance in the arrangement. In this case, the accused must have known or suspected that the complainant was no judge of her own interests. In those circumstances, he said, the accused should have done more to ensure that the complainant received adequate advice.

McMullin J said:[43]

> In New Zealand, poverty and ignorance, lack of independent advice, illness, age, inequality of bargaining power and inadequacy of consideration have been among the factors regarded by the courts as justifying the setting aside of a bargain on the grounds of unconscionability where one party has taken advantage of the weakness or necessity of another.

42 [1986] 1 NZLR 226.
43 [1986] 1 NZLR 226, 234.

(A later court added to this list: lack of education, mental or physical infirmity, stress or anxiety.[44]) McMullin J also affirmed that unconscionability may arise where the accused passively accepted the benefit of an improvident bargain.

Somers J said that unconscionable bargain was not to assist those who repent of foolish undertakings, but to protect those under a disadvantage from those who take advantage of that fact; it looks to the conduct of the stronger party. Once more, we might note, this is about relative weakness.

He also said that the doctrine applied not just when the accused knew of the complainant's material disability and its effect, but when he reasonably ought to have known. If the circumstances are such, he said, as fairly to lead a reasonable person to believe that the other is under a serious disadvantage affecting his ability to protect himself, then he is bound to make inquiry, and will be taken to know whatever such inquiry would have disclosed.

This suggests that constructive knowledge of the complainant's weakness suffices, contrary to the recent Australian decision of *Kakavas.*

When remitted,[45] the trial judge found that the accused was well aware of the complainant's weakness, yet was content passively to accept the benefit of a transaction manifestly one-sided. (So it was a case of actual rather than constructive knowledge after all.) It was not consistent with good conscience, said the judge, for the accused to retain its benefit, so the agreement was set aside.

The guidance of the Court of Appeal in *Nichols v Jessup* has been regularly followed in the New Zealand case law as regards the sufficiency of both constructive knowledge[46] and passive acceptance.

We shall consider what the subsequent cases add to *Nichols v Jessup.*[47]

In *Bowkett v Action Finance Ltd*,[48] the court said that the more startling the inadequacy of consideration, the less significant the disability of the complainant might need be, and vice versa. More broadly, in *Contracts Bonding Ltd v Snee*,[49] there appears a tendency to see unconscionable bargain not as a list of requirements, as in English and Australian law, but perhaps as a bundle of relevant factors, some of which may carry more or less weight on the facts of the particular case.

But it was confirmed, in *Attorney-General v 'R'*,[50] that there will (must?) necessarily be: serious disadvantage on the part of the complainant known to the accused, and exploitation of that disadvantage in circumstances amounting to equitable fraud. Thus, we might note, the imbalance of the transaction, or the inadequacy of consideration, is seemingly not essential, consistently with Australian case law. But, said the court in *'R'*, it is often relevant, and something capable of putting the accused on notice of the complainant's weakness.

44 *Bartle v G E Custodians* [2010] 3 NZLR 601, [166].

45 *Nichols v Jessup (No 2)* [1986] 1 NZLR 237.

46 Although the point was thought open to debate in *Walmsley v Christchurch CC* [1990] 1 NZLR 199, 206.

47 Previous case law consistent with *Nichols v Jessup* includes *Moffat v Moffat* [1984] 1 NZLR 600.

48 [1992] 1 NZLR 449.

49 [1992] 2 NZLR 157.

50 [2002] 2 NZLR 91, a point not developed on appeal to the Privy Council [2003] UKPC 22.

Another relevant factor identified in the case law is independent advice:

In *Bowkett v Action Finance Ltd*,[51] the court said that adequate independent advice would normally be deemed to overcome any disability. (As we saw, a similar point was made in the English case of *Jones v Morgan*.) In *Paki v Attorney-General (No 2)*,[52] the court said that where the transaction is imbalanced, its justification by the accused will likely require him to show that the complainant received independent legal advice. In *ASB Bank Ltd v Harlick*,[53] it was seemingly suggested that, where independent advice has been given, the accused can reasonably rely on the adequacy of that advice. Perhaps it is better to add, as does English law, that this applies only where the transaction is one which a competent solicitor could advise in favour of.

In *Dark v Boock*,[54] the transaction was a gift of the complainant's house to the use of the accused for the latter's life. The transaction was enabled by the accused's solicitor. The court said that the solicitor was put on inquiry, both as to the complainant's dementia, and to the fact that the transaction was potentially disadvantageous to her. Because the transaction was not in the complainant's best interests, the court set it aside.

Dark v Boock was 'a cautionary tale for solicitors'. This is reminiscent of the English case of *Fry v Lane*. So too is the fact that the court in *Dark v Boock* said that the accused herself had acted in complete good faith, and no order of costs was made against her. But that is inconsistent with *Nichols v Jessup*, which expressly acknowledged the need for moral fraud.

Finally, in *Gustav & Co Ltd v Macfield Ltd*,[55] the court said that the time for considering unconscionability was when entering into the transaction, or a subsequent variation. (The same point has been made in Canadian law.) But once the contract was concluded, the accused was not required to continue to make inquiries.

Summary

The New Zealand case law emphasises two things.

First, the complainant must be under a serious disadvantage, and the accused must know of this disadvantage and of its effects, or they ought reasonably to know of it. This marks a difference from the recent Australian position, which requires knowledge or wilful ignorance and not merely constructive knowledge. But consistently with the Australian position, disability is described in terms of the complainant being unable to assess or protect their best interests. Talk of the 'stronger party' again suggests that, in New Zealand, it is relative weakness which matters.

51 [1992] 1 NZLR 449.
52 [2015] 1 NZLR 67.
53 [1996] 1 NZLR 655.
54 [1991] 1 NZLR 496.
55 [2008] 2 NZLR 735.

Second, it must be unconscionable for the accused to retain the benefit of a transaction derived from this disadvantage, either because the accused actively procured the transaction by exploiting the disadvantage, or because they passively accepted its benefit when it was against conscience to do so. Either way, this requires moral obloquy on the part of the accused. (Both English and Australian law also countenance the notion of passive acceptance of an unconscionable bargain.)

Transactional imbalance and inadequacy of consideration are not necessary requirements, but it can be relevant (for example, it can provide evidence of a weakness exploited). This is consistent with the position in Australia, but contrary to the position in England.

As for legal advice, the position is similar to English law: absence of independent advice does not necessarily show the transaction to be unconscionable, but its presence is highly relevant because, if adequate, it balances out the complainant's weakness, allowing the parties to meet on equal terms.

2.4 Hong Kong case law

The central case in the Hong Kong case law is *Lo Wo v Cheung Chan Ka*.[56]

Three elderly and illiterate sisters from rural China were persuaded to sell their inherited half-share in a Hong Kong flat to a developer for a 60% discount. The agreement was signed in haste without independent advice. The accused was even appointed the complainants' attorney. The transaction was set aside.

The judge referred to the English and Australian case law. Without setting out a definitive test, the judge said that the following factors were relevant.

First, a serious disadvantage suffered by the complainant giving rise to an opportunity for the accused to take unconscionable advantage. As for what counts as serious disadvantage, the judge gave a non-exhaustive list: age, poverty, ignorance, lack of assistance or independent advice, or inability to judge what is in one's best interests.

Second, the terms of the bargain were oppressive. (As we have seen, this is seemingly a free-standing requirement in English law.) The judge said that this was to 'reinforce' the view that the complainant was at a serious disadvantage or that the accused acted in a morally culpable manner; impropriety might be inferred from the terms of the transaction, in the absence of any innocent explanation. In this case, we might note, it may be that oppressive terms are not essential, just good evidence of weakness and exploitation (as is the case in Australian and New Zealand law).

56 [2000] 2 HKLRD 370. Note also, that just as English law has the Unfair Contract Terms Act 1977, and related consumer legislation, so too Hong Kong has the Unconscionable Contracts Ordinance (Cap 458). The common law doctrine of unconscionable bargain is still relevant when considering the Ordinance: *Shum Kit Ching v Caesar Beauty Centre Ltd* [2003] 3 HKLRD 422; *Star Cruises (HK) Ltd v Tung Ho Wah* [2006] HKCU 465 (DC), [44]–[45]; *Swiss Finance Mortgages Services Ltd v Wong Kam Fan* [2016] HKCU 3124 (CFI), [26].

Third, morally culpable conduct on the part of the accused. The judge said that exploitation is the foundation of the doctrine of unconscionable bargain; the conduct must shock the conscience of the court. He said that this required the accused to be aware of the opportunity for exploitation, and to have taken advantage of that opportunity. Whether it sufficed that the accused ought to have known was, said the judge, an area of some difficulty, and he preferred to rest his decision on the accused's subjective (i.e. actual) knowledge.

Most subsequent decisions have applied *Lo Wo* or have followed the same approach. Often those three elements have been treated as all essential requirements.[57]

In *Tong Kwok Cheong v Tong Wai Lin*,[58] the court said that there was no presumption that bargains involving expectant heirs were unconscionable. That must be right – otherwise, by parity of reasoning, the same would apply to transactions with people who are poor or illiterate or in need. A rule which presumptively vitiated all transactions with people in need would deny them the very assistance which would relieve their need.[59]

Instead, the court said, any 'presumption' of fraud arises only upon facts proved by the complainant, such as morally culpable conduct by the accused. Only then did the burden switch to the accused to show that the transaction was fair, just and reasonable.[60]

An unequal or weak position is not enough to ground unconscionable bargain.

In *Beacon College Ltd v Yiu Man Hau*,[61] the evidence showed a lack of bargaining power on the part of the complainants, who felt they had no practical alternative but to sign their contracts. This, said the court, fell far short of establishing unconscionable bargain. It failed to show that the accused was aware of any weakness, or how it took advantage of it, or whether it behaved in a morally culpable manner.

In that case, the accused was a tutorial college that enforced negative covenants against the complainants against working for rivals when they left its employment.

57 *China Finance & Assets Management Ltd v Lafe Properties (Hong Kong) Ltd* [2015] HKEC 300; *Bank of China (Hong Kong) Ltd v Tsang Sheung Bun* [2012] HKEC 1586; *Shum Kit Ching v Caesar Beauty Centre Ltd* [2003] 3 HKLRD 422; *Citibank NA v KCL Chemical Ltd* [2017] HKCU 338 (CFI), [32]; *Freeway Finance Co Ltd v Lai Sau Kei* [2016] HKCU 1546 (CFI), [137], [140]–[142]. But in *Standard Chartered Bank v Shem Yin Fun* [2002] HKEC 582, the court said that inadequacy of consideration was not an essential ingredient.

58 [2014] 1 HKLRD 339.

59 Thus *Goff & Jones* must surely be wrong to say that equity presumes bargains with expectant heirs to be unconscionable: Mitchel et al. (eds), *Goff & Jones: The Law of Unjust Enrichment*, 9th edn (London: Sweet & Maxwell, 2016) [11–60]. Enonchong is surely right when he says that there is no special protection for expectant heirs: *Duress, Undue Influence, and Unconscionable Dealing* (London: Sweet & Maxwell, 2012) [15–029].

60 On the burden shifting to the accused to show that the transaction was fair, just and reasonable, see too: *Tong Kwok Cheong v Tong Wai Lin* [2014] 1 HKLRD 339; *LZX v WYL* [2012] 5 HKLRD 29; *Wong Yung v Hui Kwok Nam* [2003] HKEC 337; *Standard Chartered Bank v Shem Yin Fun* [2002] HKEC 582.

61 [2002] HKEC 1509.

The court said that the complainants could always find work in secondary schools; the fact that rival tutorial colleges might have been more profitable did not make it unconscionable to enforce the restrictive covenants.

In *Standard Chartered Bank v Shem Yin Fun*,[62] the court said that, in dealing with the question whether the complainant suffers any disabling circumstances, the best approach is very often a comparison of the relative position of the parties; however, mere inequality of bargaining power is not enough.

Similarly, a transaction will not be set aside just because there was an absence of independent advice and consideration was inadequate. It is an essential requirement that the accused engaged in an unconscientious use of power.[63]

Despite the uncertainty expressed in *Lo Wo*, a number of cases address the question of whether actual or constructive knowledge, or passive acceptance, suffices.

In *Shum Kit Ching v Caesar Beauty Centre Ltd*,[64] the court said that the accused must know of the complainant's weakness and knowingly take advantage. This was fulfilled, said the court, by actual knowledge, or constructive knowledge that a person should reasonably have possessed. On the facts of the case, the accused had actual knowledge of the complainant's weakness (she was easily persuaded to part with money on credit she could not afford).

In *Semana Bachicha v Poon Shiu Man*,[65] the complainant was a foreign domestic helper, treated abusively by her employer, and constructively dismissed. The parties attended a conciliation meeting at the Labour Department, after which the complainant signed a settlement agreement under which she was paid about 95% less than she was due. The employer had alleged that the complainant walked out of her job. In this case, said the Labour Department officer chairing the meeting, the complainant would owe money to the employer. The officer advised the complainant to accept the compromise, which she did.

But the court said that the employer knew the true circumstances of the complainant's constructive dismissal, and took advantage of the officer's faulty advice and the complainant's ignorance – which, we might add, could only mean ignorance of the law – to secure an oppressive agreement by unconscionable means. The agreement was set aside. This case might also be viewed as the accused passively accepting the benefit of the faulty advice.

Sometimes legislation deems a transaction illegal so as to protect a class of persons from being exploited. In other words, illegality may flag up unconscionable conduct:

In *Estinah v Golden Hand Indonesian Employment Agency*,[66] a foreign domestic helper was able to recover the difference between the higher amount illegally

62 [2002] HKEC 582.

63 *Standard Chartered Bank v Shem Yin Fun* [2002] HKEC 582; *Bank of China (Hong Kong) Ltd v Tsang Sheung Bun* [2012] HKEC 1586.

64 [2003] 3 HKLRD 422.

65 [2000] 2 HKLRD 833.

66 [2001] 4 HKC 607.

demanded by the employment agency for introducing her to her new employer, and the lower statutory maximum which the agency could demand. Although her payment was illegal, she did not know this, and the legislation existed to protect her. The court said that the agency had pressured her into payment (i.e. there was duress), or had exploited her comparatively weak position.[67]

Summary

In Hong Kong, most of the case law suggests a need for three factors.

First, the complainant was at a serious disadvantage relative to the accused. This is not merely an inferior bargaining position, let alone the case where the complainant has other options, even if those other options are less financially attractive.

Second, the accused knew of this weakness, and knowingly took advantage of it in a morally culpable manner. Although the possibility of constructive knowledge has been canvassed, actual knowledge has been present on the facts. In terms of acting in a morally culpable manner, this seems to include both active exploitation, and passive acceptance of a benefit in unconscionable conditions.

Third, most cases talk about the need for the transaction to be oppressive, but that might simply be useful evidence, as *Lo Wo* suggests, to support the contention that the complainant was disadvantaged or the accused acted exploitatively.

Put shortly, where English, Australian and New Zealand law take differing positions, Hong Kong law has not yet unequivocally taken sides.

2.5 Canadian case law

As for the doctrine of unconscionable conduct in Canadian law, its condition has been lamented as one of conceptual and jurisprudential paucity.[68] With that introduction, there are two cases upon which most subsequent case law is founded.

First, in *Morrison v Coast Finance Ltd*,[69] the complainant was an elderly widow who was persuaded by two men, 'comparative strangers', to borrow money from the finance company, secured by a mortgage on her house, and give that money to the men, in part to repay their debts to the same finance company. The transaction was set aside. Davey JA said that unconscionable bargain required (i) proof of inequality of the parties, arising out of ignorance, need or distress, leaving the weaker in the power of the stronger, and (ii) substantial unfairness in the bargain. This then raises a presumption of fraud (presumably, equitable fraud), which the stronger must rebut by showing the transaction to be fair, just and reasonable. He cited *Aylesford v Morris* and *Fry v Lane*.

He noted that the terms of the loan were standard, and so not on their face objectionable. Rather, the point was that the complainant gained nothing from

67 See too: *Andayani v Chan Oi Ling* [2001] 1 HKC 252.

68 Bigwood, 'Antipodean Reflections on the Canadian Unconscionability Doctrine' (2005) 84 Can Bar Rev 171, 172.

69 [1965] BCJ No 178.

the transaction herself. In other words, we might say, what was unconscionable was not the terms of the contract, but the fact that the contract was procured at all (as acknowledged in the Australian case of *Amadio*). 'Substantive unfairness' seems a poor way to express this point.

Further, Davey JA said that the finance house took advantage of the complainant's obvious ignorance and inexperience. Presumably this is an additional requirement: the question of inequality becomes redundant, surely, if no advantage is taken of this inequality. Otherwise, the test would simply involve one question: was the bargain substantively unfair.

That singular approach was adopted by Lambert JA in the second principal case, *Harry v Kreutziger*.[70] There a native Indian, of limited education and inexperienced in business, was persuaded, with false or reckless assurances, to sell his fishing boat and licence for about a third of its true value. The transaction was set aside.

McIntyre JA simply restated the approach of the court in *Morrison*. But Lambert JA went further. Unconscionable bargain, he said, comes down to a single question: whether the transaction is sufficiently divergent from community standards of commercial morality that it should be rescinded.

This approach looks unprincipled. Only afterwards do parties know whether their transactions are enforceable, and then only by submitting to the moral evaluation of a judge. This is less the rule of law, more the unbridled discretion of an unaccountable individual. For similar reasons I have argued against a justification defence for intimidation (in Chapter 1), and a defence of lesser evil necessity (in Chapter 4).

Further, even if we feel that judges have a reliable and up-to-date sense of moral intuition generally, what reassurance is there that they have, specifically, a sense of *commercial* moral intuition? Judges are legal professionals, not business people. Lambert JA said that the standard of commercial morality is to be identified by examining the fact patterns of previous *Canadian* cases in which an unconscionable bargain was found. That risks cutting Canadian law off from developments elsewhere in the common law. More than that, unless the case at hand is precisely on all fours with a previous instance of litigation, which seems highly improbable,[71] the judge will still have to wander into unchartered territory.

In *Harry*, the final judge, Craig JA, agreed with both McIntyre and Lambert JJA, seemingly endorsing the more structured approach of *Morrison* and the looser approach of Lambert JA. In *Norberg v Wynrib*,[72] the Supreme Court also seemed content with both approaches (there discussed in the context of sexual assault). In *Canadian Imperial Bank of Commerce v Ohlson*,[73] unconscionable

70 [1978] BCJ No 1318.

71 Not least because parties are very unlikely to litigate the case at hand if the outcome is clearly predicted by an identical precedent.

72 [1992] 2 SCR 226.

73 [1997] AJ No 1185.

bargain was described, nakedly, as the application of judicial discretion to excuse a party from a contract. After citing both *Morrison* and *Harry*, the court refrained from endorsing a single determinative test, in order to retain flexibility in the exercise of that discretion.

However, subsequent cases, including *Cain v Clarica Life Insurance Co*,[74] did appear to prefer a more structured approach, by asking: was the transaction grossly unfair; was there an overwhelming imbalance in bargaining power caused by the complainant's disability; did the accused knowingly take advantage; and (sometimes added) did the complainant lack independent legal advice?[75]

Most recently, in *Downer v Pitcher*,[76] the court said that it was appropriate to eschew any rigid linguistic formulation of a test for unconscionable bargain. Nevertheless, the court did not agree that Lambert JA's formulation was sufficient. In effect, its judgment does represent the most detailed examination of the doctrine, and a restatement of the law.

The court said that there must be such a special vulnerability that the weaker party cannot protect their own interests, which the other party takes advantage of, unfairly or unconscionably, to procure the resulting transaction.

The vulnerability must be special, i.e. outside the reasonably tolerable differences and risks which characterise normal human interaction, and it must be sufficiently significant that unfair advantage can be taken. (Seemingly, one cannot take *unfair* advantage of an insignificant weakness.) Such a weakness might stem from age, immaturity, senility, mental weakness, ignorance, physical disability, severe financial need, or dependence on a relationship of trust.

The court accepted developments in Australian law to state that the resulting bargain need not, after all, be substantively unfair – although unfairness was evidence from which one might infer weakness or exploitation. This was said also to be more in keeping with the early English decisions like *Chesterfield v Jansen*. It is, of course, also in keeping with the actual facts of *Morrison*.

But the court said that constructive knowledge of weakness would suffice. This was because, said the court, the doctrine was primarily concerned with protecting the vulnerable; and anyway, it seems, constructive knowledge was sufficient 'fault' to justify relief. In this the court expressly departed from the Australian position in *Kakavas*, discussed above. It also expressly departed from the previous Canadian decision of *Cain*, which itself seems to be framed in terms of the need for actual knowledge.[77]

The court also said that legal advice may level the playing field, but its presence did not disentitle relief automatically; for example, the advice may have been

74 [2005] ABCA 437.

75 *Lydian Properties Inc v Chambers* [2007] ABQB 541; *Teitelbaum v Dyson* [2000] OJ No 4583, affirmed [2001] OJ No 3483; *603262 BC Ltd v Eiyom Properties Ltd* [2014] BCSC 1152.

76 [2017] NLCA 13.

77 See too: *603262 BC Ltd v Eiyom Properties Ltd* [2014] BCSC 1152; *Ginew Housing Authority Inc v Zenke Investment Ltd* [2016] MBQB 199.

incompetent, or superficial. But rather than ask what advice was actually received, and be drawn off on collateral inquiries, indeed into areas usually governed by privilege, we might instead follow the English position, and ask objectively whether the transaction was one which a reasonably competent lawyer could advise in favour of.

Otherwise, said the court, the accused could show that the transaction was fair, or that the complainant, knowing of the disadvantage, voluntarily chose to proceed with the transaction.

We might conclude that, thanks to *Downer v Pitcher*, the Canadian doctrine, which was marred by a vague and discretionary approach, has now been returned to the common law mainstream.

2.6 The rationale for unconscionable bargain

Shortly I shall suggest that the best rationale for unconscionable bargain, consistent with the case law, is the moral proscription of exploitation. But first let us consider rival accounts.

(1) Smith argues for a distinct 'state of necessity' defence, and suggests that this is grounded in a concern to reverse unjust enrichments.[78] He says that the non-consensual creation of contractual rights can give rise to an unjust enrichment, when those rights benefit one person at the expense of another; for example, when the terms are not equivalent in value.

However, an unconscionable bargain is not usually created non-consensually. The case law testifies to the fact that the complainant is often all too ready to contract, indeed needing to contract, as in *Jansen*. Perhaps sometimes the complainant did not like the terms he was presented with, but again cases like *Fry v Lane* show that all too often the complainant had no original objection to the terms.

Further, the unjust enrichment analysis is inconsistent with the modern law of unjust enrichment:

First, as Edelman and Bant originally put it, a contractual right is not an enrichment when matched at the same time by a contractual obligation.[79] Without any enrichment, there can be no *unjust* enrichment.

Second, to the extent that payment under a contract fulfils and so discharges the contract, the payee, from whom restitution is sought, can raise a defence of change of position (having now lost any right to sue under the contract).[80]

78 Smith, *Contract Theory* (Oxford: Clarendon Press, 2004) ch 9. See too: Bamforth, 'Unconscionability as a Vitiating Factor' [1995] LMCLQ 538, 556.

79 Edelman and Bant, *Unjust Enrichment in Australia* (Melbourne: Oxford University Press, 2006) 345; see now Edelman and Bant, 'Receipt in Satisfaction of a Right' in *Unjust Enrichment*, 2nd edn (Oxford: Hart, 2016) 156–158.

80 *Lloyd's Bank plc v Independent Insurance Co Ltd* [2000] QB 110, 126; *Yukio Takahashi v Cheng Zhen Shu* (2011) 14 HKCFAR 558, [39].

Third, a contractual entitlement to payment precludes unjust enrichment. Although the language varies, the latter point is supported by case law,[81] and academic commentary.[82] To recover anything, the contract must be set aside. It is then a separate question, after a contract has been set aside, whether there is then a cause of action in unjust enrichment to recover anything paid over.[83] In other words, unjust enrichment is not the reason why the contract is set aside. Rather, the contract must first be set aside before any cause of action in unjust enrichment might afterwards arise.

(2) Other theories for unconscionable bargain focus on the difference between the contract price and the market price.

Thus Smith, in the alternative, says that it is important for our well-being to lead an autonomous life, which includes making plans.[84] These plans, he says, are built upon our material foundations or purchasing power. When contractual terms are unfair, he says, as measured against the normal market price, they erode our material foundations and so defeat our plans. This is what makes them liable to be set aside.

But, Smith accepts, all this is true only if we know the market price and plan accordingly. So for example, selling a Rembrandt, which the seller thought was worth nothing, far below market price, does not upset expectations. However, we might note, such a stance is inconsistent with the fact that ignorance is a relevant weakness, as recognised in cases like *Blomley v Ryan* and *Nichols v Jessup*; ignorance can be exploited so as to produce an unconscionable bargain.

Smith also says that contract is a facilitative institution provided by law to help people achieve their goals, and there is no reason why the law should support unfair contracts. Gordley makes a similar point, albeit couched in language of commutative justice.[85] And certainly the courts have a long history of controlling

81 *Barclays Bank Ltd v WJ Simms, Son and Cooke (Southern) Ltd* [1980] QB 677, 695; *The Evia Luck* [1992] 2 AC 152, 165; *Portman Building Society v Hamlyn Taylor Neck* [1998] 4 All ER 202, 208; *Kleinwort Benson Ltd v Lincoln City Council* [1999] 2 AC 349, 408; *Lloyd's Bank plc v Independent Insurance Co Ltd* [2000] QB 110, 130, 132; *Jones v Churcher* [2009] EWHC 722, [41]–[42], [48]; *Yukio Takahashi v Cheng Zhen Shu* (2011) 14 HKCFAR 558, [38]–[39]; *Madoff Securities International Ltd v Raven* [2013] EWHC 3147 (Comm), [376]; *Electricity Generation Corp v Woodside Energy Ltd* [2013] WASC 36, [201] and the wealth of Australian cases there cited, reversed on appeal on a different point at (2014) 306 ALR 25.

82 Virgo, 'Demolishing the Pyramid – Presence of Basis and Risk-Taking in the Law of Unjust Enrichment', in Robertson and Tang (eds), *The Goals of Private Law* (Oxford: Hart, 2009) 479, 488–504; Burrows, *The Law of Restitution*, 3rd edn (Oxford: Oxford University Press, 2011) 88–89; Tettenborn, *Law of Restitution in England and Ireland*, 3rd edn (London: Cavendish, 2002) 20–31; Mitchel et al. (eds), *Goff & Jones: The Law of Unjust Enrichment*, 9th edn (London: Sweet & Maxwell, 2016) ch 3; Edelman and Bant, *Unjust Enrichment*, 2nd edn (Oxford: Hart, 2016) ch 7; Tamblyn, 'Unjust Enrichment, Leapfrogging and a Defence of Entitlement' [2014] HKLJ 551; Webb, *Reason and Restitution* (Oxford: Oxford University Press, 2016) 152.

83 Tamblyn, 'Separating Rescission and Restitution' (2016) 33 J Contract Law 135.

84 Smith, 'In Defence of Substantive Unfairness' (1996) 112 LQR 138.

85 Gordley, 'Equality in Exchange' (1981) 69 California LR 1587.

unfairness; for example, through the rules about incorporating written terms, or rules about invoking implied terms.[86]

But for Smith (and Gordley), unfair contracts are defined in terms of their divergence from the market price. Yet some people might be happy to pay above the market price to secure what they want (for example, when buying property through sealed bids). So we can ask: when would a person who does not want to contract at a divergent price nevertheless do so? Perhaps because they were in a position of weakness or ignorance or necessity which the other exploited. The analysis brings us back to focus on exploitation (not price).

(3) Some see unconscionable bargain as merely an instance of a doctrine which responds to inequality of bargaining power between the parties.

In *Lloyd's Bank v Bundy*,[87] an elderly farmer charged his assets to the bank to support his son's indebtedness. That transaction was set aside for undue influence. Alone of the three judges in that case, Lord Denning MR referred to duress of goods, unconscionable bargain and undue influence, before gathering them together to suggest that they all rest on the single thread of inequality of bargaining power.

He said that relief is given to those who enter a contract upon terms which are very unfair, or for a consideration which is grossly inadequate, when their bargaining power is grievously impaired by reason of their own needs or desires or ignorance or infirmity, coupled with undue influences or pressures brought to bear. Those undue pressures need not involve wrongdoing. Independent advice, he said, might not save every transaction, but its absence may be fatal.

Lord Denning sought to apply his own test in subsequent cases, but other members of those courts said nothing about it,[88] or distinguished it.[89] His approach has received some support at first instance,[90] but it was distinguished in *Alec Lobb*, and was disapproved by Lord Scarman in *National Westminster Bank plc v Morgan*,[91] for three reasons. First, because equality of bargaining power was not the litmus test in cases of undue influence either. Second, this new formula was not suited to gifts. Third, rebalancing bargaining power was something for the legislature, and indeed an area of increasing legislative activity (for example, with legislation addressing unfair contract terms and consumer protection).

In the Australian case of *Berbatis*, discussed above, while not referring explicitly to *Lloyd's Bank v Bundy*, Gleeson CJ nevertheless said that taking advantage of a superior bargaining position was not the same as an unconscientious exploitation of another's inability to conserve their own interests. Most contracts, he said, are made between parties of unequal bargaining power, and good conscience

86 Waddams, 'Unconscionability in Contracts' (1976) 39 MLR 369; Barton, 'The Enforcement of Hard Bargains' (1987) 103 LQR 118.

87 [1975] QB 326.

88 *Davis (Clifford) Management Ltd v WEA Records Ltd* [1975] 1 All ER 327.

89 *Avon Finance Co Ltd v Bridger* [1985] 2 All ER 281.

90 *Backhouse v Backhouse* [1978] 1 All ER 1158, 1166.

91 [1985] AC 686.

does not require parties to contractual negotiations to forfeit their advantages or neglect their own interests. Dillon LJ made a similar point in the English case of *Alec Lobb*, and this was echoed in the Hong Kong case of *Standard Chartered Bank v Shem Yin Fun*. And although *Lloyd's v Bundy* has received more receptive treatment in Canada, in *Downer v Pitcher*, above, the court emphasised that mere bargaining imbalance was not enough.

We might make the following further negative comments about Lord Denning's test, in light of the case law.

First, we have seen how inadequacy of consideration, though often present, need not be an essential ingredient of unconscionable bargain, at least in Australian and New Zealand and Canadian law.

Second, unconscionable conduct focuses on the complainant's 'special' weakness, something beyond the ordinary urges upon which people act, as the Australian case of *Kakavas* makes clear. Simply because someone's 'desires' put them in a weaker bargaining position, perhaps because there are only limited outlets to satisfy that desire, is insufficient on its own to engage the protection of equity.

Third, ever since *Hart v O'Connor*, moral wrongdoing has been confirmed as an essential ingredient in unconscionable bargain.

Fourth, there is no requirement in unconscionable bargain that the accused bring undue influence or pressures to bear. It can suffice that the accused simply accepts the benefit of an unconscionable transaction offered to him. The notion of passive acceptance has been recognised in a number of jurisdictions. Further, while it may often be that the complainant is under external pressures, it is inapposite to describe these as 'undue' when, for example, they are a consequence of the complainant's own previous lifestyle choices, as in *Blomley v Ryan* (intoxication) or *Earl of Aylesford v Morris* (profligacy). Further still, equity intervenes even in the absence of pressures, as where the complainant's weakness is their own mental disability, as in *Dark v Boock*.

Chen-Wishart says that to require exact equality of bargaining power would leave no contract standing.[92] Andrews says that rebalancing the market is a matter for the legislature.[93] It is a political act, he says, requiring economic sophistication and ideological decisions, presumably, for example, about the relative importance of equality and market capitalism. Thal says that bargaining power requires a broad review of the market in general, for which the courts are ill-suited.[94] And, we might add, a decision in one case about market power will set precedents for other similar transactions too. Whereas, says Thal, a doctrine grounded in the weakness of the complainant is limited to the facts and parties of the individual case. That is proper ground for judicial inquiry.

92 Chen-Wishart, *Contract Law*, 5th edn (Oxford: Oxford University Press, 2015) 341.

93 Andrews, *Contract Law*, 2nd edn (Cambridge: Cambridge University Press, 2015) 316.

94 Thal, 'The Inequality of Bargaining Power Doctrine' (1988) 8 OJLS 17, 29. Similar concerns about the limits of the courts' structural and constitutional competence led us to reject the defence of justification to the tort of intimidation (Chapter 1), and the putative defence of lesser evil necessity (Chapter 4).

Trebilcock bemoans the economic illiteracy underlying a doctrine of inequality of bargaining power.[95] Standard terms, for example, imposed rather than negotiated, might simply reflect the desire for efficiency by reducing the considerable transaction costs that would come with negotiating each contract from scratch. And in a perfectly competitive market, he says, with a homogenous product, all terms would be the same, i.e. there would be no power to negotiate better terms. Further, he says, even when power is rebalanced in favour of the consumer, for example through legislation, that simply increases the costs to the producer, costs which will be passed back to the consumer, in higher prices, if the producer is to remain profitable. In other words, a free market cannot be cheated.

Overall, Lord Denning's would-be doctrine of inequality of bargaining power should not be adopted.

(4) Bigwood argues that unconscionable bargain would be better viewed as responding to 'transactional neglect': a contract should be vitiated when the accused fails to take reasonable precautions against foreseeable transactional harm to the complainant, when the complainant is contracting, as the accused knows, under circumstances making exploitation possible.[96]

Note that he is not arguing in favour of taking reasonable precautions against causing the other party foreseeable transactional harm. In general, parties are still free to drive a hard bargain. Rather, he is arguing in favour of such a duty only when that other party is known to be in a position making exploitation possible.

But is the other party exploited?

If the complainant is exploited, then the doctrine of unconscionable bargain already applies. There is no suggestion in the case law that the accused might have a defence of taking reasonable precautions against exploitation if in fact they did still exploit the complainant.

Alternatively, if the complainant is not exploited, i.e. if unconscionable advantage is not taken of any weakness, then in effect the complainant is in the same general position as any other contractor – the weakness is irrelevant because not acted upon. And, as Bigwood accepts, there is no general duty to take reasonable precautions against resulting transactional imbalance.

In other words, the theory of transactional neglect reduces to a focus on exploitation after all.

However, reasonable precautions are relevant.

If the accused knows that the complainant has received seemingly proper independent advice, that usually goes in favour of the accused, even to the point where the advice is taken to have overcome or rebalanced any weakness on the part of the complainant. So the accused can shore up their position in any transaction through the reasonable precaution of ensuring that the accused obtains proper independent advice. This is as long as the transaction is one which a reasonably competent lawyer could advise in favour of.

95 Trebilcock, 'The Doctrine of Inequality of Bargaining Power' (1976) 26 U Toronto LJ 359.

96 Bigwood, 'Contracts by Unfair Advantage: From Exploitation to Transactional Neglect' (2005) 25 OJLS 65.

But if the accused still has actual knowledge that the advice was improper, or that the advice failed to rebalance any weakness, then a hard bargain might still be exploitative. Legal advice – or any other form of reasonable precaution – is not a cure-all.

(5) Chen-Wishart says that the doctrine of unconscionable conduct protects the complainant's (future) autonomy.[97] This is because, she says, grossly unfair contracts have a long-term adverse effect by pushing the complainant below a social minimum. In similar vein, she says, we have rules of bankruptcy to allow a party a fresh start, rather than be burdened by the long-term consequences of crippling debt.

Certainly many of the cases do concern transactions which might deprive a complainant of almost all their assets. However, this explanation does not differentiate the fact that unconscionable bargain does not relieve parties of improvident transactions, even catastrophic ones, as cases like *Amadio* make clear. There must also be exploitation of weakness.

Alternatively, Chen-Wishart says, unconscionable bargain reflects the Kantian idea of treating people with respect, as ends in themselves, and never only as a means (in this case, to a quick profit).[98] This is an attractive justification. The case law does indeed stress that the courts look to the conduct of the accused, and ask whether they are morally culpable for exploiting the complainant's weakness.

Note, however, that unconscionable bargain requires not just exploitative behaviour by the accused, which alone might satisfy a Kantian approach. It also requires weakness on the part of the complainant, whereas the Kantian imperative applies to all people, not just those in a position of weakness.

Nevertheless we might square this by acknowledging that exploitation can only occur on one side if there is weakness on the other. This is especially so when we accept, as does the case law, that weakness can include ignorance or need of assistance. In other words, it only makes full sense to talk of exploitation if there is something to exploit. One cannot exploit a victim who is advertent to it and has the means to follow through their choice to resist it. Exploitation and weakness are two sides of the same coin.

2.7 The boundaries of unconscionable bargain

Across the various jurisdictions, the case law leaves a number of unresolved issues. First, whether the accused must have actual knowledge of the complainant's weakness, as in Australian law, or whether constructive knowledge suffices, as in New Zealand law (and probably Canadian law). Second, what counts as weakness? Third, whether the terms of the contract need to be oppressive, as in English law, or whether instead that is only evidence of weakness or exploitation,

97 Chen-Wishart, 'The Nature of Vitiating Factors in Contract Law' in Klass et al. (eds), *Philosophical Foundations of Contract Law* (Oxford: Oxford University Press, 2014) 303–304.

98 Chen-Wishart, 'The Nature of Vitiating Factors in Contract Law', in Klass et al. (eds), *Philosophical Foundations of Contract Law* (Oxford: Oxford University Press, 2014) 303.

as in Australian and New Zealand and Canadian law. Fourth, what is the meaning of exploitation? We shall take each topic in turn.

Knowledge

Should actual or constructive knowledge suffice for liability?

Bigwood suggests that an accused cannot exploit someone's weakness if he should have known, but did not in fact know, of that weakness.[99] In *Kakavas*, the court indicated that wilful ignorance taints a transaction as much as actual knowledge, and that seems appropriate. But otherwise the point remains: can we really talk about exploitation when the accused, honestly albeit unreasonably, did not know of the complainant's weakness?

It seems to me that there is a difference between, on the one hand, getting a good deal, and on the other hand, getting too good a deal. When the deal is too good, surely most people ask: is it me, or the other person, who is missing something? Once assured that we have not missed something, that leaves the other person's ignorance as the likely explanation. And cases like *Blomley v Ryan* and *Nichols v Jessup* and *Downer v Pitcher* confirm that ignorance is a relevant weakness. If the accused continues with a transaction which is too good, they are exploiting the other's weakness of ignorance, even if they cannot specify with precision why or in what ways the complainant is ignorant. Or at the least, they are proceeding with a wilful blindness to the situation.

What marks a good deal from too good a deal? No doubt that will be fact sensitive and contentious. But every doctrine, known and explained primarily through its obvious instances, will have to face marginal cases which sit on the boundary. Nevertheless, the accused can always take the reasonable precaution of ensuring that the complainant first receives proper independent advice. In this case, any weakness is shored up. This is so, at least, as long as the transaction remains one which a competent solicitor could advise in favour of. That, perhaps, is the tipping point: a deal is too good if no competent solicitor for the other party could support it.

So now we can see that there are two ways of approaching the question of actual knowledge: either the accused knows of a particular weakness, such as necessity or drunkenness or infatuation, or the accused knows more generally that the complainant must have some unspecified impairment because the deal is simply too good, and the complainant has not, to the accused's knowledge, received independent advice which could competently support the transaction. While it might be reasonable for an accused to plead honest ignorance of a specific weakness, it will be very rare for them to be able to credibly plead honest ignorance that the deal was too good. Yes, the marginal cases will remain hard fought, but the more advantageous the transaction to the accused, the less credible will be any assertion that they did not notice this.

99 Bigwood, 'Contracts by Unfair Advantage: From Exploitation to Transactional Neglect' (2005) 25 OJLS 65, 71.

What about when the accused should have noticed that the complainant was under a specific weakness? A failure to notice would be negligent. Is this morally culpable? Does negligence 'shock the conscience of the court', as required in *Alec Lobb* and *Lo Wo*? And in fulfilling a duty to take reasonable care to notice any weakness, must a contracting party ask their counterpart – what? Are you an alcoholic? Are you ignorant? Are you poorer than me? All of this hints at the unworkability and inconsistency of allowing constructive knowledge to ground liability.

Overall, the better approach is, consistent with Australian position in *Kakavas*, to require the accused to have actual knowledge or wilful blindness to the complainant's weakness. If the moral wrong is the accused exploiting the complainant's weakness, then the accused has done nothing objectionable if they do not exploit a weakness because they did not know of it. Rarely if ever will this enable an accused to get away with an unconscionable transaction once we appreciate that a relevant weakness is revealed simply by the transaction being, not just a good deal, but too good a deal, and one which no competent lawyer could advise in favour of. And the better the deal, the less credible will be any accused who says that they did not notice this.

Note that, while knowledge might be a subjective inquiry, unconscionability is an objective test. There is no requirement that the accused intended to behave unconscionably. If the accused knew of the complainant's weakness and took advantage, that might suffice, even if the accused themselves thought they were doing nothing wrong. (This might be the better explanation of *Fry v Lane* and *Dark v Boock*.)

Weakness

Here we explore some specific issues about weakness.

Thal suggests that ignorance is not about having less information, but about having no information.[100] I doubt this: a party who has no idea of the transaction they are entering may be able to plead *non est factum*, but if they do understand something of the transaction, still it might be an unconscionable bargain if exploitative.

In similar vein, Thal further suggests that necessity is not about whether there are reasonable alternatives, but about whether there are no alternatives.[101] But there are always alternatives: the person in necessity can refuse the transaction and accept their fate. Rather, necessity in tort (see Chapter 4) and duress in crime (see Chapter 5) both ask whether the party had any reasonable alternatives to the course of action they ultimately took. That seems appropriate here: necessity is not an absence of all alternatives, but an absence of reasonable alternatives.

100 Thal, 'The Inequality of Bargaining Power Doctrine' (1988) 8 OJLS 17, 31.
101 Thal, 'The Inequality of Bargaining Power Doctrine' (1988) 8 OJLS 17, 31–32.

Beale says that being poor or less highly educated does not of itself indicate weakness.[102] That must be true: there are people who start without money or education and, through business acumen, generate considerable fortunes. This is consistent with the approach of the court in the Hong Kong case of *Tong Kwok Cheong*: being an expectant heir does not of itself give rise to any presumption of exploitation.

Beale says that the older cases tended to focus on ignorance specific to the transaction, like the value of property, or the nature of the obligation. However, I would suggest that a weakness need not be specific: a general weakness, like a limited capacity for understanding, can infect everything. There is nothing in the case law to suggest that a complainant cannot rely on a general weakness which has consequences in a particular transaction. The complainant does not need to show that, beyond the general weakness, there was an additional or separate weakness specific to this transaction. For example, the relevant weakness in *Blomley v Ryan* was alcoholism, and in *Dark v Boock* it was dementia, but in neither case was there a specific incompetence in property sales.

However, even if the weakness need not be specific to the transaction, it must still be relevant. Spark makes the point that there must be causation explicit.[103] The weakness must affect the complainant's ability to look after their interests in this transaction. That in turn must have had some impact on the transaction subsequently produced. Spark suggests that the weakness need only be a contributory cause of the ensuing contract. This seems appropriate: it is consistent, I shall argue, with the position in contractual duress (see Chapter 3), and it is suitable for unconscionable bargain, given that another requirement of this doctrine is morally culpable behaviour by the accused.

Burrows suggests that a complainant's disability can boil down to one of two symptoms: mental weakness, or a difficult position (like a state of necessity).[104] Burrows includes inexperience within mental weakness. He would have to include ignorance as well, to reflect the case law. But mental weakness does not seem an appropriate label for inexperience or ignorance. For example, there are plenty of young people with fine minds who would still benefit from the maturity which experience and further knowledge bring. The Australian and Canadian case law puts it better: it boils down to whether the complainant is able to judge or preserve or advance their own best interests.

Substantive fairness

Must the impugned contract be substantively unfair or oppressive?

McKendrick says that unconscionable bargain should focus on procedural unfairness.[105] First, he says, it is easier to identify procedural tactics which are

102 Beale, 'Inequality of Bargaining Power' (1986) 6 OJLS 123.

103 Spark, *Vitiation of Contracts* (Cambridge: Cambridge University Press, 2013) 294–295.

104 Burrows, *A Restatement of the English Law of Contract* (Oxford: Oxford University Press, 2016) § 41.

105 McKendrick, *Contract Law*, 11th edn (London: Palgrave, 2015) 307.

unfair, than substantive unfairness. Thal makes a similar point.[106] But this misses the reality that often the courts infer the (procedural) exploitation from the substantive outcome, as the case law explicitly confirms. Indeed, it is often easier to look at the undisputed outcome, i.e. the terms of the transaction itself, than to identify the knowledge and mental state of the accused.

Second, says McKendrick, responding to procedural unfairness gives the doctrine a sound justification. But, in response, if this means that substantive fairness requires an ideological commitment which procedural unfairness does not, this is doubtful. Atiyah says that our idea of a fair outcome depends on our views about procedural fairness.[107] So if, he says, we thought it permissible to play the plausible rogue, and dissemble during negotiations, that would produce different results, but ones which we would then find acceptable. In other words, our ideological commitment to what constitutes substantive fairness presupposes an ideal of procedural fairness. Neither is philosophically more straightforward than the other.

Chen-Wishart says that substantive unfairness is a necessary condition for relief, even if the procedural unfairness is clear. Here we have to be careful. As cases like *Amadio* and *Morrison* suggest, some transactions can be fair *on their own terms* and yet still unconscionable. For example, a guarantee may be on standard terms, but a third party gets the benefit, and the guarantor all the burden. The moral wrong may have been procuring the guarantor to enter the transaction at all.

Where we can agree, as regards the role for substantive unfairness, is as follows. Chen-Wishart says that substantive unfairness is the best predictor of unconscionability, enabling the court to infer weakness and exploitation.[108] Similarly, Capper says that transactional imbalance, i.e. an unfair outcome, is powerful evidence of what really matters, namely relational imbalance and unconscionability.[109] The preponderance of case law, across all jurisdictions considered in this chapter, certainly attests to the forensic importance of substantively unfair terms from which exploitation can be inferred.

In summary, the better approach is that found in Australian and New Zealand and Canadian law: substantive unfairness is evidence of weakness and exploitation. Contrary to English law, it should not be an essential, free-standing ingredient, or it misses the point that it might be unconscionable to procure a contract at all, even if it otherwise has fair terms.

Exploitation

What is meant by exploitation?

Burrows seems to prefer bad faith to exploitation, meaning dishonestly taking advantage of the complainant's weakness.[110] But dishonesty seems an inapposite

106 Thal, 'The Inequality of Bargaining Power Doctrine' (1988) 8 OJLS 17, 24.
107 Atiyah, *Essays on Contract* (Oxford: Oxford University Press, 1986) 334.
108 Chen-Wishart, *Contract Law*, 5th edn (Oxford: Oxford University Press, 2015) 364–365.
109 Capper, 'Undue Influence and Unconscionability: A Rationalization' (1998) 114 LQR 479.
110 Burrows, *The Law of Restitution*, 3rd edn (Oxford: Oxford University Press, 2011) 300.

test here. Dishonesty in the tort of deceit means telling lies.[111] But exploitation can be open and brazen, yet still unconscionable; for example, there is nothing to suggest that, in cases like *Earl of Aylesford v Morris*, the accused was anything but clear and forthright in the contractual terms he was demanding.

That said, in criminal law, the definition of dishonesty is appallingly circular: in effect, did the accused realise that what they were doing was dishonest according to the standards of honest people?[112] What this really comes down to is: did the accused realise they were acting contrary to social norms? So too, Capper suggests that the test for unconscionability is whether the transaction, seen as a whole, is sufficiently divergent from community standards of morality that it ought not to stand,[113] echoing the approach of Lambert JA in the Canadian case of *Harry v Kreutziger*.

It seems inevitable that the concept of exploitation must remain open-textured, not least to flow with changing social attitudes. It will also be highly context dependent. This need be no cause for concern:

First, we might say the same thing of 'reasonable', a term so embedded within contract and tort that we treat it as familiar and indispensable.

Second, we should recall that, with unconscionable bargain, it is not marginal cases upon which the court intervenes, but extreme ones: cases which no competent lawyer could advise in favour of, as in *Fry v Lane* and *Boustany v Pigott* and *Dark v Boock*; cases which shock the conscience of the court, as stipulated in *Alec Lobb* and *Lo Wo*. There might be little controversy here.[114]

Third, the question of exploitation does not stand alone. Contrary to Lambert JA in *Harry*, we do not look solely at divergence from community morality. Courts do not have an unfettered discretion to set aside contracts which clash with their personal moral evaluations. Rather, it is exploitation of a known weakness, relative to the accused, which prevents the complainant from judging or promoting their best interests. The question of exploitation is not a naked value judgement, but a contextual inquiry.

2.8 Conclusions

Let us put aside alternative doctrines like inequality of bargaining power, which has problems of its own. The best justification for a doctrine of unconscionable conduct is not couched in terms of a desire to reverse unjust enrichments, or a comparison with market price. Rather, unconscionable bargain seeks to uphold

111 Specifically, the accused made a false representation knowingly or without belief in its truth: *Derry v Peek* (1889) 14 App Cas 337.

112 *R v Ghosh* [1982] QB 1053.

113 Capper, 'The Unconscionable Bargain in the Common Law World' (2010) 126 LQR 403, 415.

114 Indeed, the only case discussed in this chapter about whose outcome I have reservations is *Creswell v Potter*, as explained above. But otherwise, there appears no criticism in the academic literature that the courts are regularly producing contestable decisions.

the dignity of the complainant as an end in itself, to prevent the complainant being treated as an object for exploitation, or merely a means to a quick profit.

The precise requirements for the doctrine of unconscionable bargain have fluctuated in the case law, and there are a few points of divergence between the jurisdictions. But the best account, in terms of fit, and coherence in principle, is as follows.

The complainant must suffer a special weakness. In general terms, this is when the complainant is unable to judge or advance their best interests. But the special weakness must go beyond the personal or idiosyncratic urges and predilections which everyday lead us to transact. A condition of basic need or necessity is a special weakness. Otherwise, the special weakness is judged relative to the accused, because the ability of the accused to take advantage of the weakness is of central importance. A wide range of relevant weakness is acknowledged, including ignorance, and diminished mental capacity or fortitude.

The accused must know of the weakness. This includes both actual knowledge and wilful blindness. It should not include knowledge which the accused reasonably should have known, but did not know. Also, the weakness must be causatively relevant to the transaction, so that the accused takes advantage of it, unconscionably, in procuring the transaction, though this need only be a contributory cause of what results. Note that exploitation can be active, or it can be passive acceptance of a benefit in unconscionable circumstances.

The terms of the transaction should not need to be unfair in themselves; simply procuring the transaction might be unconscionable. But substantive unfairness is strong evidence from which weakness and exploitation can be inferred. Further, the more unfair the contract, the less credible any assertion by the accused that they did not perceive or exploit any weakness.

Behaviour which is unconscionable or exploitative is abhorrent to current standards of social morality. It is not a marginal case of misbehaviour. Rather, it shocks the conscience of the court.

Upon proof of the above, unconscionable bargain is presumptively made out. The accused then bears the burden of showing the transaction to be fair and reasonable.

Proper advice can enable a complainant to judge and advance their best interests after all. In other words, it can compensate for, and so eliminate, many relative weaknesses. But advice on its own cannot obviate a basic need or state of necessity. Also, independent advice does not make a transaction fair and reasonable, if the advice is ignored, or is advice which no competent lawyer could proffer.

An accused who knows that a complainant has received independent advice is entitled to assume that the advice was properly given and acted upon. But the transaction must be one which a competent solicitor could advise in favour of. The assumption is not available to the accused if they know the advice to be inadequate or ineffective, or if the transaction is one which no competent solicitor could advise in favour of. The latter is presumably yet further evidence of exploitation.

This leaves one more question: in terms of identifying a weakness relevant to unconscionable bargain, what is a state of necessity? In crime and tort, as we shall see, necessity is best understood as framed in terms of serious danger to the person, whether to the complainant themselves or to anyone for whom they reasonably feel responsible.

But otherwise we should note that unconscionable bargain can be more generous than the defences of duress or necessity in crime and tort. This is because, in crime and tort, the defendant is alleging duress or necessity as a reason to exculpate behaviour which causes harm or loss to an innocent third party. That possibility should be narrowly circumscribed. But with unconscionable bargain, we are concerned with protecting the complainant against exploitation, and the doctrine takes effect only against the exploiter himself. Thus:

First, it should not matter that the complainant's state of necessity has been brought about by their own prior choices. (Prior fault precludes the defences in crime and tort.) Nor should it be determinative that the complainant could reasonably have found an alternative party to transact with. (The fact that they did not find someone else to contract with might only reveal a further weakness or ignorance.) Neither situation is any justification for exploitation.

Second, it should suffice that the complainant honestly perceives a danger, even if the danger is not real. (For private necessity in tort law, the danger must be real.) After all, unconscionable bargain requires the accused to know of the complainant's weakness, which in this case would mean knowing that the complainant mistakenly believed themselves to be in danger. In the absence of real danger, the accused would still be exploiting the complainant's known fear or ignorance.

3 Contract

Duress

The law of duress has developed piecemeal.[1] The common law early on recognised duress to the person, involving threats of physical violence against, or detention of, the complainant. As for duress to goods, typically involving threats to seize or detain the complainant's property, for a time there appeared to exist a conflict, that a *payment* of money under duress to goods was recoverable,[2] but an *agreement* to pay money under duress to goods was enforceable.[3] Then it was resolved that duress to goods could render a contract voidable after all. And at the same time, it was accepted that economic pressure could amount to duress, including threats to breach contract. More recently, there has been discussion whether threats to do something lawful could sustain a plea of duress.

At the same time, equity was developing further forms of relief from such illegitimate pressures as threats to prosecute a family member unless the complainant paid money. Some of those cases invoked the language of undue influence, although Winder says it is better to see threats of prosecution as a distinct equitable doctrine of pressure.[4] Whatever the name, the modern consensus tends to suggest that the equitable doctrine has merged into the common law doctrine of duress.[5] Nevertheless, I shall suggest that threats of litigation and prosecution do raise distinctive issues which make them a discrete category.

We begin by discussing the English case law to identify the test for contractual duress. That overall test conceals a number of further controversies, which we

1 For a survey of the historical development of duress, see: Dawson, 'Economic Duress – An Essay in Perspective' (1947) 45 Michigan LR 253.

2 *Astley v Reynolds* (1731) 2 Str 915, 93 ER 939; *Maskell v Horner* [1915] 3 KB 106.

3 *Skeate v Beale* (1841) 11 Ad & E 983, 113 ER 688. But this case might be better seen not as a payment under compulsion, but as the compromise of a dispute: *North Ocean Shipping Co Ltd v Hyundai Construct Co Ltd, The Atlantic Baron* [1979] QB 705, 716, quoting Lord Denman CJ in *Wakefield v Newbon* (1844) 6 QB 276, where Lord Denman, himself the judge in *Skeate v Beale*, cast doubt on the breadth of that judgment. See too: Beatson, *The Use and Abuse of Unjust Enrichment* (Oxford: Clarendon Press, 1991) 104–106.

4 Winder, 'Undue Influence and Coercion' (1939) 3 MLR 97, 111.

5 Birks, *An Introduction to the Law of Restitution* (Oxford: Clarendon Press, 1989) 184; Bigwood, 'Four Questions on the Demise of Lawful Act Duress in New South Wales' (2008) 27(2) U Queensland LJ 41, 78; Peel (ed), *Treitel, The Law of Contract*, 14th edn (London: Sweet & Maxwell, 2015) [10-002 n 3].

then take in turn in greater detail: whether threats to breach a contract are always illegitimate; whether lawful act duress might be recognised; and what is the proper test of causation. As we go along, comparison is made to other jurisdictions, and reference is made to the academic commentary. After that, those other jurisdictions are considered on their own terms, to get a full picture of their comparative approaches. Finally, drawing on the case law, we shall explore why, in theory, contract law might recognise a doctrine of duress, and its possible relationship to the doctrine of undue influence. The conclusion draws everything together.

3.1 The test for contractual duress

It is usual to discuss separately the various forms which duress can take (duress to the person, duress to goods, etc.). Certainly the controversies around threats to breach contract and lawful act duress require them to have additional and detailed consideration. But in terms of identifying the overall test for contractual duress, it is not helpful to separate the different forms. For a start, the case law is interwoven. For example, *Barton v Armstrong*, a leading case of duress to the person, is central in various judgments discussing economic duress. Further, some authors suggest that duress to goods is now subsumed within economic duress,[6] so that the test is the same.[7] Others suggest that a threat to breach a contract might even be lawful act duress.[8] And anyway, if the accused threatens to do lawful acts, they must still be acts against the complainant's person or property or economic interests. Finally, as Andrews says, there is no good reason why a larger range of threats might not be recognised as coercive; he gives the example of threats to damage the environment.[9]

So we begin the modern case law with *Barton v Armstrong*,[10] an appeal to the Privy Council from Australia. In that case, the accused threatened to kill the complainant, to induce the complainant to enter an agreement to buy out the accused's interest in their company. There was also a commercial necessity for the complainant to enter the agreement.

The complainant sought a declaration that the agreement was void. This could mean: either that duress renders a contract void, or that it renders a contract voidable, and the complainant had in fact avoided the contract, which was thus now void.[11] Subsequent case law has been unanimous in stating that duress renders a contract voidable, without drawing any distinction between the types of threat.

Duress was made out. Lords Wilberforce and Simon, dissenting in the outcome, in a passage often repeated since, said that there were two steps to prove duress:

6 Burrows, *The Law of Restitution*, 3rd edn (Oxford: Oxford University Press, 2011) 266.
7 Peel (ed), *Treitel, The Law of Contract*, 14th edn (London: Sweet & Maxwell, 2015) [10–004].
8 Lee, 'Compromise and Coercion' [2012] LMCLQ 478, 479.
9 Andrews, *Contract Law*, 2nd edn (Cambridge: Cambridge University Press, 2015) 289.
10 [1976] AC 104.
11 Burrows agrees: *The Law of Restitution*, 3rd edn (Oxford: Oxford University Press, 2011) 263 n 62.

First, an illegitimate 'means of persuasion'. But it would be tidier to say that there must be illegitimate *threats*. That would be consistent with tort and crime. And after all, contractual duress involves threats from another person, even if the attendant circumstances can also add to the complainant's feeling of compulsion. In *Barton v Armstrong*, the illegitimate 'means of persuasion' were threats to the complainant's life.

Second, a 'relationship' between the illegitimate means used and the response. But it would be better to acknowledge that this consists of two elements, as we shall see: causation, and coercion.

Finally, they said:[12]

> In life, including the life of commerce and finance, many acts are done under pressure, sometimes overwhelming pressure, so that one can say that the actor had no choice but to act. Absence of choice in this sense does not negate consent in law: for this the pressure must be one of a kind which the law does not regard as legitimate.

Threats to the person are rare in modern English case law.[13] Burrows says that this is not surprising, since the complainant could always sue in trespass or intimidation.[14] It can amount to duress if threats are made against the complainant's employees or crew.[15] The better approach, again following tort and crime, might be to say that a threat can sustain a plea of duress if made against anyone for whom the complainant reasonably feels responsible.

Threats to the person need not be limited to threats of violence. *'R' v Attorney-General* was an appeal to the Privy Council from New Zealand.[16] It involved a soldier who sought to set aside a confidentiality agreement he had signed as a requirement for him remaining in the special forces. Without it, he would have been 'returned to unit'. This was usually a penalty for disciplinary offences, or indicated professional unsuitability for the special forces.

Lord Hoffmann delivered the judgment. He was prepared to accept that the soldier signed the agreement under compulsion, indeed under 'overwhelming pressure', and with no practical alternative. But the threat was lawful, the Crown having the discretion to return a soldier to unit. And the demand, he said, could also be justified, because anyone unwilling to sign the confidentiality agreement could reasonably be regarded as unsuitable for the special forces.

12 [1976] AC 104, 121.

13 Another example is *Antonio v Antonio* [2010] EWHC 1199 (QB). See too the New Zealand cases of *Dandoroff v Rogozinoff* [1988] 2 NZLR 588 (duress to the person, also intimidation), and *Somme Ltd v Central House Movers Ltd* [2012] NZAR 295 (duress to the person and to goods).

14 Burrows, *The Law of Restitution*, 3rd edn (Oxford: Oxford University Press, 2011) 264.

15 *Royal Boskalis Westminster NV v Mountain* [1997] 2 All ER 929; *Gulf Azov Shipping Co Ltd v Idisi* [2001] EWCA Civ 491. Both also involved duress to goods. In the Canadian case of *Saxon v Saxon* [1976] 4 WWR 300, threats were made against the complainant's children. See too threats of prosecution, discussed below.

16 [2003] UKPC 22.

'R' can be seen as a case of duress to the person, not threats of physical violence, but humiliation and loss of self-esteem. We saw in Chapter 1 that such a notion is recognised within tortious intimidation.

Similarly for *Halpern v Halpern*.[17] There a Jewish family sought to settle an inheritance dispute by referring the matter to a Jewish arbitration. The arbitrator threatened the complainant with a religious oath, to avoid which he settled with the other party. The court accepted that rescission of the agreement could be possible. This again seems best categorised as duress to the person, involving a threat to the complainant's moral integrity.

In *Halpern*, it was the arbitrator who made the threat, but the other contracting party who took the benefit. The academic consensus tends to the view that duress should vitiate the contract where the contracting party has actual or constructive knowledge of the duress brought to bear on the complainant.[18] I shall suggest below that constructive knowledge is not enough. In *Halpern*, the contracting party would have had actual knowledge that the settlement agreement was entered only because of the arbitrator's threat to require a religious oath.

Returning to the chronological development of duress in English law: after *Barton v Armstrong*, the English courts began to recognise that duress can include threats to goods or economic interests, or to breach a contract.

In *The Siboen*,[19] ship charterers were alleging that they would go bankrupt unless the ship owners agreed to reduce the charter rates. The owners did so agree. The owners' subsequent claim for misrepresentation was made out.

Referring to a line of early Australian decisions, the judge also said that duress extended to duress to goods, and beyond. Relevant factors, he said, included: whether the complainant made any protest; whether he treated the settlement as closing the transaction or whether he regarded the position as still open. In this case, the judge concluded, the complainant was acting under great pressure, but only commercial pressure, and not under any duress.

In *The Atlantic Baron*,[20] a ship builder threatened to terminate the contract unless the buyer agreed, which it did, to pay 10% more when the contractual currency was devalued. The judgment began with a discussion of duress to goods, acknowledging that this could vitiate a contract. Then the judge recognised that a threat to break a contract could amount to economic duress, again relying on the line of early Australian cases. Duress was made out: the buyer had a lucrative

17 [2006] EWHC 603 (Comm), [85], [87], on appeal at [2007] EWCA Civ 291.

18 Andrews, *Contract Law*, 2nd edn (Cambridge: Cambridge University Press, 2015) 291; Burrows, *A Restatement of the English Law of Contract* (Oxford: Oxford University Press, 2016) § 39; Burrows, *The Law of Restitution*, 3rd edn (Oxford: Oxford University Press, 2011) 255, 257; Virgo, *Principles of the Law of Restitution* (Oxford: Oxford University Press, 2015) 210. Peel recognises *Halpern* as a case of duress by a third party: Peel (ed), *Treitel, The Law of Contract*, 14th edn (London: Sweet & Maxwell, 2015) [10–036].

19 *Occidental Worldwide Investment Corp v Skibs A/S Avanti, The Siboen and Sibotre* [1976] 1 Lloyd's Rep 293.

20 *North Ocean Shipping Co Ltd v Hyundai Construct Co Ltd, The Atlantic Baron* [1979] QB 705.

charter for the ship, and the builder had declined the invitation to arbitrate the dispute. But the judge also found that the variation had been affirmed by a delay: there was no protest for nine months after delivery of the ship.

The next case was *Pao On v Lau Yiu Long*,[21] an appeal to the Privy Council from Hong Kong. In that case, the accused refused to complete an agreement to sell a building unless the complainant entered into a guarantee, which it did. That guarantee was later called upon.

Lord Scarman, delivering the judgment of the Board, once again affirmed that commercial pressure was not enough to constitute duress (in keeping with statements to that effect, as we have just seen, in *Barton v Armstrong* and *The Siboen*). Relevant factors, he said, included: whether the complainant protested; whether there was an alternative course open to him, such as an adequate legal remedy; whether he was independently advised; and whether he took steps to avoid the contract.

We might note that independent advice need not alleviate duress. It might simply confirm that the complainant has no other choice. (Similarly, we noted in Chapter 2 that legal advice does not necessarily cure an unconscionable bargain.) Also, an absence of protest does not mean that the complainant acted free of coercion.[22] As Lord Scarman himself said in a later case: 'the victim's silence will not assist the bully, if the lack of any practicable choice but to submit is proved'.[23] Whether the complainant took steps to avoid the contract is relevant to affirmation, as in *The Atlantic Baron*. As for other legal remedies, these might not be adequate: for example, an injunction might not be useful where the accused or the goods are outside the jurisdiction,[24] or where the dispute is too complex for an interim injunction,[25] or where delays at court preclude a timely judicial resolution of the dispute,[26] or where the accused has declined to arbitrate the dispute,[27] or more generally where the complainant cannot afford the time and expense of litigation, or has good reason to believe that they will not be able to realise any judgment.[28]

In *Pao On*, duress was not made out. Rather, said the court, the complainant considered the matter thoroughly, chose to avoid litigation, and formed the

21 [1980] AC 614.
22 *Kolmar Group AG v Traxpo Enterprises Pvt Ltd* [2010] EWHC 113 (Comm), [92].
23 *The Universe Sentinel* [1983] 1 AC 366, 400.
24 *The Alev* [1989] 1 Lloyd's Rep 138, 146.
25 *Adam Opel GmbH v Mitras Automotive UK Ltd* [2008] EWHC 3205 (QB), where an interim application for an injunction without notice was refused, seemingly because of uncertainty over what specific performance of the contract entailed. It was sought without notice because of the fear that notice might provoke the accused into carrying out its threat. See too the Australian case of *Electricity Generation Corp v Woodside Energy Ltd* [2013] WASCA 36, reversed on appeal on a different point (2014) 306 ALR 25.
26 *Borelli v Ting* [2010] UKPC 21.
27 *The Atlantic Baron* [1979] QB 705.
28 See the Canadian case of *Stott v Merit Investment Corp* [1988] OJ No 134, [56], where it was said that, in the majority of cases, redress to the courts is 'illusory' for these reasons.

opinion that the risk in giving the guarantee was more apparent than real. There was no coercion. Which, we might note, reveals coercion to be a further necessary ingredient in contractual duress.

In *The Universe Sentinel*,[29] a union blacklisted a ship, so that it could not be serviced in port, until the ship owners paid back wages to its crew and a contribution to the union welfare fund. It was agreed between the parties that this amounted to economic duress. The question for the court was whether the activity was otherwise legitimated by trade union legislation.

Even so, the court said that economic pressure can amount to duress. Lord Scarman, dissenting on the facts, said that there were two elements: pressure, the practical effect of which is compulsion or absence of choice; and the illegitimacy of the pressure. Lords Diplock and Cross, though not quite so explicit, spoke in similar terms.

Note that *Barton v Armstrong* spoke of the threats being a reason for the transaction, whereas *The Universe Sentinel* talks about absence of choice. This is not the same thing. If threats are a contributory reason for acting, that suggests that other reasons can be relevant too, as indeed was the case in *Barton v Armstrong*, whereas absence of choice suggests no room for other reasons.

Further, *The Universe Sentinel* suggests that compulsion and absence of choice are synonymous, but this is not so either. In *Pao On*, the complainant had no choice but to provide the guarantee, at least if it wanted the contract to proceed, but still the court found that there was no coercion, and so no duress.

Again, as previously noted, the clearest approach is to say that duress requires an illegitimate threat, which is coercive, and which causes the complainant to transact.

Then we come to *The Evia Luck*,[30] which was essentially a re-run of *The Universe Sentinel*, but with events taking place, not in England, but in Sweden, and without the protection of trade union legislation. Lord Goff said that threats to goods and economic pressure could amount to duress, provided 'at least' that the economic pressure was illegitimate and 'a significant cause' of inducing the subsequent transaction. This was seized upon, in *Huyton SA v Peter Cremer GmbH & Co*,[31] to suggest a 'but for' test of causation for economic duress, and to discuss whether bad faith was a yet further necessary ingredient for a finding of duress.

In *Huyton v Cremer*, Mance J said that a complainant who perceives that the accused is acting in bad faith may be more likely to feel coerced. No doubt this is right. But Mance J also noted, correctly, how, in *The Siboen*, counsel had argued for the relevance of bad faith, but the judge had rejected his submissions as 'much too wide'. We might add, in the 20 years between *The Siboen*

29 *Universe Tankships Inc of Monrovia v International Transport Workers Federation, The Universe Sentinel* [1983] 1 AC 366.

30 *Dimskal Shipping Co SA v International Transport Workers Federation, The Evia Luck* [1992] 2 AC 152. See too: *Vantage Navigation Corp v Suhail and Saud Bahwan Building Materials LLC, The Alev* [1989] 1 Lloyd's Rep 138, a case of both duress to goods and economic duress.

31 [2004] EWHC 1625 (Comm).

and *Huyton v Cremer*, no court considering a case of contractual duress had felt moved to discuss the relevance of bad faith.

Mance J said that it was difficult to accept that good faith could override illegitimate pressure, but not difficult to accept that bad faith could be relevant to lawful act duress. Below I shall suggest that malice, i.e. spite or ill-will (rather than generic bad faith), could be relevant to lawful act duress.

As for the facts of *Huyton v Cremer*, the accused buyer refused to pay for a cargo, which had already been delivered up to a sub-buyer, unless the complainant carrier agreed to give up its right to arbitrate various disputes, which it did.

The judge found primarily that the accused was in the right, and not in breach of contract. Alternatively, he found that the complainant's concerns were largely generated by its own false perception of what was happening. And anyway, it was not greatly affected financially, having passed on up the contractual chain the extra costs sought by the accused. The complainant was prepared to accept and live with the consequences of the contract. (We might say, the complainant was not coerced, similarly to *Pao On.*) Duress was not made out.

The final principal case we need to consider in this section is *DSND Subsea Ltd v PGS Offshore Technology AS*,[32] where Dyson J said as follows:

> The ingredients of actionable duress are that there must be pressure, (a) whose practical effect is that there is compulsion on, or a lack of practical choice for, the victim, (b) which is illegitimate, and (c) which is a significant cause inducing the claimant to enter into the contract ... In determining whether there has been illegitimate pressure, the court takes into account a range of factors. These include whether there has been an actual or threatened breach of contract; whether the person allegedly exerting the pressure has acted in good or bad faith; whether the victim had any realistic practical alternative but to submit to the pressure; whether the victim protested at the time; and whether he affirmed and sought to rely on the contract. These are all relevant factors. Illegitimate pressure must be distinguished from the rough and tumble of the pressures of normal commercial bargaining.

This concise approach has made it a favoured starting point for discussion in subsequent cases and commentary.[33] It notes three requirements of illegitimate pressure, compulsion or coercion, and causation. But otherwise, caution is needed:

First, the test of causation is controversial, as we shall see.

Second, as for bad faith, we have just seen how it has played no part in any decision to date, and was treated with caution in *Huyton v Cremer*, and is probably

32 [2000] All ER (D) 1101, [131].

33 Although a judge in a subsequent case said 'I do not understand that summary to have been presented as a precise analytic tool': *Adam Opel GmbH v Mitras Automotive UK Ltd* [2008] EWHC 3205 (QB), [26].

limited to lawful act duress. (The relevance of bad faith was also rejected in the Canadian case of *Fredericton*, discussed below.)

As for the facts, duress was not made out. The complainant had practical alternatives, like finding an alternative trading partner, or terminating the contract and litigating, in that regard having the benefit of a parent company guarantee. There was also an amicable atmosphere between the parties, and no protest. In other words, we might say, there was no coercion. And at any rate, even if there was duress, the judge found that the complainant had affirmed the contract. It is also worth noting that there was no actual finding that the accused had threatened any breach of contract either.

In summary, the cases tend to talk about illegitimate pressure, or illegitimate means of persuasion. But that pressure is always applied by another person making demands for compliance backed up with an 'or else' ultimatum. So it is more consistent with tort and crime to speak in terms of illegitimate threats which coerce the complainant. Further, the threats must cause the complainant to enter the demanded transaction. Forensic indicators of duress include such matters as whether the complainant made any contemporaneous protest, and whether they had alternative options or remedies to complying with the demand.

However, there remain a number of areas of controversy. Which threats are illegitimate? It seems clear that threats to the person or to goods are always illegitimate. After all, these would ordinarily be threats to do something tortious or criminal. Further, threats to the person need not be limited to threats of violence, but seemingly can include threats of humiliation or to self-esteem or moral integrity. (All this is consistent with the tort of intimidation.)

But are threats to breach contract always illegitimate? What about threats to do something lawful? Or threats to prosecute or litigate? And what is the proper test for causation? We consider these questions in the following sections.

3.2 Threats to breach contract

Supposedly, this is the problem: on the one hand, contracts should be dependable, so threats to breach them should not be countenanced; on the other hand, contracts do sometimes need modifying, to the benefit of both parties, and this might come to light only against a background of threatened breach.

The latter point was expressed clearly by Griffiths LJ in *B&S Contracts and Design Ltd v Victor Green Publications Ltd*:[34]

> Many commercial contracts are varied during their currency because the parties are faced with changing circumstances during the performance of the contract, and it is certainly not on every occasion when one of the parties unwillingly agrees to a variation that the law would consider that he had acted by reason of duress.

34 [1984] ICR 419, 425.

A well-known example of a renegotiated contract is *Williams v Roffey Bros & Nicholls (Contractors) Ltd*.[35] A carpenter working in a block of flats ran into difficulty because the job was priced too low. His contractor offered to pay him more money to complete the work on time, and so itself avoid penalties for late completion in its contract up the chain. The carpenter substantially completed the work and sued for the extra money promised. It was held that the practical benefit of timely completion was sufficient consideration to support the claim for the extra money. The court suggested that fraud or duress was better placed to regulate such matters than a blunt rule about past consideration. But duress was not pleaded.

So is there a middle ground that enables threatened breach of contract to be sometimes legitimate, sometimes illegitimate? Dyson J's summary of contractual duress in *DSND Subsea* seems to suggest as much, but without any explicit discussion. There are a number of suggested approaches, but I submit that none are successful.

(I) Birks says that the test for illegitimacy should be whether the pressure was applied in bad faith, which means, he says, intending to exploit the complainant's weakness rather than to solve the accused's problems.[36] But the exploitation of weakness is addressed through the doctrine of unconscionable bargain. Indeed, in the Australian case of *Crescendo v Westpac*, which we discuss in detail below, one suggestion was to import unconscionability into the test for duress. There is some academic support for this,[37] despite other Australian cases, such as *Karam*, suggesting that the two doctrines should be kept distinct.

In practical terms, if unconscionable bargain were imported into duress, that risks making duress redundant. Birks himself acknowledged this, saying that such an approach might reduce to recovery for fraud (presumably, equitable fraud) rather than duress.[38] Duress would be redundant because it would require making out unconscionable bargain, and then some.

Phillips goes further, saying that unconscionable bargain should replace duress entirely. He says that the language of illegitimacy in duress masks a concern for preventing the unconscientious taking of advantage of the weaker party's position.[39] But there is a conceptual distinction: duress is about coercion, usually by threatening to do something unlawful, whereas unconscionable bargain is about exploitation of weakness, with or without coercion, and even if what the accused is doing is otherwise lawful.

(II) Burrows modifies Birks' approach, adding that a threat to breach a contract might not be illegitimate if the varied terms proposed by the accused are a

35 [1991] 1 QB 1. See too: *Antons Trawling Co Ltd v Smith* [2003] 2 NZLR 23.

36 Birks, *An Introduction to the Law of Restitution* (Oxford: Clarendon Press, 1989) 183.

37 McKeand, 'Economic Duress – Wearing the Clothes of Unconscionable Conduct' (2001) 17 J Contract L 1; Phang, 'Undue influence – Methodology, Sources and Linkages' [1995] JBL 552, 571–573.

38 Birks, *An Introduction to the Law of Restitution* (Oxford: Clarendon Press, 1989) 183.

39 Phillips, 'Protecting Those in a Disadvantageous Negotiating Position' (2010) 45 Wake Forest LR 837, 851.

reaction to circumstances that almost constitute frustration, or amend what was clearly a bad bargain.[40]

Similarly, Chen-Wishart says that contractual modifications should be enforceable where there has been a significant change in circumstance, albeit short of frustration.[41] This is because, she says, a party facing impending insolvency has no incentive to perform if this would merely exacerbate their indebtedness, while the other party may wish to secure the performance even at the new rate. (As Birks says, it may minimise waste and inconvenience to stick with this partner.[42])

So too, Aivazian et al. suggest that modification should be allowed where there has been a change in circumstances, and, at the time of contracting, the risk of this happening was too remote to provide for, or the party better able to bear the risk was not easily identifiable.[43]

This is also consistent with a discussion, for example, in the New Zealand case of *McIntyre v Nemesis*, discussed below, that care must be taken to distinguish illegitimate threats from legitimate warnings; a legitimate warning might be where one party to a contract warns the other that, as a matter of commercial reality, it will not be able to perform its contractual obligations unless changes are agreed to.[44] Or in other words, we might say, with warnings, the party is giving notice of an inevitable outcome; with threats, the duressor has the power whether or not to bring about that outcome.[45]

In all this, the argument continues, the party seeking a variation can require only a reasonable modification.[46] This is because a reasonable modification would meet the change of circumstances. Anything more would not be due to the change of circumstances, but the greedy additional demands of the duressor.

There are a number of reasons to reject these approaches.

First, frustration automatically discharges both parties from the contract when there is a supervening event, without the fault of either party, for which the contract makes no provision, which event makes the contract not merely more

40 Burrows, *The Law of Restitution*, 3rd edn (Oxford: Oxford University Press, 2011) 273–275.

41 Chen-Wishart, *Contract Law*, 5th edn (Oxford: Oxford University Press, 2015) 326.

42 Birks, 'The Travails of Duress' [1990] LMCLQ 342, 346, where he also warns that the possibility of later renegotiation should be not a license for parties to bid too low to start with.

43 Aivazian et al., 'The Law of Contract Modifications' (1984) 22 Osgoode Hall LJ 173.

44 However, the contract in *McIntyre v Nemesis* itself contained a clause allowing the parties to initiate a process aimed at agreeing a variation. The accused's warning was thus in context, and not out of the blue. Also, the court found that the accused's behaviour did not amount to, and was not construed by the complainant as, a threat to breach the contract.

45 Beatson, *The Use and Abuse of Unjust Enrichment* (Oxford: Clarendon Press, 1991) 119; Smith, *Contract Theory* (Oxford: Clarendon Press, 2004) 318–319; Chen-Wishart, *Contract Law*, 5th edn (Oxford: Oxford University Press, 2015) 326.

46 Chen-Wishart, *Contract Law*, 5th edn (Oxford: Oxford University Press, 2015) 331–332; Bar-Gill and Ben-Shahar, 'The Law of Duress and the Economics of Credible Threats' (2004) 33 J Leg Stud 391, 400; Spark, *Vitiation of Contracts* (Cambridge: Cambridge University Press, 2013) 223.

expensive but radically different.[47] Thereafter, there is a statutory sharing of losses between the parties as the court considers just.[48]

In contrast, what is being suggested here is that one party might unilaterally force a variation, to its benefit, to rescue it from a performance specified in the contract, when that performance is not radically different, but at worst more expensive than it envisaged. That is not so much a position short of frustration, as almost antithetical. Why should that be legitimate?

There are cases against such an approach, like *The Atlantic Baron*, which involved a supervening currency devaluation, and the Australian case *Sundell v Yannoulatos*, discussed below, which involved a hike in the market price for the goods which the accused had promised to supply. Yet in both cases, duress was made out.

Second, what is a reasonable modification anyway? Enough to stave off insolvency? Enough to cover costs so that the accused breaks even on this project? Or is the party seeking variation expected to cross-subsidise projects? What about costs plus a modest profit? How will the parties know, at the time of the demand, if the request is reasonable? If they cannot know, then they also cannot tell whether the agreed modification is binding. Without that reassurance, the incentive to persist with performance disappears.

Third, and more generally, the fact that the accused is genuinely seeking to solve their own problems does not mean that it is legitimate to do so at the expense and contrary to the contractual rights of the complainant. Those problems might have nothing to do with the complainant.

Fourth, as for amending what was clearly a bad bargain, if the party seeking variation had been initially exploited, they would have a remedy anyway through the doctrine of unconscionable bargain. But if they had not been exploited, why should they be permitted to force a variation on the other party? Why permit them to escape responsibility for the contract they agreed? In *The Atlantic Baron*, the accused made a commercial error in choosing the contract currency, which then devalued, and yet duress was still made out.

Here are two more examples where duress was successful despite the accused making a bad bargain.

In *Atlas Express Ltd v Kafco (Importers and Distributors) Ltd*,[49] the complainant was a supplier to a chain of retail outlets. It agreed with the accused a rate of carriage to transport its goods to the retail outlets. A month later the accused said that it would not carry anything unless the complainant agreed to pay a higher price. It seems that the accused simply made a calculating error when advising on the carriage price, and so initially proposed a figure which was commercially unsustainable. The complainant agreed to the higher price, but later pleaded duress, successfully: the accused was threatening to breach its contract,

47 *National Carriers Ltd v Panalpina (Northern) Ltd* [1981] AC 675.
48 Law Reform (Frustrated Contracts) Act 1943.
49 [1989] QB 833.

at Christmas, when alternative carriers were not available, all of which would have threatened the complainant's contract with the retailer.

In the Australian case of *Electricity Generation Corp v Woodside Energy Ltd*,[50] the accused sought a higher price to continue its gas supply to the complainant after a fire reduced the accused's capacity to supply gas. The accused was in breach (though it genuinely thought otherwise), which was sufficient to make out economic duress. (But on the facts, the complainant had not avoided the contract.)

In short, the law provides a solution to changing circumstances through the doctrine of frustration. If, for the accused, there was no initial exploitation, and only now does the contract reveal itself to be a bad bargain, and yet the accused falls short of the plea of frustration, there is no persuasive reason why that should justify the accused unilaterally threatening to breach the complainant's contractual rights.

(III) There is a body of opinion which suggests that the absence of any practical alternative to submission is what makes economic pressure illegitimate.[51] Indeed, the absence of any realistic alternative is emphasised in the Canadian case law, below. But this is inconsistent with cases like *Barton v Armstrong* and *The Siboen* and *Pao On*, which have repeatedly said that even overwhelming pressure is not necessarily enough. It is also inconsistent with other types of duress, as follows.

As for duress to the person, the courts have never led any discussion as to whether the complainant ought to consider practical alternatives, for example, like going to the police. This is despite the discussion being highly visible in tort and criminal law. Thus it seems unlikely that practical alternatives are relevant when it comes to contractual duress to the person.

As for duress to goods, in the old case of *Astley v Reynolds*,[52] the court said that a complainant '*might* have such an immediate want of his goods, that an action of trover would not do his business' (my emphasis). In other words, litigating might not have been a reasonable alternative. In that case, the complainant pawned plate which the pawnbroker refused to return until the complainant paid more interest than was lawful. But the complainant had been without the plate for three years, and there was a further delay of 'some months' between the first refusal to return the plate, and the subsequent payment. Those facts suggest no immediate want of the goods at all. Thus it seems likely that practical alternatives are also irrelevant when it comes to contractual duress to goods.[53]

At any rate, is a lack of reasonable alternatives an indicator for or against duress? The tenor of the views above suggest that it is an indicator of duress. And yet there is a rival view which says that having no reasonable alternative is precisely when the complainant does want the modification to be binding, and

50 [2013] WASCA 36, reversed on appeal on a different point (2014) 306 ALR 25.

51 Birks, 'The Travails of Duress' [1990] LMCLQ 342, 346–347; Beatson, *The Use and Abuse of Unjust Enrichment* (Oxford: Clarendon Press, 1991) 122; Chen-Wishart, *Contract Law*, 5th edn (Oxford: Oxford University Press, 2015) 323.

52 (1731) 2 Str 915, 93 ER 939.

53 Burrows agrees: *The Law of Restitution*, 3rd edn (Oxford: Oxford University Press, 2011) 272.

not voidable for duress. This is because procuring the performance, even at the higher price, is thus by definition the best option.[54]

Spark says that the availability of reasonable alternatives is merely evidence going to the question of whether the complainant consented.[55] Another view is that it goes to the question of causation.[56] But I suggest that it is evidence going to the question of coercion: the more alternatives the complainant had, the less likely the threat was coercive. Put another way, the more alternatives, the less credible any plea of coercion. And this is relevant across all types of duress. Even with threats to the person or to goods, if those threats were not coercive, for example if the complainant shrugged them off, then duress is not made out.

Bigwood seems to suggest that coercion *means* lack of reasonable alternatives.[57] But presumably, coercion being subjective, it means lack of known reasonable alternatives. Yet a number of commentators say otherwise: it should be about objectively reasonable alternatives, because this aligns with the rules of mitigation.[58] We might put the argument like this: with mitigation, a claimant cannot recover compensation for loss which they ought reasonably to have avoided; so too with duress, we might say, a complainant cannot obtain rescission of a contract which they ought reasonably to have avoided entering (by pursuing an alternative to submission).

The error here is that rescission is not subject to mitigation. There is nothing in the case law or textbooks to suggest that a decision to rescind must be taken reasonably. The orthodox approach gives the innocent party a free choice whether to rescind, subject only to specified bars to rescission, including affirmation – but no bar considers the reasonableness of the decision itself to rescind.[59] It is the same with repudiatory breach: the innocent party can choose

54 Halson, 'Opportunism, Economic Duress and Contract Modifications' (1991) 107 LQR 649, 654; Bar-Gill and Ben-Shahar, 'The Law of Duress and the Economics of Credible Threats' (2004) 33 J Leg Stud 391, 392–393.

55 Spark, *Vitiation of Contracts* (Cambridge: Cambridge University Press, 2013) 229.

56 Smith, *Contract Theory* (Oxford: Clarendon Press, 2004) 322; Virgo, *Principles of the Law of Restitution*, 3rd edn (Oxford: Oxford University Press, 2015) 225.

57 Bigwood, 'Coercion in Contract: The Theoretical Constructs of Duress' (1996) 46 U Toronto LJ 201, 209.

58 Macdonald, 'Duress by threatened breach of contract' [1989] JBL 460, 467; McKendrick, 'The Further Travails of Duress' in Burrows and Rodgers (eds), *Mapping the Law: Essays in Memory of Peter Birks* (Oxford: Oxford University Press, 2006) 192; Morgan, *Great Debates in Contract Law*, 2nd edn (London: Palgrave, 2015) 199. See too: Halson, 'Opportunism, Economic Duress and Contract Modifications' (1991) 107 LQR 649, 671–672. I myself have previously made this point: *Hong Kong Contract Law* (Hong Kong: Rights Press, 2014) 153.

59 Where a contract is voidable for misrepresentation, the court can declare the contract subsisting, if equitable to do so: s 2(2) Misrepresentation Act 1967 (UK). The court must have regard to the loss that would be caused if the contract were upheld, as well as to the loss that rescission would cause to the other party. But the need for statutory intervention proves the common law rule that rescission is otherwise a free choice. Further, as regards s 2(2): first, it does not apply to fraudulent misrepresentation, where the complainant still has a free choice; second, the complainant is provided with an alternative remedy of damages in lieu.

whether to accept the breach and thereby terminate the contract, or whether instead to keep the contract alive. It may be that the innocent party can keep the contract alive only if they have a legitimate interest in performing their side of the bargain anyway,[60] but there is no matching requirement that the choice to terminate be reasonable.[61] The principal restriction is again simply whether the innocent party has instead affirmed the contract.

In short, the availability of reasonable alternatives goes to the question of whether the complainant was coerced. But if they were coerced, and submitted, the accused ought not to escape the consequences of their unlawful conduct by arguing that the complainant should not have submitted as the accused wanted and sought.

***

So is there a middle ground that enables threatened breach of contract to be sometimes legitimate, sometimes illegitimate? There is no consensus in approach, and no persuasive theory. Indeed, this led the Canadian court in *Fredericton*, below, to reject any test of 'illegitimacy'. But that is an overreaction. Instead, there are two bright lines we could draw with threats to break a contract.

(I) Threats to break a contract are never illegitimate. The complainant should resist, and recover damages for breach. And if the real concern is to prevent the accused from exploiting the complainant's vulnerability, that is already addressed through the doctrine of unconscionable bargain. However, the case law stands firm against this approach: as a matter of precedent, threats to breach a contract are definitely capable of amounting to duress.

(II) Threats to break a contract are always illegitimate.[62] Despite all the discussion, this is consistent with the case law. It is explicitly the position in Australian law, as we shall see, whose case law was cited with approval in the English cases of *The Siboen* and *The Atlantic Baron* (the latter a case of threatened breach of contract).[63] Indeed, there is no case in which a threatened breach of contract was nevertheless held legitimate. Even in the Canadian case of *Fredericton*, below, which said (obiter) that threats to breach contract are lawful, nevertheless duress was made out.

60 *White & Carter (Councils) Ltd v McGregor* [1962] AC 413.

61 Peel says that the choice to terminate is an 'absolute right' not subject to any implied term that it be exercised in good faith: *Treitel, The Law of Contract*, 14th edn (London: Sweet & Maxwell, 2015) [18–078]. See too: Tilbury, 'Money Remedies for Breach of Contract in Hong Kong', in Chen-Wishart et al. (eds), *Studies in the Contract Laws of Asia* (Oxford: Oxford University Press, 2016) 269.

62 Andrews, *Contract Law*, 2nd edn (Cambridge: Cambridge University Press, 2015) 291; Burrows, *A Restatement of the English Law of Contract* (Oxford: Oxford University Press, 2016) § 37; Smith, *Contract Theory* (Oxford: Clarendon Press, 2004) 320.

63 Other examples in English law where threatened breach of contract resulted in duress include: *B&S Contracts and Design Ltd v Victor Green Publications Ltd* [1984] ICR 419; *Atlas Express Ltd v Kafco (Importers and Distributors) Ltd* [1989] QB 833; *Kolmar Group AG v Traxpo Enterprises Pvt Ltd* [2010] EWHC 113 (Comm); *Progress Bulk Carriers Ltd v Tube City IMS LLC* [2012] EWHC 273 (Comm).

All this is also consistent with tortious intimidation which, as we saw in Chapter 1, applies to threats of any unlawful act, including threats to breach contract.

So how do we account for contractual modifications? Not every varied contract will be voidable or litigated. First, because in most cases freely renegotiated contracts between satisfied parties will not be the subject of litigation which costs time and money. Second, not every variation is preceded by an unlawful act or a threat, as *Williams v Roffey Bros* shows. Third, not every threat is obviously a threat of breach, as in *Huyton v Cremer*, or the New Zealand case of *Moyes & Groves v Radiation New Zealand*, discussed below, and so parties who find themselves in dispute may reach a compromise. Fourth, because in some cases the threatened breach of contract will not be coercive, the other party being content to concede a modification, as in *Pao On*.

Of course there will be borderline cases where it becomes factually challenging to distinguish between duress on the one hand, and compromise or concession on the other. But the courts have shown themselves able to do just that, and the case law reveals that there are factual details which, forensically, tend to point one way or the other: whether there was any protest; the complexity of the issue disputed, because that might encourage the parties to settle when there are arguments on both sides, or whether instead the breach was obvious; whether there were negotiations, or instead the agreement was unilaterally imposed or abnormally one-sided;[64] what other options there might have been, like litigating, or passing on the costs, or finding a new contract partner.

3.3 Lawful act duress

Should the threat of a lawful act be illegitimate? The case law seems to countenance such a possibility.

In *The Universe Sentinel*, Lord Scarman said that duress can 'of course' exist if the threat is one of lawful action, as long as the demand is illegitimate. He referred to the speech of Lord Atkin in *Thorne v Motor Trade Association*,[65] which was a case of blackmail. Similarly, in *Huyton v Cremer*, Mance J also said that, if the threat is of lawful action, it could be illegitimate if it involves potential blackmail, referring to *Thorne*.

In *Thorne*, Lord Atkin said that a blackmailer ordinarily had a right to do what he threatened, i.e. communicate information to a third party. Sometimes he even had a duty, like reporting a crime to the authorities. What the defendant had to justify was not the threat, but the demand. The gravamen of the charge, he said, is the demand without reasonable and probable cause.[66] Lord Atkin referred to

64 See too: Dalzell, 'Duress by Economic Pressure' (1942) 20 N Carolina LR 237 & 341, 375; Atiyah, *Essays on Contract* (Oxford: Oxford University Press, 1986) 346.

65 [1937] AC 797.

66 The modern law of blackmail is found in s 21 Theft Act 1968. A person is guilty of blackmail if, with a view to gain, or intent to cause loss, he makes an unwarranted demand with menaces. A demand is unwarranted if made without belief: that there are reasonable grounds for the demand; and that menaces are a proper means of reinforcing the demand.

Ware & De Freville v Motor Trade Association[67] and *Sorrell v Smith*.[68] They were both cases involving lawful act conspiracy.

All of this suggests that an appropriate model for the development of lawful act duress might draw upon blackmail, and lawful act conspiracy.

Further or alternatively, might bad faith render a lawful threat illegitimate? We saw earlier how such a possibility was countenanced in *Huyton v Cremer*.

In *CTN Cash and Carry Ltd v Gallaher Ltd*,[69] the accused regularly sold cigarettes to the complainant wholesaler. Each sale was under a separate contract. The accused also extended credit to the complainant. When a cargo of cigarettes was stolen, the accused demanded that the complainant pay for it, even though it eventually turned out that the cargo was not, at the time, at the complainant's risk. If the complainant did not pay, the accused threatened to withdraw its credit, as it was entitled to do. So the complainant paid. Nicholls VC said explicitly that, in practical terms, the complainant had no other option. But duress was not made out.[70]

In rejecting duress, Steyn LJ said that it was 'critically important' that the accused was acting in good faith, i.e. it believed that the cargo was at the complainant's risk, and indeed had been so advised by counsel. Steyn LJ said that its motive was commercial self-interest. He likened the situation to a settlement agreement. He seems to have suggested that the relevant inquiry to finding lawful act duress in such circumstances was whether the accused's conduct was morally or socially unacceptable. This, we might note, is more the province of unconscionable bargain.

And yet duress was still not made out in *Alf Vaughan & Co Ltd v Royscot Trust plc*.[71] The accused terminated vehicle hire-purchase agreements, as it was contractually entitled to do, when the customer went into receivership. It threatened to recover possession of the vehicles. The receiver offered to buy out the remainder of the hire-purchase agreements, which would have cost around £34k. It wanted to sell the business, and needed the vehicles. The accused insisted on a figure of £82k. (How they reached that figure does not appear from the judgment.) The case was pleaded as duress to goods. No doubt economic duress could have been asserted too (which was presumably the form of duress in *CTN Cash and Carry*). But duress was not made out. The judge repeated that, where the threat is not tortious, it must at least be immoral or unconscionable.

67 [1921] 3 KB 40.

68 [1925] AC 700.

69 [1994] 4 All ER 714.

70 *National Merchant Buying Society Ltd v Bellamy* [2012] EWHC 2563 (Ch) was another case involving withdrawal of credit facilities which did not amount to duress. And see too the New Zealand case of *Shivas v Bank of New Zealand* [1990] 2 NZLR 327, where the complainant was threatened with foreclosure on their home unless they provided personal guarantees for their company's debts; that too did not amount to duress. Further still, there is a line of Hong Kong cases, discussed below, where the accused was threatening ways of calling in debts, as it was entitled to do, without any finding of duress.

71 [1999] 1 All ER (Comm) 856.

Yet it was surely borderline unconscionable behaviour to extract more than double the agreed price, by leveraging the complainant's financial predicament, simply because it could. Indeed, Chen-Wishart suggests that this case is a clear example of the accused acting in bad faith.[72] And still duress was not made out.

Let us consider three further cases which discuss lawful act duress.

In the Australian case of *Westpac Banking Corp v Cockerill*,[73] the accused threatened to appoint a receiver over the complainant unless the latter entered into a refinancing agreement which contained a term agreeing to release the accused from any claims against it. Kiefel J acknowledged that lawful pressure might operate as duress,[74] citing the English cases of *The Universe Sentinel* and *CTN Cash and Carry*. The judge concluded that threatening to appoint a receiver, or demanding a release, was not wrongful, nor could it 'have operated as coercive'. Perhaps he meant that the threats were not illegitimate.

In *'R' v Attorney-General*, as we have seen, a soldier sought to set aside a confidentiality agreement he had signed as a requirement for him remaining in the special forces. Lord Hoffmann said that threats of lawful action are not necessarily legitimate, citing *Thorne*. And in this case, the threat was lawful, since the Crown had discretion to return a soldier to unit. But the demand, he said, could also be justified, because anyone unwilling to sign the confidentiality agreement could reasonably be regarded as unsuitable for the special forces. Duress was not made out.

A final case to consider is *Progress Bulk Carriers Ltd v Tube City IMS LLC*.[75] There the complainant chartered a named vessel from the accused for a carriage of scrap to China. The charter party gave no right to substitute another vessel, but the accused sought to do that anyway, in repudiatory breach. The complainant chose to keep the contract alive, not least because the accused offered reassurances that it would indemnify the complainant against any consequent losses. The accused then offered an alternative ship, but only if the complainant agreed to waive any claims, which it did. Duress was made out.

The judge treated the case as one of lawful act duress, presumably because what the accused was doing was offering a substitute, rather than threatening anything. But of course, the accused was already in breach of contract, and leveraged that in order to force the complainant into a position to which it had no practical alternative, as the judge expressly found.

This is important to emphasise. When faced with a repudiatory breach, a party can choose to terminate the contract, or keep it alive. If it chooses to keep the contract alive, that does not waive the previous breach of contract. Indeed, the

72 Chen-Wishart, *Contract Law*, 5th edn (Oxford: Oxford University Press, 2015) 334.

73 (1998) 152 ALR 267.

74 Similarly acknowledged in *Cadbury Schweppes Pty Ltd v Australian Liquor Hospitality & Miscellaneous Workers' Union* (2000) 185 ALR 480, [19].

75 [2012] EWHC 273 (Comm).

affirming party can still sue upon that breach.[76] The only thing it cannot now do is terminate. So in *Progress Bulk*, although the contract was kept alive, it was still a case of continuing actual breach of contract – more than that, the accused also threatened to continue in breach unless the settlement agreement was entered. This is not a case of lawful act duress, but at the very least a case of actual and threatened breach of contract.

So the case law purports to recognise the concept of lawful act duress, but no case has been made out on that basis. As a matter of theory, when should the threat of a lawful act be illegitimate?

Birks says that the only viable basis for discriminating between legitimate and illegitimate threats of lawful action is social morality. He says that the courts are willing to apply a standard of impropriety (rather than technical illegality) where they can be confident of a general consensus.[77] That seems true with unconscionable bargain, where the threshold is set very high: behaviour to shock the conscience of the court. A high threshold means confidence in a general consensus.

Perhaps no similar threshold is available for duress. In over 40 years since the notion of lawful act duress was first recognised, there has been no case decided on that basis, apart from genuine threats of criminal prosecution.[78] But those cases are best explained on other bases anyway, as we shall see.

It is notable that unconscionable bargain does not require the accused to do anything unlawful. The lawful / unlawful divide does not apply to unconscionable bargain. Instead, that doctrine applies a standard of social morality, with a high threshold. It seems more readily suited to the task of regulating lawful acts than any notion of lawful act duress. It is unsurprising then to find academic support for the idea that lawful acts should not sound in duress, but should be treated instead through unconscionable bargain.[79] This position is also advocated in the Australian case law, below.

The case law tends to refer to blackmail, and the case of *Thorne*, as an example of lawful act duress, as we have seen. Bigwood says that blackmail-type situations are the common thread through lawful act duress: a seriously disjunctive relationship between means used and end sought.[80] Except, of course, that blackmail is a crime, and a threatened crime is illegitimate because unlawful. There may be no

76 *Chitty on Contracts*, 32nd edn (London: Sweet & Maxwell, 2015) [24-010]; Andrews, *Contract Law*, 2nd edn (Cambridge: Cambridge University Press, 2015) 244; Peel (ed), *Treitel, The Law of Contract*, 14th edn (London: Sweet & Maxwell, 2015) [18–081].

77 Birks, *An Introduction to the Law of Restitution* (Oxford: Clarendon Press, 1989) 177.

78 Threats of criminal prosecution which are not made genuinely may be a threat to do something unlawful, i.e. a threat of malicious prosecution. See further below.

79 Virgo, *Principles of the Law of Restitution*, 3rd edn (Oxford: Oxford University Press, 2015) 218; Phillips, 'Protecting Those in a Disadvantageous Negotiating Position' (2010) 45 Wake Forest LR 837, 852.

80 Bigwood, 'Four Questions on the Demise of Lawful Act Duress in New South Wales' (2008) 27(2) U Queensland LJ 41, 60.

academic consensus as to why blackmail should be a crime.[81] But crime it is, and that suffices to render the threat illegitimate.

Might there be other suggestions for developing lawful act duress?

Beatson says that a threat not to contract, if made maliciously, might be duress. He says that there are similarities to lawful act conspiracy: that tort might 'indicate the prognosis' for lawful act duress.[82] And, as we have seen, *Thorne* itself refers to two cases of lawful act conspiracy. Lawful act conspiracy is best understood as an instance of abuse of rights, where the accused acts to inflict harm on the complainant from malice or spite.[83] It is notable that some theories of blackmail speak in similar terms: that although what the accused threatens to do is otherwise lawful, what makes the totality criminal is the accused's motive, that what they threaten to do is not for its proper purpose, but in order to inflict harm on the complainant deliberately and maliciously.[84] (And we explored in Chapter 1 the relationship between malice and abuse of rights.)

Similarly, Chen-Wishart suggests that a test for lawful act duress might ask whether the threat has been used to further an improper purpose, or whether there is a mismatch between the means used and ends sought.[85] Again, the former tends towards abuse of rights, the latter towards blackmail. Similarly, Bigwood[86] and Dalzell[87] suggest that lawful act duress might be best approached as an instance of abuse of rights. As does Neyers,[88] who characterises abuse of rights as the targeted infliction of gratuitous harm.

In summary, we might say as follows:

(i) Threats of blackmail are threats to act unlawfully.
(ii) Using threats of lawful action to procure a contract or variation is best addressed through the separate doctrine of unconscionable bargain.
(iii) There seems little further need for lawful act contractual duress. But if it is to have a separate existence, the most encouraging account sees it as an instance of abuse of rights, where the accused acts maliciously so as to inflict injury

81 For an overview of the variety of approaches, see: Herring, *Criminal Law*, 7th edn (Oxford: Oxford University Press, 2016) 601–602; *Blackmail Symposium* (1993) 141 U Penn LR 1565; Ormerod and Laird, *Smith and Hogan's Criminal Law*, 14th edn (Oxford: Oxford University Press, 2015) 1071.

82 Beatson, *The Use and Abuse of Unjust Enrichment* (Oxford: Clarendon Press, 1991) 133–134.

83 Tamblyn, 'Lawful Act Conspiracy: Malice and Abuse of Rights' [2013] SJLS 158.

84 Lamond, 'Coercion, Threats and Blackmail', in Smith and Simester (eds), *Harm and Culpability* (Oxford: Oxford University Press, 1996) 231–232; Berman, 'The Evidentiary Theory of Blackmail: Taking Motives Seriously' (1998) 65 U Chicago LR 795.

85 Chen-Wishart, *Contract Law*, 5th edn (Oxford: Oxford University Press, 2015) 336–337.

86 Bigwood, 'Coercion in Contract: The Theoretical Constructs of Duress' (1996) 46 U Toronto LJ 201, 222.

87 Dalzell, 'Duress by Economic Pressure' (1942) 20 N Carolina LR 237 & 341, 364.

88 Neyers, 'Explaining the Inexplicable? Four Manifestations of Abuse of Rights in English Law', in Nolan and Robertson (eds), *Rights and Private Law* (Oxford: Hart, 2012).

on the complainant. (This would be consistent with lawful act intimidation, as discussed in Chapter 1.) Malice sets a high threshold, and not inappropriately, since what the accused is threatening is otherwise lawful. And a high threshold is also consistent with the absence of any proven case of lawful act duress in the case law.[89]

3.4 Threats of prosecution and litigation

When is it illegitimate, and so duress, to threaten criminal prosecution or civil litigation? We take each in turn.

Criminal prosecution

If what the accused is threatening to do would amount to the tort of malicious prosecution, it would be threatening an unlawful act. That would be illegitimate pressure for the purposes of duress. That tort requires prosecution without reasonable and probable cause, and from malice. Malice here means spite, or an improper motive such as using the process of the court for an ulterior benefit other than bringing a person to justice.[90]

An example might be the Hong Kong case of *Tam Lup Wai v Vong Shi Ming*.[91] In that case, there was a twelve-hour meeting, during which there was 'more than one person nagging' at the complainant. He was threatened with civil and criminal proceedings, in order to procure a business agreement. The threatened proceedings would have brought in its train negative media publicity, not just to the complainant, but also to his wife and a family friend. Duress was made out.

The best explanation for this case is that the accused was threatening malicious prosecution and abuse of process; the court said that the threatened proceedings were based upon 'illegitimate and unfounded' accusations of fraud.

In similar vein, an attempt to buy off a prosecution could constitute the crime of seeking to pervert the course of justice.[92] And while a threat to report misconduct to the police is not itself unlawful,[93] a threat to report the complainant to a law enforcement agency, such as the Inland Revenue, unless a bargain were struck, could amount to the crime of blackmail, and so for that reason be illegitimate.[94]

But what if there are good grounds for the prosecution?

89 Coming close is the New Zealand case of *Haines v Carter* [2001] 2 NZLR 167. There the court suggested that threats to inflict gratuitous harm, in that case, to cause trouble for the complainant with his bank, might be an illegitimate form of pressure.
90 *Gibbs v Rea* [1998] AC 786, 797; *Williamson v Attorney General of Trinidad and Tobago* [2014] UKPC 29, [12].
91 [2002] HKEC 1076.
92 *Panayiotou* [1973] 1 WLR 1032.
93 *Scolio Pty Ltd v Cote* (1992) 6 WAR 475, discussed in *Carrier v Georges* [2013] NSWSC 401, [25].
94 *Haines v Carter* [2001] 2 NZLR 167.

The starting point is *Williams v Bayley*.[95] There a son forged his father's signature on promissory notes given to a bank. The promissory notes were not honoured and the forgery was discovered. The bank insisted upon the father paying the debt and providing security for it, on the understanding that the son would otherwise be prosecuted for fraud, with a certainty of conviction, and carrying with it the punishment of transportation for life. The father agreed to pay the debt and provide security in consideration of the promissory notes being delivered up to him. The agreement was declared invalid.

The principal explanation of this case, from the judgments, was that the arrangement involved an agreement to stifle a prosecution, which made it illegal or invalid as a matter of public policy.[96]

In the New Zealand case of *Pharmacy Care Systems Ltd v Attorney-General*,[97] the court said that a threat of criminal prosecution is generally an improper means of inducing a party to make an agreement, even if there is honest belief in his guilt, indeed even if he is guilty.[98]

In contrast is *Flower v Sadler*.[99] There a person was employed to collect rents but failed to account for a sizeable sum. His employer threatened to prosecute him for embezzlement, and to secure the debt the employee endorsed bills of exchange. That arrangement was upheld. The court found that there had been no *agreement* to stifle a prosecution, and said that a creditor was entitled to threaten his debtor in strong terms so as to secure the debt.

In short, threatening a third party, in an arrangement which stifles a prosecution, will be invalid, but threatening the miscreant, in order to procure what they always should have done, is probably tolerable (at least, without any promise to stifle the prosecution).

In *Mutual Finance Ltd v John Wetton & Sons Ltd*,[100] a finance house obtained a guarantee from a family company to secure a debt incurred by the son who had forged signatures to an earlier guarantee. This was obtained by threatening to arrest the son for forgery. The finance house knew that the later guarantee was given only because the father was in such a state of ill health that the criminal prosecution of his son was likely to endanger his life.

The court held that the guarantee could be set aside for undue influence. However, it looks more like unconscionable bargain: the finance house took advantage of the father's ill health in order to extract the guarantee.

In the Hong Kong case of *Diners Club International (Hong Kong) Ltd v Ng Chi Sing*,[101] the elderly complainant was visited by three men unannounced at his home 'determined' to persuade him to sign a guarantee relating to the credit card

95 (1866) LR 1 HL 200.
96 See too: *Jones v Merionethshire Permanent Benefit Building Society* [1892] 1 Ch 173.
97 (2004) 2 NZCCLR 187.
98 *Pharmacy Care Systems Ltd v Attorney-General* (2004) 2 NZCCLR 187, [94].
99 (1882) 10 QBD 572.
100 [1937] 2 KB 389.
101 [1987] 1 HKC 78.

debts of his son. They deliberately misrepresented the extent of the guarantee. They refused to leave or allow him to talk with his son. They threatened to report the son to the police.

The court said that the guarantee could be set aside for undue influence. That might be accurate, if the complainant's resistance was broken down until he was prepared to do as he was bid. But it is also notable that the accused were acting unlawfully: they committed fraud (which would have been enough to set aside any agreement), and they were (threatening to continue) committing the torts of trespass, and probably false imprisonment.

In summary:

(i) If the accused is threatening malicious prosecution, or any other tort (such as false imprisonment), or crime (such as blackmail), that is a threat to do something unlawful, and that could amount to duress consistently with the analysis in this chapter.

(ii) If the accused is making a genuine threat of prosecution, against the miscreant, in order to procure what that person should have done anyway, duress seems inapplicable, following *Flower v Sadler*.

(iii) If the accused is making a genuine threat of prosecution, not against the miscreant but against a third party, and the arrangement entails an agreement to stifle a prosecution, that will be invalid as a matter of public policy. Payment made thereunder might be recoverable by the complainant, for example, on the basis that they were not equally to blame (having been threatened into the agreement).[102] Otherwise, the complainant might be able to plead undue influence or unconscionable bargain. There seems little need for a plea of duress; indeed, the case law appears to have managed without it.

Civil litigation

It is not duress to threaten to sue in respect of legal rights which the party genuinely claims to hold,[103] let alone for money which is plainly due.[104] It is not improper pressure to threaten recovery proceedings, including bankruptcy or winding-up, in good faith to persuade a debtor to pay what is due.[105]

102 An example of money being recovered following the cancellation of an agreement to stifle a prosecution is *Davies v London and Provincial Marine Insurance Co* (1878) 8 Ch D 469. See too: *Chitty on Contracts*, 32nd edn (London: Sweet & Maxwell, 2015) [8–050].

103 *William Whitely Ltd v R* [1908–10] All ER Rep 639; *Mason v New South Wales* (1959) 102 CLR 108, 144; *News Ltd v Australian Rugby Football League Ltd* (1996) 135 ALR 33; *McKay v National Australia Bank Ltd* [1998] 4 VR 677. *William Whitely* was doubted in *Woolwich Equitable Building Society v Inland Revenue Commissioners* [1993] AC 70, but only to the extent that it involved demands for taxes by public officials. *Woolwich* otherwise confirmed that threats to sue do not amount to duress: [1993] AC 70, 161 (Lord Keith), 165 (Lord Goff), 184 (Lord Jauncey).

104 *Wing Hang Bank Ltd v Crystal Jet International Ltd* [2002] HKEC 537.

105 *Beerens v Bluescope Distribution Pty Ltd* (2012) 39 VR 1; *CSI Investment Management Ltd v Ke Jun Xiang* [2005] HKEC 2125. Nor is it duress to threaten to appoint a receiver, as in the Australian case of *Westpac Banking Corp v Cockerill* (1998) 152 ALR 267.

Chitty says that, since recourse to law is the remedy for redress provided by the law itself, a threat to enforce one's legal rights by instituting civil proceedings cannot be an illegitimate threat.[106] But this is only half true: if one has a legal right to do something, it does not follow that threatening to do it is a legitimate way of procuring a benefit.

For example, in *Norreys v Zeffert*,[107] Atkinson J said that the mere fact that a person may have a legal right to do something which will injure another is not sufficient justification for the demand of money as the price of not doing it. In that case, the accused threatened to report the complainant to his social club unless he agreed to pay a gambling debt. The judge held that no agreement was reached anyway. But if it had been, he said, it would not have been an agreement which the court would enforce. It was a threat to injure the complainant. It was not a threat to invoke the usual process in relation to unpaid gambling debts (such as notifying other bookmakers to exclude the complainant until his debt was paid). The judge also referred to the blackmail case of *Thorne*.

Civil litigation is, as *Chitty* says, the remedy for redress provided by the law. Obviously it is legitimate to *activate* that process. But *threatening* it might only be legitimate where the party seeks to obtain that which litigation itself might ultimately provide. In those circumstances, the demand is proper to the threat. In contrast, there is a tort of abuse of process. This applies to those proceedings, even if well founded, whose purpose is not the vindication of the claimant's rights in those proceedings, but some ulterior purpose outside the ambit of the claim, so that the suit is used as an instrument of extortion in an unconnected matter.[108]

Returning to the tort of malicious prosecution, traditionally its main remit was criminal law (see above), applying only to 'a few special cases' of civil process, in particular winding-up petitions. According to *Clerk & Lindsell*, the common feature of such claims was that the very institution of those proceedings, which rest on an *ex parte* legal process, may cause immediate and irreversible damage to the claimants.[109] However, the modern position is now that malicious prosecution does indeed apply to civil proceedings generally.[110]

Some case law has suggested that if the creditor knew the proceedings to be groundless or unfounded, that might amount to illegitimate pressure for the purposes of duress,[111] perhaps too if the demand backed by the threat of litigation was exorbitant.[112] But elsewhere a court has said that there is no general tort of knowingly bringing an unfounded claim.[113]

On balance, consistency across the law would suggest that threats of civil litigation can ground duress only if the litigation would amount to the torts of

106 *Chitty on Contracts*, 32nd edn (London: Sweet & Maxwell, 2015) [8–051].
107 [1939] 2 All ER 187.
108 *Speed Seal Products Ltd v Paddington* [1986] 1 All ER 91.
109 *Clerk & Lindsell on Torts*, 21st edn (London: Sweet & Maxwell, 2014) [16–08].
110 *Willers v Joyce (No 1)* [2016] UKSC 43.
111 *Beerens v Bluescope Distribution Pty Ltd* (2012) 39 VR 1.
112 *Pharmacy Care Systems Ltd v Attorney-General* (2004) 2 NZCCLR 187, [95].
113 *Metall und Rohstoff AG v Donaldson Lufkin & Jenrette Inc* [1990] 1 QB 391, 470.

abuse of process or malicious prosecution. Then, of course, the accused would be threatening an unlawful act, which is illegitimate pressure for duress as a matter of orthodoxy.

Further, there is an inconsistency or circularity in a complainant being party to litigation to vitiate a contract which they say was coercively procured by the threat of being party to litigation. Instead, the complainant should have defended the threatened litigation first time. Dalzell suggests that there is even something underhand in submitting to the pressure, in order to obtain the performance wanted, only to resile later, the performance now in the bag, instead of resiling at the time.[114]

Of course, if there is some weakness which inhibits the complainant from defending the earlier litigation, which weakness was overcome to enable the later litigation, that is a different matter. In such a case, it is not so much the threat of litigation which is relevant, as the complainant's inability to participate in that litigation. And that might sound in other doctrines, like unconscionable bargain, or undue influence.[115]

3.5 Causation, and burden of proof

In *Barton v Armstrong*, the court said that the threats need be only a contributory reason for the resulting transaction. Then in *The Evia Luck*, Lord Goff said that the threat must be 'a significant cause' inducing the complainant to enter the contract.[116]

What is 'a significant cause'? A similar phrase is used in criminal law, but only in distinction to a cause which is insignificant or trivial.[117] In criminal law, a significant cause need not be the sole or predominant cause, nor need it be shown that the defendant's acts alone would have produced the result.[118] And indeed, reference in *The Evia Luck* to 'a' significant cause might be taken as admitting that other causes could also have played a part. In so saying, Lord Goff referred to *Barton v Armstrong*, and the Australian case of *Crescendo v Westpac*. Both those cases confirmed that the threats need be only a contributory cause of the complainant contracting. Perhaps there is no difference between these tests.[119]

114 Dalzell, 'Duress by Economic Pressure' (1942) 20 N Carolina LR 237 & 341, 368.

115 An example being *Drew v Daniel* [2005] EWCA Civ 507.

116 This test has tended to be repeated in subsequent cases without further elaboration: *DSND Subsea Ltd v PGS Offshore Technology AS* [2000] All ER (D) 1101; *Bank of India v Riat* [2014] EWHC 1775 (Ch), [58]; *Dawson v Bell* (21 May 2014), [74], annexed to the judgment on appeal at [2016] EWCA Civ 96. In the New Zealand case of *Haines v Carter* [2001] 2 NZLR 167, the court said that any threat must be an 'appreciable factor' in influencing the complainant to contract, citing *Barton v Armstrong*. And the threat must be 'sufficiently coercive', sometimes described, said the court, as the complainant having no practical choice. The court also put the question this way: whether the threat had any 'significant impact' on the complainant's decision to contract.

117 *R v Cheshire* [1991] 3 All ER 670.

118 *R v Warburton* [2006] EWCA Crim 627.

119 That was the view of Stock JA in *Esquire (Electronics) Ltd v Hong Kong and Shanghai Banking Corp Ltd* [2007] 3 HKLRD 439, [157].

But then in *Huyton v Cremer*, Mance J said that the test of causation in economic duress ought to be the 'but for' test, in the sense that the contract would not otherwise have been made but for the threats. This is a novel approach, going beyond what was said in previous cases. (It was repeated subsequently in *Kolmar v Traxpo.*) Mance J acknowledged that this created a different test for economic duress, relegating the test in *Barton v Armstrong* to duress to the person.

As for the 'but for' test of causation, Mance J accepted that this failed to differentiate the situation where the complainant would not have acted but for the threats, but still had a real choice to act otherwise.

However, this problem is easily accounted for when we acknowledge that, as well as causation, there must also be coercion. Indeed, Mance J went on to say that it was necessary to consider the 'qualitative impact' of the pressure, and whether the complainant had a practical or reasonable alternative. He referred to *Pao On*, saying that, in that case, but for the pressure the complainant would not have provided the guarantee, but that the 'relationship' (perhaps echoing the words in *Barton v Armstrong*) between the pressure and the subsequent act was not of a sufficient nature or quality to 'deflect' the will.

Again, it would have been clearer simply to say that there must be both causation and coercion.

So, must any threat be a contributory cause of the subsequent contract, as in *Barton v Armstrong*, or a significant cause, as in *The Evia Luck*, if that means anything different, which seems unlikely, or a 'but for' cause, at least for economic duress, as in *Huyton v Cremer*?

Peel says that the more illegitimate the pressure, the lower the causal threshold, so that duress to goods and economic duress (which he says share the same test anyway) should require a 'but for' test of causation.[120] Similarly, Spark says that we can have a sliding scale of causation, according to the illegitimacy of the pressure.[121] He says it should be the 'but for' test for economic duress, a contributory cause for duress to the person, and something in-between (what?) for duress to goods.[122] Presumably he does not equate duress to goods with economic duress. Virgo says that there should be a stricter test for economic duress because it is a less serious type of threat.[123]

But McKendrick says that threatened economic interests can be very coercive,[124] i.e. no less serious in terms of their threatened consequences. That is surely true: threats to significant economic interests are potentially worse than threats to insubstantial property. It is worse to threaten bankruptcy than to snap a pencil. And for some people, a threat to ruin them financially might be more coercive than a threat of minor or transient personal injury.

120 Peel (ed), *Treitel, The Law of Contract*, 14th edn (London: Sweet & Maxwell, 2015) [10–006].

121 Spark, *Vitiation of Contracts* (Cambridge: Cambridge University Press, 2013) 212–213.

122 Spark, *Vitiation of Contracts* (Cambridge: Cambridge University Press, 2013) 227.

123 Virgo, *Principles of the Law of Restitution*, 3rd edn (Oxford: Oxford University Press, 2015) 210.

124 McKendrick, 'The Further Travails of Duress' in Burrows and Rodgers (eds), *Mapping the Law: Essays in Memory of Peter Birks* (Oxford: Oxford University Press, 2006) 187.

Further, Bigwood says that a higher test of causation for more serious threats ignores the fact that all threats have already passed an illegitimacy test, which might be easier for duress to the person than economic duress.[125] (Indeed, even the 'slightest touching' can count as trespass to the person in crime and tort.[126])

We are edging here towards the correct position.

First, the best explanation for contractual duress, discussed below, is that it requires the accused to do or threaten something unlawful, such as a crime or tort or breach of contract. (We concluded above that lawful act duress falls better within the province of unconscionable bargain.) Unlawfulness is the threshold. There is no sliding scale of illegitimacy. Yes, threatening death might be more 'serious' than threatening breach of contract. But both are sufficient to ground contractual duress. Meanwhile, the more serious the threat, the more likely it will incur further liability as well, outside contract law. For example, threatening death might incur criminal liability.

Second, contractual duress requires not just unlawfulness, but also causation *and coercion*. The more serious the threat, the more likely it is to be coercive. The less serious the threat, the less likely it is to be coercive. We do not need to have an adjustable test of causation when the matter is already regulated by the separate requirement of coercion.

Third, the 'but for' test does not work anyway. For example, any threat to breach a contract will usually be the sole cause of any subsequent modification. This is because, without the threat, the contract would have remained as initially agreed. There is no case in which the complainant would have modified the contract as demanded, with the threat merely providing a welcome opportunity. Where there is already a contractual relationship, a threatened breach will be not merely the 'but for' cause, but the sole cause. Yet still that is not enough for duress. The threat must also be coercive. All this was seemingly admitted by the judge in *Huyton v Cremer*. So for example, if the complainant agreed the modification without thinking it of sufficient consequence, as in *Pao On*, duress is not made out. Causation is not enough. The threat must also be coercive.[127]

Sindone suggests that 'a contributory reason' test of causation brings duress into line with misrepresentation and undue influence.[128] At least, actual undue influence and fraud need be only a contributory reason for the subsequent transaction.[129] With other types of misrepresentation, there is seemingly some uncertainty as to whether the misrepresentation need be only a contributory

125 Bigwood, 'Coercion in Contract: The Theoretical Constructs of Duress' (1996) 46 U Toronto LJ 201, 255.

126 *Collins v Wilcock* [1984] 3 All ER 374, 378.

127 See too: Peel (ed), *Treitel, The Law of Contract*, 14th edn (London: Sweet & Maxwell, 2015) [10–009]; Bigwood, 'Coercion in Contract: The Theoretical Constructs of Duress' (1996) 46 U Toronto LJ 201, 207.

128 Sindone, 'The Doctrine of Economic Duress' (1996) 14 Australian Bar Review 34 & 114.

129 Peel (ed), *Treitel, The Law of Contract*, 14th edn (London: Sweet & Maxwell, 2015) [9–024], [10–017]; *Chitty on Contracts*, 32nd edn (London: Sweet & Maxwell, 2015) [7–039], [8–072].

reason,[130] or the 'but for' reason, or indeed whether both positions are simultaneously compatible.[131] For unconscionable bargain, again it might only be a contributory reason.[132]

The better position is surely to adopt a single consistent test of causation across all types of contractual duress. Indeed, there is nothing else in the law of contractual duress to suggest that the type of duress matters. The test of causation most established in the case law is this: the accused's threat need be only a contributory cause of the subsequent contract. (This is also the position in Australian law.) Beyond that, contractual duress already recognises the varying power of different types of threat by additionally requiring any threats to be coercive. It is the requirement of coercion, not causation, which responds to the seriousness of any threat.

A related point is who bears the burden of proof. In *Barton v Armstrong*, Lord Cross, for the majority, said that the complainant might have entered the agreement had there been no threats. Nevertheless, the threats were a contributory reason, and that was sufficient. The complainant did not have to establish that he would not have made the agreement but for the threats. (This aligns with the criminal law test of causation, noted above.) On the contrary, the accused had to establish that the threats contributed nothing to the complainant's decision.[133]

In light of this, it has been suggested, with duress to the person at least, that the accused bears the burden of disproof. But this probably draws too much from Lord Cross. After all, once the complainant has showed that threats were a contributory cause, it is simply the corollary for the accused to prove that they were no cause at all.

Further, Lords Wilberforce and Simon, dissenting in the outcome in *Barton v Armstrong*, were prepared to agree that the threats need be only a contributory reason, and not the predominant or clinching reason, for entering the contract. They also agreed that the question should not be whether the complainant would have entered the contract without there being threats, because, given that there were threats, the question was whether the threats had any influence. But they otherwise appear to suggest that the burden of proof remains on the complainant.

In *Halpern*, which, I have suggested above, is also a case of duress to the person (at least to his moral integrity), the judge said that the complainant bore the burden of proof. And in all other cases, again, the complainant has borne the burden of proof.

130 Chen-Wishart, *Contract Law*, 5th edn (Oxford: Oxford University Press, 2015) 221; Peel and Goudkamp, *Winfield and Jolowicz on Tort*, 19th edn (London: Sweet & Maxwell, 2014) [12–048].

131 Peel (ed), *Treitel, The Law of Contract*, 14th edn (London: Sweet & Maxwell, 2015) [9–024]–[9–025]; McKendrick, *Contract Law*, 11th edn (London: Palgrave, 2015) 228–229; *Chitty on Contracts*, 32nd edn (London: Sweet & Maxwell, 2015) [7–037]–[7–038]; *Clerk & Lindsell on Torts*, 21st edn (London: Sweet & Maxwell, 2014) [2–20].

132 Spark, *Vitiation of Contracts* (Cambridge: Cambridge University Press, 2013) 294–295.

133 A similar approach can be found in the New Zealand case, discussed below, of *Pharmacy Care Systems Ltd v Attorney-General* (2004) 2 NZCCLR 187.

There seems no good reason to eschew the usual approach to the burden of proof: the complainant should prove everything. This is unlikely to be onerous. Having proven an unlawful and coercive threat, it will usually be easy to persuade the court that the threats were at least a contributory reason for acting. The evidential burden will then rest heavily on the accused to show that their unlawful and coercive threats, intended to procure the resulting contract, in fact did not.[134]

3.6 Australian case law

We have already made useful comparison to foreign jurisdictions when discussing English law, above. But to avoid a piecemeal presentation of the foreign law, in these following sections we consider them on their own terms, to appreciate their comparative value in full.

We begin in this section with Australian law.

As mentioned above, the English cases of *The Siboen* and *The Atlantic Baron* were relied on a line of earlier Australian decisions. Those are as follows.

In *Smith v William Charlick Ltd*,[135] the Wheat Board was a government monopoly for selling wheat. It threatened not to supply the complainant with any more wheat in the future unless it paid a supplemental price for wheat already delivered and paid for. The complainant could not buy from anyone else, and without wheat would have been unable to carry on business as a miller. It paid under protest. Its claim for duress was not made out.

The majority of the court said that there was no threat to the person or property or legal rights of the complainant, nor to any other person related to or in affinity with the complainant. The money was paid not to have done that which the accused was legally bound to do, but in order to induce it to do that which it was under no legal obligation to do. Specifically, the majority found that the Wheat Board had no obligation to sell any wheat to anyone. Comparing the position to a highwayman who demands 'your money or your life', Higgins J (who dissented on the facts) said that a property owner has a right to refuse to sell, whereas the highwayman has no right to take life. A threat not to sell, he said, was justified or legitimate.

The decision can be contrasted with *White Rose Flour Milling Co Pty Ltd v Australian Wheat Board*.[136] In that case, the complainant had a contract with the Wheat Board, which threatened not to fulfil the contract unless the complainant agreed to a higher price, which it did. Duress was made out. Rich J, who was also a judge in *Smith v Charlick*, distinguished the latter. In the present case, the accused had an obligation to supply wheat, and nothing in the contract allowed it to charge a higher price than agreed.

134 Even with unconscionable bargain, the burden of proof shifts to the accused to show that the transaction was fair, just and reasonable only once the complainant has otherwise made out their claim. So too with undue influence. It would be out of keeping, among the vitiating factors of contract law, for duress alone to have the accused bear the full burden of disproof from the outset.

135 (1924) 34 CLR 38.

136 (1944) 18 ALJ 324.

In *Nixon v Furphy*,[137] the complainant paid an extra price, above what was agreed, to complete a contract for the sale of land, under a threat by the vendor otherwise to cancel the agreement. Duress was made out. The judge said that the payment was made by the complainant, not intending to give up its rights, nor to close the transaction, but on the contrary, in endeavouring to preserve its legal rights as far as it could without jeopardising the sale and thus incurring further liability to its own sub-purchaser. This was a threat, said the judge, to interfere with the complainant's contractual and proprietary rights. The complainant was paying to have done that which the accused was already legally bound to do.

In *Re Hooper & Grass' Contract*,[138] again the accused threatened to cancel a contract for the sale of land unless the complainant paid a sum of money for an irrigation charge subsequently imposed. At trial this sum was held to be more than the complainant's share on a proper construction of the contract. Duress was made out. Fullager J said that the accused was not threatening to exercise a legal right, as in *Smith v Charlick*, but to withhold that which the other party was legally entitled to. It made no difference, he said, that the accused honestly believed that it was entitled to the amount demanded.

In *TA Sundell & Sons Pty Ltd v Emm Yannoulatos (Overseas) Pty Ltd*,[139] the seller demanded an increased price to fulfil a contract to sell iron, following an increase in the market price. Again duress was made out. The court said, following *Nixon v Furphy*, that duress of any legal right included a threat to refrain from performing a contractual duty.

In summary, these cases stand strongly for the following propositions. First, a threat to breach contract is always illegitimate, as I argued above. Second, a threat not to contract does not support a plea of duress, because a person is entitled not to contract.

After those early cases, we move forward to *Crescendo Management Pty Ltd v Westpac Banking Corporation*.[140] This is the grounding decision for most subsequent cases, and was cited with approval in the English case of *The Evia Luck*.

In *Crescendo v Westpac*, the complainant alleged that it entered into a mortgage with the accused bank only because the latter withheld money due to it from the sale of property. The detention of the money was held to be unlawful, but duress was not made out, since the mortgage was entered into before the money was detained (i.e. there was no causation).

McHugh JA said that the proper approach to duress was to ask whether the pressure induced the complainant to enter the contract, and whether the pressure went beyond what the law is prepared to countenance as legitimate. He said that pressure will be illegitimate if it consists of unlawful threats or amounts to unconscionable conduct.

137 (1925) 25 SR (NSW) 151.
138 [1949] VLR 269.
139 (1956) 56 SR (NSW) 323.
140 (1988) 19 NSWLR 40.

If this means that duress must incorporate the test for unconscionable bargain, then as argued above, duress risks becoming redundant. This is because a complainant would have to prove unconscionable bargain, and then some. Why go that extra distance when unconscionable bargain provides the same remedy (rescission) as contractual duress?

Otherwise, McHugh JA said that even overwhelming pressure will not necessarily constitute economic duress (quoting Lords Wilberforce and Simon in *Barton v Armstrong*). He also said that any pressure need be only a contributory cause of the resulting contract, and that once illegitimate pressure was shown, the burden lies on the accused to show it made no contribution to the complainant entering the contract.[141]

In *Westpac Banking Corp v Cockerill*,[142] the accused threatened to appoint a receiver over the complainant unless the latter entered into a refinancing agreement which contained a term agreeing to release the accused from any claims against it. In considering what constituted illegitimate threats, Kiefel J referred to *Crescendo v Westpac*, but said that the judge there, in talking about threats which were unlawful or 'unconscionable', was not to be taken as referring to the distinct doctrine of unconscionable bargain. Duress, he said, focuses on the effect of the pressure on the complainant's consent, whereas unconscionable bargain focuses on the conduct of the accused.

I doubt whether this is a helpful distinction. Bad conduct is not the preserve of unconscionable bargain; with duress, to threaten unlawful acts is still reprehensible conduct by the accused. Also, reluctant consent is not the preserve of duress; with unconscionable bargain, the complainant may be just as aware of their predicament, and contract just as reluctantly. This is not a successful way of distinguishing the two doctrines.[143] But the judge was otherwise right to maintain the two doctrines as distinct.

The appeal was resolved on the basis that the complainant had pleaded only duress, whereas the judge had found instead unconscionable bargain, as a preliminary issue on the basis of an admission which could not sustain that finding.

In *Australia & New Zealand Banking Group Ltd v Karam*,[144] the complainant, in a perilous financial position, sought further financing with the accused bank,

141 This also finds support in the earlier case of *J&S Holdings Pty Ltd v NRMA Insurance Ltd* (1982) 41 ALR 539. That was a case of duress to property (land). The accused refused to discharge a mortgage until the complainant paid more money than was due. Duress was made out. It did not detract from duress that the accused also threatened to present a winding-up petition, which the court thought might have been an even more effective threat.

142 (1998) 152 ALR 267.

143 Duress is about coercion, whereas unconscionable bargain is about exploitation, which need not involve any threats.

144 (2005) 64 NSWLR 149.

which the latter was prepared to offer only if the complainant's directors provided personal security, which they did. The court held that there was no unconscionable bargain. This was so even though the terms of the further financing were unusual. This was because, said the court, the greater the financial risk, the greater the justification for increased security.

Otherwise the court said that threats of unlawful conduct should be addressed through the doctrine of duress. Threats can be against person or property or commercial and financial interests, whereas, illegitimate pressure which was not unlawful should be addressed through the separate doctrine of unconscionable bargain.

Some subsequent cases, without further argument, continued to treat the question of whether behaviour was 'unconscionable', so as to amount to illegitimate pressure for the purposes of duress, as importing the doctrine of unconscionable bargain.[145] Other cases have endorsed the approach in *Karam.*[146]

Finally, as with *Pao On*, so too the Australian courts also recognise the need for coercion. For example, in *Deemcope Pty Ltd v Cantown Pty Ltd*,[147] it was found on the facts that any pressure was not sufficiently coercive, given that the complainant negotiated down the price demanded, and successfully resisted demands for a personal guarantee, and when anyway he had practical alternatives.

In summary, Australian law closely tracks English law in requiring an illegitimate threat which is coercive and which causes the resulting transaction. Otherwise, Australian law tends to support my arguments above in terms of the better position for English law: the threat need be only a contributory cause; threats to breach contract are always illegitimate; and the ascendant position is probably that threats to do something lawful are better addressed through unconscionable bargain rather than duress.

3.7 New Zealand case law

The New Zealand decisions have tended to follow English law closely, with particular reference made to *Pao On* and *The Universe Sentinel* and *'R'*, the latter a decision of the Privy Council on appeal from New Zealand. We shall here consider the New Zealand cases which advance the discussion.

145 *Fair Work Ombudsman v National Jet Systems Pty Ltd* [2012] FCA 243; *O'Toole v Kent* [2015] VSC 470, [35].

146 *Magnacrete Ltd v Douglas-Hill* (1988) 48 SASR 565, 592 (an earlier case presaging the same point); *Mitchell v Pacific Dawn Pty Ltd* [2007] QCA 74, [7]; *A v N* [2012] NSWSC 354, [509]; *Electricity Generation Corp v Woodside Energy Ltd* [2013] WASCA 36, reversed on appeal on a different point (2014) 306 ALR 25.

147 [1995] 2 VR 44.

In *Pharmacy Care Systems Ltd v Attorney-General*,[148] the court said:

> In summary, the elements of duress in New Zealand law today are these: First, there must be a threat or pressure. Secondly, that threat or pressure must be improper. Thirdly, the victim's will must have been overborne by the improper pressure so that his or her free will and judgment have been displaced. Fourthly, the threat or pressure must actually induce the victim's manifestation of assent. Fifthly, the threat or pressure must be sufficiently grave to justify the assent from the victim, in the sense that it left the victim no reasonable alternative. Sixthly, duress renders the resulting agreement voidable at the instance of the victim ... Seventhly, the victim may be precluded from avoiding the agreement by affirmation.

The court also said that the threat need be only *an* inducement, and not the sole cause, of the resulting agreement, following *Barton v Armstrong*.[149]

On the facts, the agreement was found affirmed.

In *McIntyre v Nemesis DBK Ltd*,[150] those seven 'elements' listed in *Pharmacy Care* were described as better regarded merely as legal propositions 'of relevance' to duress. It noted that *Pharmacy Care* had attracted scholarly criticism for adding undue complexity;[151] also, that the Supreme Court had refused leave to appeal that decision, taking the view that the law was sufficiently clear and settled by *'R'*. In light of this, the court said, the test to adopt was: whether there was illegitimate pressure on the complainant, and if so, whether it resulted in the complainant being coerced into the subsequent variation.[152]

The court said that duress is concerned with the permissible limits of coercion in society, and the extent to which society can legitimately require people to stand up to threats rather than submit and litigate afterwards.[153]

Now, criminal law requires a duressee to stand up to threats. But it might be thought less applicable to contract law. With criminal law, the complainant seeks to escape liability for a crime committed against an innocent third party. In those circumstances, some stoical resistance might be reasonably required against the duressor. But in contract, the plea of duress is made only against the duressor. It seems a little generous to allow a duressor to argue that a complainant should have resisted submitting to the duressor's own threats which sought that very submission.

148 (2004) 2 NZCCLR 187, [98].

149 But a subsequent case noted, without deciding, the question whether economic duress required a stricter test of causation: *Barnes v Barnes* [2012] NZCA 255, [2012] NZFLR 617, [42].

150 [2009] NZCA 329; [2010] 1 NZLR 463.

151 Bigwood, 'When Exegesis Becomes Excess' (2005) 21 J Contract L 208.

152 One subsequent case quoted the *Pharmacy Care* list with approval: *Barry v Carlisle* (2015) 16 NZCPR 449, [122]. Other cases have tended to follow the retrenchment of *McIntyre v Nemesis*: *Magsons Hardware Ltd v Concepts 124 Ltd* (CA 671/2010); *Barnes v Barnes* [2012] NZCA 255, [2012] NZFLR 617; *Vervoort v Spears* [2015] NZHC 808, [2015] NZFLR 525, [40 n 13].

153 The court cited Atiyah, 'Duress and the Overborne Will Again' (1983) 99 LQR 353.

On the facts of *McIntyre v Nemesis*, the court found no illegitimate threat, no coercion, and, anyway, affirmation. It said that the complainant agreed to the variation, not because of any duress, but because that was the best option in bringing their joint venture to completion.

In similar vein, in *Shivas v Bank of New Zealand*,[154] the court said that, simply because the complainant was faced with an unpalatable choice, in that case between providing a personal guarantee, or selling their home, that alone did not constitute duress. Presumably, what the accused was threatening was lawful. And anyway, any threats in that case were held not causative, the guarantee being provided three months after any threats had been made – presumably by then the threats had 'expired' or lost their coercive potency.

There has been a line of cases where the court has concluded that the contract between the parties arose not by reason of any duress, but as a settlement of their dispute.[155]

In *Moyes & Groves Ltd v Radiation New Zealand Ltd*,[156] the complainant ordered some goods from the accused, who in turn ordered them from India. By the time the goods arrived two years later, both parties had forgotten about the contract. Meanwhile, the cost of production had increased. The accused asked a higher price for the goods, which the complainant paid under protest.

The court acknowledged that economic duress could be a ground for avoiding liability under a contract. But, it said, it should not be found lightly – a phrase regularly repeated since in the New Zealand case law. As for the facts, while the complainant alleged breach of contract, it was far from certain whether the contract was still existent, rather than abandoned. There were good arguments on both sides, genuinely held. The court found that the parties had entered a fresh contract, at the higher price, not under duress, but as a 'prudent and sensible compromise of a difference on which there was much to be said on both sides'.

A similar interpretation might be placed on *Walmsley v Christchurch City Council*.[157] The accused council engaged the complainant to produce a souvenir programme for its air show. The complainant was to bear the costs of production, but would be paid a share of sales revenue. When the programme was delivered, it was full of typographical errors. The accused rejected it, and engaged another printer. The parties were then reconciled with a further agreement. Under that agreement, the complainant reprinted the programme at its own cost, but was guaranteed a minimum sales return. This agreement the complainant sought to set aside for duress.

The court said that the accused was threatening to breach the contract in refusing to accept the programme. Yet it also held that the accused was entitled

154 [1990] 2 NZLR 327.

155 See too: *Aotearoa International Ltd v Scancarriers A/S* [1985] 1 NZLR 513; *Mann v Buxton* (CA 49/90).

156 [1982] 1 NZLR 368.

157 [1990] 1 NZLR 199.

to reject the programme. As what had arisen was never contemplated, said the court, the parties had to negotiate what was to happen next, and there were really only two options: use another printer, or for the complainant to reprint. Although there was pressure, it was legitimate and unavoidable. Thus we might see the final agreement as a compromise to a situation where both sides had good arguments to make.

In summary, the New Zealand case law is aligned with that in England and Australia: there must be an illegitimate or improper threat, which is coercive, and which causes or induces the subsequent transaction. It emphasises the distinction between, on the one hand, a variation procured by duress, and on the other hand, parties who find themselves in a genuine dispute with good arguments on both sides who enter into an agreement in order to settle or resolve that difference of opinion.

3.8 Hong Kong case law

Beyond *Pao On*, which was an appeal to the Privy Council from Hong Kong, the Hong Kong case law testifies to the potential breadth of circumstances involving duress.

There was duress to goods when a consignee threatened to destroy them unless the seller accepted a reduced price.[158] There was duress to the person when the complainant was kidnapped by triads.[159] There was duress to goods, and to the person, when the complainant's property was damaged, and the complainant himself assaulted, to procure his agreement to a reduced share of compensation upon the sale of ancestral land.[160] There was duress when the accused threatened to prevent the complainant getting further work from a third party, which would mean a severe blow to her career as an artiste, and to her finances.[161] But embarrassment and wounded pride do not constitute duress.[162] And yet, we have seen in the English case law how humiliation or loss of self-esteem might be sufficient for duress.

In *Mir v Mir*,[163] there was duress to the person when the complainant was assaulted at home by her partner. The impugned deed was signed ten days later. Although in the interim there was no further violence or threat of violence, the court said that the pressure continued, because the partner 'took advantage of the violence which had previously occurred' by moving in with the complainant for that period. The court also said that this rendered the deed voidable, not void, despite any reading of *Barton v Armstrong* to the contrary.

158 *Tang Yat Keung v Yunnan Provincial Import and Export Corp* [2003] HKEC 1439.
159 *Wa Lee Finance Co Ltd v Staryork Investment Ltd* [2004] HKEC 735.
160 *Tang Che Tai v Tang On Kwai* [2007] HKEC 674.
161 *Kwok Wing Kiu v Boxing Promotions Ltd* [2013] HKEC 798.
162 *Lam Yuk Wing v Yu Lai Wa* [2015] HKEC 2777, [95].
163 [2012] 1 HKLRD 671.

A couple of cases, such as *Esquire (Electronics) Ltd v Hong Kong and Shanghai Banking Corp Ltd*[164] and *Zebra Industries (Orogenesis Nova) Ltd v Wah Tong Paper Products Group Ltd*,[165] give a thorough recitation of the English and Australian case law, but without themselves offering any definitive exposition. Indeed, in *Zebra Industries*, the judge said:[166]

> The above brief survey suggests that economic duress is an area of law shaped by relatively high-level principles rather than readily applicable tests. There are few hard and fast rules. Each case has to be decided on its own facts based on the guidance provided by the cases.

In that case, the judge thought the following questions pertinent: was the complainant impecunious; did the accused know this; did the accused apply pressure; did this arise from a breach of contract; did the complainant have a practical alternative; did it have access to independent advice; did it protest; was the pressure illegitimate; was it a cause of the subsequent agreement? At least from these questions we can see that the court was engaged on familiar lines of inquiry.

The judge said that it was not essential to establish that the accused appreciated that the complainant was acting under duress. He also said that settlement agreements can be vitiated by duress, but extra care needed to be taken, for two reasons. First, settlement agreements are reached by two parties in dispute. They are opponents rather than collaborators, threatening litigation, bringing sometimes 'ruthless pressure' to bear on each other to reach a resolution. Second, there is good public policy in upholding compromise agreements which, as part of the machinery of the administration of justice, bring disputes to an end without need for further litigation.

In *Esquire (Electronics) Ltd v Hong Kong and Shanghai Banking Corp Ltd*,[167] Stock JA said that there must be illegitimate pressure. It was not enough for the pressure to be overwhelming commercial pressure exercised by a party in a stronger bargaining position. He then quoted from the Australian case of *Crescendo v Westpac* that pressure will be illegitimate if it consists of unlawful threats or amounts to unconscionable conduct. As for unconscionable conduct, he then quoted from the Australian unconscionable conduct case of *Amadio*, which might thereby suggest that the test of unconscionable bargain be imported into duress. But he also cited *Karam*, which, as we have seen, suggested that economic duress and unconscionable bargain be kept separate.

As for causation, Stock JA thought there no difference between a contributory cause, from *Barton v Armstrong*, and a significant cause, from *The Evia Luck*. He noted that a 'but for' test was preferred in *Huyton v Cremer*, but said there was no need in the present case to decide which test to prefer.

164 [2007] 3 HKLRD 439.
165 [2015] HKEC 1807.
166 [2015] HKEC 1807, [87].
167 [2007] 3 HKLRD 439.

On the facts of *Esquire*, the accused was threatening to call in a mortgage unless the complainant refinanced. This the accused was perfectly entitled to do.[168] There was no illegitimate pressure. And there was no causation, the complainant acting as it did for its own interests.

Similarly to *Esquire*, there is a line of cases in which the accused was threatening to do what it was entitled to do. So there was no economic duress when the accused was seeking payment of a judgment debt.[169] The court said that the complainant could have paid the debt, or if unable, it could instead have invoked the usual liquidation remedies under the companies legislation. In other cases, there was no duress when the accused was threatening legal proceedings for money which was plainly due,[170] or simply demanding repayment of a debt, even though the complainant was in financially difficult circumstances,[171] or when threatening to wind-up the complainant unless outstanding licence fees were paid.[172] In the latter case, the court said that it made no difference that the complainant was vulnerable, having just been through a debt restructuring, because that 'was not [the accused's] problem'.

In summary, there is no definitive exposition of the Hong Kong law of contractual duress, but it draws heavily on the English and Australian discussions. There is a strong line of cases holding that it is not illegitimate to threaten to do what one is entitled to do, such as call in a debt. Similarly to New Zealand law, there is also acknowledgment that, where there is a genuine argument on both sides, any subsequent agreement might not be the result of duress, but rather a compromise to close out the transaction. *Zebra Industries* reminds us that compromise agreements are reached by parties acting as adversaries not collaborators; heated circumstances need not preclude a binding settlement.

3.9 Canadian case law

Three principal cases are worth discussing here.

First, in *Stott v Merit Investment Corp*,[173] the court said that the pressure must be illegitimate, and must amount to a coercion of the will, alternatively, it must result in the complainant having no realistic alternative but to accede to the demand. The court endorsed the cases of *Pao On*, *Universe Tankships* and *The Atlantic Baron*. On the facts, the court found that, although there had been initial duress, the complainant had subsequently affirmed the arrangement by his conduct.

168 Similarly, in the Australian case of *McKay v National Australia Bank Ltd* [1998] 4 VR 677, it was not duress when a secured creditor made a threat to exercise rights conferred by the security.

169 *Padmilla Chien Mateo v Chan Choi Hing* [1997] HKLRD 539.

170 *Wing Hang Bank Ltd v Crystal Jet International Ltd* [2002] HKEC 537.

171 *DBS Bank (Hong Kong) Ltd v Young & Fortune Ltd* [2016] HKCU 115 (CFI); *Lam Yuk Wing v Yu Lai Wa* [2016] HKCU 4 (CFI), [92].

172 *CSI Investment Management Ltd v Ke Jun Xiang* [2005] HKEC 2125.

173 [1988] OJ No 134.

An example of legitimate pressure is *Morton Construction Co v Hamilton (City)*.[174] There the complainant sought payment for repairing pavements which it had originally laid down, under threat by the city that if the repairs were not carried out (for free), the complainant would receive no further work. The court held that this was a threat which the city was entitled to make.

Second, in *Gordon v Roebuck*,[175] the court, following *Pao On*, found that, first, the complainant protested, second, there was no alternative course open to him, third, independent advice would not have assisted, and fourth, the complainant promptly took steps to set aside the contract. On this basis, said the court, economic duress was made out. But, the court continued, one must still determine whether the coercion was legitimate. The court concluded that the economic duress was justified.

This is a strange way of defining duress. *Pao On* is better understood as identifying a set of evidential factors which are of forensic utility in determining the credibility of the complainant's assertion of coercion. They are not themselves the legal test for duress, indeed as a subsequent Canadian case has confirmed.[176] It is awkward to talk of economic duress being made out, but otherwise legitimate or justified and so without remedy. It confuses the factual inquiry (for example, was there coercion?), with the legal inquiry (was there duress?). Instead, a holding of duress should be the legal conclusion, necessarily incorporating the decision that the pressure was illegitimate.

Third, in *Greater Fredericton Airport Authority Inc v NAV Canada*,[177] the court held that a variation to a contract can be enforceable without fresh consideration, as long as it was not procured by duress. Here, however, duress was made out.

The court accepted that tortious and criminal conduct is unlawful pressure, but otherwise rejected the idea that there might be a broader notion of illegitimate pressure. In particular, the court said that threatened breach of contract was *lawful*. This point was under-developed. The court said that there was a right to breach a contract, if compensation was paid. But this denies the court's ability to order specific performance. At any rate, it does not explain why it is lawful to *threaten* breach of contract. (As we saw in Chapter 1, this is tortious.)

The court said that economic duress must (i) result from pressure, such that (ii) the complainant had no practical alternative but to agree. These were 'threshold' requirements, with the 'ultimate question' being whether or not the complainant consented to the variation. That involved asking whether there was any consideration, or any protest, or if steps were taken to disaffirm the agreement. That the accused acted in good faith was said to be no defence.

174 (1961) 31 DLR (2d) 323, [34].
175 [1992] OJ No 1499.
176 *Bell v Levy* [2011] BCCA 417, [57]–[58].
177 [2008] NBCA 28.

The approach in *Fredericton* is probably gaining the ascendancy.[178] And yet it seems insufficient.

The case law in other jurisdictions, like *'R'* and *Crescendo v Westpac*, indeed even in Canada, like *Morton v Hamilton*, recognises that parties can be under heavy pressure, and without any practical alternative, but without that necessarily being something for which the accused must accept a vitiated contract. For example, you have missed your train, and now risk missing your flight, so a taxi offers to take you to the airport, for its usual fee. Why should that have passed the 'threshold' for duress?

Why should it further buttress your position that you complained at the time, and upon arrival at the airport sought to disaffirm the contract? Protest may or may not be evidence of acquiescence, but just because one party stamps their feet, that alone cannot convert the other's conduct into something unenforceable.

In this example, the taxi has provided consideration, by driving you to the airport. But it is difficult to see why consideration should hold the sway. First, *Fredericton* itself held that a variation could be enforceable without consideration (which is probably just a more honest approach to what the English court did in *Williams v Roffey Bros*). Second, all the other case law on duress is premised on the admission that the contract was otherwise binding. Consideration had been forthcoming. It was precisely because the complainant was otherwise bound to the contract that they were pleading duress. Or to approach it from the other end, if there were no consideration, the contract would not be binding anyway, and there would be no need to discuss duress.

In short, the Canadian exposition of contractual duress seems to be moving away from its description in the other common law jurisdictions – but through case law which is muddled, failing as it does to reveal a singular approach, and on ideas that are under-developed and unsatisfactory.

3.10 The rationale for contractual duress

Shortly I shall suggest that contractual duress shares the same rationale as tortious intimidation, in that it polices coercion which seeks to leverage unlawful activities. But first we consider alternative theories.

We begin with theories of overborne will.

In *The Siboen*, the judge said that the complainant's consent must be overborne by threats. In *Pao On*, the court said that duress is coercion of the will so as to vitiate consent, an approach which finds support in the Canadian case of *Stott v*

178 *Jonathan's Aluminium & Steel Supply Inc v Retail Alloy Metal & Plastic Plus Ltd* [2015] ONSC 6485; *Keating Construction Co v Ross* [2015] NSSC 173; *Burin Peninsula Community Business Development Corp v Grandy* [2010] NLCA 69; *Haskayne v Resort Development Funding Corp* [2012] ABPC 287; *Bonne Bay Fish Farms Inc v Nutreco Canada Inc* [2010] NBQB 108. Although continuing support can still be found for *Gordon v Roebuck*: *Ekum-Sekum Inc v Bel Air Excavating & Grading Ltd* [2017] ONSC 540; *Ramdial v Davis* [2015] ONCA 726; *Freshwest Equities Trading Corp v Dosanjh* [2015] BCSC 952.

Merit Investment. In the New Zealand case of *Pharmacy Care*, the court said that the victim's will must have been overborne by the improper pressure so that his or her free will and judgement have been displaced. In *Huyton v Cremer*, the judge spoke of duress deflecting the will, citing a criminal law case in support.[179] (Similar language is even found in a recent unsuccessful case of tortious intimidation.[180])

However, in the Australian case of *Westpac v Crescendo*, McHugh JA rejected the overborne will theory. Were the will truly overborne, he said, that would render the contract void, whereas duress renders a contract merely voidable. He said that the complainant usually knows only too well what he is doing, but chooses to submit rather than take the alternative course of action. Similarly, in *The Universe Sentinel*, Lord Scarman said that duress involved an intentional submission to the accused's demands, arising from the complainant's realisation that he has no practical choice.[181]

In *The Evia Luck*, Lord Goff approved of *Westpec v Crescendo*, and doubted that it was helpful to talk of vitiated consent or coercion of the will. Also, in the New Zealand case of *McIntyre v Nemesis*, the court said that talk of 'overborne will' was apt to mislead. Duress, it said, did not require the complainant to be 'psychologically crippled', or completely deprived of any free will.

Birks calls coercion of the will a 'plausible sounding but inscrutable expression'.[182] Further, an overborne will, whatever that might mean, is inconsistent with the facts that: the resulting contract is voidable, and not void (as noted in *Crescendo v Westpac*); and duress need not be the sole cause of the resulting contract.[183] In the latter regard, if the will were overborne, at least in the sense of being completely defeated, there would be no room for the complainant having residual will to act on any other reason.

Similarly in criminal duress, as we shall see, there is also talk of the overborne will. But there too it does not prevent the defendant otherwise committing a crime with the requisite *mens rea*. Neither criminal duress, nor contractual duress,[184] is a form of automatism.

The notion of an overborne will is too imprecise and poetic, and goes too far. It is better simply to talk about a threat which is coercive.

Any focus not on the will but on consent, seems equally misplaced. It is well noted that we never have total freedom of choice or unfettered consent.[185]

179 *DPP v Lynch* [1975] AC 653.

180 *Dawson v Bell* [2016] EWCA Civ 96.

181 [1983] 1 AC 366, 400.

182 Birks, 'The Travails of Duress' [1990] LMCLQ 342, 342.

183 Chen-Wishart, *Contract Law*, 5th edn (Oxford: Oxford University Press, 2015) 323; Morgan, *Great Debates in Contract Law*, 2nd edn (London: Palgrave, 2015) 195; Sindone, 'The Doctrine of Economic Duress' (1996) 14 Australian Bar Review 34 & 114.

184 Macdonald, 'Duress by Threatened Breach of Contract' [1989] JBL 460, 463–464.

185 Dalzell, 'Duress by Economic Pressure' (1942) 20 N Carolina LR 237 & 341, 239; Chen-Wishart, 'The Nature of Vitiating Factors in Contract Law' in Klass et al. (eds), *Philosophical Foundations of Contract Law* (Oxford: Oxford University Press, 2014) 298; Morgan, *Great Debates in Contract Law*, 2nd edn (London: Palgrave, 2015) 196.

It is not possible in life to avoid contracts completely. And the case law affirms that it is not enough simply that contracts are made under everyday commercial pressures, even overwhelming ones. Anyway, contract law requires, not consent, but an *intention* to contract.[186] And we know from criminal law that intention is not the same as want or desire.[187] Hence again the recognition in the case law that parties intentionally submit to demands in order to avoid threatened consequences.

Cartwright says that duress is unfair pressure which interferes with the complainant's freedom to form an independent judgment about the contract.[188] But a complainant might be under no illusion as to the undesirability of the contract. More accurately, we might say, the pressure interferes with the complainant's ability to say 'no'.

Dalzell says that a contract procured by duress is tainted, not because of some difference in the nature of consent, but because of the impropriety of the alternative presented.[189] Similarly, Chen-Wishart says that duress is about the nature and acceptability of the choices left to the complainant.[190]

Certainly the case law stresses the relevance of whether or not the complainant had any reasonable alternatives to submission. But it is equally clear that a lack of choice does not equate with duress. Even overwhelming pressure, or unpalatable choices, do not amount to duress. So it is not about preserving a sphere of choice. And ultimately, the complainant does retain some choice after all: agree the contract, or refuse and suffer the threatened consequences.

Smith says that an accused who has obtained a contractual right by virtue of their wrongdoing has been unjustly enriched, and that ought to be reversed.[191] Duress, he says, is restitution for wrongs, the accused being required to return the contractual right to the complainant. But we might make a number of criticisms here.

First, it seems unnatural to talk about returning contractual rights. Second, the remedy for contractual duress is rescission. That accords more with the idea of setting aside contractual rights, rather than returning them.[192] Third, as Edelman and Bant originally put it, a contractual right is not an enrichment anyway when matched at the same time by a contractual obligation.[193] Without any enrichment,

186 Peel (ed), *Treitel, The Law of Contract*, 14th edn (London: Sweet & Maxwell, 2015) ch 4; Simpson, 'Innovation in Nineteenth Century Contract Law' (1975) 91 LQR 247, 263–265.
187 *Moloney* [1985] AC 905, 926.
188 Cartwright, *Unequal Bargaining* (Oxford: Clarendon Press, 1991) 151.
189 Dalzell, 'Duress by Economic Pressure' (1942) 20 N Carolina LR 237 & 341, 240.
190 Chen-Wishart, *Contract Law*, 5th edn (Oxford: Oxford University Press, 2015) 322. See too: Birks, 'The Travails of Duress' [1990] LMCLQ 342, 344; Bigwood, 'Coercion in Contract: The Theoretical Constructs of Duress' (1996) 46 U Toronto LJ 201, 227, 230.
191 Smith, *Contract Theory* (Oxford: Clarendon Press, 2004) 317–318.
192 The idea that rescission *is* restitution is controversial: see the views collected at Tamblyn, 'Separating Rescission and Restitution' (2016) 33 J Contract Law 135–136.
193 Edelman and Bant, *Unjust Enrichment in Australia* (Melbourne: Oxford University Press, 2006) 345; see now Edelman and Bant, 'Receipt in Satisfaction of a Right' in *Unjust Enrichment*, 2nd edn (Oxford: Hart, 2016) 156–158.

there can be no *unjust* enrichment. Fourth, Smith's approach is inconsistent with the orthodox view of restitution for wrongs:[194] first, the wrong must be independently actionable, and second, the remedy is a restitutionary measure of damages (not rescission).

The better rationale for contractual duress is the same as tortious intimidation, as follows.

Contractual duress polices coercion. As we saw in Chapter 1, coercion is wrong to the extent that it forces a complainant to change their behaviour for the selfish reasons of the accused. This denies the complainant the (residual) freedom to choose their own goals. It also denies them the dignity of an equal status, because it fails to respect them as having the capacity to choose such goals. And it deprives them of the chance to use or develop that capacity, when doing so is personally fulfilling and socially inspiring.

So coercion is a moral wrong. But we still need to distinguish illegitimate coercion from legitimate if forceful persuasion.

Contractual duress polices coercion by drawing a line consistent with the rest of the law: it outlaws the leveraging of activities which other areas of the law have already proscribed, such as crime, tort and breach of contract. To this extent, unlawful act contractual duress is law enforcement. Not in the way that the police might enforce the criminal law for the protection of society. Rather it is the law, through its own internal workings, ensuring that what it proscribes elsewhere is being observed.[195] We might ask, for example, what is morally wrong with violence against the person.[196] But the doctrine of contractual duress does not need to answer such questions. It suffices that those acts have been designated unlawful, for whatever reason. All duress has to do is act consistently. In contract law, this simply means rendering the contract voidable.[197]

Note the following. Doing something unlawful is, obviously, unlawful. Threatening to do something unlawful, whether or not that might involve a specific crime or tort like assault (i.e. threatening violence), nevertheless will also be the tort of intimidation, and so, again, unlawful. Contractual duress polices all such unlawful behaviour.

Lawful act duress might involve the moral wrong of coercion; but without leveraging unlawful activities, we lack the ingredient to distinguish unlawful coercion from forceful but legitimate persuasion. That extra ingredient, I have suggested, could be malice, because that would convert what would otherwise be

194 Burrows, *The Law of Restitution*, 3rd edn (Oxford: Oxford University Press, 2011) ch 23; Virgo, *The Principles of the Law of Restitution*, 3rd edn (Oxford: Oxford University Press, 2015) ch 16.

195 In this regard, duress also operates to deny the accused the fruits of any threatened wrongdoing: Morgan, *Great Debates in Contract Law*, 2nd edn (London: Palgrave, 2015) 199; Smith, *Contract Theory* (Oxford: Clarendon Press, 2004) 317.

196 Tamblyn, 'Why is Killing Morally Wrong?' (2014) 25 King's LJ 454.

197 By making the contract voidable, rather than void, the needs of the victim are taken into account – or, more precisely, the victim has the option of affirming the contract (if that is in their better interests).

the exercise of lawful rights into an abuse of rights. But then again, contract law already has the doctrine of unconscionable bargain which renders illegitimate the exploitation of a victim albeit through otherwise lawful means.

A consequence of this suggested rationale is that duress should apply only when the accused applied the coercion, or had actual knowledge that coercion was applied by a third party. Constructive knowledge seems less appropriate. If central to the moral wrong of coercion is the accused's manipulation of the complainant to their own ends, then a party seemingly has done nothing wrong who neither has effected that manipulation nor takes the benefit of another's known manipulation. We saw, in Chapter 2, that a similar analysis applies to unconscionable bargain, and the same reasoning applies here.[198]

Where constructive knowledge is relevant is in property law.[199] A subsequent legal right is trumped by an earlier equitable right if the owner of the legal right had actual or constructive knowledge of the equitable right. Disputed property must be allocated to one of the two disputants (it cannot be left unattributed). But if two parties have entered a contract, it should stand; the fact that one party was manipulated prior to entering the contract, but not by the other party, and not to their knowledge, seems no reason to burden that innocent party with the consequences of another's moral wrong. After all, the complainant can sue the actual duressor in tortious intimidation.

3.11 The relationship with undue influence

What is the relationship between contractual duress and undue influence?

There are two ways of proving undue influence: with a presumption, when it tends to be called presumed undue influence, and without a presumption, when it tends to be called actual undue influence.

Presumed undue influence requires a complainant to show a relationship of trust and confidence, and a transaction which calls for an explanation. Thereafter, it is presumed that the transaction was brought about by undue influence, unless the accused can convince the court otherwise. There seems little overlap here with duress, not least because: duress does not require a relationship of trust and confidence; with duress, there is nothing in the case law to suggest any requirement that the impugned transaction calls for an explanation or is otherwise substantively unfair.

Actual undue influence is approached in a different way. It has been said to require proof of the following:[200] the accused had the ability to influence the

198 Also, we saw that unconscionable bargain can attach to an accused who passively (yet still knowingly) accepts the benefit of an unconscionable bargain. The same language and approach would be equally apposite with contractual duress.

199 *Kakavas v Crown Melbourne Ltd* (2013) 87 ALJR 708, discussed in Chapter 2 above.

200 *Bank of Credit and Commerce International SA v Aboody* [1990] 1 QB 923.

complainant; the accused exercised this influence; such exercise was undue; the undue influence caused the complainant to enter the transaction. The undue influence need be only a reason, not the 'but for' reason, for entering the transaction.[201]

Actual undue influence can be exercised by way of overt threats, and modern examples include the following: verbal abuse and threats of physical violence;[202] threats not to allow the complainant to return to his lodgings after discharge from hospital;[203] emotional pressure, and the elderly complainant's fear of not being cared for;[204] wounding language which amounted to emotional blackmail, and fear of divorce.[205]

Historically, when the common law of duress recognised only threats of physical violence, equity allowed a wider range of threats to count for undue influence. In modern times, duress has been expanded. Hence the suggestion that all threats now be governed singularly by the law of duress.[206] But as Burrows says, that would leave actual undue influence 'virtually bereft of case examples',[207] and so presumably teetering on redundancy.

Further, we can see from the previous examples, that allocating them to duress would involve duress recognising a much greater range of poor behaviour than has hitherto been the case. That may be little strain where the poor behaviour is unlawful (for example, harassment). But actual undue influence does appear to capture behaviour which might not otherwise be independently unlawful. Chen-Wishart's insight seems perceptive, that what makes such low-level coercion legally relevant is that it happens in a relationship of influence.[208] Duress does not require such relationships, suggesting a residual need for undue influence.

There is no consensus over the rationale for undue influence. For example, some suggest it focuses on the complainant's lack of autonomy,[209] others that it centres upon the exploitative conduct of the accused,[210] which has led still others

201 *UCB Corporate Services v Williams* [2002] EWCA Civ 555; Peel (ed), *Treitel, The Law of Contract*, 14th edn (London: Sweet & Maxwell, 2015) [10–017]; Enonchong, *Duress, Undue Influence, and Unconscionable Dealing* (London: Sweet & Maxwell, 2012) [8–031]; Virgo, *The Principles of the Law of Restitution*, 3rd edn (Oxford: Oxford University Press, 2015) 261–262.

202 *Clarke v Prus* (8 March 1995).

203 *Re Killick* [1999] All ER (D) 395.

204 *Langton v Langton* [1995] 2 FLR 890.

205 *Bank of Scotland v Bennett* [1997] 1 FLR 801, on appeal at [2001] UKHL 44.

206 Birks and Chin, 'On the Nature of Undue Influence', in Beatson and Friedmann (eds), *Good Faith and Fault in Contract law* (Oxford: Clarendon Press, 1995) 63.

207 Burrows, *The Law of Restitution*, 3rd edn (Oxford: Oxford University Press, 2011) 283.

208 Chen-Wishart, 'Undue Influence: Vindicating Relationships of Influence' (2006) 59 CLP 231, 265.

209 Birks and Chin, 'On the Nature of Undue Influence', in Beatson and Friedmann (eds), *Good Faith and Fault in Contract law* (Oxford: Clarendon Press, 1995).

210 Bigwood, 'Undue Influence: Impaired Consent or Wicked Exploitation?' (1996) 16 OJLS 503.

to commend it being merged with unconscionable bargain.[211] Some authors say that it looks both ways, to the effect on the complainant and the conduct of the accused,[212] others that its purpose is to uphold important social relationships of trust and confidence.[213] Indeed, any rationale would surely have to give a dominant place to the relationship of trust and confidence, given its central role in the legal test for presumed undue influence.

As for the case law, although the courts have not always used the same language, nevertheless a common theme emerges on how actual undue influence is characterised. Thus, the complainant's decision to transact 'must be the offspring of her own volition, not a record of someone else's'.[214] There must not be 'complete domination by [the accused] over [the complainant] so that the mind of the latter became a mere channel through which the wishes of the former flowed'.[215] The situation to avoid is where 'the pen may have been the pen of [the complainant], the mind was the mind of [the accused]',[216] or where there has been such domination that the complainant 'acts as the mere puppet of the dominator'.[217]

Such characterisation is quite different from duress. In broad terms, we might summarise the different focal instances as follows: undue influence works from the inside, usually between parties who ought to be on the same side, whereas duress works on the outside, tending to put the parties in an adversarial relationship.

It may be that some threats can support both pleas. But it seems that the threats travel along a different pathway, or, if we prefer, they have a different pathology. The rationales for duress and undue influence are likely different, with the latter probably focusing on the need for a relationship of trust and confidence, which is no requirement for duress. Undue influence also continues to respond to lesser levels of coercion than the unlawfulness required for duress. All of this suggests that it might be appropriate to maintain rather than merge the two doctrines.

211 Capper, 'Undue Influence and Unconscionability: A Rationalization' (1998) 114 LQR 479. But the Australian case of *Commercial Bank of Australia Ltd v Amadio* (1983) 57 ALJR 358, discussed in Chapter 2, suggests that undue influence and unconscionable bargain, while they might overlap on certain facts, also have different focal instances. With undue influence, the complainant does not act independently; with unconscionable bargain, the complainant can act independently, but the transaction is still impugned due to the accused taking unconscientious advantage of the complainant's disadvantaged position.

212 Enonchong, *Duress, Undue Influence, and Unconscionable Dealing* (London: Sweet & Maxwell, 2012) [7–006]; Virgo, *The Principles of the Law of Restitution*, 3rd edn (Oxford: Oxford University Press, 2015) 259.

213 Chen-Wishart, 'Undue Influence: Vindicating Relationships of Influence' (2006) 59 CLP 231.

214 *Drew v Daniel* [2005] EWCA Civ 507, [36].

215 *Tufton v Sperni* [1952] 2 TLR 516, 519, 532.

216 *Dunbar Bank plc v Nadeem* [1998] 3 All ER 876, 883.

217 *Lloyd's Bank Ltd v Bundy* [1975] QB 326, 342.

3.12 Conclusions

The best approach to contractual duress, consistently with the case law and principle, is as follows.

A contract is voidable for duress. Duress is where the accused makes a demand of the complainant, threatening to otherwise commit an unlawful act if the complainant does not comply with the demand. It is notable that this scenario, of threatening an unlawful act to procure compliance with the demand, is itself an unlawful act, namely tortious intimidation. The threat must coerce the complainant, and be a contributory cause of the resulting transaction. The complainant should bear the burden of proof. Of course, the accused can always seek to show that any threats were, after all, no cause of what subsequently transpired.

Contractual duress is not about an overborne will. Nor is best explained as concerned with consent. Rather, as with tortious intimidation, it polices coercion. Coercion is wrong for denying the complainant the dignity of an equal status, by depriving them of the (residual) freedom or autonomy to choose their own goals, and of the exercise of their capacities in that regard.

In distinguishing between illegitimate coercion and forceful yet legitimate persuasion or threats, contractual duress polices coercion by drawing a line consistently with the rest of the law: it provides a remedy when the accused seeks to leverage activities which are already unlawful. This includes threats to the person. That need not be restricted to threats of physical violence. As with tortious intimidation, it might include threats of humiliation or to self-esteem or moral integrity. Certainly it can include threats of blackmail. It should also include, like crime and tort, threats to another person for whom the complainant reasonably feels responsible. Duress also includes threats to goods or to economic interests. More generally, we might say that duress responds to threats of crime or tort.

It also responds to threats to breach contract. While the case law has discussed the possibility of a threat to breach contract being nevertheless legitimate in some circumstances, those circumstances have never been properly identified, and no case has held a threatened breach to be legitimate. And after all, a threat to breach contract can itself amount to tortious intimidation – which thus constitutes unlawful behaviour.

This does not mean that every varied contract is voidable or will lead to litigation. First, freely renegotiated contracts between satisfied parties will not likely be the subject of litigation. Second, not every variation is preceded by a threatened breach. Third, not every threat is obviously a breach, and so parties who find themselves in dispute may reach a compromise. Fourth, in some cases the threatened breach of contract will not be coercive, the other party being content to concede a modification.

With lawful act duress, of course, the accused does not threaten anything unlawful. So a different ingredient is needed to identify illegitimate coercion. The best candidate is malice, because that would convert what would otherwise be the exercise of lawful rights into an abuse of rights. But then again, contract law already has the doctrine of unconscionable bargain, which renders illegitimate the exploitation of a victim through otherwise lawful means. Meanwhile, genuine threats of criminal prosecution are best understood as a distinctive category: they will usually include, in return for payment, an agreement not to prosecute, and that is invalid anyway as a matter of public policy.

Otherwise, threats of criminal prosecution or civil litigation should constitute duress only if what is threatened is malicious prosecution or abuse of process – in other words, if what is threatened is otherwise unlawful.

Bad faith on the part of the accused might make the complainant feel more coerced. And bad faith in the form of malice might be relevant to lawful act duress. But otherwise bad faith has no confirmed role to play in contractual duress, and has not been pivotal in any case.

The principal lines of distinction are between, on the one hand, duress, and on the other hand, compromise and concession. These can be investigated forensically by searching for such probative facts as: whether there was any protest, or instead whether the complainant felt the demand to be of inconsequence; the complexity of the issue disputed, because that might encourage the parties to settle when there are arguments on both sides, or whether instead the breach was obvious; whether there were negotiations, or instead the agreement was unilaterally imposed or abnormally one-sided; what other options there might have been, like litigating, or passing on the costs, or finding a new contract partner. In all this, it should also be remembered that compromise agreements are reached by parties acting as adversaries not collaborators, and so are often attended by circumstances of pressure.

Whether the complainant knew that it had reasonable alternatives goes to the question of coercion (i.e. the credibility of alleging it felt coerced). But otherwise it should hardly be a defence for an accused to say that the complainant should not have submitted to threats which the accused intended the complainant to submit to.

As with unconscionable bargain, duress should taint a contract only when the other party applied the coercion or had actual knowledge that coercion had been applied to procure the contract. Constructive knowledge, i.e. what the accused might reasonably have known, is relevant when it comes to determining priorities of property interests. But otherwise, if the accused did not actually know of any coercion, then they are not guilty of any manipulation sufficient to constitute the moral wrong of coercion.

4 Tort and crime

Necessity

This chapter begins by considering the tortious defence of necessity. This is where the defendant acts upon the victim's person or property for the benefit of the defendant (private necessity), or for the benefit of a third person or the public more generally (public necessity). Some authors say that private necessity is no defence,[1] but the cases below demonstrate the contrary. These tortious defences are similar to the criminal defence of duress of circumstances. (That defence is considered in the next chapter, alongside the criminal defence of duress by threats, because the criminal case law tends to see both as governed by the same principles.) After identifying the ingredients for the tortious defence of necessity, we shall then explore its theoretical rationale.

It is possible to identify a further two types of tortious necessity. Because of the fact patterns in which these issues have arisen, the legal position appears to be coextensive in both tort and crime (hence the title of this chapter). Those two types are:

First, where the defendant acts upon the victim's person or property for the benefit of the victim. Although it uses the language of necessity, it is better understood as a separate defence, with a distinctive rationale, where necessity is only an ingredient rather than a motivating theme. So here it is called 'best interests intervention'.

Second, where the defendant acts upon the victim's person or property to avoid something even worse. This is usually called lesser evil necessity. It has the potential to absorb all other necessity defences, which might also explain why some authors identify the tortious defence of private necessity as lesser evil necessity instead.[2] Nevertheless, I argue against the adoption of a defence of lesser evil necessity.

A couple of further preliminary remarks are warranted.

1 Peel and Goudkamp, *Winfield & Jolowicz, Tort*, 19th edn (London: Sweet & Maxwell, 2014) [26–043]; Witting, *Street on Torts*, 14th edn (Oxford: Oxford University Press, 2015) 342; Epstein, 'Defenses and Subsequent Pleas in a System of Strict Liability' (1974) 3 J Legal Stud 165, 169.

2 Williams, 'The Defence of Necessity' (1953) 6 CLP 216, 224.

Necessity can be an ingredient in other defences, like self-defence, or it can be a defence in its own right. We are here concerned with necessity as a defence in its own right.

There are, additionally, 'backdoor' defences of necessity. As Glazebrook says of criminal law,[3] crimes which proscribe behaviour done 'dishonestly', or 'without reasonable excuse', or 'unlawfully', might allow for arguments from necessity. (We might add, something similar could be said about torts which impose liability only for unreasonable behaviour.) So too, he says, it might be thought a principle of statutory interpretation that any proscription is not intended to apply where compliance would produce more harm than would contravention.[4] However, we are here concerned with necessity as a general defence, that is, a free-standing defence potentially available to all crimes and torts, however those crimes and torts are worded.

The different types of necessity have not always been clearly demarcated. The case law is interwoven, and often the legal tests overlap. But the rationales are different. We shall take each type of necessity in turn.

4.1 Private necessity in tort

Private necessity is where the defendant acts upon the victim's person or property for the benefit of the defendant.

There are only a few examples of private necessity in the case law.

In *Mouse's Case*,[5] passengers were travelling by barge on a river when a storm blew up. They were in danger of being drowned, so threw property overboard to lighten the barge. It was proved that the passengers would have drowned had this not been done. The owners of the property sued in trespass. The court said that the passengers were permitted to throw the property overboard, in case of necessity, for the safety of their lives. If the ferryman had overloaded the barge, the owners of the property could sue him, otherwise everyone was to bear their own loss.

In *Romney Marsh v Trinity House*,[6] a ship was wrecked against a sea wall. There was valuable property on board, which the ship owners removed with reasonable speed, before breaking up the ship; the delay did damage to the sea wall. It was held that the ship owners were entitled to remove the property, and having acted reasonably were not liable for damage to the wall for not breaking up the ship sooner. In other words, though the ship found itself 'using' the sea wall, it could continue to do so while the ship owners preserved their cargo.

3 Glazebrook, 'The Necessity Plea in English Criminal Law' (1972) 30 Cambridge LJ 87.

4 See too the Australian case of *Leichhardt Council v Geitonia Pty Ltd (No 6)* [2015] NSWLEC 51, [137].

5 (1609) 12 Co Rep 63, 77 ER 1341.

6 (1870) LR 5 Exch 204, affirmed (1872) LR 7 Exch 247.

However, the fact that the ship came to rest against the wall in the first place was on account of the ship's earlier negligent navigation, and for that reason, said the court, the ship owners were liable for all the damage.

In *Cope v Sharpe (No 2)*,[7] the claimant, an owner of land, let the shooting rights to another, whose head gamekeeper was the defendant. A fire broke out on the land, and the defendant set fire to strips of heather to create a fire break to protect nesting pheasants. In the event, the fire was extinguished and the fire break was not needed. The claimant sued in trespass, unsuccessfully.

The court said that necessity was not to be judged in hindsight. The test was whether there was a real and imminent danger to property as entitled its owner to act, and whether those acts in response were reasonable.

But on the question of imminence, the real point is whether the defendant can avoid the danger lawfully. The less imminent, the more opportunity to escape or seek assistance. But if there are no lawful alternatives, then it should not matter whether the danger is imminent, if the only way to escape its inevitability is to act now.[8]

The court also said that there must be an actual danger, not merely an honest belief, nor seemingly even a reasonable belief,[9] nor mere good intentions. The need for an actual danger seems appropriate. The defendant has deliberately destroyed the victim's property. Why should the victim bear the costs of the defendant's mistake?

Kennedy J also said that, when considering the legality of destroying property to preserve another, their relative values were relevant. In this case, the damage to the land was adjudged only nominal.

In *Esso Petroleum Co Ltd v Southport Corporation*,[10] an oil tanker was stranded in a river estuary and, to prevent her breaking her back, she jettisoned some of her oil cargo, which washed upon the foreshore, causing damage. The foreshore owners sued in trespass, nuisance and negligence. At first instance, Devlin J said that he was not satisfied that a defence of necessity allowed one person to damage another's property simply to preserve his own property, without compensation. He also doubted the approach of comparing the relative values of such property.

7 [1912] 1 KB 496.

8 This point is discussed more fully in the criminal case law (see Chapter 5).

9 Such was also the interpretation of *Cope v Sharpe (No 2)* by Clarke MR in *Ashley v Chief Constable of Sussex* [2006] EWCA Civ 1085, [41]. *Ashley* was a case about self-defence. In the House of Lords, it was held that a minimum of reasonable belief was needed to invoke self-defence in a civil claim, but a majority indicated that it was an open question whether an actual danger might be needed there too: [2008] UKHL 25, [20] (Lord Scott), [55] (Lord Rodger), [89]–[90] (Lord Neuberger). And yet, in *Davis v Commissioner of Police for the Metropolis* [2016] EWHC 38 (QB), the judge said that *Ashley* had decided that a reasonable belief sufficed for the tortious defence of self-defence.

10 [1956] AC 218.

However, he said, in this case the crew were endangered:

> The safety of human lives belongs to a different scale of values from the safety of property. The two are beyond comparison and the necessity for saving life has at all times been considered a proper ground for inflicting such damage as may be necessary upon another's property.

This would not be so, he said, if the predicament were due to the ship's negligence – which in the event was not proven. Thus necessity was a defence to the claims in trespass and nuisance, a point confirmed by Earl Jowitt on appeal to the House of Lords (which otherwise considered only the issue of negligence).

In the Canadian case of *Ramsahai-Wing v Weenen*,[11] the defendant trespassed onto the claimant's property when pouring concrete intended to shore up the defendant's wall.[12] The court said that necessity was available only in situations of imminent peril, when any reasonable person would have concluded that there was no alternative to the act of trespass. In other words, this case acknowledges that imminence is really about the availability of lawful alternatives. (Necessity was not made out on the facts.)

In the Australian case of *Simon v Condran*,[13] it was seemingly accepted that necessity might allow a person to enter another's land in order to rescue their dog. But in that case there was no defence, because the owner was negligent in allowing her dog to escape to the neighbour's property in the first place. In other words, it was a case of prior fault (like *Romney Marsh*).

Finally, we must consider a case which looms large in discussions of private necessity, and tends to be read as precluding or severely limiting any such defence.

In *Southwark LBC v Williams*,[14] squatters moved into and repaired derelict houses owned by the local council, who sought to eject them. The squatters pleaded necessity. This was rejected.

Lord Denning MR said that, in case of imminent danger, in order to preserve life, the law will permit an encroachment on private property. But not, he said, when a starving man enters a house to take food – which would be theft. In support, he cited Hale.

Any reliance on Hale must be treated with caution, for a number of reasons.

First, Hale himself expressly acknowledged that there were other English lawyers who held views, contrary to his own, that necessity would be a defence, for example, to stealing food.[15]

Second, Hale noted that English ships sailing abroad could, on grounds of necessity, take provisions by force, albeit upon making reasonable satisfaction, because they could not otherwise have their needs fulfilled.

11 [2016] OJ No 1906.

12 A similar case in Hong Kong is *The Incorporated Owners of Fu Fai Court v Henble Ltd* [2003] HKCU 1164, [8].

13 [2013] NSWCA 388.

14 [1971] Ch 734.

15 Hale, *The History of the Pleas of the Crown* (1736) 54–56.

Third, this corresponds with one of the reasons why Hale thought there was no necessity defence in English law, because sufficient provision was supposedly made for the supply of necessities by collections for the poor, and by the power of the civil magistrate (something not available to ships overseas). But that claim was questionable in Hale's day and remains questionable today. Even in a modern welfare state, situations of necessity can arise when official protection or assistance is simply not available. The case law is testament to that.

Fourth, Hale was writing almost 300 years ago, and the law has much evolved since then. If it was ever the law that a starving person commits theft when they take bread, probably today they would have a defence.[16]

Lord Denning MR also said that 'if homelessness were once admitted as a defence to trespass, no one's house could be safe'.[17] He said that it would not be only those in extreme need who would enter, but also those who imagine or invent a need. We can dismiss these latter concerns: *Cope v Sharpe (No 2)* stands clearly for the proposition that the defendant must face an actual danger, not an imagined or invented one.

And what about the academic's favourite, the mountaineer in dire need who takes shelter in another's lodge?[18] The difference between the two scenarios might be put thus: the mountaineer is in a temporary situation, whereas homelessness is otherwise a more prolonged state. Edmund Davies LJ made this explicit.[19] Necessity, he said, deals with urgent situations of imminent peril, and might justify an initial entry, but not a continuing occupation for an indefinite period. Similarly, in the Australian case of *Bonaccorso v Strathfield Municipal Council*,[20] it was acknowledged that necessity could be a defence to nuisance, but not to a long continuing nuisance.

Yet to permit the defence would not allow the squatters in *Southwark v Williams* to remain indefinitely (assuming they could enter initially). Any danger might abate. Or it might come to be reasonably avoidable by alternative and lawful means (like renting accommodation). Or the local authorities might have provided for them. Or a necessity defence might be trumped by a statutory duty on the local authorities to eject the squatters in order to use that accommodation to house others on their waiting list.

16 Ormerod and Laird, *Smith & Hogan's Criminal Law*, 14th edn (Oxford: Oxford University Press, 2015) 414; Allen, *Textbook on Criminal Law*, 13th edn (Oxford: Oxford University Press, 2015) 196. See too: http://www.bbc.co.uk/news/world-europe-36190557 ('Italian court rules food theft "not a crime" if hungry').

17 Christie similarly thinks that the destitute may be owed a moral duty of charity, but have no right to take for themselves: Christie, 'The Defense of Necessity Considered from the Legal and Moral Points of View' (1999) 48 Duke LJ 975, 1010.

18 Introduced by Feinberg: 'Voluntary Euthanasia and the Inalienable Right to Life' (1978) 7 Phil & Pub Aff 93, 102. The general consensus appears to tolerate this situation. For example, 'anyone may take temporary shelter to avoid an immediate catastrophe': Simester et al., *Simester and Sullivan's Criminal Law: Theory and Doctrine*, 5th edn (Oxford: Hart, 2013) 807.

19 [1971] Ch 734, 746.

20 [2003] NSWSC 408, [52].

Megaw LJ said that the council were keeping the properties empty pending regeneration of the whole area. Whether this was a good use of the property or not, he said, it was the policy adopted by the democratically elected council. Those interested could challenge that policy democratically. (Other options might have included judicial review, or application to the government housing minister.) Necessity does not allow, he said, the squatters intentionally to defeat council policy. But, we might note, democratic challenge is a slow process, and hardly obviates urgent need.[21]

Homelessness is an emotive topic. It seems callous for someone sitting comfortably in their own home or courtroom to abandon the homeless to the dangers of the street. Yet homes are a place of special sanctity – their special status is acknowledged in American law, as we shall see. And what of those home owners who give to homeless charities, or who pay taxes, some of which goes to housing the needy? Are some to be singled out to provide yet further support, at their own additional expense?[22] And what about difficult questions of prior fault, as to why someone might find themselves homeless? In *Southwark v Williams*, Lord Denning MR noted that some of the squatters had left accommodation elsewhere in the country and come to the borough without any advance preparation.

All this said, homelessness does not ground a defence of necessity. Neither does hunger. Nor is it a question of relative need. Necessity does not seek to redistribute property according to a balance of utility. The touchstone is not convenience or advantage. What triggers the defence of necessity is a relevant *danger*. And the response must be reasonable, and without lawful alternative, and, in English law, without prior fault. It *would* be only those in extreme need who could enter. How much room for anarchy does that leave?

Nevertheless, perhaps some problems are of a kind which, fairly, can be solved only at a political level. Until then, the problem remains a moral stain on society. But so long as each of us is contributing our share to the solution, probably the law should not allow individuals to be singled out arbitrarily for a greater burden than others.[23] The challenge, of course, is in identifying which problems so qualify. Homelessness might be such a problem.

Summary

There must be an actual danger. It is not enough that the defendant believes, even reasonably, that there is a danger. This is appropriate too: the victim should not have to bear the burden of the defendant's own mistake. Further, it does

21 And at that time, homeless people had no vote. See now Representation of the People Act 1983, s 7B. And what of the likelihood of homeless people being able to mount a public law challenge? See Woolf, 'Judicial Review: A Possible Programme for Reform' [1992] PL 221, 226–227.

22 Sugarman suggests more generally that a necessity defence is akin to the defendant arbitrarily forcing the victim to be their benefactor: Sugarman, 'The Necessity Defence and the Failure of Tort Theory' (2005) 5(2) Issues in Legal Scholarship 47.

23 See too: Tamblyn, 'The Duty to Help the World's Poor' (2012) 23 King's Law Journal 312.

not matter that, after the event, the defendant's response was shown unnecessary after all (as long as there was an actual danger at the time). In other words, the danger need not come to pass. But otherwise, the danger must threaten the defendant's life. Seemingly, it may also threaten the defendant's property, but we shall have more to say about that below.

The defendant's response to the danger must be reasonable, which seems to mean both that the response was a reasonable way to behave, for example there being no lawful alternatives, and that it was carried out with reasonable care.[24]

The cases regularly repeat that the danger must be imminent, but the better position is that imminence is only forensically relevant to the questions whether there was an actual danger, and whether alternative responses were available.

In all the cases discussed, the defendant acted upon the victim's property, not their person. We shall have more to say about this below as well. Necessity provides a complete defence, so that the defendant does not have to pay compensation. The defence is precluded if the danger was caused by the defendant's prior negligence. It may be that the defence permits only temporary, rather than prolonged, use of the victim's property, though the precise point when temporary becomes prolonged is not clear. For example, if a lost hiker can take shelter in a mountain lodge, after how many days must they leave? And what if the unfavourable situation still has not improved?

4.2 Private necessity in American tort law

In this section we consider the position under the *Restatement (Second) of Torts*, and the case law upon which the relevant articles are founded.

The American position is usually described as an 'incomplete privilege'. In other words, the defendant is entitled or privileged to use another's property, but still has to pay for any damage done. On the other hand, in English law, as we have seen, necessity is a complete defence; the successful defendant need pay no compensation.

Section 197 states that a defendant is privileged to use land in another's possession if it is necessary, or reasonably appears to be necessary, to prevent serious harm, to the defendant or that other person or a third party, or any of their property, but not where the defendant knows, or has reason to know, that the person for whose benefit he acts is unwilling for him so to act. Where the defendant acts for the benefit of himself or a third party, he is liable for any harm done. This, the notes reveal, is drawn from the case of *Vincent v Lake Erie Transport Co*,[25] more on which below. The defendant need not pay if the threat of harm was caused by the tort of the possessor of the land.

24 Hence necessity is no defence to negligence, since necessity's requirement that the defendant respond reasonably, if made out, negates any breach of a duty of care: Virgo, 'Justifying Necessity as a Defence in Tort Law', in Dyson et al. (eds), *Defences in Tort Law* (Oxford: Hart, 2015) 155; Klar, 'The Defence of Private Necessity in Canadian Tort Law' (2005) 5(2) Issues in Legal Scholarship 6.

25 (1910) 109 Minn 456, 124 NW 221.

Comment (a) states that the defendant must act reasonably. Otherwise he incurs liability for harm under § 214. This seems superfluous, or at any rate it is no incentive to behave reasonably, since the defendant has to pay for any harm done anyway, at least where he acts for himself or a third party.

Comment (c) says that, in determining reasonableness, the probable gain to the defendant must be weighed against the probable detriment to the possessor. Comment (h) states that reasonableness demands more when the land involved is a dwelling, thus recognising the special sensitivity of people's homes.

Comment (d) says that the privilege is available even though the danger was caused by the defendant's own negligence. Pausing here, English law requires there to be an actual danger, not caused by the defendant's negligence, otherwise, the defendant has to pay. In American law, the defendant has to pay anyway, so it can be more lenient, such that a reasonable belief in danger suffices, and prior fault is irrelevant.

Comment (g) says that the defendant has the subsidiary privilege to use force, for example to break and enter, which seems appropriate, since that is still making necessary use of land in order to gain a position of safety.

But comment (g) also says that force can be used even against the person of the possessor. Comment (j) says that the possessor may not resist. This is a balance strongly in favour of the defendant, who need have only a reasonable belief that he faces danger, whereas the land owner, strictly, may not resist, and if he does, may be overcome with force.

Perhaps that balance is appropriate where the defendant seeks to save life at the expense of another's property. But where he seeks only to save property? The defendant may be obliged to pay for harm done, but that might be little comfort to the property owner:

In *Latta v New Orleans & NW Rly Co*,[26] the court held that there was *no* legal entitlement in the defendant to save his property by destroying another's. (And so presumably the other person could have resisted.) It was not sufficient, said the court, merely to say that the more valuable property was saved. That ignored the question of the comparative ability of the parties to sustain the loss. And what, said the court, if the destroyed property was all that the other party owned?

Similarly, Christie says that a property owner should be able to resist if they do not believe that the defendant has accurately assessed what it is reasonable to use or take, or if the owner is apprehensive about the defendant's ability to replace the property, or their ability to pay.[27] Alternatively, what if the defendant is penniless, and the victim is a billionaire? Christie says that morality is more subtle than a blanket rule that the defendant should pay. Indeed, we might add, what if the owner needs the property themselves in order to survive?

26 (1912) 131 La 272.

27 Christie, 'The Defense of Necessity Considered from the Legal and Moral Points of View' (1999) 48 Duke LJ 975, 1007–1009.

The same incomplete privilege is created in respect of chattels by § 263. Comment (d) adds that reasonableness also considers the likelihood that the defendant's acts will be effective to prevent the threatened harm.

So far, we have discussed acting upon another's property. Sections 74, 63 and 64 combine in a way which is far from clear, but seemingly as follows. When a defendant reasonably believes that another is about to inflict substantial bodily harm intentionally or negligently, they may use reasonable force to defend themselves against that other person, and also intentionally make substantially harmless contact with a third party, although they are still liable to that third party for any harm. The comments cite no case in support, but indicate that it is an equivalent provision to § 197. That is unconvincing. Section 74 seems to address intentional but harmless side-effects of self-defence. Otherwise, § 73 expressly states that there is no privilege to inflict substantial, or perhaps even slight, bodily harm on another person to avoid harm from a third source. In other words, necessity is no defence when acting upon another's person.

Let us consider the principal cases upon which these articles are based.[28]

In *Depue v Flateau*,[29] the claimant, after having dinner with the defendant, took ill, and asked to stay the night. The defendant refused, and set the claimant upon his cart. The defendant then started the horses off down the road. The claimant was found the next morning, fallen from the cart, by the roadside, nearly frozen to death. Several fingers required amputation. The court held that the defendant owed a duty of care to the claimant, not to send him out from their property when they knew, or reasonably should have known, of his dangerous condition.

In the Canadian case of *Ploof v Putnam*,[30] the claimant was out sailing with his family when a storm arose. To save the ship and passengers from danger, he moored at the defendant's dock. The defendant unmoored the ship, with the result that the ship was damaged and the family were injured. The claimant sued in trespass and negligence, and the court held that he had a good cause of action. It stressed the need to preserve life, and that necessity justified entry upon another's land.

Klar sees these two cases as examples, not so much of necessity, but of 'host liability':[31] while there is no general duty to (let) rescue, a host might have a responsibility to ensure that their guests are in a fit state to care for themselves before they are turned out.[32] That seems a good explanation of *Depue v Flateau*. But 'host' liability seems a misnomer for cases like *Ploof v Putnam*, where the necessitous party is uninvited.

28 For criticism that the cases cited in these *Restatement* articles do not support them, see: Christie, 'The Defense of Necessity Considered from the Legal and Moral Points of View' (1999) 48 Duke LJ 975; Friedmann, 'Restitution of Benefits Obtained Through the Appropriation of Property or the Commission of a Wrong' (1980) 80 Columbia LR 504, 543.

29 (1907) 100 Minn 299.

30 (1908) 81 Vt 471.

31 Klar, 'The Defence of Private Necessity in Canadian Tort Law' (2005) 5(2) Issues in Legal Scholarship 25–27.

32 The leading Canadian case is *Jordan House Ltd v Menow* [1974] SCR 239.

However, guest or trespasser, what both cases do suggest is a tension between causes of action. Thus, I may eject a trespasser from my land using reasonable force, to vindicate my property rights. But presumably when I act upon him, I must use reasonable care also. So for example, I cannot eject the trespasser onto a busy road without taking care for their safety. Once I start physically manhandling a person, I assume a duty of care towards them.

Now, *Ploof v Putnam* is usually taken to support the notion that a land owner cannot eject a necessitous trespasser. But perhaps all that the case stands for is that a land owner cannot, by their ejection, unreasonably endanger the trespasser. Given that the trespasser is sheltering from danger, reasonable ejection might be rare. But nevertheless, reasonable ejection is possible in theory, and recognising this results in a rebalancing in favour of the property owner, who is no longer strictly forbidden to defend their property.

For example, in the Australian case of *Beckingham v Port Jackson & Manly Steamship Co*,[33] the claimant bought a submarine for public display, and moored it at the defendant's dock. When a storm arose, the defendant, thinking the submarine a danger to the wharf and to itself, towed it into open waters, where it was wrecked. This was held to be a defence to what would otherwise be trespass, as long as the defendant used reasonable care. In other words, the dock owner could defend his own property, and could eject the submarine, at least as long as he took reasonable care of the submarine too.

In *Vincent v Lake Erie Transport Co*,[34] a ship was lawfully alongside a dock unloading cargo. By the time the cargo was unloaded, a storm arose. The court said that 'no master would have been justified' in sailing from the dock, that it would have been 'highly imprudent' to leave or drift away, and that in holding the vessel fast to the dock those in charge 'exercised good judgment and prudent seamanship'. It was indeed a terrible storm.[35]

In order to hold the ship to the dock, as lines parted they were replaced. The majority held that the ship must nevertheless pay for the damage to the dock. Yet they said that, if the vessel had been in the harbour and thrown against the dock, the dock owners would have had to bear the loss. So too, they said, if the lines had parted, and in the absence of replacement, the ship was then thrown against the dock. Either would have been unavoidable accident. But because the ship owners had 'deliberately and by their direct efforts' kept the ship against the dock and so 'preserved the ship at the expense of the dock', they were liable for the damage.

The dissenting judge could see no sufficient difference between, on the one hand, renewing ropes to keep the ship at the dock, and on the other hand, having used sufficiently strong ropes in the first place such that no replacements were

33 [1957] SR (NSW) 403.

34 (1910) 109 Minn 456.

35 It took 36 lives and 18 ships: Sugarman, 'The Necessity Defence and the Failure of Tort Theory' (2005) 5(2) Issues in Legal Scholarship 8.

needed – when presumably there would have been no liability, the ship then having taken no deliberate and direct steps to preserve itself when the storm later arose. The judge said that a person who constructs a dock and contracts with ships to moor there takes the risk of a ship being caught there in a storm and doing damage which could not be avoided with reasonable care.

In the Canadian case of *Munn & Co Ltd v m/v Sir John Crosbie*,[36] a ship was again lawfully moored at another's wharf when a storm blew up, and the ship, pressed by a gale, damaged the wharf. The court held that no compensation was payable. The court said that the ship had acted neither negligently nor wilfully to preserve itself at the expense of the wharf. That would be consistent with the majority approach in *Vincent*, since the ship in *Munn* took no further active steps once the storm arose. Nevertheless, the court also said that it agreed with the approach of the dissenting judge in *Vincent*, that any risk of non-negligent storm damage was borne by the dock owner.

In the English case of *Romney Marsh v Trinity House*,[37] discussed above, a ship was wrecked against a sea wall. The ship owners delayed breaking up the ship, in order to save cargo. This delay caused more damage to the wall. This would not have attracted compensation (but for the ship's prior negligence). In permitting the deliberate preservation of the ship while the cargo was rescued, without the need to pay for the further damage, the case is inconsistent with the result in *Vincent.*

Finding a cause of action to support the outcome in *Vincent* is no easy task, as we shall see shortly. But the approach in *Munn* and *Romney Marsh* is no easier. If the dock owner bore the risk of damage, then presumably he could also transfer that risk, for example when contracting with the ships which use the dock, or, to cover situations like *Ploof v Putnam*, with a sign to the effect that users of the dock must pay for any damage. Any visitor who disagreed might be denied access. But the whole point of a necessity defence is that it entitles the necessitous person to use property even against the wishes of its owner. Which only returns us to square one. And it is not obvious that the dock owner is the one who naturally bears the risk. Why not say that anyone who sails takes the risk of causing damage by their boat should a storm arise?

There is some academic support for the idea that English law ought to follow the American position.[38] (Incomplete privilege is also the rule in German and French law.[39]) How do we account for it in theory?

Sugarman decries any need for an incomplete privilege.[40] The reality, he says, is that property is insured, and so the cost is already spread throughout society.

36 [1967] 1 Ex CR 94.

37 (1870) LR 5 Exch 204, affirmed (1872) LR 7 Exch 247.

38 Virgo, 'Justifying Necessity as a Defence in Tort Law', in Dyson et al. (eds), *Defences in Tort Law* (Oxford: Hart, 2015) 153; Edelman and Dyer, 'A Defence of Duress in the Law of Torts?', in Dyson et al. (eds), *Defences in Tort Law* (Oxford: Hart, 2015) 174.

39 Gordley, 'Damages Under the Necessity Doctrine' (2005) 5(2) Issues in Legal Scholarship 7–8.

40 Sugarman, 'The Necessity Defence and the Failure of Tort Theory' (2005) 5(2) Issues in Legal Scholarship 110–111.

But this does not quite work. For example, if lost hikers can use mountain lodges, then the cost is spread, through premiums, on the owners of mountain lodges. Insurance is not free. The cost is still borne by one class of people for the benefit of another class. And another example: when it comes to ships damaging docks, still the question remains unanswered: should it be the ship or the dock that insures against storm damage to the other?

Bohlen, who coined the phrase 'incomplete privilege', and who was Reporter for the American Law Institute when it adopted that language for the *Restatement of Torts*, simply says that requiring the defendant to pay is 'fair'.[41] But why?

Keeton says that what is blameworthy is not so much the activity as the lack of willingness to pay should foreseeable risks materialise.[42] But this creates a second locus of tort liability: one in the defendant's act, another in the defendant's attitude. It would mean a victim could sue, for example, either for an unlawful activity, or for a lawful activity which produced loss which the defendant was not willing to pay for. This amounts to strict liability for the foreseeable consequences of lawful acts. It would cover events like unavoidable accidents, or even business competition. It is surely too broad.

Feinberg suggests that the victim's rights have been infringed, hence the need for compensation, but not violated, because using the property was justifiable.[43] Does this mean that all rights can be traversed at two levels? Can we infringe, but not violate, a contract right? And how do we tell when an act is an infringement rather than a violation? What makes necessity a mere infringement (other than definitional fiat)?

Coleman too invokes a distinction between infringement and violation. As for a doctrine of necessity, he says that 'only someone who had no understanding of human need and motivation' could deny it existence.[44] But then, why is it only an incomplete privilege, and not a complete defence?

Epstein sees the incomplete privilege as supporting his theory of strict liability: the defendant caused loss, and that is enough, as a matter of fairness and efficacy, for prima facie liability, absent any defence.[45] It is fairer, he says, for the defendant to bear the loss, because the defendant had the choice of harming or being harmed when the victim did not.[46] Let us accept that the defendant did indeed have a choice. But it is a choice between a rock and a hard place. It is not necessarily 'fair' to abandon the defendant to that situation. We have already seen with contractual duress, and will see again with criminal duress, that a remedy or

41 Bohlen, 'Incomplete Privilege to Inflict Intentional Invasions of Interests of Property and Personality' (1926) 39 Harv LR 307.

42 Keeton, 'Conditional Fault in the Law of Torts' (1959) 72 Harvard LR 401. See too: Keating, 'Property Rights and Tortious Wrong in *Vincent v Lake Erie*' (2005) 5(2) Issues in Legal Scholarship.

43 Feinberg, 'Voluntary Euthanasia and the Inalienable Right to Life' (1978) 7 Phil & Pub Aff 93, 102.

44 Coleman, *Risks and Wrongs* (New York: Oxford University Press, 2002) 283.

45 Epstein, 'A Theory of Strict Liability' (1973) 2 J Legal Stud 151.

46 Epstein, 'Defenses and Subsequent Pleas in a System of Strict Liability' (1974) 3 J Legal Stud 165, 169.

defence is still provided, even though, technically, the party involved has a choice (albeit an unpalatable one).

Klepper develops further the notion of choice beyond mere invocation of fairness.[47] He grounds his argument in a Kantian notion of respect for individuals and their autonomy in terms of the risks they choose to adopt in pursuing their ends. He says that the wrongfulness is the defendant choosing which risks he takes for his benefit, while imposing risks upon the victim who has no such choice.

In similar vein, Fletcher sees the incomplete privilege as evidencing a paradigm which he says underlies much tort law: the right to recover for loss caused by a non-reciprocal risk.[48] But he acknowledges a doctrine of emergency, when a defendant is caught in an unexpected, personally dangerous situation not of his making.[49] So perhaps he recognises a complete privilege where life is at stake. He also says that the victim's loss is not just the damage, but the fact that in law he was required to sacrifice his right to expel the defendant from his property.[50]

The difficulty here, for Fletcher and Klepper, at least when it comes to necessity, is that they do not start at the beginning. The first question is whether the defendant can make use of the victim's property. The second question is whether they must compensate. All seem to assume, in answer to the first question, that the defendant does nothing wrong in using the property. Why not? They provide no explanation. And yet the answer to the second question must be consistent with any answer to the first question.

So if, for example, the victim's property interests yield to the defendant's personal necessity, as I shall argue below, then the defendant is entitled to use the victim's property. In this case, the victim suffers no legitimate harm to their interests in that property because, at that point, they have no such interests at all. This also means that no risk is imposed on the victim, nor right sacrificed. There is then no question of compensation.

Weinrib says that the incomplete privilege is best explained as an example of restitution (rather than tort).[51] Others are similarly in favour of restitution.[52]

Indeed, not only does the *Restatement (Second) of Torts* speak of liability for harm done, but so too does § 40 of the *Restatement (Third) of Restitution and Unjust Enrichment.* The latter states that a person who obtains a benefit by an act

47 Klepper, 'Torts of Necessity: A Moral Theory of Compensation' (1990) 9 Law & Phil 223.

48 Fletcher, 'Fairness and Utility in Tort Theory' (1972) 85 Harvard LR 537, 546.

49 Fletcher, 'Fairness and Utility in Tort Theory' (1972) 85 Harvard LR 537, 552.

50 Fletcher, 'The Search for Synthesis in Tort Theory' (1983) 2 Law & Phil 63, 87.

51 Weinrib, *The Idea of Private Law* (Oxford: Oxford University Press, 2012) 198–200.

52 Keating, 'Property Rights and Tortious Wrong in *Vincent v Lake Erie*' (2005) 5(2) Issues in Legal Scholarship; Sussmann, 'The Defence of Private Necessity and the Problem of Compensation' (1967) 2 Ottawa LR 184; Friedmann, 'Restitution of Benefits Obtained Through the Appropriation of Property or the Commission of a Wrong' (1980) 80 Columbia Law Review 504; Williams, 'The Defence of Necessity' (1953) 6 CLP 216, 231, 233; Brudner, 'A Theory of Necessity' (1987) 7 OJLS 338, 362.

of trespass is liable in restitution. It might be thought that the incomplete privilege in tort precludes any trespass arising. But the notes to § 40 state expressly that it applies to situations like *Vincent*.[53] The notes concede that this reflects the academic uncertainty as to whether liability under the incomplete privilege arises in tort or restitution. In other words, we might say, the American Law Institute is hedging its bets.

How might restitution work? Weinrib says of *Vincent* that use of the dock was not the free gift of the dock owner, but was mandated by law, and having benefitted from its use, however faultlessly, the ship must now remove the detrimental effects. Or, as Finan and Ritson express it, the gain to the ship is measured by damage to the dock.[54]

Virgo is against any restitutionary analysis of the qualified privilege.[55] Indeed, it is notable that leading English authors on restitution, though their books contain chapters addressing necessity, make no mention of *Vincent*.[56] Virgo's reasons are as follows. First, if the defendant is permitted to use another's property, then there is no tort, and so no restitution for a wrong. Second, says the academic consensus, an entitlement or legal basis to any enrichment precludes a claim in unjust enrichment.[57] So here, if a defendant were permitted or entitled to use another's property, for that reason there could be no claim in unjust enrichment. Third, correspondence between gain and loss is an organising feature of unjust enrichment, because the defendant's gain must be at the expense of the property owner. But in *Vincent*, the dock's damage was not the ship's gain.

Nor can the gain be the continued existence of the defendant's property, because they owned that already.[58] Rather, the defendant's gain is the use of the victim's property, while the victim similarly loses out in having what is otherwise his exclusive property used by another. Only here, in use of the property, is there a correspondence between gain and loss. At most, the victim should recover a

53 Originally it appeared as § 122 in the *Restatement (First) of Restitution*, where it stated explicitly that a person acting under the tortious incomplete privilege owed a duty of restitution for harm done.

54 Finan and Ritson, 'Tortious Necessity: The Privileged Defence' (1992) 26 Akron LR 1, 7.

55 Virgo, 'Justifying Necessity as a Defence in Tort Law', in Dyson et al. (eds), *Defences in Tort Law* (Oxford: Hart, 2015) 154.

56 Virgo, *Principles of the Law of Restitution*, 3rd edn (Oxford: Oxford University Press, 2015); Burrows, *The Law of Restitution*, 3rd edn (Oxford: Oxford University Press, 2011); Mitchel et al. (eds), *Goff & Jones: The Law of Unjust Enrichment*, 9th edn (London: Sweet & Maxwell, 2016).

57 Virgo, 'Demolishing the Pyramid – Presence of Basis and Risk-Taking in the Law of Unjust Enrichment', in Robertson and Tang (eds), *The Goals of Private Law* (Oxford: Hart, 2009) 479, 488–504; Burrows, *The Law of Restitution*, 3rd edn (Oxford: Oxford University Press, 2011) 88–89; Tettenborn, *Law of Restitution in England and Ireland*, 3rd edn (London: Cavendish, 2002) 20–31; Mitchel et al. (eds), *Goff & Jones: The Law of Unjust Enrichment*, 9th edn (London: Sweet & Maxwell, 2016) Pt 2; Edelman and Bant, *Unjust Enrichment*, 2nd edn (Oxford: Hart, 2016) ch 7; Tamblyn, 'Unjust Enrichment, Leapfrogging and a Defence of Entitlement' [2014] HKLJ 551; Webb, *Reason and Restitution* (Oxford: Oxford University Press, 2016) 152.

58 Klimchuk, 'Necessity and Restitution' (2001) 7 Legal Theory 59, 72; Weinrib, *The Idea of Private Law* (Oxford: Oxford University Press, 2012) 198; *Yeoman's Row Management Ltd v Cobbe* [2008] UKHL 55, [41]; *Greenwood v Bennett* [1973] QB 195.

rental price.[59] But of course, this does not hold them harmless against damage, and was not the result in *Vincent*.

Nevertheless, if we want to explain the incomplete privilege, there are perhaps two approaches.

One develops an idea from Klimchuck.[60] Necessity requires the defendant to act reasonably. Presumably that includes taking no more than they need. If they fail to pay (assuming they can pay), then they have taken more than they need after all. At least, they have ended up with more than they needed. In this case, the defence of necessity fails retrospectively, and compensation is due.

But my preference is to focus on remedies. For example, in contract, breach may lead to specific performance, but only at the court's discretion. Or it may lead to damages, but still subject to remoteness, and the duty to mitigate. And restitutionary damages are again discretionary in contract law. In some cases, contract provides a remedy of rescission, but that can sometimes be overridden by the court, as with misrepresentation, or lost, for example through affirmation. Why not a similar range for tort? So we might say that, with necessitous trespass, the remedy is damages, but an injunction, which is already at the court's discretion, will not be granted, and the self-help remedy of ejection will be lost.[61] Thus it is not that the defendant's act is right-but-wrong-enough for compensation; rather, their act is wrong throughout, a trespass, but with restricted remedies.

This is how we might explain an incomplete privilege. But we still need a justification, both for the privilege at all, and for its partial application. We turn to that below, after discussion of public necessity.

4.3 Public necessity in tort

Public necessity is where the defendant acts upon the victim's person or property for the benefit of a third person or the general public.

Where the Crown, using its prerogative, takes property, even for defence of the realm, usually it has to pay compensation.[62] But what is the position when others act for the benefit of the public?

In *The Case of the King's Prerogative in Saltpetre*,[63] the court said that any person may come onto his neighbour's land to make bulwarks and trenches in

59 *Penarth Dock Engineering Co Ltd v Pounds* [1963] 1 Lloyd's Rep 359 (QBD); *Ministry of Defence v Ashman* (1993) 66 P & CR 195 (CA).

60 Klimchuck, 'Property and Necessity', in Penner and Smith (eds), *Philosophical Foundations of Property Law* (Oxford, Oxford University Press, 2013) 55–56.

61 See too: Stevens, *Tort and Rights* (Oxford: Oxford University Press, 2007) 103–104; Goldberg and Zipursky, *Torts* (New York: Oxford University Press, 2010) 239–241.

62 *Attorney-General v De Keyser's Royal Hotel Ltd* [1920] AC 508; *Nissan v Attorney-General* [1968] 1 QB 286; *Burmah Oil Company Ltd v Lord Advocate* [1965] AC 75, reversed by War Damage Act 1965. See: 'The Burmah Oil Affair' (1965) 79 Harv LR 614; Jackson, 'War Damage Act' (1965) 28 MLR 584.

63 (1606) 12 Co Rep 12, 77 ER 1294.

defence of the realm, but had to remove them afterwards. 'A thing for the commonwealth every man may do without being liable to an action.'

In *Dewey v White*,[64] a house had been damaged by fire, and a stack of its chimneys was in immediate danger of falling on the highway and neighbouring houses, and thereby a risk to life and limb. It was necessary, for the safety of other people, immediately to remove the chimneys, and this the firemen did. This caused damage to an adjoining house, whose owner sued in trespass. The firemen were held not liable for unavoidable damage.

In early cases,[65] the courts said repeatedly that a house could be pulled down, seemingly by anyone, to prevent the spread of fire from a neighbouring house, in necessity to save the town. In *Burmah Oil Company Ltd v Lord Advocate*,[66] Lord Upjohn thought such a principle to be obsolescent, given that people can now call the fire brigade.[67]

In *Carter v Thomas*,[68] a fire brigade, provided by an urban authority, was extinguishing a fire. A member of a volunteer fire brigade arrived, and when refused entry to the premises, forced an entrance. This amounted to assault, his good intention notwithstanding. The court said that statute gave the authority fire brigade control over the premises, such that the volunteer was lawfully excluded. The volunteer could not justify his behaviour. To force an entrance might have been possible, in other circumstances, said the court, if this were necessary to save life, or if there were insufficient force on the premises to extinguish the fire, or if the duty of those present was being neglected so as to endanger life or property.

Some public problems are more appropriately addressed through democratic processes:

In *Monsanto plc v Tilly*,[69] the claimant was licensed to grow genetically modified crops. The defendants pulled up some of the crops in protest. The claimant sought an injunction. The defendants pleaded necessity, but unsuccessfully.

Stuart-Smith LJ said that the danger must be immediate and obvious, and that a reasonable person would conclude that there was no alternative to trespass. In this case, the defendants were acting to draw publicity to their cause. They sought to change government policy, and that, said the judge, should have been by democratic means, or perhaps through judicial review.

Pill LJ said that there was no imminent danger. Mummery LJ said that the defence was available only in cases of emergency, where it was necessary to act in the face of immediate and serious danger to life or property, and the defendant must act reasonably. Trespass will not likely be reasonable or necessary if there exists a public authority one could turn to (in this case, the government department which licensed the crops).

64 (1827) M & M 56, 173 ER 1079.

65 *Maleverer v Spinke* (1538) Dyer 35b, 73 ER 79; *Mouse's Case* (1609) 12 Co Rep 63, 77 ER 1341; *The Case of the King's Prerogative in Saltpetre* (1606) 12 Co Rep 12, 77 ER 1294.

66 [1965] AC 75, 164.

67 That position was endorsed by Stuart-Smith LJ in *Monsanto v Tilly* [1999] All ER (D) 1321.

68 [1893] 1 QB 673.

69 [1999] All ER (D) 1321.

Mummery LJ also said that the plea was not justiciable in these circumstances, because the issues strayed beyond the constitutional function and indeed structural competence of the court to decide. The potential risks and rewards of genetically modified crops were a matter of state policy and political judgement, which called for wide-ranging inquiry beyond the limited evidence and issues pleaded by adversarial parties in a private dispute.

Similarly, in the New Zealand case of *Attorney-General v Leason*,[70] the defendants entered a government communications facility and deflated a satellite dome cover. They said it was being used to collect information for wars overseas, leading to deaths of civilians. They pleaded necessity, unsuccessfully, because there was no imminent peril, the protest being symbolic. Also, there was no basis for saying that their actions were reasonable, since there was no evidence at all to suggest it achieved their goals. Further, they had other democratic ways of voicing their concerns.

The proper authorities can themselves invoke a defence of necessity:

In *Rigby v Chief Constable of Northamptonshire*,[71] a psychopath had broken into a gun shop. To flush him out, the police fired gas canisters into the shop. This caused a fire and serious damage to the shop, whose owners sued in trespass and negligence. The court said that, while necessity is a defence to trespass, it must not have been brought about by the defendant's negligence. The police were then held liable in negligence for not having sufficient fire-fighting capacity to hand.

But we need to distinguish two matters in *Rigby*. First, the need to flush out the psychopath was not caused by police negligence. So use of the gas canisters in itself was covered by the defence of necessity. Second, the police response to the necessity was not reasonably carried out, because of insufficient fire-fighting equipment. Thus the police were held liable for the *extra* damage which could have been avoided by having sufficient equipment to hand. This was not a case of prior fault, but a case of responding unreasonably to necessity.

In another New Zealand case, *Dehn v Attorney-General*,[72] the police forced an entry into a house, contrary to the wishes of those living there, after receiving a phone call that suggested that an elderly inhabitant might have suffered serious harm. The judge said that a person may enter the land of another if he has a good faith and reasonable belief that it is necessary to preserve life, or to prevent serious harm, or to render assistance to someone who has suffered serious harm. Cases involving apprehended danger to property, said the judge, may require stricter criteria. The method of entry and conduct must be reasonable and proportionate to the apprehended danger and urgency of the situation.[73]

70 [2013] NZCA 509.

71 [1985] 1 WLR 1242.

72 [1988] 2 NZLR 564, appealed on a different point [1989] 1 NZLR 320.

73 In *Shattock v Devlin* [1990] 2 NZLR 88 it was said that any common law right of the police to enter another's land had been superseded by statute. This was doubted in *Edwards v Police* [1994] 2 NZLR 164. The approach in *Dehn* was confirmed in *R v Fraser* [2005] 2 NZLR 109.

Similarly, in the American case of *The People v Roberts*,[74] the court held that it was sufficient for the police to force an entrance if they had a reasonable belief that someone inside was in need of assistance.

In all these cases, the defendant was acting on the property, not the person, of the victim.

But in *Austin v Commissioner of Police for the Metropolis*,[75] the police, expecting a breach of the peace to follow from a rally, rounded up protesters in the street, holding them there for many hours. Included in that number were people who posed no risk. This was held lawful.

The case has attracted criticism.[76] Nevertheless, it is sometimes given as another example of a defence of necessity. But it is not an example of necessity as a defence in its own right. Rather, the case concerned how the police might discharge their duty to prevent a breach of the peace. If a breach of the peace was reasonably thought imminent, and all possible prior preparations had been taken, and there was a reasonable belief that no other means were available, then the rights of innocent third parties caught up in the event could be curtailed, if reasonably necessary and proportionate. In short, necessity was an ingredient in how the police used their breach of the peace powers, and not a separate defence, as indeed the court made explicit.[77]

American law on public necessity is broadly in keeping with the cases mentioned above, so we can consider it here too.

By § 196 of the *Restatement (Second) of Torts*, a defendant is privileged to enter land, if it is necessary, or if the defendant reasonably believes it is necessary, to avert an imminent public disaster. (Section 262 similarly applies to use of chattels.)

Comment (b) states again that the defendant may use reasonable force against the person if it appears reasonably necessary to accomplish the purpose for which the privilege is given. Comment (e) says that the defendant must use reasonable care, otherwise he is liable for harm done (under § 214). And if public authorities have taken control of the situation, it would ordinarily be unreasonable for the defendant to exercise the privilege on his own initiative.

The defendant incurs no liability for any harm done. What about the municipality for whose benefit he acts?

In *Jarvis v Pinckney*,[78] a ship and her cargo were burned to stop the spread of cholera. Although this was necessary to save life, still the cargo owners were entitled to compensation. 'There is no principle more deeply founded in policy and justice, than that where the public service requires . . . the destruction of

74 (1956) 47 Cal 2d 374.

75 [2007] EWCA Civ 989, on appeal on a different point at [2009] UKHL 5.

76 Feldman, 'Containment, Deprivation of Liberty and Breach of the Peace' [2009] Cambridge LJ 243; Mead, 'Of Kettles, Cordons and Crowd Control' [2009] EHRLR 376.

77 [2007] EWCA Civ 989, [49]. See too the Australian case of *New South Wales v McMaster* (2016) 328 ALR 309, where necessity was discussed, but which was clearly a case of self-defence.

78 (1836) 3 Hill (SC) 123.

private property, compensation should be made to the owner, unless he is in default.' The same sentiment can be found in *Bishop & Parsons v The Mayor and City Council of Macon.*[79] Except, the court said, no compensation is payable if the owner's property would have been lost anyway to the public disaster (for example, consumed in a spreading fire).

But cases like *McDonald v City of Red Wing* state that a municipality cannot be held responsible except by statute.[80] In *Seavey v Preble*,[81] no action lay by the owner of a building against a city physician for advising, to prevent the spread of disease, the destruction of wallpaper in rooms where smallpox patients had been treated. Similarly, in *The State v Mayor and Aldermen of Knoxville*,[82] the public authority was not liable in nuisance for burning clothing and bedding contaminated with infectious disease.

Similar is the more recent Canadian case of *Lapierre v Attorney-General.*[83] There the claimant was vaccinated against measles as part of a government programme, and through statistical bad luck contracted viral encephalitis. She argued that since she incurred a cost (her illness), for the benefit of the community (through a socially desirable vaccination programme), the community should provide compensation. The court, dismissing the claim, thought this notion an 'excellent thing' but without any basis in Quebec law.

Hence comments (h) and (g) to § 196, which say that, while the municipality which benefits from the averted disaster ought morally to compensate for any harm done, usually they are protected by rules as to governmental immunity. If compensation is payable, it says, that is usually under statute.

Summary

There must be a serious danger to another's person or to the public generally. The English and Commonwealth cases mention that danger to property might suffice, but the successful cases concerned only danger to the person. The defence does not cover political protests.

Must there be an actual danger? That would be consistent with private necessity. But in *Dehn* it was explicitly accepted that a reasonable belief would suffice, at least when it involves danger to another person. The facts of *Dehn* show that that is indeed appropriate. It finds further support in the *Restatement.* This extra degree of latitude seems warranted when the defendant is acting reasonably and from the praiseworthy motive of saving others (rather than just themselves).

The defendant must respond to the danger reasonably. So for example, there must be no lawful alternatives, and no one else to hand better placed to

79 (1849) 7 Ga 200.
80 (1868) 13 Minn 38.
81 (1874) 64 Me 120.
82 (1883) 80 Tenn 146.
83 [1985] 1 SCR 241 (Quebec).

act (like a rescue service). The response must be likely to address the danger. Seemingly it does not matter that, after the event, the defendant's response was shown not to be needed after all. The defendant must also act with reasonable care, and proportionately in light of the danger and urgency. Probably the defence is precluded if the danger was caused by the defendant's own negligence (though presumably they would still have an incentive to abate a worse catastrophe).

Seemingly, public necessity is a complete defence, at least if done by a private individual.[84] 'The public champion is in no position to distribute the cost among the public benefitted if he were made to pay.'[85] Perhaps, at most, following the case of *Saltpetre*, if the defendant brings something onto another's land, they must remove it again afterwards. Then again, there is no suggestion that firemen must afterwards drain any water.

There is a tidy logic that, if action is carried out for the public benefit, then the public ought to pay, or at least their municipal council.[86] After all, such a public authority is well placed to recoup the cost, for example through taxes. But, Crown prerogative aside, there is no support for that in the law. It would need to be brought about by legislation. Even in American law, public necessity is a complete defence.

4.4 The rationale for tortious necessity

Why should necessity be a tortious defence at all? There has been little attention to that question. One approach is to say that tort law should follow criminal law.[87] However, we might say that criminal and tortious liability are different levels:

84 Bohlen, 'Incomplete Privilege to Inflict Intentional Invasions of Interests of Property and Personality' (1926) 39 Harv LR 307, 318; Keeton, 'Conditional Fault in the Law of Torts' (1959) 72 Harvard LR 401, 430; Cohan, 'Private and Public Necessity and the Violation of Property Rights' (2007) 83 N Dakota LR 651.

85 Sappideen and Vines (eds), *Fleming's The Law of Torts*, 10th edn (Pyrmont NSW: Thomson Reuters, 2011) 108–109.

86 Hall and Wigmore, 'Compensation for Property Destroyed to Stop the Spread of Conflagration' (1907) 1 Illinois LR 501, 515.

87 Virgo, 'Justifying Necessity as a Defence in Tort Law', in Dyson et al. (eds), *Defences in Tort Law* (Oxford: Hart, 2015). Virgo says that necessity in crime is a justification, which thus makes necessitous conduct lawful. But, as we shall see, I reject as unhelpful theories of justification and excuse in criminal law, at least when it comes to duress and necessity. Bohlen also says such theories should have no place in tort law: 'Incomplete Privilege to Inflict Intentional Invasions of Interests of Property and Personality' (1926) 39 Harv LR 307, 308. But there is a broader academic appetite for comparing or aligning crime and tort: Virgo, 'We Do This in the Criminal Law and That in the Law of Tort: A New Fusion Debate' in Pitel et al. (eds), *Tort Law: Challenging Orthodoxy* (Oxford: Hart, 2013); Klar, 'The Defence of Private Necessity in Canadian Tort Law' (2005) 5(2) Issues in Legal Scholarship 16; Smith, J C, 'Civil Law Concepts in the Criminal Law' (1972) 31 Cambridge LJ 197, 197; Dyson (ed), *Unravelling Tort and Crime* (Cambridge: Cambridge University Press, 2014); Dyson (ed), *Comparing Tort and Crime* (Cambridge: Cambridge University Press, 2015); Goudkamp, *Tort Law Defences* (Oxford: Hart, 2013) 26–27.

crime is the higher level of liability, tort the lower. It would be contradictory, then, if behaviour were sufficiently trivial to avoid tort liability and yet sufficiently serious to attract criminal liability. But it does not also work the other way: behaviour might fall below the threshold for criminal liability, and yet still be above the threshold for tort liability. Just because there is a criminal defence, it need not follow that there should also be a tortious defence.

Klar says that, were we to deny a defence of necessity, that would be consistent with the lack in tort law of any duty to rescue.[88] If, he says, a person must use their resources to rescue another in need, or another in need can rescue themselves from someone else's resources, that should be a policy decision, taken democratically, and promulgated through legislation. But, in response, a defence of necessity certainly does exist already, as the case law shows, so we must find a theoretical justification for it.

We might simply accept that we have a moral duty of compassion, and reflect that in a legal duty. Not a full legal duty of compassion, whatever that might mean, nor even a duty to rescue, but at least the more minimal duty to allow another, when death or serious injury is at risk, to use our property. And there should be little controversy about the worthiness of compassion, since it is extolled in most of the world's great religions and philosophies.

Nevertheless, there are more technical approaches we might adopt.

A first approach is grounded in property theory:

What entitles a person to exclude others from a piece of property? A familiar notion is that of 'first come, first served'. But why should that entitle the first person to exclude others for all time? Why does it not reveal instead that the first person has already used up their turn, and now it is for someone else to use? In short, it seems morally arbitrary to give property rights to someone simply because they were there first. Or because they arrived most recently. Or because they were stronger.[89]

Locke says that, in order to justify us taking property from its state of nature and turning it into private property from which we can exclude others, we must leave enough and as good for others.[90] That proposition seems intuitively attractive. As Cohen says, resistance to appropriation is likely to focus on its impact on others, rather than, say, the method of appropriation. If its impact on others is at worst harmless, then it will be difficult to criticise the appropriation.[91] Yet even Locke bolstered it, such that those in necessity have a 'right' in charity to relief from another's plenty.[92]

88 Klar, 'The Defence of Private Necessity in Canadian Tort Law' (2005) 5(2) Issues in Legal Scholarship.

89 A property owner can use force to exclude others, but cannot use force to become a property owner in the first place. Otherwise, our legal system, rightly, proscribes violence.

90 Locke, *Two Treatises of Government*, Laslett (ed) (Cambridge: Cambridge University Press, 1988) II:27.

91 Cohen, *Self-ownership, Freedom, and Equality* (Cambridge: Cambridge University Press, 1995) 75.

92 Locke, *Two Treatises of Government*, Laslett (ed) (Cambridge: Cambridge University Press, 1988) I:42. As to which, see also: Cohen, *Self-ownership, Freedom, and Equality* (Cambridge: Cambridge University Press, 1995) 190; Tierney, *The Idea of Natural Rights* (Grand Rapids, MI: William B Eerdmans Publishing Co, 1997) 70–76.

Nozick, in developing Locke, in effect says that 'enough and as good' is not a one-time question at the moment of appropriation, but continues to apply even as circumstances change. He gives the following example: if all wells in the desert were fairly appropriated, but then all the others dry up, our ownership of the remaining well now runs afoul of the Lockean proviso.[93] It is not, he says, that our property rights in the well are overridden, but that 'considerations internal to the theory of property itself' now govern use of the property.

In short, we might say that any justification for the privatisation of property from its natural state is only defensible if there is an exception such that others in necessity can still use the property. Indeed, the need for a justifying necessity proviso can be found, not just in Locke and Nozick, but also in Aquinas,[94] and in Grotius according to Klimchuck,[95] and in the Late Scholastics (such as de Soto, de Molina and Lessius) according to Gordley.[96]

In other words, my necessity does not override your property rights. Rather, necessity is the exception to your property rights, and that exception is the reason you can have property rights at all. Within that exception, I am free to act.

Alternatively, we might adopt the short and tidy logic of Brudner.[97] He says that the basis of private rights is moral personality, i.e. our capacity for purposiveness. Property helps us achieve our purposes. Thus property rights are derivative of personal rights, and so must yield to them when in conflict. This is perhaps consistent with Devlin J's intuitive remark in *Esso v Southport* that the safety of human lives belongs to a different scale of values from the safety of property.

All of this suggests that necessity is an absolute defence, with no duty to pay compensation. (Or more accurately, it suggests that no tort has been committed in the first place.) But it is primarily concerned with saving life by using another's property. What about saving life by using another's person?

The authors of *Fleming* consider that it might be possible to inflict personal injury on a victim, if slight, in order to avoid very serious harm to the defendant.[98] Bohlen suggests that a defendant might act upon another's person, to save himself or his property, but seemingly only where the harm to that other person is at most trivial. And because it is not possible accurately to weigh one bodily harm against another – especially, we might add, in an emergency – he says that the victim should not lose his right to resist.[99]

93 Nozick, *Anarchy, State, and Utopia* (New York: Basic Books, 1974) 180–181.

94 Aquinas, *Summa Theologica*, Part II-II, Q66, A7.

95 Klimchuck, 'Property and Necessity', in Penner and Smith (eds), *Philosophical Foundations of Property Law* (Oxford: Oxford University Press, 2013).

96 Gordley, 'Damages Under the Necessity Doctrine' (2005) 5(2) Issues in Legal Scholarship 16–19.

97 Brudner, 'A Theory of Necessity' (1987) 7 OJLS 338, 362.

98 Sappideen and Vines (eds), *Fleming's The Law of Torts*, 10th edn (Pyrmont NSW: Thomson Reuters, 2011) 110.

99 Bohlen, 'Incomplete Privilege to Inflict Intentional Invasions of Interests of Property and Personality' (1926) 39 Harv LR 307, 319–324.

However, acting upon another person to preserve ourselves would mean, in Kantian terms, using another as a means, as a tool, for self-protection, like a life-raft. It would fail to respect them as a person. And this too rebounds on us: we would also be letting ourselves down, since our inability to appreciate the qualities in other people which make them worthy of respect indicates a failure properly to acknowledge and act upon those qualities in ourselves.[100] This would seem an absolute prohibition against using other people to attain our own safety. Indeed, it is notable that none of the law considered in this chapter seeks to legitimise such conduct. (Further, the prohibition against using other people solely as a means is the same reason we identified for grounding the doctrine of unconscionable bargain in contract law.)

Finally, what about saving property by using another's property? Weinrib argues as follows.[101] He says that Kantian right regards an owner's use of property as the realisation of his free and purposive agency. But to use property, one must first preserve it. So an owner has two rights, to use his property, and, logically prior to that, to preserve it. To comply with the Kantian formula of universal law, these same rights must be conceded to others. Thus, he says, the right to preserve property trumps the right to exclusive use.

We might make two points.

First, the argument does not do the work Weinrib claims. The formula of universal law might well mean that everyone should have the same rights, and that those rights include the rights to preserve and use property. But it does not follow that, in exercising my right to preserve my property, I can use your property. Yes, we could have a universal law in such terms. But equally we could have a universal law which says the opposite, as Kant himself admits.[102] Though preservation is logically prior to use, that works only when we are talking about the self-same property. It is not logically prior that I must preserve my property before you can use yours.

Second, as Weinrib would explain it, still it fails to provide a solution when one property can only be preserved, not by using another property, but only by damaging or destroying it, at which point that property's own need to be preserved is engaged – and we end in stalemate.

An alternative, utilitarian, position, implicit perhaps in the requirement that a defendant act proportionately, is that it is better for society to end up with a net preservation of property.[103] This might be said to justify saving more valuable

100 For a fuller discussion of Kant, see Chapter 1.

101 Weinrib, *The Idea of Private Law* (Oxford: Oxford University Press, 2012) 200.

102 Though for prudential reasons Kant suggests that we might help others because in turn we might need help ourselves: Gregor (trans and ed), *Immanuel Kant: Groundwork of the Metaphysics of Morals* (Cambridge: Cambridge University Press, 1997) 33 [4:423]. See further: Herman, 'Mutual Aid and Respect for Persons', in Guyer (ed), *Kant's Groundwork of the Metaphysics of Morals: Critical Essays* (Lanham, MD: Rowman & Littlefield, 1998) 133; Tamblyn, 'The Duty to Help the World's Poor' (2012) 23 King's Law Journal 312, 315–319.

103 Cohan, 'Private and Public Necessity and the Violation of Property Rights' (2007) 83 N Dakota LR 651, 655.

property at the expense of less valuable property. Although, as Christie says, how do we compare a Van Gogh painting against a family heirloom?[104] At any rate, I fail to see why moral superiority is conferred simply by a higher price tag. Life is beyond measure and should be saved. But not all property need be saved. Life in danger creates a necessity to act. But property in danger need not. Surely, at best, only danger to *necessary* property creates an imperative to act. A defence or privilege of necessity should not be about rich owners preserving their luxuries at another's expense.

The most necessary property is that on which life depends. Examples might include a life support system in use at a hospital, or perhaps the hospital itself when treating patients, or an ambulance responding to an emergency, or a submerged submarine with people inside, or an airborne plane with passengers. Also, other property, if not preserved, might endanger life, like a power station, or a nuclear warhead. All of which simply returns us to the proposition that in necessity we can act upon another's property in order to preserve life, when life is threatened either directly with bodily harm, or indirectly through risk to those objects upon which life depends.

Yet some cases do recognise an entitlement to protect property at the expense of other property, like *Romney Marsh* and *Cope v Sharpe* (although in the latter case the damage was nominal). But other cases express disquiet, like *Esso v Southport* and *Latta v New Orleans.* And in American law, following *Vincent*, compensation does have to be paid for the other property damaged.

So let us return, as an example, to *Ploof v Putnam*, and the idea that a necessitous user cannot be ejected. We can now see that the facts of that case can be addressed in two ways.

First, that case is better understood not as denying a right to eject, but in requiring the ejector to act with reasonable care. If, in *Ploof v Putnam*, the family were taken ashore, could the dock owner have unmoored the ship after all, to protect his dock?

Second, if one person's property is threatened with damage, to avoid which they damage another's property, is that other property not now threatened with damage also, to avoid which its owner can act, in necessity, even on the first property, perhaps by ejecting it?

This is the stalemate we identified in Weinrib's argument. It is notable that no case has had to square up to it. In *Ploof v Putnam* there was life at risk. In *Vincent*, seemingly, there was no objection at the time from the dock. In *Cope v Sharpe* the

104 Christie, 'The Defense of Necessity Considered from the Legal and Moral Points of View' (1999) 48 Duke LJ 975, 1000. But sentimental value has its own problems: individual defendants could then rely upon their personal preferences to increase subjectively the value of their property and thereby legitimise a greater range of interference with other people's property. Thus a philatelist might claim that, because they value their stamp collection for sentimental reasons above its market price or social significance, this therefore entitles them to cause yet more damage in necessity to others' property. An individual should not be able to set for themselves the limits of their own legal duty not to interfere with other people's property.

land owner was fighting fire elsewhere. In *Romney Marsh*, the owners of the sea wall sued after the event, and recovered.

In summary, the only convincing theoretical justification(s) support a defence of necessity, when seeking to preserve life, by acting upon another's property. In those circumstances, it is a complete defence or privilege, and there is no compensation payable.[105] Also, the property owner cannot resist.

In all other circumstances, there is no convincing reason why tortious necessity should be a defence. In this case, rights should be upheld, compensation paid, and defence of self or property permitted. It should not be possible to act upon another's person. It should not be possible to preserve one's own property at another's expense. All of which is substantially consistent with the outcomes of the case law. And though an incomplete privilege might be technically explicable, as discussed above, there seems no successful argument in principle for its half-way house position.

4.5 Best interests intervention in crime and tort

Best interests intervention is where the defendant acts upon the victim's person or property for the benefit of the victim.

In most cases of best interests intervention, the courts have had to consider the defendant's liability in both crime and tort. This has produced a unified approach to the topic. Many of the cases which discuss best interests intervention concern medical treatment. There are also some cases which arise from different circumstances. We consider them all in this section, starting with the medical cases.

As regards the medical cases, it is not my purpose here to be side-tracked into specialist questions of medical ethics, and topics such as euthanasia,[106] though we must inevitably touch upon them. Rather, the purpose is to identify the structuring principles of best interests intervention, and thus know the remit of that doctrine, in comparison to a general defence of necessity.

There was some earlier case law which can be taken as support for the notion of best interests intervention. Thus a doctor was not behaving 'unlawfully' when carrying out an abortion if done in good faith for the purpose of preserving the

105 One exception might be where the property belongs to a 'professional rescuer' like a pharmacist. Sugarman says that they should get paid when their property is used by defendants in necessity. Otherwise, if every time a pharmacist's wares saved a life, and it had to be free, they would never get paid. We need professional rescuers, and they must earn a living: Sugarman, 'The Necessity Defence and the Failure of Tort Theory' (2005) 5(2) Issues in Legal Scholarship 63–64.

106 Euthanasia is now, beyond doubt, a matter for legislative deliberation rather than judicial development of the defence of best interests necessity. See further the debate in: Stark, 'Necessity and *Nicklinson*' [2013] Crim LR 949; Lewis, 'The Failure of the Defence of Necessity as a Mechanism of Legal Change on Assisted Dying in the Common Law World', in Baker and Horder (eds), *The Sanctity of Life and the Criminal Law* (Cambridge: Cambridge University Press, 2013); Dennis, 'On Necessity as a Defence to Crime' (2009) 2 Crim Law & Phil 29; Ost, 'Euthanasia and the Defence of Necessity: Advocating a More Appropriate Legal Response' [2005] Crim LR 355; Herring, 'Escaping the Shackles at the End of Life' (2013) 21 Medical LR 487.

physical or mental life of the mother.[107] So too a doctor would not be aiding and abetting underage sex by prescribing contraceptives to a child if, in the exercise of their clinical judgement, they honestly believed it to be necessary in the best interests, physical, mental and emotional, of the patient.[108]

In *Re F (Mental patient: sterilisation)*,[109] a mentally handicapped woman who resided as a voluntary patient at a mental hospital had formed a sexual relationship with another patient. The staff considered that she would be unable to cope with the effects of pregnancy and giving birth. Contraception was thought unsuitable, so too restricting her freedom of movement and association. They sought a declaration that it would be lawful to perform an operation to sterilise her. Her mother supported this. She herself lacked capacity to consent. The declaration was given.

Lord Bridge said that doctors should not be put in the dilemma that, if they administer treatment in the best interests of their incompetent patients, they run the risk of trespass, but if they withhold treatment, they may be in breach of their duty of care. In effect, we might note, once the treatment was declared to be no trespass, the dilemma never arose.

Lord Goff formulated the following test: there must be a necessity to act when not practicable to communicate with the assisted person; and the action must be what the reasonable person would take, acting in the best interests of the assisted person.

In determining what is in the best interests of the assisted person, the courts now approach that question from the viewpoint of the patient themselves.[110]

This test, said Lord Goff, was apt to cover such situations as dragging a person from the path of an oncoming vehicle, or dressing and feeding mentally disordered patients. No doubt, we might add, it would also extend to the unconscious victim of a car crash admitted to hospital. But, said Lord Goff, though an emergency might explain why it is not possible to communicate with the person assisted, nevertheless an emergency was not a prerequisite. Rather, the defence can also apply to those incapable of communication permanently or for a prolonged period.

Further, Lord Goff said that this defence did not justify officious intervention, when another, more appropriate person, is willing and able to act.

However, it might be fairer to the well-meaning intervener to preclude the defence only where they knew, or perhaps ought reasonably to have known, that there was another person more suited to intervene. To hold them strictly

107 *Bourne* [1939] 1 KB 687; *Davidson* [1969] VR 667.

108 *Gillick v West Norfolk and Wisbech Area Health Authority* [1986] AC 112. See now: Sexual Offences Act 2003, s 73.

109 [1990] 2 AC 1. And see too the American *Restatement (Second) of Torts*, § 892D 'Emergency Action Without Consent'.

110 *Re J (A Minor) (Wardship: Medical Treatment)* [1991] Fam 33; *Portsmouth Hospitals NHS Trust v Wyatt* [2005] EWCA Civ 1181; *Aintree University Hospitals NHS Foundation Trust v James* [2013] UKSC 67.

liable despite the limits of their reasonable knowledge might discourage necessary intervention, like first aid at an accident. The person assisted remains well protected, because the defence still otherwise requires that the intervention be in their best interests.

Further, we should say, that there is no one else *to hand* better placed to act. A doctor about to carry out a necessary operation need not ensure that they are, in comparison to all other doctors, the best at this operation. It suffices that they are able to act with reasonable care and advance the patient's best interests. Perhaps a more felicitous expression of this principle is as follows: it must reasonably appear to the defendant that they are a suitable person to intervene in the circumstances.

Finally, Lord Goff said that the defence cannot be invoked against the known wishes of the assisted person.

In this regard, other case law has been explicit in upholding a patient's right to refuse medical treatment, even if the reasons for refusal are irrational, indeed even in the absence of any reasons, as long as the patient has sufficient mental capacity.[111] So strong is this right, it applies even where the patient's refusal puts at risk not only her life, but also the life of her unborn child.[112] Similarly, a prisoner can go on hunger strike without any duty on the prison to provide nutrition or hydration.[113]

A competent patient can refuse treatment, or insist upon its withdrawal, even if it means her death.[114] In complying with the patient's wishes, the doctor does not thereby assist suicide,[115] because to act upon the patient contrary to their wishes would itself be unlawful. But the law has drawn a distinction between, on the one hand, refraining from or withdrawing treatment, such that death results, and administering death on purpose, even with the consent of the patient. The latter remains a crime, even where the victim, suffering irreversible physical difficulties, has for that reason a settled and considered wish to die.[116] Nevertheless, a doctor who administers drugs for palliative care, with the consequence that life is also thereby shortened, is not necessarily taken to intend death.[117]

In *Airedale NHS Trust v Bland*,[118] the patient had been in a persistent vegetative state for a number of years without any chance of improvement. The hospital and parents sought a declaration that it would be lawful to discontinue all medical treatment except that necessary to enable the patient to die peacefully.

The declaration was granted. The argument ran as follows: discontinuance was an omission;[119] an omission is not unlawful unless in breach of duty; one may act

111 *Re C (Adult: refusal of medical treatment)* [1994] 1 All ER 819.
112 *St George's Healthcare NHS Trust v S* [1999] Fam 26.
113 *Secretary of State for the Home Department v Robb* [1995] Fam 127.
114 *Re B (Adult: Refusal of Treatment)* [2002] EWHC 429 (Fam).
115 *Airedale NHS Trust v Bland* [1993] AC 789, 864 (Lord Goff).
116 *Nicklinson* [2014] UKSC 38, [130].
117 *Adams* [1957] Crim LR 365.
118 [1993] AC 789.
119 Nor did it amount to 'deprivation of life' for the purposes of Art 2 ECHR: *NHS Trust v A* [2001] 1 All ER 801.

upon a patient unable to consent only if acting was in that patient's best interests; since any further treatment was not in this patient's best interests, further treatment was not lawful; thus it must be discontinued, entailing no breach of duty.[120]

Drawing a distinction between act and omission has been criticised.[121] And the fine line between letting die and euthanasia has also attracted academic attention.[122] But my purpose here is to investigate more closely the concept of best interests.

In *Bland*, Lord Keith said that being in a persistent vegetative state was not a benefit to the patient. Similar sentiments appear in the judgments of Lord Lowry and Lord Browne-Wilkinson. Lord Keith further said that it must be a matter of complete indifference to someone with no cognitive capacity whether he lives or dies.

We need to be careful with our approach here. 'Best interests' suggests that a person's interests are best served when adopting this rather than that course of action. But, as Epicurus points out,[123] upon death, there is no person at all, to have any interests, best or otherwise. Only a living person has interests. Death is in no one's best interests, because death precludes there being anyone to have interests.

Now it may be that a course of action makes it worse for a living person, in which case we might refrain. If the consequence is death, we are still not saying that death is better for them than being alive. This is because upon death there is no 'them' to appreciate being better off. They will be too dead to notice. What we are saying is that any action might, for example, lead to a situation of intolerable or unbearable pain, literally, and so for that reason we refrain, and the natural consequences follow.[124]

Alternatively, a course of action may be pointless, so that we refrain for that reason. There is no value in giving a pill which has no effect. In *Bland*, Lord Goff said that the life-prolonging treatment was medically useless, because the patient was totally unconscious without prospect of improvement. But the care

120 This reasoning was also adopted in *Aintree University Hospitals NHS Foundation Trust v James* [2013] UKSC 67.

121 Wilson, *Criminal Law*, 5th edn (Harlow: Pearson, 2014) 85; Keown, 'Restoring Moral and Intellectual Shape to the Law after Bland' (1997) 113 LQR 482, 485. But McGee says that there is a sound difference between a positive act of euthanasia, which is a death earlier than would otherwise naturally occur, and withdrawing treatment which was unnaturally prolonging life: 'Finding a Way Through the Ethical and Legal Maze: Withdrawal of Medical Treatment and Euthanasia' (2005) 13 Med LR 357, 383.

122 Wilson, 'Is Life Sacred?' (1995) 17 J Social Welfare and Family Law 131; Finnis, '*Bland*: Crossing the Rubicon?' (1993) 109 LQR 329.

123 Epicurus, Letter to Menoeceus.

124 Which was precisely the reasoning in the case of *Re J (A Minor) (Wardship: Medical Treatment)* [1991] Fam 33. But while the question of intolerable pain is obviously relevant, 'best interests' is a broader concept, encompassing medical, emotional and other welfare issues: *Portsmouth Hospitals NHS Trust v Wyatt* [2005] EWCA Civ 1181. We might put it this way: pain need not render a patient's life meaningless.

was having an effect: it was keeping him alive. And for the patient in *Bland*, the situation was not intolerable, because he was suffering no pain.

Keown says that we must draw a distinction between whether the treatment is worthwhile, a legitimate question, and whether the patient's life is worthwhile, which is illegitimate.[125] But this does not work. As McGee says, kidney dialysis might be futile in terms of failing to cure the underlying condition, but it is worthwhile because it keeps the patient alive.[126] Alternatively, treatment might be effective in keeping the patient alive, but productive of so much pain that life becomes intolerable. The effects of treatment, and its impact on quality of life, are inseparable – because medical treatment takes place upon a human life.

Lord Mustill said that the patient in *Bland* had no best interests of any kind. Finnis rejects this,[127] saying that the patient could not be simply thrown out with the rubbish. Keown adds, colourfully, nor could the patient be used as a sideboard.[128] But why not?[129] The patient would never have known. He would never have been aware of any indignities. Are they even his indignities if he is never conscious? Certainly, treating the patient in those ways would reflect upon us, and to the extent that our actions form our character we would have to wonder whether we would want to be the sort of person who behaves that way.

The unarticulated concern is whether the care was pointless because the patient was devoid of all cognitive capacity. This is not to say that life has no value without consciousness. Trees and plants have value. But this is, in effect, the level at which the patient in *Bland* was living since the accident. 'Persistent *vegetative* state' is accurate: a human living on a lesser cognitive plane of existence (and not necessarily a lesser plane *simpliciter*). Ought this to be prolonged? That is a moral question, and I see no reason why it might not be 'yes' rather than 'no'.

The family in *Bland* felt one way, but no family can insist that one of its adult members should now die. The court pointed out that it too had no inherent jurisdiction to make decisions on behalf of any adult patient. And let us be clear, this is not a question of resources.[130] Yes, the NHS might not have deep pockets – but it could do. This is one of the richest nations in the history of humanity. We could spend more on the NHS, and we could raise taxes. So ultimately this is a political question, of how we should treat people in persistent vegetative states. The court in *Bland* called upon the legislator. Now we have the Mental Capacity Act 2005.

125 Keown, 'Restoring Moral and Intellectual Shape to the Law after *Bland*' (1997) 113 LQR 482. For a rebuttal, see: Price, 'Fairly *Bland*: An Alternative View of a Supposed New "Death Ethic" and the BMA Guidelines' (2001) 21 LS 618.

126 McGee 'Finding a Way Through the Ethical and Legal Maze: Withdrawal of Medical Treatment and Euthanasia' (2005) 13 Med LR 357, 379.

127 Finnis, '*Bland*: Crossing the Rubicon?' (1993) 109 LQR 329.

128 Keown, 'Restoring Moral and Intellectual Shape to the Law after *Bland*' (1997) 113 LQR 482.

129 Could we have stuffed him and mounted him in a glass cabinet as a curiosity, like the body of Jeremy Bentham?

130 On how tight budgets risk distorting the principle of the sanctity of life, see: Wilson, 'Is Life Sacred?' (1995) 17 J Social Welfare and Family Law 131.

But s 5, which covers acts in connection with care or treatment, is still couched in terms of the patient's best interests, which takes us no further forward.

Another decision, questionable for its treatment of the concept of best interests, is *Re Y (Mental Incapacity: Bone Marrow Transplant)*.[131] There it was held lawful to make the defendant, a mentally incompetent adult, a bone marrow donor for her sister. The donation was said to be in the defendant's best interests, because it may save the life of the sister, who would thereby be 'eternally grateful', and preserve the frail health of the mother, who 'clearly wishes it to take place'. This in turn, so it was said, would lead to better relations between the parties, to the defendant's benefit. But would the relationships have soured, if the defendant's autonomy had been upheld, because the mother and sister did not get their own way? What is objectionable here is the implicit notion that the defendant's best interests depended upon pleasing other people by doing their bidding.[132]

Necessity can provide for ongoing intervention, as long as the necessity is also ongoing:

In *Bournewood*,[133] it was held that a defence of necessity would permit an agitated autistic person to be detained in hospital for psychiatric treatment in his best interests. But that was later held to be a deprivation of his human right to liberty, unlawfully so, given the total absence of any fixed procedural rules for his admission, detention, review or treatment.[134] In similar vein, in the Hong Kong case of *Attorney-General v Chan Yuen Lung*,[135] the 'inmate' of an old people's home was manacled to the bed. The court said that necessity might have been an available defence, if the victim were violent and not amenable to reasonable restraint, but only pending the arrival of police, and not as a long-term option. And in the Australian case of *New South Wales v Riley*,[136] while the initial detention of a man discharging a firearm might have been justified by necessity, there was no warrant for binding him too tightly, or for failing to explain the situation to him once he was suitably restrained.

The cases so far involve acting upon the assisted person themselves. What about acting upon their property?

131 [1997] Fam 110.

132 The judge stressed the close-knit nature of the family. But the sister visited only 'occasionally', and their relationship was admittedly not particularly strong, while the mother visited 'almost' once a week, and even then, the defendant 'does not appreciate that this lady is in fact her mother'. If a bone marrow donation was acceptable in *Re Y*, why not mine patients like *Bland* for their healthy organs?

133 *R v Bournewood Community and Mental Health NHS Trust, ex p L* [1998] 3 All ER 289.

134 *HL v UK* (2004) 40 EHRR 761. The government's response was the Mental Capacity Act 2005. In *H v Commissioner of Police for the Metropolis* [2013] EWCA Civ 69, applying the Mental Capacity Act 2005, it was held not to be in the best interests of an autistic boy who was visiting a swimming pool to be detained by police.

135 [1989] 1 HKC 470.

136 [2003] NSWCA 208.

In *Kirk v Gregory*,[137] the relative of a deceased person, being in the house at the death, removed some jewellery from one room to another, in good faith for its preservation. The executor sued in trespass. The relative had no defence: it had to be shown that the interference was required or necessary, and that it was reasonably carried out.

In contrast, there was a defence in the Australian case of *Proudman v Allen*.[138] The defendant saw a car rolling downhill, about to crash into another car. To prevent the collision, he opened the door, grabbed the steering wheel, and redirected the car. The collision was avoided, but the car continued into the sea, causing more damage than had the collision occurred. Nevertheless the defendant was exculpated. The court said that the defendant acted reasonably to an urgent necessity of damage to property. He was not to be blamed because, in the excitement of the moment, it might appear in retrospect that he picked the wrong course of action. Further, it did not matter that the defendant was a stranger to the property involved.

In another Australian case, *Beckingham v Port Jackson & Manly Steamship Co*,[139] discussed above, the claimant bought a submarine for public display, and moored it at the defendant's dock. When a storm arose, the defendant, thinking the submarine a danger to the wharf and to itself, towed it into open waters, where it was wrecked. Thus the defendant was acting in defence of his own property, and to preserve the submarine (in its owner's best interests). This was held to be a defence to what would otherwise be trespass, as long as the defendant used reasonable care.

If the property owner objects to his property's preservation, then the default position, once again, is that intervention is not allowed.[140] However, while the medical cases show that a patient's decision to refuse treatment is paramount, in property cases, there is a suggestion that it might just be possible to intervene despite the owner's refusal.

Thus in *Cope v Sharpe (No 2)*, Kennedy J said that in the case of a volunteer it would require very special circumstances to justify a trespass against the will of an owner, even on the ground of reasonable necessity.

So too in the Canadian case of *Sherrin v Haggerty*,[141] the court said that it would take very special circumstances to justify a volunteer, entering on land against the will of the owner, in order to protect the owner's property, when the owner knew of the danger and had elected to do nothing about it. In that case, the defendant moved the claimant's lodge inland, when it was overhanging a crumbling river bank. The claimant had previously refused consent to do this. This was trespass, although since the property was saved, damages were nominal.

137 (1876) 1 Ex D 55.
138 [1954] SASR 336.
139 [1957] SR (NSW) 403.
140 *Maleverer v Spinke* (1538) Dyer 35b, 73 ER 79.
141 [1953] OWN 962 (Ontario).

What are those special circumstances which justify acting against the owner's consent? The courts do not say. An example might be where property, although privately owned, ought to be preserved in the public interest, like an invaluable piece of art, or an important scientific discovery, or evidence of a serious crime. But this is not best interests intervention so much as public necessity – acting in the general public interest to preserve property. So it seems doubtful that intervention could ever be legitimate when done only for the benefit of the property's owner, when the owner themselves objects.

Summary

It must be necessary to act, to preserve or advance the best interests of another, assessed from the viewpoint of that other, when not possible to obtain their consent. The necessity must be real. This might seem a high threshold, but that must surely be appropriate, at least when the defendant acts upon another's person.

It need not be an emergency; this doctrine applies even in prolonged situations. There is no minimum threshold of 'danger'; the doctrine applies to matters of routine care. If the other person refuses consent, their autonomy trumps, and no intervention is permissible, no matter how vital. Any intervention must be carried out with reasonable care. It must reasonably appear to the defendant that they are a suitable person to intervene in the circumstances. This doctrine allows intervention upon another's person or their property.

As for medical treatment, an operation which keeps a patient alive might nevertheless not be in their best interests if it results, for example, in a life of unbearable pain. In this case, the operation cannot be carried out, even if the consequences are death. But death itself is in no one's best interests; death and best interests are conceptually incompatible.

The justification for a doctrine of best interests intervention seems clear: a person should not be denied willing assistance, which is necessary to preserve or advance their best interests, judged from their perspective, just because it is not possible to communicate with them beforehand. Emergency dangers would go un-averted. The needy would be denied care. This is not about overriding their interests, but upholding them, when they themselves are unable to. It is not a duty to rescue. It is merely a pragmatic solution which enables a willing volunteer to assist lawfully when such assistance is necessary.[142]

4.6 Lesser evil necessity in crime and tort

Lesser evil necessity, in general terms, is where the defendant commits a wrong upon the victim's person or property to avoid something even worse.

142 The volunteer need not be amateur or unpaid: a doctor, employed at hospital, thereby assumes a duty to care for those brought through the door, and gets paid for doing so. But an off-duty doctor in the street, no less than any other person, is under no duty to assist the victim of a road accident they happen to pass. But if a willing volunteer does pass by, the doctrine of best interests intervention enables them lawfully to assist.

Its modern origins lie with Stephen. He wrote, in the first edition of his *A Digest of the Criminal Law* in 1877, that an act which would otherwise be a crime may be excused if: it was done only to avoid consequences which could not otherwise be avoided; and which would have inflicted inevitable and irreparable evil,[143] upon the defendant or others whom he was bound to protect; that no more was done than was reasonably necessary for that purpose; and the evil inflicted was not disproportionate to the evil avoided.[144]

And yet, in *A History of the Criminal Law of England*, published in 1883, Stephen declared the law on 'compulsion by necessity' so vague that if cases raising the question should ever occur, judges would be able to lay down any rule which they considered expedient.[145] This he wrote despite himself having set out a test of lesser evil necessity, as we have just seen, in the first edition of the *Digest*. Thus Stephen's own test of necessity in the *Digest* must not be treated as a restatement of the law, but cautiously, as his own personal suggestion of what an expedient test might be. It clearly reflects Stephen's avowed utilitarianism.[146]

In justifying his proposed test in the first edition of the *Digest*, Stephen cited Bacon's *Maxims* for the proposition that, if two drowning men are on a plank large enough to support only one person, it is no crime for one to push the other off. Stephen otherwise cited only two authorities to illustrate his test of necessity, but neither provides direct support for it.

The first authority referred to by Stephen was *R v Stratton*,[147] where the governor of Madras was assaulted while being deposed by his council. In the *Digest*, Stephen made reference to the judgment of Lord Mansfield. That judgment got extended, and glowing, coverage in the *History*. Yet in that part of the judgment so praised by Stephen, Lord Mansfield appeared to deny the possibility of *any* defence of necessity in England (which Lord Mansfield said was without any precedent) because there is always an official authority to which one can turn for assistance (instead of acting in self-help). Lord Mansfield accepted that a defence might exist outside England, for example in India where there is no superior to turn to for help, but still the necessity must be imminent and extreme and the action taken for the benefit of society *as a whole*. Stephen echoed this latter qualification in his *Digest* illustration when he said that the Madras council would have a defence only if it sought to avoid irreparable mischief to *the establishment* at Madras.[148]

The second authority referred to by Stephen was the American case of *Commonwealth v Holmes*.[149] In that case, a lifeboat had too many people on

143 Whatever 'evil' might mean: see Greig, 'Criminal Responsibility and the Concept of Evil' (1996) 3 Psychiatry, Psychology and Law 163.

144 Stephen, *A Digest of the Criminal Law*, 1st edn (London: Macmillan & Co, 1877) 19.

145 Stephen, *A History of the Criminal Law of England*, vol 2 (London: Macmillan & Co, 1883) 108.

146 As to which, see: Stephen, *Liberty, Equality, Fraternity* (London: Smith, Elder & Co, 1873).

147 (1779) 21 St Tr 1045.

148 Might there be a separate, or more generous, defence of criminal necessity for those acting in a public or official capacity? There is nothing in the case law to suggest as much. But see the discussion of public necessity in tort law, above at 4.3.

149 (1841) 26 Fed Cas 360.

board, so the sailors threw some of the passengers overboard. The court held that sailors should have been sacrificed before passengers, but otherwise those on board should have drawn lots. Although Stephen referred to this case, he doubted the decision and the correctness of drawing lots, and expressly following Stephen's lead, so too did the court in *R v Dudley and Stephens*.[150]

In that case, four shipwrecked sailors were cast adrift in a lifeboat without food or water or prospects of a timely rescue. To stay alive, two sailors killed and ate the cabin boy. They survived, were rescued and convicted of murder. The decision is usually taken as denying a defence of necessity to murder.

In the fourth edition of the *Digest*, which was the last edition of his lifetime, Stephen described his own test of necessity as 'not vague enough' to represent fully the vagueness of the law, and added the rider that 'the extent of this principle [of necessity] is unascertained'.[151] Stephen made reference to only one additional case, that being *Dudley and Stephens* itself, and he took issue with the court's reasoning (but not the outcome). But perhaps more important is how the court in *Dudley and Stephens* took issue with Stephen. Although the judgment in *Dudley and Stephens* was largely confined to circumstances where the defendant kills in order to avoid his own death, there is little suggestion that there might be a broader defence of necessity of the type suggested by Stephen for lesser crimes than murder. Rather, the whole tenor of the judgment is against a doctrine of necessity. The court also confined to its particular facts the judgment of Lord Mansfield in *Stratton*, so impressive to Stephen, and dismissed as unsound the proposition of Bacon, otherwise relied upon by Stephen, and expressly said that it was prepared to depart from Stephen's formulation of necessity anyway. (In *R v Howe*,[152] which applied *Dudley and Stephens*, Lord Hailsham also dissented 'profoundly' from Bacon's maxim.)

Thus Stephen's test of necessity was the personal proposal of an avowed utilitarian and not the codification of a law which he himself thought too vague and uncertain. The only supporting precedent limited the defence to political coups abroad necessary to achieve social stability. And the contemporaneous decision of the Divisional Court in *Dudley and Stephens* did not embrace Stephen's approach, but instead rejected the foundations of Stephen's test in Lord Mansfield and Bacon, and rather set itself against a defence of necessity at all.

Nevertheless, a stream of case law continued to address the question of whether necessity might be a defence after all, though not always consistently. A mother might have had a defence to carrying her infected child in the street had it been necessary to get medical attention, but there was no such evidence.[153] A drunken passenger could not take control of a parked car when he awoke to

150 (1884) 14 QBD 273, 285.
151 Stephen, *A Digest of the Criminal Law*, 4th edn (London: Macmillan & Co, 1887) 24.
152 [1987] AC 417, 431.
153 *Vantandillo* (1815) 4 M&S 73, 105 ER 762.

find it rolling downhill.[154] A fire engine responding to an emergency could not jump a red light.[155] But a police officer could direct people to disobey traffic regulations if reasonably necessary to protect life or property.[156] And a police driver might have been entitled to drive on the hard shoulder, had there been sufficient evidence of necessity.[157]

In *R v Pommel*,[158] the defendant was charged with being in unlawful possession of a gun. He claimed that he had taken it from another man to prevent him from shooting a third.[159] The court said that a defence should lie where one person commendably infringes the law in order to prevent the commission of a greater evil.

In *R v Shayler*,[160] a former spy disclosed documents to a newspaper in breach of the Official Secrets Act. The Court of Appeal phrased a defence in terms of acting to prevent a greater evil – although the House of Lords, where no such question of necessity was thought to arise, distanced itself from the Court of Appeal's analysis.[161]

The most explicit modern treatment of a defence of lesser evil necessity is found in *Re A (Children) (Conjoined twins: surgical separation)*.[162] In that case,[163] conjoined twins were taken to hospital. Without surgical separation, both would die. With separation, the weaker twin would certainly die, but the stronger twin would probably live.[164] The hospital sought a declaration that separation would be lawful; it would otherwise be tortious, perhaps murder. The twins were too young to consent. The parents resisted the separation on religious grounds. The declaration was given.

Ward LJ said that the doctors were under a conflict of duties,[165] to operate for the benefit of the stronger twin, and not to operate for the benefit of the weaker twin. The law, he said, must allow an escape through choosing the lesser of the two evils. (Robert Walker LJ also said he would be prepared to extend the defence of necessity in this way.)

154 *R v Kitson* (1955) 39 Cr App R 66.

155 *Buckoke v GLC* [1971] 2 All ER 254, 258. On traffic lights, see now: Traffic Signs and General Directions Regulations 1984 (SI 1984/859), reg 34(1). And on exceeding speed limits, see: Road Traffic Regulations Act 1984, s 87.

156 *Johnson v Phillips* [1975] 3 All ER 682.

157 *Wood v Richards* [1977] RTR 201 (where he was nevertheless given an absolute discharge).

158 [1995] 2 Cr App R 607.

159 In similar vein is the Canadian case of *Kerr* [2004] SCJ No 39, where the defence of necessity was available to a defendant possessing a dangerous weapon. He said that he had armed himself for imminent self-defence.

160 [2001] EWCA Crim 1977.

161 [2002] UKHL 11, [17] (Lord Bingham), [39] (Lord Hope), [117] (Lord Hutton).

162 [2001] Fam 147.

163 For similar cases, see: Huxtable, 'Separation of Conjoined Twins: Where Next for English Law?' [2002] Crim LR 459; *State of Queensland v Alyssa Nolan (an infant)* [2001] QSC 174.

164 She did live: http://www.dailymail.co.uk/news/article-2780371/Separated-twin-living-life-says-judge-ordered-operation-killed-conjoined-sister.html.

165 In the Canadian case of *Perka* [1984] 2 SCR 232, Wilson J, in the minority, wanted to keep open the possibility of a necessity defence when a defendant faced a conflict of legal duties.

Note, however, that this was not a defence of lesser evils *tout court*. In effect, the defence was 'conflict of duties', in which case the defendant was obliged to choose the lesser evil.

That conflict arose only because the patients were conjoined. For example, it may be that patient A needs a heart transplant, and patient B is a refusing but suitable donor. We cannot say that the doctor is under a duty to operate for the benefit of patient A, but under a duty not to operate for the benefit of patient B. This is because there are two separate operations to justify. The operation on patient A is acceptable, if A consents, or the doctors can otherwise invoke the doctrine of best interests intervention. But the operation on patient B cannot be justified in the face of their refusal. Whereas with the conjoined twins, it was the self-same operation to save one which would have killed the other.

How did Ward LJ chose the lesser evil? He said that the weaker twin was 'doomed' or 'designated for death'. This is not accurate. Both twins were designated for an early death by the consequence of being born conjoined. Indeed, the evidence indicated that the stronger twin would die first. Brooke LJ similarly said that the weaker twin was self-designated for death. This is even worse, since it implies a choice on her part which was entirely absent, and, in light of the prohibition against assisted suicide, probably irrelevant. Ward LJ also said that the weaker 'parasitic' twin had little right to be alive because she sucked the lifeblood from her twin. But she was not a parasite, and the stronger twin was not a host. They had been born together in a single whole with shared blood.

Robert Walker LJ relied on the doctrine of double effect. The death of the weaker twin was not the intention or the purpose of the surgery, which was to save the stronger twin. (Nevertheless, we might note, the death of the weaker twin was foreseen as an inevitable consequence. And this would satisfy the test of oblique intention set out in *R v Woollin*,[166] sufficient to support a conviction for murder.) But the doctrine of double effect, he said, would work only if the operation was also in the best interests of the weaker twin. The operation would give the weaker twin bodily integrity, he said, and for that reason was in her best interests. (Brooke LJ made a similar point about the value of bodily integrity.) This latter point does not convince. As Harris says, bodily integrity is about protecting the body against violations, not changing it through surgery.[167] And as Watt says, it represents a new low in how we view disability or difference: killing someone to make them look 'normal'.[168]

Brooke LJ set out the following test of necessity, which, he said, was satisfied in this case (agreeing with the reasons of Ward LJ):[169]

> (i) The act is needed to avoid inevitable and irreparable evil; (ii) no more should be done than is reasonably necessary for the purpose to be achieved; (iii) the evil inflicted must not be disproportionate to the evil avoided.

166 [1999] AC 82.
167 Harris, 'Human Beings, Persons and Conjoined Twins' (2001) 9 Medical LR 221, 227.
168 Watt, 'Conjoined Twins: Separation as Mutilation' (2001) 9 Medical LR 237, 238.
169 [2001] Fam 147, 240.

This, said Brooke LJ, was Stephen's test.[170] However, Brooke LJ did not accurately adopt Stephen's test, but made it worse.

First, in Stephen's test the defendant must act *in order to* avoid greater evil; whereas in Brooke LJ's test, it suffices that greater evil was in fact avoided. This is inconsistent with the principle in *R v Dadson*,[171] and cloaks with legality a defendant who commits a crime for dastardly reasons yet fortuitously produces a good result.

Second, Stephen's test applies only when the defendant themselves, or someone whom they are bound to protect, is threatened with evil, whereas Brooke LJ's test allows anyone to intervene, and thus has no restraint on the officious intermeddler.

Third, Stephen's test requires the defendant to take the least alternative course, whereas in Brooke LJ's test it suffices simply that greater evil was avoided, even if there were better ways of achieving the same result.

Having pointed out these inconsistencies, they could of course be cured. But still, the justification for Brooke LJ's test purports to rest solely on Stephen's authority,[172] yet we saw above just how weak that authority turned out to be. And there are further problems still:

Brooke LJ's test would have permitted the killing in *Dudley and Stephens*, even while the court in *Re A* purported to uphold that decision. I am not averse to a contrary outcome in *Dudley and Stephens*. But the judicial inconsistency, on the one hand purporting to stand by the outcome in *Dudley and Stephens*, and on the other hand, promulgating a test which would have reversed that same decision, should sound alarm bells.

Moreover, the test of lesser evil necessity is avowedly utilitarian. This is not the place for a full rebuttal of that philosophy.[173] But I have always been alarmed by how an innocent third party, unrelated to unfolding events, can be sacrificed for a breezy mathematics. For example, authors have noted how this test of lesser evil necessity would permit an innocent person to be killed so that their organs might be harvested to save the lives of several others.[174] This is morally wrong. At any rate, such a calculus is flatly opposed to individual rights, and such rights are undeniably the fundamental baseline of modern jurisprudence.

170 Stephen's test was also purportedly adopted in the Australian criminal case of *Loughnan* [1981] VR 443 (see Chapter 5).

171 (1850) 14 JP 754. In that case, the defendant shot an escaping felon, which would have been lawful, except that the defendant did not know that the victim was a felon, and so the defendant was guilty of wounding.

172 See too the Hong Kong case of *Attorney-General v Chan Yuen Lung* [1989] 1 HKC 470, which also purported to adopt Stephen's test of lesser evil necessity (but was not made out on the facts).

173 Smart and Williams, *Utilitarianism: For and Against* (Cambridge: Cambridge University Press, 1973); Scheffler (ed), *Consequentialism and Its Critics* (Oxford: Oxford University Press, 1988); Glover (ed), *Utilitarianism and Its Critics* (New York: Macmillan, 1990). See too my critique of the reification of happiness in Tamblyn, 'Why is Killing Morally Wrong?' (2014) 25 King's LJ 454.

174 Brudner, 'A Theory of Necessity' (1987) 7 OJLS 338, 365; Simester et al., *Simester and Sullivan's Criminal Law: Theory and Doctrine*, 5th edn (Oxford: Hart, 2013) 802.

Further, Wilson says that there are rule of law concerns, if laws can be ignored, subject to retrospective ratification as a lesser evil by politically unaccountable judges.[175]

Further still, judges are not often best placed to decide questions of lesser evil. We saw above how, in *Monsanto v Tilly*, when the defendants pulled up the claimant's genetically modified crops, Mummery LJ thought it beyond the competence of the court to adjudge the moral merits of the defendants' action. Is genetically modified food a good thing or a bad thing, and for whom, and over what period, and according to what reckoning?

Similar concerns can be felt behind the Court of Appeal's decision in *R v Jones*,[176] where the defendants unsuccessfully pleaded necessity to a charge of criminal damage, committed at a military airbase in protest at the war in Iraq.[177] Was the war in Iraq good or bad, and for whom, and over what period, and according to what set of values?[178]

These concerns are what Gardner calls the democracy problem[179] – unelected judges making political decisions about what activities or policies are best for society. In the Canadian case of *R v Perka*,[180] the court said that, to allow ostensibly illegal acts to be validated on the basis of their expediency would import an undue subjectivity into the criminal law. It would invite the courts to second-guess the legislature and to assess the relative merits of social policies underlying criminal prohibitions, a role which does not fit well with the judicial function.[181]

To avoid the difficulties of weighing 'evils', Gardner suggests instead that necessity might be structured by reference to rights: lesser rights can be sacrificed to protect superior rights.[182] Thus, he says, a property right might be sacrificed to sustain a right to life. But that is already permitted, as we have seen, as private or public necessity. If we are looking to go beyond the limits of those doctrines, to a broader defence of lesser evil necessity, we are still left with a whole host of incommensurable rights. For example, what is the order here:

175 Wilson, *Criminal Law*, 5th edn (Harlow: Pearson, 2014) 200.

176 [2005] Crim LR 122, on appeal at [2006] UKHL 16.

177 And yet there is evidence that, in other courts, necessity has been providing a defence to politically motivated protest crimes: Keating et al., *Clarkson & Keating: Criminal Law*, 8th edn (London: Sweet & Maxwell, 2014) 389 (climate change); Norrie, *Crime, Reason and History*, 3rd edn (Cambridge: Cambridge University Press, 2014) 217 (Iraq war).

178 Similarly, the courts have often declared themselves unable or ill-suited, or otherwise at risk of usurping the legislature, if asked to determine whether political goals are for the public benefit so as to support the recognition of a trust as charitable: *Bowman v Secular Society Ltd* [1917] AC 406, 442; *McGovern v Attorney-General* [1982] Ch 321, 336–337; *Southwood v Attorney-General* [2000] All ER (D) 886.

179 Gardner, S, 'Necessity's Newest Inventions' (1991) 11 OJLS 125, 133.

180 [1984] 2 SCR 232.

181 *Perka* did recognise a defence of 'necessity', but not lesser evil necessity, rather duress of circumstances (see Chapter 5).

182 Gardner, S, 'Direct Action and the Defence of Necessity' [2005] Crim LR 371; Gardner, S, 'Necessity's Newest Inventions' (1991) 11 OJLS 125, 130–132.

the right to privacy, the right to a fair trial, the right to education? And what about other laws which enshrine such values as protection of the environment or freedom of conscience? And if the rankings are decided by judges, does this not simply restore the democracy problem? Further, this approach breaks down when faced with balancing the same right. For example, one could never kill one person to save a thousand because the *right* to life is the same in both cases.[183] (This is precisely the reasoning in German law.[184])

Another suggested way of comparing harms is by reference to the maximum punishments meted out.[185] But that assumes that the punishments attached to different crimes are rationally defensible, which seems doubtful.[186] And it still fails to resolve the problem of commensurability when different crimes attract the same sentence.[187] So yet another way of ranking harms is the living standards analysis: the seriousness of harms depends on its effect upon living standards, the most serious being those which affect physical integrity at the level of subsistence.[188] No doubt this reinforces the claim that defences like necessity or duress should respond only to serious threats to life or well-being. But it still fails to direct how we resolve conflicts between harms at the same level.

In my view, the long list of objections should be seen as fatal to recognising lesser evil necessity as an appropriate defence of general application. (For the same reasons, in Chapter 1, I rejected a defence of justification to the tort of intimidation.) And the defence is not needed. Most cases can be addressed through the criminal defence of duress of circumstances (see Chapter 5). Even in *Re A*, only one judge out of three felt the need to resort to lesser evil necessity. Added to this are also the defences of tortious necessity, and best interests intervention. There is no obvious gap which needs filling.

And yet, it might be asked, are not the tortious defence of necessity and the defence of best interests intervention also about avoiding a greater evil? (Could we say the same for yet more defences, like self-defence?) Yes, at a higher level of generality, we might hope that such defences, when acted upon, do indeed avoid the greater evil. But it is precisely that higher level of generality which is objectionable. A defence of lesser evil necessity never descends from that higher level of generality. It authorises any act as long as the end result is a lesser evil, whatever that means, and no matter what happens in order to get there.

183 Brudner, 'A Theory of Necessity' (1987) 7 OJLS 338, 365.

184 Bohlander, 'In Extremis – Hijacked Planes, "Collateral Damage" and the Limits of Criminal Law' [2006] Crim LR 597, 588–589; Hornle, 'Hijacked Planes: May They Be Shot Down?' (2007) 10 New Crim LR 582.

185 Simon, 'Exploring the Intricacies of the Lesser Evil Defense' (2005) 24 Law & Phil 645, 647.

186 For example, why does fraud attract a maximum punishment of ten years in prison, but theft only seven years? Why do both grievous bodily harm (s 20 Offences Against the Person Act 1861) and (lesser) actual bodily harm (s 47) have the same maximum punishment of five years?

187 For example, robbery and arson and rape and manslaughter all have a maximum punishment of life in prison. What is their ranking?

188 Dennis, 'On Necessity as a Defence to Crime' (2009) 2 Crim Law & Phil 29; von Hirsch and Jareborg, 'Gauging Criminal Harms: A Living Standard Analysis' (1991) 11 OJLS 1.

Its rationale is purely utilitarian. In contrast, the defences of tortious necessity and best interests intervention each have a specific and separate rationale, which is reflected in the constraining detail of their legal tests. Their driving force and key moving parts are constructed on concepts notably different from a utilitarian test of lesser evil necessity.

4.7 Conclusions

We should reject a defence of lesser evil necessity. Its utilitarian calculus is capable of producing outcomes which are morally unacceptable. And it requires judges to take policy decisions about which rival activities or rights are best for society beyond their constitutional competence.

Best interests intervention should be viewed, not as a defence of necessity, but as a distinct doctrine, even if its ingredients have some resort to the language of necessity. It has its own rationale: it enables a willing volunteer to provide necessary assistance to someone then unable to ask for help, so that the needy are not otherwise abandoned to their fate

The legal test for best interests intervention is as follows. It must be necessary to act to preserve or advance the best interests of another, assessed from the viewpoint of that other, when not possible to obtain their consent. If the other person refuses consent, that is the end of the matter. The doctrine allows intervention upon another's person or property. The necessity must be real. It need not be an emergency, and there is no minimum threshold of danger. Any intervention must be carried out with reasonable care. It must reasonably appear to the defendant that they are suited to intervene in the circumstances.

As for the tortious defences of private and public necessity, the analysis in this chapter reveals that the tests for those two branches are almost identical. More than that, it reveals, as we shall see in the next chapter, that the defence is akin to the criminal defence of duress of circumstances.

There must be an actual danger, of death or serious injury. Except that, where the defendant acts for the benefit of a third person, or the public generally, it suffices that the defendant reasonably believes there is a danger. The defendant's response to the danger must be reasonable, which involves a number of considerations. The response must likely be effective. It must reasonably appear to the defendant that there are no lawful alternatives, and the less imminent the danger, the more likely there are alternatives (or indeed, the less real the danger). The response must be carried out with reasonable care. Where the defendant acts for the benefit of a third party, or the public generally, it must reasonably appear to the defendant that they are suited to act in the circumstances. It does not matter that, after the event, the defendant's response was shown unnecessary after all.

This type of necessity proper provides a complete defence in tort, so that the defendant does not have to pay compensation. The defence is precluded if the danger was caused by the defendant's prior negligence. While usually the defence is expressed in terms of permitting only temporary use of another's property, the more honest approach might be to recognise that some persistent problems can fairly be addressed only collectively at a political level, rather than necessitous use imposing long-term burdens on individual third-party victims arbitrarily. Homelessness might be such a problem.

Necessity allows the defendant to act upon another's property. A person in necessity making use of another's property does not traverse any property rights, but is free to act as upon any property in its natural state. It is this necessity proviso which justifies the institution of private property, and an owner's ability otherwise to exclude others. Alternatively, property rights are derivative of – they exist only to support – personality rights, and so have to yield when the latter are threatened by death or serious injury.

A person in necessity cannot act upon another's person. That would fail to respect the victim, since it would be using them only as a means, as a tool for self-protection.

And the better view is that no one can protect their property by sacrificing another's property, because it creates a stalemate: the second property now endangered could then preserve itself at the expense of the first. The cases which did seem to allow the protection of property were easy cases which never had to square up to this predicament. Nor is there any good reason to resolve this conflict simply by stipulating that the more expensive property should be saved, rather than, for example, the more necessary property, or even on the basis of the ability of the parties to sustain the loss.

Characterising necessity as an incomplete privilege, while technically possible in legal terms – my preference is to say that necessitous use remains a trespass but bars the remedy of ejection, otherwise provides no further argument or justification for its half-way-house position.

5 Criminal law

Duress

Duress by threats has long been recognised. It is where the duressor commands the defendant to commit a crime, otherwise threatening them with bad consequences if they do not comply. (To this extent, it shares the same coercive 'or else' element as tortious intimidation and contractual duress.)

Duress of circumstances was recognised more recently. It is where the defendant commits a crime of their own initiative, in order to escape the bad consequences of the position in which they find themselves. It often involves driving offences, such as dangerous driving to escape threats of violence,[1] or driving while intoxicated or over the speed limit in order to get an injured person to hospital.[2]

The courts have often said that duress by threats and duress of circumstances are subject to the same legal test.[3] Authors tend to agree.[4] Indeed, cases of one type are often discussed by the court when explaining the legal test for cases of the other type. The case law for the two types is inextricably interwoven. One difference might be whether, for duress by threats, the duressor must nominate the crime. But if they do not, and the defendant picks the crime to avoid the threats, then the defendant can usually slide across to duress of circumstances.[5]

1 *Willer* (1986) 83 Cr App R 225; *Conway* [1989] QB 290.

2 See the Canadian cases of *Costoff* [2013] NSJ No 630, and *Pleau* [2013] NSJ No 630. In contrast, in the English case of *DPP v Hicks* [2002] 2 All ER (D) 285, it was no defence that a person driving when intoxicated was doing so in order to get medicine for a sick child, since the sickness did not amount to the threshold danger of serious injury. Whereas in the Australian case of *White* (1987) 9 NSWLR 427, the child was 'gravely ill'. See too *DPP v Pipe* [2012] EWHC 1821 (Admin) and the New Zealand case of *Police v Kawiti* [2000] 1 NZLR 117 (where the defendant drove herself to hospital).

3 *Quayle* [2005] EWCA Crim 1415; *Howe* [1987] AC 417, 429; *Conway* [1989] QB 290; *Abdul-Hussain* [1999] Crim LR 570; *Re A* [2001] Fam 147, 200.

4 Ormerod and Laird, *Smith & Hogan's Criminal Law*, 14th edn (Oxford: Oxford University Press, 2015) 424; Herring, *Criminal Law*, 8th edn (Basingstoke: Macmillan, 2013) 304; Herring, *Criminal Law*, 7th edn (Oxford: Oxford University Press, 2016) 653; Allen, *Textbook on Criminal Law*, 13th edn (Oxford: Oxford University Press, 2015) 194; Dennis, 'On Necessity as a Defence to Crime' (2009) 2 Crim Law & Phil 29.

5 *Cole* [1994] Crim LR 582; Allen, *Textbook on Criminal Law*, 13th edn (Oxford: Oxford University Press, 2015) 174. Similarly in Australian law, the defence of duress only applies when the defendant

However, I shall argue below for an important but hitherto unnoticed difference: with duress by threats, the defendant can act upon another's person or property; but with duress of circumstances, the defendant can only act upon another's property, and not also their person.

There is no clean separation of language when it comes to duress and necessity in criminal law. Various cases use, as interchangeable labels for the same defence, duress of circumstances and necessity,[6] sometimes even duress by threats and necessity.[7] Indeed, sometimes they mix the language to refer to 'necessity by circumstances',[8] or 'duress by necessity'.[9] When this happens, necessity is usually being used as a synonym for duress of circumstances.

There is some suggestion of a genus defence of necessity, with duress and self-defence as species.[10] Clarkson has suggested that they be collapsed together into one defence of 'necessary action'.[11] This has not happened. After all, duress and self-defence have different focal instances: with self-defence, the defendant acts on the source of the threat, whereas with duress, the defendant avoids the threat by acting on a third party.[12] And the leading explanation for self-defence is that there is a moral right to resist someone who, because they themselves are an unjust threat to our person, has forfeited their own rights.[13] As we shall see below, that is not a rationale shared by duress.

The criminal defence of duress was restated in *Hasan*.[14] It was said to include the following elements:

is threatened by another person into committing the crime, rather than where the defendant commits a crime of their own initiative in order to avoid danger: *Dawson* [1978] VR 536; *Lorenz* [1998] ACTSC 81, [38]–[41]. However, where the defendant acts of their own initiative, they might still plead necessity as an alternative: *Lorenz* [1998] ACTSC 81, [42], referred to as 'duress of circumstances' by counsel in *Clarkson* [2007] NSWCCA 70, [87].

6 *Pommel* [1995] 2 Cr App R 607; *Hasan* [2005] UKHL 22, [19]; *Howe* [1987] AC 417, 429; *Conway* [1989] QB 290; *Hammond* [2013] EWCA Crim 2709, [10]; *Martin* [1989] 1 All ER 652; *Gregory* [2011] EWCA Crim 1712, [12]; *Cairns* [1999] 2 Cr App R 137; *Ip Chung San* HCMA 318/2005; *Willer* (1986) 83 Cr App R 225.

7 *Abdul-Hussain* [1999] Crim LR 570.

8 *Quayle* [2005] EWCA Crim 1415.

9 *Rodger and Rose* [1998] 1 Cr App R 143.

10 Wilson, *Criminal Law*, 5th edn (Harlow: Pearson, 2014) 258; Dennis, 'On Necessity as a Defence to Crime' (2009) 2 Crim Law & Phil 29; *Re A* [2001] Fam 147, 253 (Robert Walker LJ).

11 Clarkson, 'Necessary Action: A New Defence' [2004] Crim LR 81. Elliott also suggests some merger of ideas: 'Necessity, Duress and Self-defence' [1989] Crim LR 611. For further discussion, see: Horder, 'Self-Defence, Necessity and Duress: Understanding the Relationship' (1998) 11 Can J Law & Juris 143; Dennis, 'On Necessity as a Defence to Crime' (2009) 2 Crim Law & Phil 29; Chan and Simester, 'Duress, Necessity: How Many Defences?' (2005) 16 King's LJ 121.

12 See too: *Hasan* [2005] UKHL 22, [19]; *Hibbert* [1995] 2 SCR 973, [50]. The Canadian case of *Ryan* [2013] 1 SCR 14, discussed below, appears to suggest that, where the defendant addresses the source of the threat, self-defence is available to the exclusion of duress.

13 Uniacke, *Permissible Killing* (Cambridge: Cambridge University Press, 1994); Leverick, *Killing in Self-Defence* (Oxford: Oxford University Press, 2006). More loosely, the court in *Hibbert* [1995] 2 SCR 973 said that the victim of self-defence was the author of his own deserts.

14 [2005] UKHL 22.

Duress is not a defence to murder, nor perhaps some forms of treason. The threat must be to cause death or serious injury. The threat must be to the defendant or their immediate family or someone close to them, or someone for whose safety they would reasonably regard themselves as responsible. The defendant's perception of the threat, and their response, must be reasonable. The defence is not available where the defendant voluntarily associated with known criminals when they ought reasonably to have foreseen the risk of them coercing them.

The defence of duress provides a full acquittal.

We can use that outline from *Hasan* to structure our discussion of English law. Each ingredient will be explored in more detail, comparison made to other jurisdictions, and improvements to the law recommended. After that, we consider those other jurisdictions on their own terms, to get a full picture of their comparative approaches. Finally, drawing on the case law, we shall explore why, in theory, criminal law might recognise a defence of duress.

Finally, before we begin, it is worth making the point that criminal law defences can be shaped by criminal law offences. As Glazebrook says,[15] crimes which proscribe behaviour done dishonestly, or without reasonable excuse, or unlawfully, might already allow for arguments akin to necessity. In this chapter, it is not possible to consider all major criminal offences, and their differences between jurisdictions. And anyway, offence definitions can or should change, and new offences get added. There is value in focusing on the generic defence on its own terms.

5.1 Types of threat

Duress is not the same as feeling under pressure.[16] (So too with contractual duress.) Rather, there must be a threat of death or serious injury,[17] or rape.[18] The following dangers are insufficient: a punch in the face,[19] assault,[20] threats to property,[21] sickness not sufficient to justify hospitalisation,[22] nor acting generally from fear or upset.[23]

Cumulative threats probably ought to be taken into account; it should not simply be the final act which triggers the defence. As Smith says, a simple threat to twist an arm is one thing, but a threat to twist an arm after 24 hours of arm-twisting is quite another.[24] Thus it may be that a series of lesser threats might together combine to produce an overall effect of serious harm.

15 Glazebrook, 'The Necessity Plea in English Criminal Law' (1972) 30 Cambridge LJ 87.
16 *A* [2012] EWCA Crim 434, [63].
17 *Hasan* [2005] UKHL 22, [21(2)].
18 *A* [2012] EWCA Crim 434, [63]; *Hammond* [2013] EWCA Crim 2709, [12].
19 *Aikens* [2003] EWCA Crim 1573, [9].
20 *Lam Yung* [2010] 2 HKLRD 384.
21 *DPP for Northern Ireland v Lynch* [1975] AC 653, 686–687 (Lord Simon); *Lam Yung* [2010] 2 HKLRD 384, where the threat was to splash the defendant's house in red paint.
22 *DPP v Hicks* [2002] 2 All ER (D) 285.
23 *Radford* [2004] EWCA Crim 2878; *Lam Yih Jiun Michael* [1996] 2 HKC 499.
24 Smith, J C, 'Individual Capacities and Criminal Liability' (1998) 6 Medical LR 138, 159.

In *Hammond*,[25] the defendant prisoner complained of sexual assault ('he squeezed my arse and things'). The defendant said that his attacker would have him 'taken care of' if he reported the matter. The court was prepared to accept that this might be a threat to kill. The defendant did not report the matter. But instead of 'dealing' (as the court put it) with these unwanted sexual approaches, he broke prison. This was held to be 'miles away' from supporting a defence.

However, no person should be obliged to 'deal with', i.e. suffer from, all criminal behaviour against them short of death or serious injury or rape. A victim must be able to complain or seek protection. But in *Hammond*, if the defendant complained, then he would be killed.

If a defendant is told 'suffer sexual assault, or complain and die', any response is not simply to avoid the sexual assault, it is also to avoid the alternative threat of death. Contrary to the court in *Hammond*, the defence of duress should have been available. (Whether the court believed the defendant is another matter.)

In *van Dao*,[26] police broke into a cannabis factory. They found workers inside. Some claimed duress. The evidence did not support those pleas. Also, provisionally, the court was inclined to say that false imprisonment was not a sufficient threat to sustain a plea of duress, without an accompanying threat of death or serious injury.

But surely it depends on the circumstances. Horrific stories make the press about people being locked in basements, without prospects of escape, for years on end, for example in Austria,[27] and America,[28] and Spain[29] and Sweden.[30] Assuming the only complaint was false imprisonment,[31] still, would the law really require the defendant to endure decades of detention, when the commission of a crime could set them free?

Put another way, surely lengthy false imprisonment counts as a serious threat to the person. It might not threaten their physical integrity, but it represents drastic harm to their freedom and autonomy. (Such harm is recognised in tortious intimidation and contractual duress.) Contrary to the court in *van Dao*, false imprisonment should be capable of sustaining the defence.

In *Jones*, the defendants were charged with conspiracy to commit criminal damage at an airbase. They said that they did this to prevent illegal war in Iraq.

25 [2013] EWCA Crim 2709.

26 [2012] EWCA Crim 1717.

27 http://www.telegraph.co.uk/news/worldnews/europe/austria/8723400/Austrian-man-locked-up-daughters-for-40-years.html (40 years detention); http://news.bbc.co.uk/1/hi/world/europe/7952275.stm (24 years); http://news.bbc.co.uk/1/hi/world/europe/5280472.stm (8 years).

28 http://www.bbc.co.uk/news/world-us-canada-22430145 (10 years).

29 http://www.bbc.co.uk/news/world-europe-35194227 (perhaps 19 years).

30 http://www.bbc.co.uk/news/world-europe-35399854 (planned 10 years).

31 Unfortunately, in many of those reported cases, the false imprisonment provided the opportunity for abuse of the captive.

The Court of Appeal said that the defence was only available when the defendant was responding to a threatened domestic crime, whereas waging war was a lawful exercise of the powers of prerogative.[32]

It is understandable, the court's reluctance to weigh in the balance the defendants' crimes against the waging of war abroad. But the court went too far in suggesting that the threat must be to commit a crime. The defence is available when the defendant faces threats which are not crimes. For example, in *Martin*,[33] duress was available when the defendant was coerced into driving while disqualified by his wife's threats of suicide. And in *DPP v Pipe*,[34] an appeal against conviction was allowed where the defendant drove over the speed limit to take to hospital a child in pain from a broken leg.

In *S*,[35] the court said that there does not need to be a specific identifiable threat. But in *Shayler*,[36] the Court of Appeal said that unspecified threats of harm to unspecified people will not likely sustain the defence. This can be reconciled as follows. The less specific the threat, the less credible it will be for a defendant to say that they reasonably believed it, and that it caused them to act, and the more difficult it will be to show that their criminal response was reasonable.

In *Valderama-Vega*,[37] the defendant was threatened with violence, and he was in debt to his bank, and he was threatened with the disclosure of his homosexuality. The court seemed to suggest that the defendant must not have acted but for the threat of violence, but beyond that, it did not matter if other factors also motivated him. That approach was questioned in *Ortiz*,[38] where the court wondered how a defendant's will can be overborne by threats if he also acted on other motives. However, I shall suggest below that an overborne will is not the rationale for duress. In this case, as long as admissible threats caused the defendant to react, it need not matter that there were additional causes as well. (With contractual duress, threats need only be a contributory cause.)

Should we dispense with the need for serious threats, and simply allow the defendant to respond reasonably to any threat?[39] That is a plausible suggestion, and indeed the Australian codes do seem to allow for any threat, as we shall see. But there are two reasons to dismiss this approach. First, it risks becoming a general defence of lesser evil necessity, and we rejected that defence in Chapter 4. Second, what usually happens with duress is that the defendant, to

32 [2005] Crim LR 122 (CA), on appeal [2006] UKHL 16 where the defence of duress or necessity was not considered.

33 [1989] 1 All ER 652. Similarly, there were threats of suicide in *Louth v Diprose* (1992) 67 AJLR 95, which raised the tortious defence of necessity, as we saw in Chapter 4.

34 [2012] EWHC 1821 (Admin).

35 [2009] EWCA Crim 85.

36 [2001] EWCA Crim 1977, on appeal at [2002] UKHL 11.

37 [1985] Crim LR 220.

38 (1986) 83 Cr App R 173.

39 Wilson, Criminal Law, 5th edn (Harlow: Pearson, 2014) 249; Horder, Asthworth's Principles of Criminal Law, 8th edn (Oxford: Oxford University Press, 2016) 229.

avoid harm to themselves, acts upon an innocent third party. That ought not to be routine, but should only apply at the limits, when the defendant is seeking to escape serious danger.

Might then we allow a broader defence for victimless crimes?[40] No doubt the absence of any victim would count in mitigation. But it seems to me that there is the following objection. Crimes only turn out to be victimless after the event. Yes, the defendant in fact did not harm any innocent third party, but they did not know it would turn out that way at the time. There are crashes even on roads which seem empty. A rule which condones victimless crimes is a rule which condones taking risks at the potential expense of third-party victims, and again that ought not to be routine, in the absence of serious danger to the defendant.

In summary, there must be serious danger to the person. This includes death and serious injury and rape, but there is no reason why this should be a closed list. It ought to include lengthy false imprisonment. And lesser dangers might count too if they have a cumulative effect. The dangers need not constitute a crime, and they probably need only be a contributory cause of the defendant's behaviour.

5.2 Pain and internal causes

In *Rodger and Rose*,[41] the defendants were in prison, having been convicted of murder. When their tariff was increased, they became suicidal, and so broke prison. Their defence of duress or necessity was denied. The court said that what caused the crime must be extraneous to the defendant, rather than his own subjective thought processes and emotions. Similarly in *Quayle*,[42] which relied on *Rodger and Rose*, the court repeated that there must be an external source of duress. In that case, pain suffered by an amputee was not such a cause as to allow a defence against using cannabis for pain relief.[43]

The court's concern in *Quayle* was put thus. If the defendant were allowed to raise a plea based upon his own subjective assessment of his own private condition, the prosecutor would be unable to disprove it, the jury would have nothing capable of objective scrutiny, and the risk would arise of abusive (i.e. fictitious) defences.[44]

And yet in *Martin*,[45] a defence was available when the defendant responded to his wife's threats of suicide. So why no defence with a defendant's own risk of suicide? And in *DPP v Pipe*,[46] a defence was available when the defendant responded to a child's pain. So why no defence with a defendant's own pain?

40 Wilson, *Criminal Law*, 5th edn (Harlow: Pearson, 2014) 249, 282. It is notable that the early cases of duress of circumstances involved 'victimless' driving offences.

41 [1998] 1 Cr App R 143.

42 [2005] EWCA Crim 1415.

43 See too: *Altham* [2006] Crim LR 633 (where the defendant was nevertheless given an absolute discharge).

44 A concern repeated in *Hasan* [2005] UKHL 22, [22].

45 [1989] 1 All ER 652.

46 [2012] EWHC 1821 (Admin).

In fact, in *Quayle*, the discussion seemed to leave open the possibility that if the pain became life-threatening, a defence might be available after all.

Further, the court in *Quayle* accepted evidence that the defendant had an extensive history of severe pain which a succession of doctors had accepted as genuine, and, we might add, a credible history of pain, since it arose following an amputation, itself a verifiable event.

In truth, in neither case was the harm caused by processes internal to the defendant. In *Rodger and Rose*, it was the external setting of prison which caused the suicidal tendencies. This is not a rare phenomenon.[47] In *Quayle*, it was an amputation which caused residual pain. No doubt the defence should be denied to those who commit crimes from internal, pathological compulsion, but these were not such cases.

Further still, the primary role of juries, in fact finding, is to determine whether or not the defendant is telling the truth. Many allegations of duress involve the defendant asserting that they were threatened by a third party, often with that third party not properly identified and not before the court. The claim that the defendant is suffering pain is no more incredible or forensically challenging. There is no reason to suppose, in either scenario, that a jury would simply accept, without more, a defendant's self-serving assertion. Indeed, in *Howe*,[48] the court accepted that juries could be trusted with spotting a bogus defence of duress.[49]

What is more, the court has held that psychological injury can count as actual or grievous bodily harm in the context of offences against the person.[50] And tort law, even contract law, has awarded damages for psychological injury and pain. None of this suggests that such matters are inscrutable.

Additionally, even if criminal law is reluctant to recognise what we might call 'background' pain or psychological suffering as sufficient for duress of circumstances, there is some suggestion that a *threat* by another to inflict psychological injury can support the defence.[51]

Further still, even with criminal duress, juries are already allowed to take account of a defendant's psychiatric condition when considering the defendant's response to any threat (see below).

47 http://www.inquest.org.uk/statistics/deaths-in-prison.

48 [1987] AC 417, 434.

49 If this were a real problem, one solution might be a reversed burden of proof, for which there is some support: Law Com No 304, [6.141] (at least on a charge of murder); Reed, 'Duress and Normative Moral Excuse', in Reed et al. (eds), *General Defences in Criminal Law* (Farnham: Ashgate, 2014) 109-110; *Hasan* [2005] UKHL 22, [20] (Lord Bingham).

50 *Ireland* [1998] AC 147.

51 *Baker* [1997] Crim LR 497. See too: Ormerod and Laird, *Smith & Hogan's Criminal Law*, 14th edn (Oxford: Oxford University Press, 2015) 390; Herring, *Criminal Law*, 8th edn (Basingstoke: Macmillan, 2013) 300; Herring, *Criminal Law*, 7th edn (Oxford: Oxford University Press, 2016) 656; Card, *Card, Cross and Jones, Criminal Law*, 21st edn (Oxford: Oxford University Press, 2014) 684. But to the contrary, see: Simester et al., *Simester and Sullivan's Criminal Law: Theory and Doctrine*, 5th edn (Oxford: Hart, 2013) 741; Wilson, *Criminal Law*, 5th edn (Harlow: Pearson, 2014) 248 n 14.

All in all, there is considerable inconsistency here. A better position might be that pain or psychological injury can support a plea of duress, as long as there is a sufficient minimum of credible (perhaps also corroborative?) evidence, and, of course, as long as it passes the threshold of serious injury. (In *Quayle*, the question would have been whether the difference in pain, between legal painkillers and illegal cannabis, amounted to serious injury.)

The better reason for the decision in *Quayle* was, as the court said, that the legislative scheme for dealing with controlled drugs was exhaustive and permitted no residual common law defence.

As for the decision in *Rodger and Rose*, there are a number of better explanations. (1) As a matter of policy, any system which uses prison as punishment and deterrence cannot allow people to escape prison because they do not like prison. (2) The defendants surely had alternatives, like consulting a doctor. People outside prison manage suicidal thoughts too. (3) The defendants laid themselves open to the duress of prison by committing an earlier imprisonable crime. (We discuss laying oneself open to duress, below.)

However, a final difficulty is where, for example, the defendant suffers pain not caused by an external event like amputation, but through a condition with which they were born. We might have considerable sympathy for such a person, and yet little sympathy for the person also born with a pathological compulsion to criminal behaviour.

It cannot be that pathological compulsion to criminal behaviour provides a full acquittal through the defence of duress.[52] It would, in effect, amount to a lifelong permission for this defendant to commit crime. Yet we face the same challenge with the permanently injured. Indeed, it seems that the crimes committed in *Quayle* had been ongoing for years. Duress cannot be used to give long-term personal immunity from laws which purport to apply to everyone without private exception.

So perhaps the proper approach here is to admit that duress can only be pleaded for single events and not for continuous states of affairs.[53] Wilson says that criminal defences respond to a crisis.[54] Similarly, Australian code jurisdictions talk about sudden emergencies (rather than persistent problems). And we saw in Chapter 4 with the tortious defence of necessity that some ongoing problems are not fairly suited to self-help, but require collective action at the political level. This was precisely the position in *Quayle*, where drug policy was enacted democratically through comprehensive legislation.

52 Morse suggests that inner compulsion is better seen as irrationality, and proposes a verdict of guilty but partially responsible, as an analogue to diminished responsibility, but available to all crimes: 'Diminished Capacity', in Shute et al. (eds), *Action and Value in the Criminal Law* (Oxford: Clarendon Press, 1993). See too: Lippke, 'Chronic Temptation, Reasonable Firmness and the Criminal Law' (2014) 34 OJLS 75.

53 See too: Simester et al., *Simester and Sullivan's Criminal Law: Theory and Doctrine*, 5th edn (Oxford: Hart, 2013) 807; Wilson, *Criminal Law*, 5th edn (Harlow: Pearson, 2014) 200.

54 Wilson, 'The Structure of Criminal Defences' [2005] Crim LR 108; Wilson, 'The Filtering Role of Crisis in the Constitution of Criminal Excuses' (2004) 17 Can J L & Juris 387.

In summary, pain and psychological injury should be capable of supporting a defence of duress if they amount to a serious danger, and are sufficiently supported by credible evidence. But the defence probably ought only to apply to one-off events rather than ongoing states of affairs; the defence should not provide long-term personal immunity from the criminal law.

5.3 Threats to whom?

Usually it is the defendant who is threatened. But it may also be his girlfriend and child,[55] or her boyfriend,[56] or a passenger in the defendant's car.[57] More generically, in *Hasan*, the court spoke of threats to the defendant's immediate family or someone close to him, or to a person for whose safety the defendant would reasonably regard himself as responsible.[58] This latter phrase could encompass strangers. For example, where a bank robber threatens to kill an unknown customer unless the clerk hands over money, a defence of duress would surely be available to the clerk.[59]

The real concern is to avoid officious intermeddling. Simply because some people are under threat, it should not follow that just anyone can get involved and commit crimes in an attempt to resolve the situation. For example, if a victim is being held hostage, the police are the proper people to deal with the situation. We saw in Chapter 4, with public necessity, and with best interests intervention, a similar concern to exclude officious intermeddlers when there were more suitable people to respond to the danger.

And of course, the more extenuated the relationship between the defendant and the person threatened, the less credible it might be that the defendant felt coerced by the threat.

5.4 Perception and response

The defendant's perception of the threat need not be accurate. They could be mistaken. But their perception must be reasonable, and not merely honest. The principal authority here is *Graham*.[60] The test is this: was the defendant impelled to act because, as a result of what they reasonably believed the duressor said or did, they had good cause to fear death or serious injury? This objective approach

55 *Cole* [1994] Crim LR 582.
56 *Wright* [2000] Crim LR 510.
57 *Conway* [1989] QB 290.
58 [2005] UKHL 22, [21(3)].
59 Ormerod and Laird, *Smith & Hogan's Criminal Law*, 14th edn (Oxford: Oxford University Press, 2015) 393; Simester et al., *Simester and Sullivan's Criminal Law: Theory and Doctrine*, 5th edn (Oxford: Hart, 2013) 747; Horder, *Ashworth's Principles of Criminal Law*, 8th edn (Oxford: Oxford University Press, 2016) 230; *Shayler* [2001] EWCA Crim 1977, [49].
60 [1982] 1 All ER 801.

was confirmed by Lord Mackay in *Howe*,[61] and by Lord Bingham in *Hasan*.[62] Note that this test contains two elements, both objective: first, a reasonable belief that a threat was made; second, good cause to fear that threat.

As for this second element, rather than talk in terms of having 'good cause' to fear the threat, a clearer approach, following Canadian law, below, might ask whether the defendant had a reasonable belief that the threat might be carried out.

So for example, a defendant might plead duress if a gun was put to their head, when they did not reasonably know that the gun was unloaded.[63] In contrast, if a prisoner the other side of bars threatens to kill a visitor, the threat is real, but there may be no cause to fear the threat, if incarceration prevents it from being carried out.

The threats must cause,[64] or impel,[65] the defendant to commit the crimes in respect of which they seek to raise the defence of duress. And there must be coercion.[66] As we saw in Chapter 3 with contractual duress, causation and coercion are not the same thing:[67] the demand may be the reason why the defendant acts, but if they want to plead duress, they must also feel coerced by the threats (rather than just shrugging them off).

After that, the test, again from *Graham*,[68] is whether a sober person of reasonable firmness, sharing the defendant's characteristics, would have responded similarly.

There is some suggestion in the case law that the defendant must act proportionately.[69] But in what proportion? Equality is a proportion (an equal one). And for example, self-defence requires a proportionate reaction, but it may still legitimise killing in defence to a non-fatal attack. There seems little need for a separate test of proportionality if the defendant is already obliged to respond reasonably.

Another question is whether we should require a reasonable response at all, given that duress already consists of a threat of death or serious injury.[70] But a grave threat should not be a free pass to commit any crime against innocent

61 [1987] AC 417.

62 [2005] UKHL 22, [21(4)], [23]. See too: *Safi* [2003] Crim LR 721; *Cairns* [1999] 2 Cr App R 137.

63 Yet potentially contrast s 31 Criminal Code (Qld), below, which appears to suggest that there must be an actual danger.

64 *Hasan* [2005] UKHL 22, [21(5)].

65 *Graham* [1982] 1 All ER 801, 806.

66 Horder, 'Occupying the Moral High Ground? The Law Commission on Duress' [1994] Crim LR 334, 341.

67 See too: Moore, 'Causation and the Excuses' (1985) 73 Cal LR 1091, 1131–1133.

68 [1982] 1 All ER 801, 806.

69 *Martin* [1989] 1 All ER 652; *Howe* [1987] AC 417; *Abdul-Hussain* [1999] Crim LR 570.

70 Clarkson, 'Necessary Action: A New Defence' [2004] Crim LR 81, 92; Smith, K J M, 'Duress and Steadfastness: In Pursuit of the Unintelligible' [1999] Crim LR 363; Smith, K J M, 'Must heroes Behave Heroically?' [1989] Crim LR 622, 628; Keating et al., *Clarkson & Keating: Criminal Law*, 8th edn (London: Sweet & Maxwell, 2014) 371.

third parties. Even if committing a crime is understandable, we can still insist that the defendant does less rather than more harm where possible.

The fortitude expected of the defendant is said to be that of a person of reasonable firmness sharing the defendant's characteristics. Similarly, Canadian law holds the defendant to a 'modified objective' standard, as we shall see. But why take any characteristics into account? It might be said that some defendants otherwise lack a fair opportunity to conform to the law.[71] No doubt the same could be said of others with a pathological compulsion to criminal behaviour. Yet in truth, we only allow some characteristics to be taken into account, not others. So which ones?

In *Bowen*,[72] the court said that age and sex were relevant.[73] How can that be? Is the reasonable man different from the reasonable woman? Is a man or a woman more or less resistant to threats? How is age relevant? (For example, a plea of duress has not always acquitted the young.[74]) The fact that I am a 40-year-old man tells you nothing about my moral strength.

The court in *Bowen* said that homosexuals were no less robust than heterosexuals. The court also said that physical health and disability *may* be relevant characteristics. But again, is a runner or a wheelchair user more or less resilient to threats? Surely there can be no generic answer to these questions.

Now a threatened punch to the stomach may be more serious for a pregnant woman than for a champion swimmer. And a threatened strike to the head may be more dangerous for an elderly stroke victim than for a professional boxer. But this goes to the separate question of whether what is threatened is serious injury. Also, the chance of escape from a duressor may be greater for an athlete than for someone with asthma. But that goes to the separate question of whether evasive action was available.[75] To be clear, even if evasive action was *not* available, the test still asks whether a person of reasonable firmness would have resisted the threat anyway.

In *Bowen*, the defendant was abnormally suggestible and had a low IQ of 68 (which would be around the bottom 2% of the population). The court said that being more susceptible to threats than a normal person was not a legitimate characteristic – unless this was due to a mental illness or impairment, or a recognised psychiatric condition.[76] This leaves us with the strange position that being susceptible to threats is irrelevant unless one is *really* susceptible to threats.

71 Wilson, *Criminal Law*, 5th edn (Harlow: Pearson, 2014) 253.

72 [1996] 4 All ER 837, 841, 845.

73 A similar approach is found in the defence of loss of control (formerly called provocation): Coroners and Justice Act 2009, s 54.

74 *N* [2007] EWCA Crim 3479 (aged 16); *Wilson* [2007] EWCA Crim 1251 (aged 13).

75 See too: Smith, K J M, 'Duress and Steadfastness: In Pursuit of the Unintelligible' [1999] Crim LR 363, 370–371.

76 Virgo and Buchanan warn of over-reliance on 'recognised' psychiatric diagnoses, whose purpose is medical rather than the attribution of moral responsibility, and which may or may not signify any loss of function: 'Duress and Mental Abnormality' [1999] Crim LR 517. Loveless also warns of 'syndromising' defendants, especially battered women, looking for a psychiatric diagnosis which reflects their experience, when the legal test of serious threat is satisfied without needing any further medical inquiry: '*R v GAC*: Battered Woman "Syndromization"' [2014] Crim LR 655.

In *Sewell*,[77] the judge said that Post Traumatic Stress Disorder (PTSD) was a relevant characteristic. The appeal against conviction did not focus on whether the judge was right to do so, and was dismissed for other reasons. In *Emery*,[78] where there was evidence of PTSD, learned helplessness and battered women's syndrome, the jury rejected a defence of duress all the same.[79] In *Walker*,[80] the court said that an anxiety state, caused by a traumatic and deprived childhood, amounting to a recognised psychological disorder, could be relevant. In *Antar*,[81] the court said the following were admissible: the defendant had a very low IQ of 51, functioned cognitively at a significantly impaired level, had moderate learning disability (the expert later downgraded this to mild), and had a level of suggestibility significantly higher than the general population. This does seem to be a softening of *Bowen*. Perhaps *Bowen* and *Antar* mark the two sides of a borderline which the court has not yet explicitly identified. Or perhaps it was the cumulative characteristics in *Antar* which altogether made it appropriate to admit these matters before the jury.

Self-induced intoxication is not a relevant characteristic.[82] This is despite alcoholism and drug abuse being recognised psychiatric illnesses.[83] Nor is being emotionally unstable or in a grossly elevated neurotic state relevant,[84] nor being unusually pliable or vulnerable to pressure,[85] not even if this was the result of a history of sexual abuse.[86] After all, said the court in *Horne*,[87] if the defendant were imbued with *all* his own characteristics, the test in *Graham*, an objective test, would become instead a subjective test.

The position here is muddled and unsatisfactory. Our inability to identify with conviction a list of morally relevant criteria suggests we might be better off without admitting personal characteristics. Asking straight whether the defendant responded reasonably would be tidier (as appears to be the position in Australian code jurisdictions). I shall suggest below that holding the defendant to a straight objective standard is defensible.

Nevertheless, I would also commend the suggestion to extend a separate defence of diminished responsibility so that it was available to all crimes (not just murder).[88] This would be a more coherent way to deal with the defendant's

77 [2004] EWCA Crim 2322.

78 (1993) 14 Cr App R (S) 394.

79 Perhaps the jury simply disbelieved the defendant's evidence.

80 [2003] EWCA Crim 1837.

81 [2004] EWCA Crim 2708.

82 *Graham* [1982] 1 All ER 801, 806; *Bowen* [1996] 4 All ER 837, 844; *Flatt* [1996] Crim LR 576.

83 See too *Dowds* [2012] EWCA Crim 281.

84 *Hegarty* [1994] Crim LR 353.

85 *Horne* [1994] Crim LR 584.

86 *Hurst* [1995] 1 Cr App R 82.

87 [1994] Crim LR 584.

88 Simester et al., *Simester and Sullivan's Criminal Law: Theory and Doctrine*, 5th edn (Oxford: Hart, 2013) 745; see too Tadros, *Criminal Responsibility* (Oxford: Oxford University Press, 2007) ch 13; Horder, 'Pleading Involuntary Lack of Capacity' (1993) 52 Cambridge LJ 298 (who recommends that diminished responsibility be a verdict alternative to guilty or not guilty).

mental idiosyncrasies. So if the defendant's plea is that the crime was caused in substantial part by their own mental impairment, that can be given proper consideration on its own terms, rather than distorted through an ill-fitting defence of duress.

In summary, the defendant must have a reasonable belief in there being a danger, and a reasonable belief that any threat will be carried out, or that the danger will materialise. This is so even if there is in fact no danger, or even if any threat is incapable of being carried out. The danger must be coercive, and cause the defendant to act. The cleaner approach is to say that the defendant's response must be reasonable. Although the case law talks in terms of taking account of the defendant's personal characteristics, no convincing list of relevant characteristics has been identified; rather, which characteristics are taken into account seems morally arbitrary. If the law ought to respond to mental impairment, that should be recognised through a separate defence.

5.5 Imminence and alternative action

In *Hudson*,[89] the defendant was charged with perjury. She said that she was threatened into giving false evidence, and that one of her duressors, with a reputation for violence, was in the public gallery in court watching her. The court said that there was no requirement that the threat be carried out instantly. The threats were 'no less compelling because their execution could not be effected in the court room if they could be carried out in the streets of Salford the same night'.

But in *Hasan*,[90] Lord Bingham cast grave doubt over whether this approach was correct. (A later court consequently assumed the decision in *Hudson* to have erred,[91] but some authors continue to support the decision.[92]) Lord Bingham said that he could not accept that a witness testifying in a Crown Court had no opportunity to avoid complying with a threat incapable of execution then and there. But that objection had already been addressed by the court in *Hudson*: it failed to distinguish between cases where police protection would be effective and where it would not. (And by way of further example, in the case of *Shepherd*,[93] the defendant was even attacked within the court precincts.)

Note that the court in *Hudson* was not saying that police protection would have been ineffective, only that the prosecution had not proved otherwise. In Australian law, as we shall see, the courts have repeatedly acknowledged that going to the police will not always or necessarily provide the defendant with effective protection; but the defendant's mere belief that police protection

89 [1971] 2 QB 202.

90 [2005] UKHL 22, [27].

91 *Batchelor* [2013] EWCA Crim 2638, [15].

92 Simester et al., *Simester and Sullivan's Criminal Law: Theory and Doctrine*, 5th edn (Oxford: Hart, 2013) 742; Keating et al., *Clarkson & Keating: Criminal Law*, 8th edn (London: Sweet & Maxwell, 2014) 372.

93 (1988) 86 Cr App R 47.

would not be effective is insufficient to ground the defence, in the absence of good reasons to justify that belief.

In *Abdul-Hussain*,[94] the court said:

> If Anne Frank had stolen a car to escape from Amsterdam and been charged with theft, the tenets of English law would not, in our judgment, have denied her a defence of duress of circumstances, on the ground that she should have waited for the Gestapo's knock on the door.

This is surely right: there was an ever-present risk of death, and it should not matter that a defendant cannot tell precisely when that threat will materialise, as long as the threat is real, or reasonably perceived to be real. Again, the Australian cases talk of a continuing and impending danger, as we shall see.

Let us further say, in this illustration, that Anne Frank knew that the Gestapo would come in precisely one month. That is not imminent. So when can she escape? Today? Next week? Or only the day before? If the only evasive action she can take is to steal a car today, surely she would have a defence. The alternative would be waiting until the day before – and missing the only chance of escape, and so enduring certain death.

What this reveals is that imminence is little more than a poor approximation for other questions: whether the defendant reasonably perceived a danger, and whether the defendant had alternative ways of escaping it. This has been acknowledged in the Australian case of *Rogers*, and now seems to be the position in Canadian law, following *Ruzic* and *Ryan*.

Now, the less imminent the threat, the more likely that there is lawful evasive action available.[95] But if no alternative escape is available between now and the threat materialising, then it should not preclude the defence that the threat is not imminent, as long as it is reasonably certain. I say 'reasonably certain' because the perception of the threat must be reasonable, as we have seen. However, in the Canadian case of *Latimer*,[96] the court spoke of the peril being 'virtually certain'.

So, there must be no alternative action which the defendant could reasonably have been expected to take.[97] Or, which is not quite the same thing, the defendant must genuinely and reasonably believe they have no other escape.[98] In *Sharp*,[99] the court spoke about escape 'without danger to himself', suggestive perhaps that the only alternatives which a defendant need consider are those which do not simply replace one threat with another danger. But there must surely be some (minor) dangers which a defendant might reasonably be expected to take in order to avoid inflicting a serious crime on an innocent third party.

94 [1999] Crim LR 570.
95 *Hasan* [2005] UKHL 22, [28].
96 [2001] 1 SCR 3.
97 *Hasan* [2005] UKHL 22, [21(6)].
98 *N* [2007] EWCA Crim 3479.
99 [1987] QB 853.

In similar vein, a defendant must desist from committing the crime as soon as they reasonably can.[100] For example, in *DPP v Jones*,[101] the defendant was driving while intoxicated. He claimed to be escaping attackers. That might have been true initially, but two miles later, he failed to ascertain whether he was still being pursued. The defence was denied him.

In summary, the defence of duress should be available where a danger is continuing and impending, even if the defendant does not know precisely when its harm might materialise. If the harm is reasonably certain to materialise in the future, and escape is available only now, the defence should still be available.

If the harm is not imminent, there might be no serious danger, or the defendant might have alternative and lawful means of escape. The defendant's response to any danger must be reasonable; this means they should take lawful means of escape, if they are effective. There should be no presumption that police protection is always effective. But a defendant ought to be able to give reasons to support any assertion that police protection will not assist in this particular case.

5.6 Laying oneself open to duress

The defence is not available to a defendant who lays themselves open to duress. (Similarly, the tortious defence of necessity is precluded by prior fault.) The cases interweave two questions as to when this proviso applies. First, must the defendant foresee the risk of coercion? Second, must this arise only from consorting with criminals?

Earlier cases suggested that the question was whether the defendant foresaw the risk of coercion *to commit crimes*.[102] This is the position in Canadian law too. In *Hasan*,[103] the court was agreed that the proviso was not so narrow that the defendant must have foreseen the risk of coercion to commit crimes *of the sort* with which he was charged. (Although something akin to that more generous position can be found in Australian law.) But Lord Bingham, with whom the majority agreed, said that the proviso applies if the defendant foresaw, or reasonably ought to have foreseen, merely the risk of coercion.

Smith makes the following objection: there is a difference between, on the one hand, foreseeing a likely beating for not paying one's drug debts, and on the other hand, foreseeing being threatened into committing crimes.[104] Two points might be made in response.

First, the defendant is already in a morally objectionable, indeed criminal, position: on this example, they are an illegal drug user. For that, we might deny

100 *Pommel* [1995] 2 Cr App R 607.

101 [1990] RTR 33. In contrast, in *DPP v Bell* [1992] RTR 335, the court held that it was not demonstrated that the defendant drove while intoxicated for longer than was necessary.

102 The discussion was not always as clear as it might have been: *Sharp* [1987] QB 853; *Ali (Mumtaz)* [1995] Crim LR 303; *Heath* [2000] Crim LR 109, *Harmer* [2002] Crim LR 401.

103 [2005] UKHL 22.

104 J C Smith, 'Commentary' [2000] Crim LR 109.

them a defence altogether. This could be analogous to the defence of illegality in tort. Thus if one engages in criminal activity, one must take full responsibility for what happens next, and not rely on the court's sympathy. So for example, in New Zealand law, it seems likely that, if the defendant is in a criminal gang, that alone might preclude the defence of duress (if it was a gang member who coerced the defendant). But in the Canadian case of *Perka*, the court said explicitly that behaving illegally did not preclude the defence of necessity; what mattered was foresight that the behaviour might give rise to the necessity.

Second, if it is reasonably foreseeable that criminals will resort to coercive violence, it is surely reasonably foreseeable that such coercive violence might be turned towards procuring criminal ends. They are criminals after all. In other words, even if duress were precluded only upon proof of foresight of coercion to commit crimes, rather than foresight of mere coercion, where the coercion is coming from known criminals, it would be a very fine line between the two tests, and sorely test the credibility of the witness who claimed that they foresaw coercion from their criminal associates, but not coercion to commit crime.

In most of the cases, the risk of coercion arose from the defendant voluntarily consorting with known criminals.[105] This is also the context in which a similar proviso applies in the statutory defences of compulsion in Canada, New Zealand and Australia. Note, however, that not all criminal gangs foreseeably use violence.[106] And in *Ali*,[107] the court suggested that what mattered was consorting with coercers rather than criminals.

Yet in *Hasan*, Baroness Hale gave an alternative example, of a battered wife who stays with her abusive husband, foreseeing the risk of further violence, but not foreseeing any risk of being coerced to commit crimes (like perjure for him).[108] Of course, domestic violence is a crime, which makes an abusive husband a known criminal, but not in the usual context of criminal gangs or conspiracies. Baroness Hale suggested that, in such cases, the defendant ought to be denied the defence only if she foresaw the risk of compulsion to commit crime, rather than just the risk of compulsion.[109]

We can identify a middle way: when consorting illegally with other criminals, as with conspiracy, or drug use, reasonable foresight of mere coercion might preclude the defence, whereas consorting legally with other criminals, as in a domestic context, the defence might be precluded only with reasonable foresight of compulsion to commit crimes.

Those who consort with known criminals may seek to withdraw their association. Thereafter, a defence of duress may be available, as acknowledged in *Sharp*.[110] But there must be a passage of time between the withdrawal and the duress.

105 *Sharp* [1987] QB 853; *Ali (Mumtaz)* [1995] Crim LR 303; *Hasan* [2005] UKHL 22.
106 *Shepherd* (1988) 86 Cr App R 47 (a gang of burglars).
107 [2008] EWCA Crim 716.
108 [2005] UKHL 22, [77].
109 See too: Ibbetson, 'Duress Revisited' (2005) 64 Cambridge LJ 530.
110 [1987] QB 853.

In *Sharp*, the defendant, who had joined a gang of robbers, sought to withdraw from the planned robbery, at which point the gang leader forced him to continue with a gun to his head. The defence was not available: the coercion followed immediately to prevent his attempted withdrawal, as might well have been expected. We might say that there must have been a genuine period of disassociation before the defendant can resort to a defence of duress by prior colleagues.

In *Lewis*,[111] the defendant was convicted of robbery. He was attacked in prison by a fellow robber, and then refused to give evidence against him for fear of reprisals. The court said that duress should have been left to the jury on the defendant's charge of contempt of court. Despite the defendant consorting with violent criminal associates, said the court, the reprisal was not so closely or immediately connected with robbery that the defendant must be taken to have voluntarily exposed himself.

This reasoning seems wrong. Surely a defendant knows that, by consorting with violent criminals, that violence might be turned against them to prevent them giving evidence against the others. But perhaps there is a policy justification for the decision. The defendant was attacked in prison, where the state was immediately responsible for his safety. It hardly seems fair to lock up a defendant with violent criminals and then lay the blame for any subsequent violence upon the defendant's continued and unavoidable association with them.

All this is only one instance of laying oneself open to duress. It is also possible to bring upon oneself duress of circumstances or a situation of necessity. So in the Canadian case of *Perka*,[112] discussed further below, the court said that the defence is precluded if the defendant foresaw or reasonably ought to have foreseen that his action would likely give rise to the necessity.

A similar English example might be *Rodger and Rose*,[113] discussed above, where one reason why the defendants' suicidal feelings as a result of their incarceration did not support the defence might have been that they had foreseeably laid themselves open to the duress of prison by committing an earlier imprisonable crime.

But note, in both *Perka* and *Rodger and Rose*, the defendant was previously engaged in an illegal activity. In *Perka*, it was importing drugs; in *Rodger and Rose*, it was the earlier imprisonable offence. Now, if some allowance ought to be made for those who lawfully consort with criminals, then so too allowance ought to be made for those pleading necessity against a background of lawful activity.

In summary, the defence should be precluded if the defendant, voluntarily engaged in an illegal activity, should reasonably have foreseen that their actions might well expose them to danger, or to the risk of being coerced by fellow criminals. But where the defendant consorts with criminals lawfully, or when they are otherwise engaged in a lawful activity, the better approach might be to preclude

111 (1993) 96 Cr App R 412.
112 [1984] 2 SCR 232.
113 [1998] 1 Cr App R 143.

the defence only if the defendant should reasonably have foreseen the need to commit crimes to escape their predicament.

Otherwise, in the case of withdrawal, there must be a genuine period of disassociation before a defendant can plead duress by a former colleague.

5.7 A defence to which crimes?

In English law, duress is not available where the statutory scheme is exhaustive or otherwise can be taken to preclude the defence, as is the case with controlled drugs,[114] or the protection of children,[115] or the control of dangerous dogs.[116] It is available to some forms of treason, but whether to all forms is unclear.[117] Otherwise the defence is available to all crimes, except murder and attempted murder. There is a longer list of exceptions in New Zealand law. So too under the Canadian Criminal Code – except some of those exceptions have now been struck down as unconstitutional.

There is some support for the notion that duress might be developed as a partial defence to murder,[118] while still a full defence to other crimes. That smacks of an unprincipled compromise; it seems morally arbitrary to draw a line there. The Law Commission rejected the suggestion,[119] primarily for the good reason that the arguments in favour of duress being any sort of a defence to murder – or, we might add, the rationale that duress be a defence at all – does not reveal any morally significant fault line which would allow the defence to be divided in this way.

I shall now argue that there is no good reason to exclude murder or attempted murder from the defence of duress by threats.

In *Dudley and Stephens*,[120] four shipwrecked sailors were cast adrift in a lifeboat without food or water or prospects of a timely rescue. To stay alive, two sailors killed and ate the cabin boy. They survived, were rescued and convicted of murder. The court rejected their plea of necessity (i.e. duress of circumstances). Three themes appear in the judgment of Lord Coleridge CJ, who gave the judgment of the court.

First, he said that the weight of learned opinion was against necessity as a defence to murder. But Walters says that this was really just a repetition of opinion

114 *Quayle* [2005] EWCA Crim 1415; *Altham* [2006] Crim LR 633.

115 *CS* [2012] EWCA Crim 389.

116 *Cichon v DPP* [1994] Crim LR 918.

117 Ormerod and Laird, *Smith & Hogan's Criminal Law*, 14th edn (Oxford: Oxford University Press, 2015) 406; Card, *Card, Cross and Jones, Criminal Law*, 21st edn (Oxford: Oxford University Press, 2014) 695; Jackson, *Criminal Law in Hong Kong* (Hong Kong: Hong Kong University Press, 2003).

118 Horder, *Asthworth's Principles of Criminal Law*, 8th edn (Oxford: Oxford University Press, 2016) 236; Allen, *Textbook on Criminal Law*, 13th edn (Oxford: Oxford University Press, 2015) 187; Card, *Card, Cross & Jones, Criminal Law*, 21st edn (Oxford: Oxford University Press, 2014) 694.

119 Law Com No 304 Pt 6.

120 (1884) 14 QBD 273.

going back to one author, Hale, as its source.[121] Lord Mackay made a similar point in *Howe*.[122] We have already cast doubt on the authority of Hale in Chapter 4.

Second, Lord Coleridge said that to allow the defence would mark an absolute divorce of law from morality. But as Simpson records, there was popular support for the defendants in *Dudley and Stephens*, and the Queen commuted their death sentence to a mere six months' labour, which was taken as vindication by the seafaring community.[123]

Third, Lord Coleridge said that there was the problem of selecting the victim. Why kill the cabin boy? We can identify some reasons: he was nearest to death, and had no family to support. And the defence of duress of circumstances is generally available despite the defendant himself choosing the crime of his own initiative – and hence also choosing the victim (if any).

Lord Mackay repeated the point in *Howe*, saying that no defendant had the right to choose one innocent life over another.[124] And yet, a person acting in self-defence can prefer his own life to that of his attacker, even where that other person is otherwise committing no crime.

Ward LJ put it this way in *Re A*: the policy of the law is to prevent one party being judge in his own cause of the value of his life over another's, and then being executioner as well.[125] However, a person killing under duress is not killing because his life is more valuable, all things considered; he is killing simply to stay alive himself.

In *Lynch*,[126] the House of Lords ruled by a majority that duress was a defence to murder as an accessory. In *Abbott*,[127] the Privy Council ruled that duress was not a defence to murder as principal. In *Howe*,[128] overruling *Lynch*, it was said definitively that duress is no defence to murder, whether the defendant was a principal or an accessory. Why? Lord Hailsham said:[129]

> I do not at all accept in relation to the defence of murder it is either good morals, good policy or good law to suggest … that the ordinary man of reasonable fortitude is not to be supposed to be capable of heroism if he is asked to take an innocent life rather than sacrifice his own. Doubtless in actual practice many will succumb … But many will not, and I do not believe that as a "concession to human frailty" the former should be exempt from liability to criminal sanctions if they do. I have known in my own lifetime of too

121 Walters, 'Murder Under Duress and Judicial Decision-making in the House of Lords' (1988) 8 LS 61.
122 [1987] AC 417, 449.
123 Simpson, *Cannibalism and the Common Law* (London: Hambledon Press, 1994).
124 [1987] AC 417, 456.
125 [2001] Fam 147, 200.
126 [1975] AC 653.
127 [1977] AC 755.
128 [1987] AC 417.
129 [1987] AC 417, 432.

> many acts of heroism by ordinary human beings of no more than ordinary fortitude to regard a law as either "just or humane" which withdraws the protection of the criminal law from the innocent victim and casts the cloak of protection upon the coward and the poltroon in the name of a "concession to human frailty".

He added to this that duress requires some proportionality between the threat and the crime committed, and that one human life was worth the same as another, so the defendant could not claim to be choosing the lesser evil. He suggested that there might instead be mitigation of sentence, an idea which has support elsewhere,[130] or use of the prerogative to reduce sentence (or, presumably, exonerate). However, as Norrie says, if conviction is retained for reasons of deterrence, then mitigation or pardon undermines that.[131]

The decision in *Howe* has received sustained criticism.[132] Lord Brandon in *Howe* declared the outcome unjust.[133] The principal objections are as follows:

First, heroism is not ordinary fortitude. Heroism goes above and beyond. A lack of heroism is not cowardice. Cowardice, even assuming it is a bad thing,[134] is the opposite end of the spectrum. Ordinary fortitude is in the middle. If many people would succumb, are they all cowards? Are all people to be divided into cowards and heroes? If many people would succumb, including perhaps even judges,[135] is this not a form of hypocrisy?[136] The current legal test is, assuredly, one of reasonable fortitude. This is not synonymous with heroism.

In Queensland, for the defence of emergency, the test explicitly asks whether an ordinary person possessing ordinary power of self-control could not reasonably be expected to act otherwise. And in the Canadian case of *Ruzic*, the court said explicitly that the defence of duress 'is designed for the common man, not for a community of saints or heroes'.[137]

Second, if one life is worth the same as another, as Lord Hailsham suggested, nevertheless killing one innocent victim to save the lives of multiple others

130 *Gotts* [1992] 2 AC 412, 424 (Lord Jauncey). Schopp says that duress should never be a defence; there should be a vindicating conviction, but a complete mitigation of punishment: *Justification Defenses and Just Convictions* (Cambridge: Cambridge University Press, 1998) 143–145. Wasik similarly says that duress should only go to mitigation: 'Duress and Criminal Responsibility' [1977] Crim LR 453.

131 Norrie, *Crime, Reason and History*, 3rd edn (Cambridge: Cambridge University Press, 2014) 222.

132 Milgate, 'Duress and the Criminal Law: Another About Turn by the House of Lords' [1988] Cambridge LJ 61; Walters, 'Murder Under Duress and Judicial Decision-making in the House of Lords' (1988) 8 LS 61.

133 [1987] AC 417, 438.

134 In some cultures, it is valued: Howell, 'To Be Angry Is Not to Be Human, But to Be Fearful Is: Chewong Concepts of Human Nature', in Howell and Willis (eds), *Societies at Peace* (Routledge, 1989).

135 Lord Coleridge admitted as much: *Dudley and Stephens* (1884) 14 QBD 273, 288.

136 Simester et al., *Simester and Sullivan's Criminal Law: Theory and Doctrine*, 5th edn (Oxford: Hart, 2013) 753.

137 [2001] 1 SCR 687, [40], a point repeated in *Aravena* [2015] ONCA 250, [64].

threatened with death might thereby warrant the defence being extended to murder after all. For example, in *Dudley and Stephens*, the death of one sustained three others.

Third, relying on administrative clemency seems cold comfort. It is said that a morally innocent person should not be left at the mercy of administrative discretion on a murder charge.[138] Of course, that depends on whether the rationale for duress casts the defendant as morally innocent. But other problems with administrative clemency remain:

In *Pommel*,[139] the court said that a prosecuting authority might prosecute after all, if it was not satisfied that the defendant was telling the truth; and then, if the defendant is vindicated and given an absolute discharge, he is still left with a criminal conviction which, for some purposes, would be recognised as such. And in *Lynch*,[140] Lord Wilberforce said that, even if the executive were minded to use the prerogative, without the defence being raised, the evidence might never come out, and certainly would not be tested in court under cross-examination. Also, he said that the risk of bogus defences was better safeguarded by the process of law than by inquiry by a government department.

In *Gotts*,[141] it was held that duress is no defence to attempted murder. That had been presaged in *Howe*, where Lord Griffiths had said that, if duress is no defence to murder, nor should it be to attempted murder, since attempted murder required an 'even more evil intent'.[142] This is because, he said, attempted murder requires an intent to kill, whereas murder requires only an intent to cause really serious injury. Lord Jauncey in *Gotts* agreed. But Lord Keith, dissenting, rejected the idea that attempt required a more evil intent. That ignores, he said, the very claim that the defendant was under duress. If the attempt fails, he said, the defendant is 'likely to be as relieved at the outcome as anyone'.

In *Ness*,[143] the court held that duress can be a defence to conspiracy to murder. Even though, we might note, that would also require an intent to (carry out the agreement to) kill. The court purported to draw a distinction between a mere agreement to kill, and an attempt to kill, the former still providing time for 'repentance, lack of opportunity and failure'. Now attempt requires an act which is more than merely preparatory.[144] But though the timescale is shortened, there is still the possibility of repentance, lack of opportunity and failure. Indeed, failure is probably why the crime is charged as an attempt, and not as actual murder.

And what about criminal damage with intent to endanger life?[145] Seemingly duress would be a defence there too.

138 Ormerod and Laird, *Smith & Hogan's Criminal Law*, 14th edn (Oxford: Oxford University Press, 2015) 408.
139 [1995] 2 Cr App R 607.
140 [1975] AC 653, 685.
141 [1992] 2 AC 412.
142 [1987] AC 417, 445.
143 [2011] Crim LR 645.
144 Criminal Attempts Act 1981, s 1.
145 Criminal Damage Act 1971, s 1(2).

So there seems an inconsistency between attempt, where there is no defence, and conspiracy, where there is a defence. (Indeed, the Australian case of *Qaumi*, below, noting that inconsistency, sought to allow the defence of duress to attempted murder after all.) And *Howe* lacks any persuasive reason for denying the defence to murder.

The Law Commission has recommended that duress be a defence to murder.[146] In Canada, the statutory exclusion of murder has since been struck down as unconstitutional. Duress is now also a defence to murder in some Australian jurisdictions. (Duress is also a defence to murder in France and Germany.[147]) In *Hasan*, Lord Bingham admitted that the logic of extending the defence to murder was 'irresistible'.[148] That logic hangs simply on the internal requirements of the defence: there must be no alternative action; the defendant must not have brought this upon themselves; and above all the defendant must act reasonably. It may be rare when killing is a reasonable response. But to preclude the debate from the outset risks a set of circumstances in which the law requires, in effect, that the defendant act *unreasonably*.

The position is well put by Lord Wilberforce in *Lynch*:[149]

> So I find no convincing reason, on principle, why, if a defence of duress in the criminal law exists at all, it should be absolutely excluded in murder charges whatever the nature of the charge; hard to establish, yes, in case of direct killing so hard that perhaps it will never be proved: but in other cases to be judged, strictly indeed, on the totality of facts.

So when might killing be defensible? Here is an example.[150] A defendant is chosen at random to drive terrorists to a killing. The defendant otherwise did not participate in the killing. Meanwhile, his wife and child are held at gunpoint. He is charged as an accessory. Surely a conviction for murder is unwarranted in those circumstances.

So far I have been discussing duress by threats. As for duress of circumstances, I shall argue below that a defendant under duress of circumstances should not be allowed to act upon another's person. That would obviously preclude killing them. However, the case law does reveal one rare exception, with its own distinctive justification:

If two or more people are virtually certain to suffer death imminently and together, from the same cause, but one or more could be saved only by killing a particular person in that group, then such killing would be lawful. (The killer does not have to be one of the group.) Formulating the principle this way also

146 Law Com No 304, Pt 6.

147 Reed, 'Duress and Normative Moral Excuse', in Reed et al. (eds), *General Defences in Criminal Law* (Farnham: Ashgate, 2014) 107–108.

148 [2005] UKHL 22, [21(1)].

149 [1975] AC 653, 681.

150 Based on true events: Allen, *Textbook on Criminal Law*, 13th edn (Oxford: Oxford University Press, 2015) 185.

reveals its underlying justification: if all life is otherwise going to be lost anyway, it is better to save at least some of that life.[151]

In such a case, the killer does not transfer any risk of their death onto an innocent victim, as concerned the court in *Howe*. Yes, they precipitate the victim's death, but the victim was going to die soon anyway and imminently. There is no problem (if indeed it is a problem) of selecting the victim, since only by killing a specific person will any life be saved. In *Dudley and Stephens*, there was perhaps no uniquely correct victim.

Another example is the case of *Re A (Children) (Conjoined twins: surgical separation)*.[152] There conjoined twins were taken to hospital. Without surgical separation, both would die. With separation, the weaker twin would certainly die, but the stronger twin would probably live. The hospital sought a declaration that separation would be lawful; it would otherwise be tortious, perhaps murder. The twins were too young to consent. The parents resisted the separation on religious grounds. Nevertheless, the declaration was given. We have already analysed, in Chapter 4, the reasons given by the court. But the outcome also supports my suggested approach: only by operating, and thereby killing the weaker twin, would any life be saved.

The requirement of a uniquely correct victim might be justified: if any three in a group of four could be saved by killing any one, then, we might say, the law ought not to cast its protection over whomever happens, arbitrarily, to be strongest or sneakiest. In order to exculpate something as serious as *killing*, the parties must show that there was simply no alternative.

What sort of alternative? In the American case of *Commonwealth v Holmes*,[153] where a lifeboat was overloaded and passengers thrown overboard, the court thought that the parties involved should have drawn lots. This was disapproved by the court in *Dudley and Stephens*.[154] But in some situations, drawing lots need not result in murder. For example, if there are four people but only enough food or water or medicine or life jackets or parachutes for three, the allocation of those necessaries could potentially be resolved consensually, even though it means one person will die. Such situations need not involve murder; it could be that the 'victim' simply accepts their death, not at the hands of another person, but through the agency of whatever danger they all faced, while allowing the others to effect their escape.

Having said this, we could make a bolder claim, that *Dudley and Stephens* was wrongly decided. Then a defence might be available even when there are several ways of producing a net saving of life. A defence might be available only if the

151 My views here were first expressed in 'Necessity and Murder' (2015) 79 Journal of Criminal Law 46. My position has been endorsed by Herring: *Criminal Law*, 7th edn (Oxford: Oxford University Press, 2016) 650. See too: Dennis, 'Duress, Murder and Criminal Responsibility' (1980) 96 LQR 208, 230.

152 [2001] Fam 147.

153 (1841) 26 Fed Cas 360.

154 (1884) 14 QBD 273, 285.

defendant chose the alternative which maximised the saving of life. Or perhaps a defence might be available whether or not the defendant made the best possible choice. All this would require a more robust acceptance that in nasty situations unpleasant events can play out along lines which are indeed morally arbitrary (e.g. according to the luck or strength of those involved). It would ensure that some life is saved when otherwise all life would have been lost.

At any rate, as I have defined the proposition, the death of the victim must save the lives of others imperilled *by the same cause*. It requires the victim and those who benefit from the killing to be 'in the same boat'. It only applies within one disaster; it does not allow one situation to be traded off against another. (For example, a doctor could not harvest organs from one healthy person to save the lives of several other people.) It is not simply about maximising life, broadly stated, but about maximising survival in one crisis. There are no lives to be valued and weighed in some utilitarian metric, nor incommensurable rights to be ranked, contrary to my criticisms in Chapter 4 of a defence of lesser evil necessity. Beyond the simple claim that it is better to save some life than lose all life, there is no further room for discretion or value judgements.

In summary, duress by threats in English law is currently no defence to murder or attempted murder. But none of the reasons given for that exclusion are persuasive, and other jurisdictions, like Canada and Australia, do extend the defence to murder. Duress of circumstances, however, should remain no defence to killing. But there is a principle, separate to any defence of duress or necessity, which might apply – the case where only by killing one person in a threatened group might any life in that group otherwise be saved.

5.8 Canadian law

We have already made comparison to foreign jurisdictions when discussing English law. That has been instructive. To avoid a piecemeal and scattered presentation of the foreign law, in these sections we consider them on their own terms, to see in full their comparative approaches. We begin in this section with Canadian law.

As for duress of circumstances:

In *Perka*,[155] the defendants were charged with importing cannabis. They said that they intended to import the drugs to Alaska, but were forced to put ashore in Canada when their ship suffered mechanical problems, worsening weather and a grounding. The majority recognised a defence of excusatory necessity (i.e. duress of circumstances). A retrial was ordered. The defence applied, said the court, when the defendant's behaviour was morally involuntary (more on which below).

In *Latimer*,[156] the defendant carried out what he considered to be a mercy killing of his severely disabled 12-year-old daughter. The defence was denied:

155 [1984] 2 SCR 232.
156 [2001] 1 SCR 3.

the defendant had the alternative course of 'struggling on', and the infliction of death to avoid manageable pain was not a proportionate response.[157]

The courts in *Perka* and *Latimer* expressed the defence of necessity in the following terms:

First, there must be urgent or imminent danger, 'when human instincts cry out for action and make a counsel of patience unreasonable'. But this requirement has surely been watered down by *Ruzic* and *Ryan*, below.

Second, there must be no reasonable legal alternative. This is appropriate, and consistent with English law.

Third, the harm inflicted must be less than (*Perka*), or at least proportionate to (*Latimer*), the danger avoided. But that too probably disappears once the defence is available to murder, again below. At any rate, it is surely the case that killing one person to avoid suffering death oneself is not a lesser harm. So it is probably more appropriate to say simply that the defendant's response was reasonable. And in this regard, the defendant must, said the court in *Perka*, show normal resistance to the pressure. In *Latimer*, the court said that this is to be judged objectively, but taking into account the situation and characteristics of the defendant, what it called a 'modified objective standard'.[158] This repeats the problems with English law, discussed above, without offering further solutions.

Also, in *Perka*, the court said that the fact that the defendant was acting illegally did not preclude the defence (that might lead to separate punishment). But prior fault does preclude the defence, it said, if the defendant foresaw or reasonably ought to have foreseen that his action would likely give rise to the necessity.

An example of prior fault is *Bartram*.[159] There the defendant broke into a trailer, claiming that he was a lost hiker in need of shelter. The defence of necessity was denied. He contributed to his own misfortune by driving off-road while intoxicated and wrecking his car. Also, he could have followed the road to safety (i.e. there were lawful alternatives), and there was no need for the level of ransacking done to the trailer (i.e. his response was not reasonable).

As for 'compulsion by threats', the Canadian Criminal Code, s 17 provides:

> A person who commits an offence under compulsion by threats of immediate death or bodily harm from a person who is present when the offence is committed is excused for committing the offence if the person believes that the threats will be carried out and if the person is not a party to a conspiracy or association whereby the person is subject to compulsion.

There then follows a long list of excluded crimes, including: treason, piracy, murder, attempted murder, sexual assault, forcible abduction, hostage taking, robbery, assault with a weapon, unlawfully causing bodily harm and arson.

157 Mercy killing was still murder in the English case of *Inglis* [2010] EWCA Crim 2637.

158 That approach was endorsed in *Hibbert* [1995] 2 SCR 973. In *Ruzic* [2001] 1 SCR 687, it was described as an 'objective-subjective standard'.

159 [2015] AJ No 1304.

In *Hibbert*,[160] the defendant was a secondary party to an attempted murder (and not the actual perpetrator of the shooting). The court said that s 17 applies only to perpetrators, not secondary parties, and the latter could rely on the common law defence of duress. This, said the court, was analogous to the defence of necessity, such that the two had the same 'juridical foundation' and were 'based on the same juristic principles'.

In *Ruzic*,[161] the defendant was charged with importing heroin. She said that she was under duress, because a man in Belgrade, where she lived in an apartment with her mother, had threatened harm to her mother if the defendant did not bring the heroin to Canada. This fact pattern did not satisfy the test in s 17, because the duressor was not present when the offence was committed. Nevertheless, the defendant was successful in striking down that requirement as unconstitutional.

The court's argument proceeded as follows: the defendant had a constitutional right not to be deprived of her liberty except in accordance with the principles of fundamental justice; moral involuntariness is such a principle; the defence of duress exculpates acts which were morally involuntary; the defendant's acts in *Ruzic* were morally involuntary, even though the duressor was not present when the defendant committed the crime; thus to the extent that the duressor's absence precluded resort to a plea of moral involuntariness or duress, it was unconstitutional.[162]

Note that the outcome in *Ruzic* effectively eliminates any requirement that the threatened harm will materialise imminently. The importation of drugs involved a passage of time during which harm to the mother was held in abeyance. (Whether the defendant had any reasonable alternative to complying with the duressor's demand is another matter.) And indeed in *Ryan*, as we shall see, the court said explicitly that any threat may be of future harm.

The approach of the court in *Ruzic* opened up the possibility of other aspects of s 17 being struck down. The exclusion for murder has been struck down on the basis that killing could also arise in circumstances which are morally involuntary.[163] So too the exclusions for robbery and assault with a weapon have been struck down.[164] In light of this, it must be doubted whether it remains valid to exclude automatically any of the crimes listed in s 17.

In *Ryan*,[165] the defendant was the victim of domestic abuse. She contracted a killing on her husband, but the hitman was an undercover officer. The court said that duress was only available when a defendant commits a crime under

160 [1995] 2 SCR 973.

161 [2001] 1 SCR 687.

162 See too *Nwanebu* [2014] BCL No 2530, where the defence was available to a person illegally entering Canada, via Germany, fleeing torture and death at the hands of Nigerian police, who were obviously not present at the time of the person entering Canada.

163 *Sheridan* [2010] OJ No 4884; *Aravena* [2015] ONCA 250.

164 *Fraser* [2002] NSJ No 400; *Allen* [2014] SKQB 402.

165 [2013] 1 SCR 14.

compulsion of a threat made for the purpose of compelling her to commit that crime. In other words, we might say, duress only applies to 'do this or else' demands. If the defendant is simply threatened, without the coercive 'or else' element, the only defence, said the court, is self-defence.

But that proceeds too quickly: if the defendant is under pressure, and acts against the source of that pressure, that would indeed be a focal instance of self-defence; but if a defendant is under pressure, and of their own initiative commits a crime to escape, presumably that would raise the plea of necessity / duress of circumstances.

The better explanation of *Ryan* might have been to say that the defendant had other alternatives to murdering her husband. If her abuse precluded her from seeing that, she might have instead a different defence based on mental impairment.

The court in *Ryan* explained that *Ruzic* did not simply strike out the offending words from s 17 but interpreted and supplemented what remained in light of the common law defence, so that the two forms were 'largely the same'. In other words, the statutory defence of compulsion by threats has largely been re-written to coincide with the common law defence of duress by threats – which, said the court in *Hibbert*, is itself aligned with the common law defence of necessity / duress of circumstances.

In effect, there is probably a single defence of duress, a blend of the common law and the criminal code. In *Ryan*, the court summarised the defence as follows:[166]

There must be an explicit or implicit threat of death or bodily harm against the defendant or a third person. (In English law, I have argued above for a wider range of recognised dangers.) The threat may be of future harm. The defendant must reasonably believe that the threat will be carried out (which is tidier than the English formulation of having 'good cause' to fear the threat).

Further, there must be a temporal connection between the threat and it being carried out: such that the threat was coercive when the crime was committed; and so as to preclude any alternative and safe avenue of escape. (This accords with my argument above in respect of English law, that imminence should not be viewed as a free-standing requirement, but as relevant to the inquiry whether there was a serious danger, and whether there might have been alternatives.)

Also, there must be proportionality between the harm threatened and the crime committed. This, and the possibility of escape, is to be evaluated on an objective-subjective standard, i.e. what might reasonably have appeared to someone with the defendant's characteristics. (Again, this merely paraphrases the problematic position found in English law, without offering further solutions.)

Finally, the defence is precluded if the defendant is party to a conspiracy or association of criminal activity whereby they are subject to compulsion and actually knew that coercion to commit an offence was a possible result. (So this proviso would not catch those consorting lawfully with criminals, like Baroness Hale's battered wife.)

166 [2013] 1 SCR 14, [55], [81].

5.9 New Zealand law

While there are naturally areas of overlap, in some important respects the law in New Zealand stands in contrast, especially to Canadian law.

Section 24 of the Crimes Act 1961 sets out the defence of compulsion:

> [A] person who commits an offence under compulsion by threats of immediate death or grievous bodily harm from a person who is present when the offence is committed is protected from criminal responsibility if he or she believes that the threats will be carried out and if he or she is not a party to any association or conspiracy whereby he or she is subject to compulsion.

Subsection 2 then sets out a long list of offences to which the defence of compulsion does not apply, including: treason, espionage, sabotage, piracy, murder, attempted murder, wounding and injuring with intent, abduction, kidnapping, robbery and arson.

In *IA*,[167] the court discussed the Canadian approach in *Ruzic*. Indeed, the facts were similar: the defendant in *IA* was charged with importing drugs, and pleaded that his family in Nigeria was otherwise threatened with harm.

The court noted that it had no power in New Zealand to strike down statutory provisions, and anyway there were differences between the New Zealand Bill of Rights and the Canadian Charter. It also rejected the notion of moral involuntariness (again, more on which below).

The court said that s 24 excluded any residual common law defence of duress or necessity based upon threats by another person. And its terms were to be read strictly. Accordingly, it did not apply on the facts of *IA*, where the duressor was not present when the offence was committed. In other words, the court reached an opposite outcome to *Ruzic*.

As for the list of excluded crimes, the court said that this was 'quintessentially' a policy question. Of course, they could say that, since the legislature had stated its position, unlike in England, and the courts could not strike it down, unlike in Canada. The court also said that, although 'a little crude', the list of precluded crimes ensured that the harm done was not disproportionate to the harm threatened. But then s 24 does not require the defendant to act reasonably, which, I suggested above, would obviate any need for a further test of proportionality.

And yet, the New Zealand courts have *added* to s 24: there must be no realistic choice other than to break the law; and the defence will not likely avail if there were reasonable opportunities to seek assistance or to escape.[168] (This is in line with English and Canadian law.)

In *Teichelman*,[169] the court said that the defence was directed at 'standover situations' where the defendant fears that instant death or grievous bodily harm

167 [2014] 1 NZLR 17.
168 *Witika* [1993] 2 NZLR 424; *Neho* [2013] NZAR 464; *Hay* [2015] NZAR 1426.
169 [1981] 2 NZLR 64.

will ensue if he does not do what he is told. So in *Richards*,[170] the defence was not available for a battered spouse when the abuser was not present at the time of the offence. Further, nothing less than a threat of grievous or really serious harm will suffice.[171] After all, that is what the statute says explicitly (though I have argued for a wider range of dangers to be recognised in English law).

In *Raroa*,[172] it was held that the defendant's belief need only be honest; whether there were reasonable grounds for the belief would of course go to credibility. This is more generous than the position in English and Canadian law, where a reasonable belief in the danger is needed, not a merely honest belief.

As for the defence of 'necessity' (i.e. duress of circumstances), in *Kapi v Ministry of Transport*,[173] the court said that, if it did exist, it required at least the following:

First, a belief, on reasonable grounds, of an imminent peril of death or serious injury. This is consistent with English and Canadian law; it stands in contrast to the merely honest belief needed to ground the defence of compulsion in New Zealand.

Second, no realistic choice but to commit the crime.

Third, the crime must be proportionate to the peril. Such a peril, said the court, could not arise out of duress by threats, which is the exclusive domain of s 24. Nevertheless, it is notable that all three elements of necessity are common also to compulsion.

The defence was held to exist in *Police v Kawiti*,[174] where the defendant, intoxicated and disqualified, drove herself to a hospital emergency department after being assaulted. In *Hutchinson*,[175] the court identified this defence as 'necessity arising out of duress of circumstances'. That court considered it an open question whether imminent peril meant immediate, as in s 24 (as the court seemed to prefer).[176] It also couched the defence in terms of requiring the peril to overbear the defendant's will.

Thus there are perhaps two main differences from English and Canadian law. First, the requirement of imminence, because New Zealand law, at least for duress by threats, is primarily and narrowly concerned with 'standover' situations. Second, a long list of excluded crimes. This the New Zealand courts seek to explain as ensuring proportionality between the danger and the crime committed to escape it. If that is the purpose, then it would be more honest, and indeed flexible, simply to require a proportionate response, as in Canadian law, or better yet just a reasonable response, as I have suggested for English law.

170 (CA 272/98).
171 *Mauriere* [2001] NZAR 431.
172 [1987] 2 NZLR 486.
173 (1991) 8 CRNZ 49 (CA). See too: *Nebo* [2013] NZAR 464.
174 [2000] 1 NZLR 117.
175 [2004] NZAR 303.
176 The English case of *Abdul-Hussain* suggested that 'imminent' gave greater flexibility than 'immediate', but the Hong Kong case of *Mbugua James Waigwa* (CACC 188/2009) suggested that both words had the same meaning.

5.10 Australian law

We begin with code jurisdictions:

In Queensland, s 31 of the Criminal Code provides that: a defendant is not criminally responsible when they act in order to save themselves or another, or their property,[177] from serious harm or detriment; inflicted by some person in a position to carry out the threat;[178] and the defendant reasonably believes that they are unable otherwise to escape the carrying out of the threat; and the crime committed is reasonably proportionate to the harm threatened. The defence does not apply to murder or grievous bodily harm. Nor does it apply where the defendant has, by entering into an unlawful association or conspiracy, rendered themselves liable to have such threats made to the person (but not to property?).

It is not sufficient that the crime was a reasonable means of escaping the threat if the defendant reasonably believed that there were other (presumably lawful, or less seriously criminal) reasonable means of escaping the threat.[179]

In Western Australia, s 32 of the Criminal Code provides that: a defendant is not criminally responsible when: they believe, on reasonable grounds, that a threat (any type?) has been made, and will be carried out, unless an offence is committed; and committing the offence is necessary to prevent the threat being carried out; and the crime is a reasonable response to the threat. But the defence does not apply when made by a person with whom the defendant voluntarily associates for the purpose of: doing an act of the kind in fact done, or prosecuting an unlawful purpose in which it is reasonably foreseeable that such a threat would be made.

Both Codes have a provision, in both cases under s 25, for emergencies. This defence expressly does not apply in circumstances covered by the sections on duress / compulsion. It applies when the defendant faces a sudden or extraordinary emergency. A sudden emergency is one which comes upon the defendant unexpectedly, catching them off-guard; whereas an extraordinary emergency is a situation of extreme gravity and unusual danger.[180] That would exclude continuous states of affairs, like the pain suffered by the defendant in the English case of *Quayle*, and, for that matter, the homelessness of *Southwark v Williams* (discussed in Chapter 4).

Thereafter, in Queensland, the question is whether an ordinary person possessing ordinary power of self-control could not reasonably be expected to act otherwise.

177 While the English criminal defence of duress only responds to dangers of death or serious personal injury, and so not damage to property, nevertheless under s 5(2)(b) of the Criminal Damage Act 1971, a defendant can destroy or damage another's property to protect their own.

178 Would this preclude the defence if, unknown to the defendant, the duressor had an unloaded gun? Surely the better position, consistent with the other jurisdictions, is whether the defendant believes, either honestly (as in New Zealand), or reasonably (as in England and Canada and Western Australia), that the duressor is able to carry out the threat.

179 *Smith* [2005] QCA 1.

180 *Johnson v State of Western Australia* [2009] WASCA 71, quoting Yeo, 'Necessity under the Griffith Code and the Common Law' (1991) 15 Criminal LJ 17.

In Western Australia, the question is whether the defendant believes, on reasonable grounds, that the emergency exists and that committing the crime is a necessary response; and whether the crime is a reasonable response.

In *Johnson v State of Western Australia*,[181] the defence was available when the defendant entered another's house without consent in order to help a friend whom he believed had been attacked with an axe. (We saw a similar permission in tort, in Chapter 4, with the New Zealand case of *Dehn*, and the American case of *Roberts*.) In *GV*,[182] the defence of emergency was available on a charge of dangerous driving when the defendant was fleeing a violent incident of road rage (like the English cases of *Willer* and *Conway*).

From all this, the following points are worthy of note.

First, these code jurisdictions seem to frame the relevant questions in objective terms: whether the defendant's belief or response was reasonable. This is clearer than the English and Canadian positions, which ask whether it would be reasonable for a person in the defendant's situation and with their relevant characteristics, without any convincing explanation of which characteristics should count.

Second, duress of circumstances explicitly only applies to sudden or extraordinary emergencies, and so to one-offs (as I suggested should be the case with English law).

In the Australian common law, the leading case on duress by threats is *Hurley and Murray*.[183] The dissenting judgment of Smith J has been regularly endorsed since, where he said:[184]

> Where the accused has been required to do the act charged against him (i) under a threat that death or grievous bodily harm will be inflicted unlawfully upon a human being if the accused fails to do the act and (ii) the circumstances were such that a person of ordinary firmness would have been likely to yield to the threat in the way the accused did and (iii) the threat was present and continuing, imminent and impending … and (iv) the accused reasonably apprehended that the threat would be carried out and (v) he was induced thereby to commit the crime charged and (vi) that crime was not murder,[185] nor any other crime so heinous as to be excepted from the doctrine and (vii) the accused did not, by fault[186] on his part when free from the duress, expose himself to its application and (viii) he had no means, with safety to himself, of preventing the execution of the threat, then the accused, in such circumstances at least, has a defence of duress.

181 [2009] WASCA 71.
182 [2006] QCA 394.
183 [1967] VR 526. See too the jury direction in *Abusafiah* (1991) 24 NSWLR 531, 544–545.
184 [1967] VR 526, 543.
185 Duress is now a defence to murder in Victoria: Crimes Act 1958 (Vic), s 9AG.
186 Once again, this might exonerate Baroness Hale's battered wife who remains with, or finds herself unable to leave, an abusive partner despite the likelihood of coercion by him. But the defence would be precluded if the defendant joined an illegal organisation: *Nguyen* [2008] NSWCCA 22, [40].

In that case, two escaped convicts took shelter in the defendant's home, holding his partner hostage while he was sent to Sydney to obtain a car. In such circumstances, said the judge, the threat to the partner was sufficiently imminent and impending.

The judge also confirmed that a threat to any person, not just to a closed list of people with a relationship to the defendant, might suffice to ground the plea of duress. (English law talks about a threat to someone for whom the defendant reasonably feels responsible, in order to preclude the officious intermeddler.)

Also, if the defendant had a reasonable opportunity to escape, then the defence is not available.[187] The courts have repeatedly acknowledged that going to the police will not always or necessarily provide the defendant with effective protection.[188] (Thereby siding with the English case of *Hudson* rather than *Hasan.*) That said, the defendant's mere belief that police protection would not be effective is insufficient, in the absence of good reasons to justify that belief.[189]

The ordinary person of reasonable firmness can be imbued with the characteristics of the defendant,[190] except perhaps the defendant's strength of mind,[191] but including, for example, that she suffers from battered woman syndrome.[192] This is again somewhat consistent with the position in English and Canadian law, but without further advance in identifying any convincing moral boundary to indicate which characteristics are relevant.

In *Qaumi*,[193] it was held that duress is a defence to attempted murder, otherwise noticing the inconsistency of allowing the defence for conspiracy to murder (as we discussed above). The only sensible line to draw, suggested the court, was where death actually resulted, thus separating murder from its inchoate counterparts.

As for laying oneself open to duress, again in *Qaumi*, the defence was held not to apply if the defendant voluntarily put themselves in a position where they knew, or ought to have known, that they might be forced by threats of violence to commit criminal offences ***of a similar kind*** to those that were in fact committed. (This is more generous to the defendant than the position in English law.)

The defence of duress only applies when the defendant is threatened by another person into committing the crime, rather than where the defendant commits a crime of their own initiative in order to avoid danger.[194] However, in such a case the defendant might still plead necessity as an alternative.[195]

187 *Lawrence* (1980) 32 ALR 72 (NSW).

188 *Lawrence* (1980) 32 ALR 72, 100; *Palazoff* (1986) 43 SASR 99, 110; *Brown* (1986) 43 SASR 33, 40 ('such situations must be considered to be the exception'); *Lorenz* [1998] ACTSC 81, [35]. See too: Criminal Code (NT), s 40(1)(d).

189 *Taiapa* [2009] HCA 53.

190 *Director of Public Prosecutions (Vic) v Parker (a pseudonym)* [2016] VSCA 101.

191 *Palazoff* (1986) 43 SASR 99, 109.

192 *Runjanjic* (1991) 56 SASR 114.

193 *Qaumi (No 64)* [2016] NSWSC 1269.

194 *Dawson* [1978] VR 536; *Lorenz* [1998] ACTSC 81, [38]–[41].

195 *Lorenz* [1998] ACTSC 81, [42]; referred to as 'duress of circumstances' by counsel in *Clarkson* [2007] NSWCCA 70, [87].

As for necessity:

In *Loughnan*,[196] Young CJ and King J seemingly endorsed Stephen's test of lesser evil necessity. I have already argued against adopting that test, in Chapter 4. The defence was said to require the following:

First, the crime must have been done only to avoid consequences which would have inflicted irreparable evil upon the defendant or others whom he was bound to protect. If this means that the defence is only available to a defendant who is under a legal duty to protect the person threatened, that seems unnecessarily strict, and is out of keeping with English law (and indeed the common law position in Australia on duress by threats).

Second, the defendant must honestly believe on reasonable grounds that he was placed in an urgent situation of imminent peril. But as to this, the court did seem to acknowledge that necessity might still permit acting now to avoid a future crime, if there was no other way of avoiding it.

Third, the response must be proportionate: would a reasonable man in the same position have considered that he had any alternative to doing what the defendant did? Both this and the previous element appear, sensibly, to be couched in straightforwardly objective terms.

In *Rogers*,[197] the test was framed as follows: whether the defendant acted as he did, honestly believing, on reasonable grounds, that his crime was necessary in order to avoid threatened death or serious injury. This is noticeably not a test of lesser evil necessity, and for that reason it is a far preferable approach. Although briefly stated, it suggests a correlation with the defences in England and Canada.

The court said that imminence of threat was not a required ingredient of the defence. Rather, it was a matter of evidence which went to the question of the defendant's honest and reasonable belief that it was necessary to commit the crime (rather than, perhaps, adopt an alternative and lawful course of action). This too is consistent with Canadian law, and what I have suggested for English law. However, the importance of imminence has reappeared in the Australian case law subsequently.[198]

Thus, as to Australian common law, duress by threats seems much like its English and Canadian equivalents. As to duress of circumstances, the more welcome authority is *Rogers*, rather than *Loughnan* which, unpromisingly, seems to prefer a test of lesser evil necessity.

Finally, we consider federal law. From the Criminal Code Act 1995 (Cth), which has also been adopted to some extent in the Australian Capital Territory and the Northern Territory, the Criminal Code provides for a defence of duress (s 10.2) and emergency (s 10.3).

196 [1981] VR 443. Sudden or extraordinary emergency is now a statutory defence to murder in Victoria: Crimes Act 1958 (Vic), s 9AI. For a recent and fulsome review of the authorities, see *Leichhardt Council v Geitonia Pty Ltd (No 6)* [2015] NSWLEC 51, [136]–[153].

197 (1996) 86 A Crim R 542 (NSW).

198 *Lorenz* [1998] ACTSC 81; *Bayley v Police* [2007] SASC 411, [53].

As for duress, the defence applies if the defendant reasonably believes that: a threat has been made that will be carried out unless an offence is committed; and there is no reasonable way that the threat can be rendered ineffective; the conduct is a reasonable response to the threat. Seemingly, any threat will suffice, even a threat to do something lawful.[199] Potentially that extends the defence considerably beyond threats of death or serious injury.

As for what constitutes a 'reasonable belief' on the part of the defendant, the majority in *Oblach* held that the actual belief held by the defendant must be objectively justifiable, taking into account the objective circumstances of the defendant, but not their personal circumstances, or the circumstances as the defendant perceived them to be.[200] That appears to be a more straightforwardly objective approach than the common law approach which seeks to take into account the defendant's characteristics. The minority in *Oblach* went further, suggesting it imposed a test of what a reasonable person might believe; and in relation to the defence of emergency (below), so too did the court in *Luong*.[201]

The defence of duress does not apply if the threat is made by a person with whom the person under duress is voluntarily associating for the purpose of carrying out conduct of the kind actually carried out. There are two points to note here.

First, the present tense indicates that the defence can be pleaded by a defendant who has ceased their involvement with any criminal gang. Again, we might say that there must have been a genuine period of disassociation before the defendant can resort to a defence of duress by prior colleagues.

Second, this is seemingly a very generous test: it is not about associating with those who might foreseeably coerce, or even coerce to commit crimes, or even coerce to commit crimes of this sort; rather, it is about associating for the purpose of committing crimes of this sort. Thus it seems that the defence might apply where a defendant voluntarily associated with criminals known to coerce others into committing crimes, as long as the defendant joined that gang for other purposes. That seems unduly generous to those who choose to join criminal conspiracies.

As for emergency, the defendant is not criminally responsible if they reasonably believe that: circumstances of sudden or extraordinary emergency exist; committing the offence is the only reasonable way to deal with the emergency; the conduct is a reasonable response to the emergency.

As Odgers notes, if it is reasonable for the defendant to believe that the only reasonable way to deal with the emergency is to commit the offence, it is difficult to imagine any circumstances in which it would not be reasonable to believe that their

199 Odgers, *Principles of Federal Criminal Law*, 3rd edn (Pyrmont NSW: Lawbook Co, 2015) [10.2.190].

200 *Oblach* (2005) 65 NSWLR 75; see too *Morris* [2006] WASCA 142; *Mirzazadeh v R* [2016] NSWCCA 65, [52].

201 *Luong v DPP (Cth)* [2013] VSCA 296, [88], referring to s 8.4(2) of the Code (which itself deals with the defence of intoxication).

conduct in committing the offence is a reasonable response to the emergency.[202] In other words, the third requirement adds nothing. However, the defence seemingly only applies if committing the crime was the *only* reasonable response. If another reasonable response would have been lawful, presumably that should indeed be the preferred course of action. But what if there are various criminal responses, all reasonable, and none inherently more risky than another?

5.11 The rationale for criminal duress

Shortly I shall suggest that duress of circumstances, like the tortious defence of necessity, is grounded in property theory, while duress by threats hinges upon the moral regard maintained for the third-party victim. First, however, we shall consider the principal rival theories for why criminal law recognises a defence of duress.

(I) We begin with theories of justification and excuse.

Since Fletcher reanimated the debate,[203] some authors seek to categorise defences as either justifications or excuses. In general terms, an act is justified when it is the right thing to do, or perhaps at least when its commission is tolerable, whereas a person is excused when not sufficiently blameworthy.

Many disclaim the value of any such distinction.[204] And in none of the cases considered in this chapter has any classification had any consequence.[205] Nevertheless, some authors do suggest that there may be the following consequences.[206]

First, it is said, justified violence cannot be lawfully resisted.

202 Odgers, *Principles of Federal Criminal Law*, 3rd edn (Pyrmont NSW: Lawbook Co, 2015) [10.3.230].

203 Fletcher, *Rethinking Criminal Law* (Little, Brown & Co, 1978) ch 10.

204 Simester et al., *Simester and Sullivan's Criminal Law: Theory and Doctrine*, 5th edn (Oxford: Hart, 2013) 673; Horder, *Ashworth's Principles of Criminal Law*, 8th edn (Oxford: Oxford University Press, 2016) 147–148, 227; Wilson, *Criminal Law*, 5th edn (Harlow: Pearson, 2014) 197, 202; Norrie, *Crime, Reason and History*, 3rd edn (Cambridge: Cambridge University Press, 2014) 231–233; Simester, 'On Justifications and Excuses', in Zedner and Roberts (eds), *Principles and Values in Criminal Law and Criminal Justice* (Oxford: Oxford University Press, 2012); Greenawalt, 'The Perplexing Borders of Justification and Excuse' (1984) 84 Columbia LR 1897; Duff, 'Rethinking Justifications' (2004) 39 Tulsa LR 829; Gur-Ayre, 'Should the Criminal Law Distinguish Between Necessity as a Justification and Necessity as an Excuse?' (1986) 102 LQR 71; Smith, J C, *Justification and Excuse in the Criminal Law* (London: Stevens & Sons, 1989) ch 1; *Re A* [2001] Fam 147, 237 (Brooke LJ), 253 (Robert Walker LJ).

205 In the Canadian case of *Perka*, the court carefully characterised necessity / duress of circumstances as an excuse. Yet even there it seemingly had no consequence. The authors of *Smith & Hogan* suggest that it merely made the court feel better to call it an excuse: Ormerod and Laird, *Smith & Hogan's Criminal Law*, 14th edn (Oxford: Oxford University Press, 2015) 423.

206 Herring, *Criminal Law*, 7th edn (Oxford: Oxford University Press, 2016) 703; Keating et al., *Clarkson & Keating: Criminal Law*, 8th edn (London: Sweet & Maxwell, 2014) 304–305; Brudner, 'A Theory of Necessity' (1987) 7 OJLS 338, 363; Jackson, *Criminal Law in Hong Kong* (Hong Kong: Hong Kong University Press, 2003); Wilson, *Criminal Law*, 5th edn (Harlow: Pearson, 2014) 197–198.

Let us consider an example. A attacks B. B can defend herself. Self-defence is usually taken to be a justification. True, A cannot resist that defence, but that is not simply because self-defence is characterised as a justification. It is because A is committing battery, and obviously cannot compound that offence by using further force to defeat B from preventing that battery. If A dislikes the violent defence, all A has to do is desist in attack, at which point B has nothing to defend against and must also desist.[207]

What if B mistakenly believes that she is being attacked, and so acts in mistaken self-defence? Surely A is not obliged to endure a beating, or even death, on account of another's mistake. But then some say that a mistake downgrades a justification to an excuse (whereupon resistance would be lawful).[208] That sounds like definitional fiat, simply to produce a desired outcome. Others take the view that some mistakes can be justified.[209] Still others say it is possible for both parties to a conflict to be justified.[210]

Second, it is said, there is no liability for assisting a justified actor.

So for example, if B is defending herself, then C can assist. But again, not because B's conduct is characterised as a justification. C can assist only where they have their own defence, such as public defence or preventing a crime.[211] There is no such thing as being an accessory to a defence. Just because B has a defence, it does not follow that C can use it parasitically. Defences are personal and not transferrable.[212] If C joined the affray simply for the thrill of the fight, they would surely have no defence.[213]

So, whether justification or excuse, the courts have attached no consequences, and the arguments in favour of automatic consequences are not persuasive. There are still further controversies:

The above suggested consequences are premised on the idea that justifications are hierarchically superior to excuses.[214] But others say that there is no reason to

207 See too: Clarkson, 'Necessary Action: A New Defence' [2004] Crim LR 81, 86–87.

208 Herring, *Criminal Law*, 8th edn (Basingstoke: Macmillan, 2013) 296; Westen and Mangiafico, 'The Criminal Defense of Duress: A Justification, Not an Excuse – And Why It Matters' (2003) 6 Buffalo Crim LR 833, 877; Robinson, 'Criminal Law Defenses: A Systematic Analysis' (1982) 82 Columbia LR 199, 239; Williams, 'The Theory of Excuses' [1982] Crim LR 732, 740.

209 Greenawalt, 'The Perplexing Borders of Justification and Excuse' (1984) 84 Columbia LR 1897, 1908; Tadros, *Criminal Responsibility* (Oxford: Oxford University Press, 2007) ch 10; Goudkamp, *Tort Law Defences* (Oxford: Hart, 2013) 97.

210 Simester et al., *Simester and Sullivan's Criminal Law: Theory and Doctrine*, 5th edn (Oxford: Hart, 2013) 675–676; Glazebrook, 'The Necessity Plea in English Criminal Law' (1972) 30 Cambridge LJ 87, 93; Dressler, 'New Thoughts about the Concept of Justification in the Criminal Law' (1984) 32 UCLA LR 61, 88–90; Tadros, *Criminal Responsibility* (Oxford: Oxford University Press, 2007) 291; Husak, 'Conflict of Justifications' (1999) 18 Law & Phil 41.

211 See too: Tadros, *Criminal Responsibility* (Oxford: Oxford University Press, 2007) 291.

212 See too: Goudkamp, *Tort Law Defences* (Oxford: Hart, 2013) 143.

213 See too: *Dadson* (1850) 14 JP 754.

214 Gardner, J, 'Justifications and Reasons', in Simester and Smith (eds), *Harm and Culpability* (Oxford: Clarendon Press, 1996) 122.

suppose any hierarchy.[215] And some say that there are other defence classifications as well: for example, there are exemptions, like insanity, and public policy defences, like testimonial immunity of witnesses, so defences need not fall into a binary hierarchy anyway.[216]

And what of necessity and duress? Most suggest that necessity can be a justification,[217] seemingly by definition, at least where the defendant chooses the lesser of two evils. But another view suggests that, unlike choosing between equal goods (when there is no right answer), it is only an excuse to choose between lesser evils.[218] What is more, while duress is often considered an excuse,[219] some think it instead a justification,[220] and others that it can be either a justification or an excuse depending on the facts.[221] Yet others suggest that the defence of duress eschews any such categorisation.[222]

There is little guidance here, only controversy. And whether we were to label duress an excuse or a justification, we still have no reason to recognise it in the first place.

(II) Duress is often said to be a concession to human frailty or weakness.[223] I will dispute this below. But certainly it is not a concession to frailty *simpliciter*,

215 Husak, 'On the Supposed Priority of Justification to Excuse' (2005) 24 Law & Phil 557; Simester, 'On Justifications and Excuses', in Zedner and Roberts (eds), *Principles and Values in Criminal Law and Criminal Justice* (Oxford: Oxford University Press, 2012) 104.

216 Yet another approach is to replace justification and excuse with an alternative binary categorisation of contextual permission and mental impairment: Colvin, 'Exculpatory Defences in Criminal Law' (1990) 10 OJLS 381.

217 Allen, *Textbook on Criminal Law*, 13th edn (Oxford: Oxford University Press, 2015) 188; Card, *Card, Cross and Jones, Criminal Law*, 21st edn (Oxford: Oxford University Press, 2014) 715; Jackson, *Criminal Law in Hong Kong* (Hong Kong: Hong Kong University Press, 2003); Williams, 'The Theory of Excuses' [1982] Crim LR 732, 740; Alldridge, 'The Coherence of Defences' [1983] Crim LR 665, 666.

218 Teichman, *Pacifism and the Just War* (Oxford: Basil Blackwell, 1986) 103.

219 Ormerod and Laird, *Smith & Hogan's Criminal Law*, 14th edn (Oxford: Oxford University Press, 2015) 389 n 37; Allen, *Textbook on Criminal Law*, 13th edn (Oxford: Oxford University Press, 2015) 181, 182; Keating et al., *Clarkson & Keating: Criminal Law*, 8th edn (London: Sweet & Maxwell, 2014) 301; Jackson, *Criminal Law in Hong Kong* (Hong Kong: Hong Kong University Press, 2003); Alldridge, 'The Coherence of Defences' [1983] Crim LR 665, 667; *Hasan* [2005] UKHL 22, [18] (Lord Bingham).

220 Westen and Mangiafico, 'The Criminal Defense of Duress: A Justification, Not an Excuse – And Why It Matters' (2003) 6 Buffalo Crim LR 833. See too: Duff, 'Rule-Violations and Wrongdoings', in Shute and Simester (eds), *Criminal Law Theory* (Oxford: Oxford University Press, 2002) 63–64; Horder, 'Self-Defence, Necessity and Duress: Understanding the Relationship' (1998) 11 Can J Law & Juris 143, 163.

221 Wilson, *Criminal Law*, 5th edn (Harlow: Pearson, 2014) 247, 257; Herring, *Criminal Law*, 8th edn (Basingstoke: Macmillan, 2013) 297–298; Simester et al., *Simester and Sullivan's Criminal Law: Theory and Doctrine*, 5th edn (Oxford: Hart, 2013) 676–677, 739–740; Greenawalt, 'The Perplexing Borders of Justification and Excuse' (1984) 84 Columbia LR 1897, 1912.

222 Keating et al., *Clarkson & Keating: Criminal Law*, 8th edn (London: Sweet & Maxwell, 2014) 356; Dennis, 'On Necessity as a Defence to Crime' (2009) 2 Crim Law & Phil 29; Chan and Simester, 'Duress, Necessity: How Many Defences?' (2005) 16 King's LJ 121, 123.

223 *Howe* [1987] AC 417; *Perka* [1984] 2 SCR 232; *Mirzazadeh v R* [2016] NSWCCA 65, [40], [60].

otherwise the more frail the defendant, the more readily the defence would be available. That is inconsistent with the case law which tends to hold the defendant to a standard of reasonable fortitude. And even if duress were about human frailty, why make the concession? For example, temptation is a human weakness, yet it affords no criminal defence. So why should duress be a defence?

(III) Some resort to character theory, which, in broad terms, says that criminal law responds to bad character. Duress, it is said, tells us nothing bad about the defendant's character, only that in response to a crisis, they behaved not unreasonably, just as other ordinary and decent people might.[224]

But character theory faces difficulties. For example, a one-off killing, statistically out of character, is still murder. So what does a one-off episode of coercion disclose? Another approach, that each of our individual acts reveals our character,[225] however previously latent, smacks of an *ex post* rationalisation. It tends to an unpersuasive fatalism: everything we do, we will be told afterwards, was previously written in our character.[226] Further, if I am cowardly one year, courageous the next, what is my settled character? Alternatively, if we accept that character changes, how can we identify something sufficiently continuous and worthy of the name 'character' in a single act?

Some prefer choice theory, which, in general terms, says that we should not blame or punish people who had no choice. This tends towards supposing an active deliberation; yet we still punish crimes committed spontaneously.[227] And a defendant under duress can choose, if they wish, to suffer the consequences. Alternatively, we might consider it unfair to punish someone who had not the fair opportunity to conform their behaviour.[228] But that turns on what we define as a 'fair opportunity'. Do drug addicts or the socially excluded have a fair opportunity? In truth, we only recognise some constraining situations as exculpating. So why duress?

(IV) Some of the cases talk of the overborne will.[229] For example: 'the will of the accused has been overborne by threats . . . so that the commission of the alleged offence was no longer the voluntary act of the accused'.[230] But all this is euphemism.

224 Wilson, 'The Filtering Role of Crisis in the Constitution of Criminal Excuses' (2004) 17 Can J Law & Juris 387; Wilson, *Criminal Law*, 5th edn (Harlow: Pearson, 2014) 196; Wilson, 'The Structure of Criminal Defences' [2005] Crim LR 108.

225 Duff, 'Choice, Character and Criminal Liability' (1993) 12 Law & Phil 345, 376–379; Gardner, S, 'The Gist of Excuses' (1998) 1 Buffalo Crim LR 575, 577.

226 An idea Diderot caricatured in *Jacques the Fatalist and His Master* (1796).

227 Horder, 'Criminal Culpability: The Possibility of a General Theory' (1993) 12 Law & Phil 193, 201.

228 Hart, *Punishment and Responsibility* (Oxford: Oxford University Press, 2008) 181. On combining choice and character theory, see: Horder, 'Criminal Culpability: The Possibility of a General Theory' (1993) 12 Law & Phil 193; Duff, 'Choice, Character and Criminal Liability' (1993) 12 Law & Phil 345; Tadros, *Criminal Responsibility* (Oxford: Oxford University Press, 2007) ch 11; Parry, 'The Virtue of Necessity: Reshaping Culpability and the Rule of Law' (1999) 36 Houston LR 397.

229 *Goldie Anne C* [2013] EWCA Crim 1472, [51]; *Graham* [1982] 1 All ER 801, 806; *Abdul-Hussain* [1999] Crim LR 570; *Ortiz* (1986) 83 Cr App R 173; *N* [2007] EWCA Crim 3479, [12]; *Re A* [2001] Fam 147, 236; *Hutchinson* [2004] NZAR 303.

230 *Hudson* [1971] 2 QB 202, 206.

There is no suggestion that the defendant must be acting physically involuntarily, for example in the sense of automatism.[231] At any rate, the will, whatever that might be, is not overborne, since the defendant still commits a crime with the requisite *mens rea*. (We saw in Chapter 3 how contractual duress similarly came to abandon talk of the overborne will.)

In the Canadian case of *Perka*, the court characterised the defence of necessity (i.e. duress of circumstances) as based upon moral involuntariness. The court said:

> [The defence] rests on a realistic assessment of human weakness, recognizing that a liberal and humane criminal law cannot hold people to the strict obedience of laws in emergency situations where normal human instincts, whether of self-preservation or of altruism, overwhelmingly impel disobedience ... [The defendant's] act is not a "voluntary" one. His "choice" to break the law is no true choice at all; it is remorselessly compelled by normal human instincts. This sort of involuntarism is often described as "moral or normative involuntariness".

When endorsing this notion of moral involuntariness, the court in *Ruzic* reasoned from physical involuntariness. But as Yeo says, physical involuntariness is total, whereas moral involuntariness still involves a choice, even if an unpalatable one.[232] It is not truly involuntary. Indeed, as Berger points out, true involuntariness would contradict the very test of duress, which still requires the defendant to respond reasonably to the danger.[233] How can a defendant fairly be required involuntarily to produce reasonable conduct?

What is more, the court in *Ruzic* acknowledged that what is morally involuntary is not necessarily free of blame. It is not, said the court, synonymous with moral innocence. So, we might ask, why exculpate after all?

The court in *Ruzic* said that a defendant under duress has no 'real' choice. But what does amount to a real choice? The following statement from the court is particularly telling:[234]

> Only voluntary conduct – behaviour that is the product of a free will and controlled body, unhindered by external constraints – should attract the penalty and stigma of criminal liability.

But most of our choices have 'external constraints', from the basic, like how much money we have to spend, to the complex, like the social opportunities which

231 McSherry and Naylor, *Australian Criminal Laws* (Melbourne: Oxford University Press, 2004) 557.

232 Yeo, 'Challenging Moral Involuntariness as a Principle of Fundamental Justice' (2003) 28 Queen's LJ 335, 346.

233 Berger, 'Emotions and Veil of Voluntarism: The Loss of Judgment in Canadian Criminal Defences' (2006) 51 McGill LJ 99, 108.

234 [2001] 1 SCR 687, [47].

reflect the circumstances of our birth and education. As we saw in Chapter 3, contract law openly acknowledges this, when it says that not every constraint or pressure, even overwhelming ones, is sufficient to invoke a plea of duress. There are degrees of pressure. As the New Zealand court said in *IA*:[235]

> [We] do not accept that recognition of moral involuntariness is a principle of fundamental justice ... Involuntariness involves questions of degree and is not easily susceptible to a binary analysis under which actions are either voluntary (and punishable) or involuntary (and not punishable).

In short, overborne will and moral involuntariness are euphemisms which thereby fail to provide the specific detail necessary to explain why we recognise duress as a criminal defence.

The better reason for recognising a criminal defence of duress by threats is as follows.

First, the defendant has been coerced. As we saw in Chapter 1, coercion is wrong to the extent that it forces a complainant to change their behaviour for the selfish reasons of the accused. This denies the complainant the freedom or autonomy to choose their own goals. It also denies them the dignity of an equal status, because it fails to respect them as having the capacity to choose such goals. And it deprives them of the personal fulfilment which comes from using or developing that capacity.

Second, any person who seeks to avoid death or serious injury, to themselves or others, acts upon a vital impulse that is surely as constitutive of human nature as any other characteristic. Life is the fundamental baseline we all share in common. It is condescending at best, ignorant at worst, to call such behaviour weakness or cowardice, when it arises from the very well-spring of our existence and reflects how much we cherish life – indeed, that we are creatures of life.

Third, let us not forget the structural pattern of the defence: the defendant did not bring this upon themselves; they had no lawful alternative; their response, even given their impeccable motivation, must be reasonable, as determined by a jury, in theory a reflection of social values.

All this might give us considerable sympathy for the duressee. To this extent, there may be some correlation with character theory, at least to the extent that we have not yet identified any cause for moral blame of the duressee, or moral involuntariness, in as much as we talk about acting upon basic human nature. But these theories, on their own terms, have problems, as we have seen. And sympathy cannot be a free pass to crime.

The tipping point comes when we appreciate that a defence of duress by threats still respects the third-party victim (upon whose person or property the duressee acts). This is what enables us to extend a defence of duress by threats.

235 [2014] 1 NZLR 17, [20].

What happens to the victim remains criminally proscribed. The duressor will be liable for procuring the crime,[236] or for encouraging it.[237] This proscription respects the victim. The deterrent effect of the criminal law continues to protect the victim. And subsequent prosecution of the duressor is still available to punish transgression and so vindicate the victim.

More than that, it is important to understand the relative moral status of both the duressee and their victim. It may be that the duressor has threatened the duressee with harm. But this is done to procure a crime against the victim. Both the duressee and the third-party victim are victims of the duressor. The duressee is not, properly speaking, transferring any risk of harm onto the victim. This is because the duressor is not threatening the duressee with harm for no reason, as if harm to the duressee were in itself the end result sought by the duressor. Rather, the intention of the duressor throughout is to commit the crime against the victim. If anything, the victim is the primary target. The duressee is a means to an end, threatened into action.

Duress of circumstances is different. Yes, the defendant will have the same motivation, in acting to preserve life; and again, they will not be the author of their predicament, and will respond reasonably, without lawful alternative. But they are not a victim of coercion. And often, the danger they face is not itself criminally proscribed. More than that, the defendant is the primary person afflicted. In the natural course of events, the victim would not ordinarily have been involved. The defendant is now transferring the risk, which was originally theirs alone, onto a third-party victim. Since the crime was committed on the initiative of the defendant, there seems little prospect of otherwise attaching criminal liability to another person or 'duressor' (at least, without doing violence to principles of causation). The defence of duress of circumstances usually precludes any likelihood of the victim being vindicated.

We need a different justification for the defence of duress of circumstances. For this, we can turn back to tort law, which recognises a defence of necessity, and in terms which are substantially the same as the criminal defence of duress of circumstances. Indeed, the rationale for the tortious defence applies equally in the criminal context. As we saw in Chapter 4, a person in necessity making use of another's property does not traverse any property rights, but is free to act as upon any property in its natural state. It is this necessity proviso which justifies the institution of private property, and an owner's ability otherwise to exclude others. Alternatively, property rights are derivative of – they only exist to support – personality rights, and so have to yield when the latter are threatened by death or serious injury.

Note that this property theory is also available to someone who acts upon another's property under duress by threats. But it only applies to acting upon another's property, hence the need for duress by threats to find a further justification for acting upon another's person.

236 Accessories and Abettors Act 1861, s 8.
237 Serious Crime Act 2007, s 44.

Thus duress of circumstances cannot justify acting upon another's person, only their property. This would otherwise treat the other person merely as a means, in this case, a tool for self-preservation. (We noted how using another solely as a means is wrong, in Chapter 4 in the context of tortious necessity, and in Chapter 2 in the context of unconscionable bargain.) In none of the cases considered in this chapter has the defence of duress of circumstances been applied to crimes against the person.

What are the consequences, in terms of resistance and assistance?

In terms of resistance, it follows that a property owner cannot resist a defendant who acts upon 'their' property under genuine duress; a property owner cannot exclude others in necessity. (A similar conclusion arises with tortious necessity, as we saw.) As for duress by threats, if a defendant acts upon a victim's person, I see no reason why that victim cannot defend themselves, just as they might had the duressor acted against them directly. There is nothing in the law of self-defence which would seem to preclude that outcome.

As for assistance, a defendant who acts under duress may be assisted by another only if that other person has their own defence. That defence might also be duress, because a party can plead duress when they act because of dangers to others.

5.12 An objective standard?

Should we hold the defendant to an objective or subjective or hybrid standard? This is relevant to a number of the elements of the defence of duress.

Should we take into account the defendant's personal characteristics when assessing the reasonableness of their response, as in English and Canadian law? Given that it seems morally arbitrary which characteristics we take into account, a normative standard might be thought appropriate.

Should the defendant perceive the threat honestly, as in New Zealand law, or also reasonably, as in English law? Some authors suggest that the test should be subjective.[238] The defendant, it is said, may have been unduly credulous or stupid, but they are no more blameworthy than a person whose fear is based on reasonable grounds.[239] But this is not accurate. They may be no less fearful than the reasonable person, but it is an open question whether we can blame them for being credulous or stupid (let alone *unduly* credulous).

Should the question of lawful alternatives or escape be judged by what the defendant actually appreciated, or what they ought reasonably to have appreciated? Again, it is said, if the defendant is not aware of the opportunity to escape, they should not be penalised for their stupidity or slow-wittedness.[240] But this is

238 Ormerod and Laird, *Smith & Hogan's Criminal Law*, 14th edn (Oxford: Oxford University Press, 2015) 394; Wasik, 'Duress and Criminal Responsibility' [1977] Crim LR 453, 463.

239 Elliott, 'Necessity, Duress and Self-defence' [1989] Crim LR 611, 615; Ormerod and Laird, *Smith & Hogan's Criminal Law*, 14th edn (Oxford: Oxford University Press, 2015) 394.

240 Ormerod and Laird, *Smith & Hogan's Criminal Law*, 14th edn (Oxford: Oxford University Press, 2015) 401.

no more accurate. The defendant is not being penalised for their stupidity; they are being convicted for committing a crime against an innocent third party. It is otherwise no defence in criminal law that a defendant only committed the crime because they were too stupid to realise they had lawful alternatives.

While the trend in criminal law generally is towards a subjective standard, nevertheless in duress, an objective standard is defensible.

First, if part of the rationale for duress is that the defendant has reacted to a situation in a way consistent with human nature, that is a claim that they acted according to a common or generalised standard.

Second, for duress by threats, the claim is that the defendant is also a victim. That rationale would tend to suggest the need for an actual danger. So too with duress of circumstances: actual necessity is the proviso which allows a person in need to use property from which they are otherwise excluded by private rights. Requiring instead that the defendant might react to what they reasonably perceive to be a danger is already an allowance.[241] It would be a double concession to allow a defendant to react to a danger merely honestly perceived.

Third, for self-defence it suffices that the defendant perceived a threat honestly, even if unreasonably. But with self-defence, the defendant is acting against the perceived threat. In contrast, with duress, the third-party victim is never a threat. Even where the defendant is mistaken as to the need to act, nevertheless they always appreciate that the victim is not the source, but an innocent third party. Extra care should be required before inflicting harm in those circumstances.

5.13 Conclusions

All jurisdictions considered in this chapter recognise a defence of duress on similar terms: there must be a grave threat such as death or serious injury; which the defendant has not brought upon themselves; when there is an absence of alternatives or escape; and the defendant's response must conform to some standard of reasonable behaviour.

The rationale for the defence of duress is best understood as follows.

First, any person who seeks to avoid death or serious injury, to themselves or others, acts upon a vital impulse that is surely as constitutive of human nature as any other characteristic. This suggests conformity to a universalised (i.e. objective rather than subjective or hybrid) standard of behaviour. But an impeccable motivation, though an important part of the story, does not give a free pass to crime.

Second, with duress by threats, the defendant's position is morally strengthened by the fact that they too are a victim of the duressor, no less than the third party they act upon. And the plight of the third-party victim is acknowledged,

241 It is an appropriate allowance. The criminal defence must surely allow a defendant to respond to a gun against their head, even if they are reasonably ignorant that the gun is unloaded. But although criminal liability is avoided, tortious liability will remain in the absence of an actual danger (see Chapter 4).

for the criminal law continues to proscribe what the duressor does, and holds the duressor accountable for procuring the harm to the third party.

Third, this is not so with duress of circumstances. However, the justification for that defence in tort law applies equally to criminal law, but thus with the same limits. So the defendant is entitled, to preserve life or health, to act upon another's property. The reason is the logical superiority of personality over property, or because the defendant does not traverse any property right, necessity being a proviso to private property, the very proviso which justifies private property.

The best account of the common law, in terms of case law and principle, is as follows.

The defendant must reasonably perceive a serious danger to the person, and reasonably believe that the danger will materialise. It does not matter, for the criminal defence, that there was in fact no danger (but that is relevant for tortious liability). The threat can be against the defendant or another person for whom they reasonably regard themselves as responsible. The latter qualification is there to prevent officious intermeddling.

The threat might be death or serious injury or rape. There is no reason why the list of serious threats should be closed. It ought to include false imprisonment. Less serious threats might also be relevant to the extent that they have a cumulative effect. The danger need not be a crime. What is not serious for one person might be very serious for another, depending on their personal circumstances (e.g. a punch to the stomach might be more serious for a pregnant woman). Serious harm should include psychological injury and pain, although the latter will likely require corroborative evidence to be credible.

Duress of circumstances should only be available for single events or one-off emergencies, and not for continuous states of affairs. It should not be used to furnish a long-term personal immunity from the law. Thus permanent states of pain would not support the defence. Nor would pathological compulsions to commit crime. Mental impairments would be more suitably addressed through an alternative defence framed for that very purpose. Other ongoing problems (like the plight of the homeless) might more honestly be acknowledged as involving policy questions to be addressed through legislation.

The defence ought to be precluded by prior fault (as with tortious necessity). Thus, the defence should be precluded if the defendant, voluntarily engaged in an illegal activity, should reasonably have foreseen that their actions might well expose them to danger, or to the risk of being coerced by fellow criminals. But where the defendant consorts with criminals lawfully, or when they are otherwise engaged in a lawful activity, the better approach might be to preclude the defence only if the defendant should reasonably have foreseen the need to commit crimes to escape their predicament. Otherwise, in the case of withdrawal, there must be a genuine period of disassociation before a defendant can plead duress by a former colleague.

There must be no alternative which the defendant ought reasonably to have taken. This might include escape or seeking protection or assistance. It might include acting in self-defence, or committing a different crime. There should be no presumption that police protection is always effective. But a defendant ought to be able to give reasons to support any assertion that the police cannot assist in this particular case. The less imminent the threatened harm, the more likely that the defendant could have sought assistance or protection, and perhaps the less real the danger, but otherwise there should be no separate requirement of imminence. In particular, the defence should be available: where a danger is continuing and impending, even if the defendant does not know precisely when its harm might materialise; and where the danger is reasonably certain to materialise in the future, and escape is only available now.

The danger must be coercive. Probably it suffices to be a contributory cause of the defendant's response. That response must be reasonable. Although the case law talks in terms of taking account of the defendant's personal characteristics, no convincing list of relevant characteristics has been identified. On the contrary, which characteristics are currently taken into account seems morally arbitrary. It would be better simply to hold the defendant to a straight objective standard.

A better alternative response might show this response to be unreasonable. But even if there was no alternative (other than suffering the threatened harm), still the defendant's response must be reasonable. Yes, the defendant faces serious harm, but that is not a free pass to commit any crime against third-party victims. That must still be a reasonable thing to do. And there should be a reasonable resilience to life's misfortunes.

When the defendant acts upon another's property, that other cannot resist. When acting upon another's person, under duress by threats, that other can resist. Another person might be entitled to assist the defendant who acts under duress, but only if they have their own defence. That defence might also be duress, for example where that other person is coerced by the fact that the defendant faces serious danger.

Duress by threats is currently no defence to murder or attempted murder in English law. But none of the reasons given for that exclusion are persuasive, and other jurisdictions, like Canada and Australia, do extend the defence to murder. The rationale for duress by threats is also consistent with the defence being so extended. Nevertheless, it will likely be rare when killing is a reasonable response to duress by threats.

Duress of circumstances, however, should remain no defence to killing. Its rationale does not extend to legitimising harm to another's person. But there is a separate principle which might apply, as we saw in Chapter 4, where it is only by killing one person in a threatened group that any life in that group might otherwise be saved. This has nothing to do with duress. It has a distinctive rationale: if all life is otherwise going to be lost anyway, it is better to save at least some of that life.

Draft criminal provisions are set out in the Appendix.

Epilogue

We have considered the evidence and argument in the individual chapters. Here in the Epilogue we draw all the analysis together. First, we disentangle the language of duress and necessity. Second, we identify overlap between the subject areas of crime, tort and contract. Third, we review the detailed conclusions of case law and theory, to show how everything fits together. Finally, we stand back to consider the overarching themes revealed by this project.

The language of duress and necessity

We begin by disentangling the language of duress and necessity.

Duress by threats is where the duressee is threatened by another person with bad consequences unless they, the duressee, capitulate to a demand. Duress of circumstances is where the duressee faces a situation with bad consequences, and, of their own initiative, they take evasive action.

Necessity can be an ingredient in other defences, like self-defence. Instead, we are here concerned with necessity as a defence in its own right. The label 'necessity' is used in the case law to refer to the following defences:

First, duress of circumstances (above).

Second, best interests intervention. This is where the defendant acts upon the 'victim', in the best interests of the victim. This is recognised both in criminal law and tort law. Necessity is merely an ingredient of best interests intervention, which is better seen as a distinct defence, with a different rationale (see below).

Third, lesser evil necessity. This is where the defendant commits a wrong to avoid something even worse. Although both criminal law and tort law have given voice to the notion of a defence of lesser evil necessity, I have argued against its adoption.

The upshot of all this, in short, is that the only real defence of necessity proper is that used synonymously with duress of circumstances.

How do the subject areas use this language?

Contract law is concerned with duress by threats, though it tends to be called simply 'duress'. Sometimes it is further sub-divided into types of duress (duress to the person, duress to goods, etc.), but this is not especially helpful. Additionally, circumstantial necessity can provide the factual setting which might lead to exploitation and so a plea of unconscionable bargain.

Criminal law recognises duress by threats. This is sometimes called compulsion. It also recognises duress of circumstances. This is often called necessity or emergency.

In tort law, the defence is most commonly called necessity. It is akin to duress of circumstances. A further distinction is sometimes drawn between a defendant acting to save themselves, which is private necessity, and acting to save others or the public generally, known as public necessity. The legal test for these two forms is substantially the same. Beyond that, the received wisdom is that tort law has no defence of duress by threats – but it could, by comparison with criminal law. And duress by threats does give rise to a cause of action in tort called intimidation.

Areas of overlap

Next, we identify overlap between the subject areas of crime, tort and contract.

First, there is an overlap between contractual duress and tortious intimidation.

In both cases, the duressor threatens to do something unlawful, or possibly something lawful maliciously, unless the duressee capitulates. With contractual duress, the capitulation takes the form of agreeing a contract or contractual variation. With intimidation, the capitulation could potentially take any form. That includes agreeing a contract. In this case, the duressee may be able to plead either contractual duress or tortious intimidation (there are examples of this in the case law).

Second, there is an overlap between criminal and tort law.

This is explicitly acknowledged by the courts when it comes to best interests intervention and lesser evil necessity. This is because the focal instances in which these defences apply inevitably give rise simultaneously to liability both in tort and in criminal law, since they tend to involve deliberate interference with another's person.

There has been little overt comparison between tortious necessity and its criminal law counterpart of duress of circumstances – and even less attempt to identify a rationale for tortious necessity. However, an analysis of the case law shows that the legal tests for tortious necessity and criminal duress of circumstances are strongly correlated. Further, a singular rationale justifies them both.

Similarly, although tort law supposedly does not recognise the defence of duress by threats, a comparison with criminal law shows that it could. Put another way, having identified a rationale for the recognition of duress by threats in criminal law, that explanation or justification would naturally extend to exculpate tortious liability as well.

Third, what about an overlap between contract and crime?

If contract law interacts with tort, and tort overlaps with crime, then it might be thought that contract and crime also have something in common, through the mediacy of tort law. Indeed, both contractual and criminal duress share similar ingredients. And both have flirted with the overborne will theory as a rationale. However, caution is needed here: contract and crime do not directly overlap, and the differences between them which prevent such overlap should not be ignored (see below).

The point of identifying overlap is as follows:

In the areas of overlap, the law should be suitably aligned, rather than productive of discord. Put another way, the subject areas of crime, tort and contract should mesh rather than collide. We ought to find rationales in common, and a similarity of ingredients in the doctrines. Equally, however, relevant differences should be acknowledged and acted upon, rather than glossed over. It is with all this in mind that we seek the most coherent position in terms of the detail of case law and theory.

Case law and theory: the key details

The tort of intimidation and contractual duress share the same rationale. Both doctrines police coercion. Coercion is wrong to the extent that it forces a complainant to change their behaviour for the selfish reasons of the accused. This denies the complainant the (residual) freedom or autonomy to choose their own goals. It also denies them the dignity of an equal status, because it fails to respect them as having the capacity to choose such goals. And it deprives them of the chance to use or develop that capacity, when doing so is personally fulfilling and socially inspiring.

Both intimidation and contractual duress react to (threats of) unlawful acts. In so doing, they police coercion by drawing a line consistent with the rest of law: they outlaw the leveraging of activities which other areas of the law already proscribe. Thus, both intimidation and contractual duress are sustained by threats of crime, tort and breach of contract. To be clear, a threatened breach of contract should always be illegitimate for contractual duress. The unlawful threatened acts do not have to be independently actionable.

It is thus unsurprising that the tests for intimidation and contractual duress are strongly correlated. In essence, they involve: a demand, backed up by the doing or threatening of something unlawful, which coerces the complainant and causes them to comply with the demand. With intimidation, the primary remedy is damages, and with contractual duress, the remedy is rescission. These are complementary remedies, not inconsistent ones. The doctrines mesh together coherently. For example, just as affirmation might preclude a plea of contractual duress, so too it would equally prevent a claim in intimidation (because it would be the complainant's actual or deemed choice to affirm which finally accounts for the transaction, rather than any prior threats).

The case law has not yet gone so far as to say that intimidation and contractual duress also respond to lawful acts. Were that to be so, an extra ingredient would be needed to draw the line between oppressive coercion and legitimate persuasion. For both intimidation and contractual duress, the most likely extra ingredient is the malicious (i.e. spiteful) infliction of harm. And the explanation is the same: someone who inflicts harm maliciously reduces their victim from a person to an object of sport, or simply a tool for self-gratification. To hide behind the lawfulness of one's act in order to inflict harm on another out of spite is a cynical misuse of the law, an abuse of rights which the law can properly censure.

But the need for so-called lawful act duress in contract law is less pressing. This is because when a party threatens to do something lawful, thereby procuring a contract, that can give rise to a plea of unconscionable bargain. That doctrine covers threats to do something lawful (usually threats not to contract at all). Unconscionable bargain embraces all forms of victimisation. It is this victimisation which makes it illegitimate to threaten what is otherwise lawful. The moral wrong with unconscionable bargain is again that the complainant is treated, not as an end in themselves, but as an object for exploitation, a means to a quick profit.

Unconscionable bargain requires that the accused took knowing and unconscionable advantage, actively or passively, of the complainant's relative weakness. In general terms, a complainant suffers such a weakness when they are unable to judge or advance their own best interests. But this is a special weakness which must go beyond the personal and idiosyncratic urges and predilections which everyday lead us to transact. A special weakness would include, for example, a condition of basic need or necessity.

Necessity is not defined in the case law for unconscionable bargain, so we can take a lead from the position in tort and criminal law. But we can also be more generous. This is because, in crime and tort, the defendant is usually alleging duress or necessity as a reason to exculpate behaviour which causes harm or loss to an innocent third party. That possibility should be narrowly circumscribed. But with unconscionable bargain, we are concerned with protecting the complainant against exploitation, and the doctrine takes effect against the exploiter themselves. So for example, in crime and tort the defence might be precluded if the defendant was at fault in creating the necessity. But with unconscionable bargain, it should not matter that the complainant's state of necessity has been brought about by their own prior choices. That is still no justification for exploitation.

As for necessity in crime and tort, we need to distinguish, as previously noted, between three situations.

First, there is best interests intervention. This applies when it is necessary to act, to preserve or advance the best interests of another, assessed from the viewpoint of that other, when it is not possible to obtain their consent. It shares the language of necessity, but really only to the extent that necessity is an ingredient in best interests intervention. It has little in common with any free-standing defence of necessity. Rather, best interests intervention has its own distinctive rationale: it enables a willing volunteer to provide necessary assistance to someone then unable to ask for help, so that the needy are not otherwise abandoned to their fate.

Second, there is the would-be defence of lesser evil necessity. This is where the defendant does something wrong in order to avoid something worse. This defence should be rejected. Its utilitarian calculus is capable of producing outcomes which are morally unacceptable. And it requires judges to take policy decisions about which rival activities or rights are best for society, beyond their constitutional competence.

(There is a similar reason to reject the defence of justification to the tort of intimidation. The notion behind that would-be defence is that, although a defendant might threaten to do something unlawful, still they might be justified in doing so. Yet the courts have said that the defence is not susceptible to definition. So instead, it seems to give the courts an unpredictable discretion to decide cases simply according to a judge's unaccountable sense of moral justice.)

Third, there is a defence of necessity proper, which in criminal law is often synonymously called duress of circumstances. Similar principles are at play in both crime and tort. There must be a grave danger such as death or serious injury. This could include psychological injury or pain, if suitably corroborated. Further, the defendant's response to the danger must be reasonable. This includes whether there were lawful or lesser alternative responses. The less imminent the danger, the more likely that there are alternatives. The defence is precluded if the danger was caused by the defendant's own prior fault.

The defence best applies to a temporary state of affairs, or one-off emergencies. Beyond that, the more honest approach might be to recognise that some persistent problems can fairly be addressed only collectively at a political level, rather than necessitous use imposing long-term burdens on individual third-party victims arbitrarily, or furnishing the defendant with long-term personal immunity from the law.

There are differences between necessity / duress of circumstances in crime and tort. Tort can take a stricter line. While criminal law might acquit, tort might still require the defendant to compensate the victim. For example, in criminal law, the defence is available even though the defendant was reasonably mistaken about the existence of the danger, whereas for private necessity in tort law, there must be an actual danger. (And yet, a reasonable mistake is allowed for public necessity, when the defendant is acting to save others rather than themselves.)

In crime and tort, necessity / duress of circumstances allows the defendant to act only upon another's property. The possible rationales are the same in both subject areas. First, a person in necessity making use of another's property does not traverse any property rights, but is free to act as upon any property in its natural state. It is this necessity proviso which justifies the institution of private property, and an owner's ability otherwise to exclude others. Alternatively, property rights are derivative of – they exist only to support – personality rights, and so have to yield when the latter are threatened by death or serious injury. All of this also reveals that the property owner cannot resist the defendant who acts under genuine necessity or duress.

In tort, the better view is that no one can protect their own property by sacrificing another's property. This is because it creates a stalemate: the second property is now endangered, and could then preserve itself at the expense of the first. Nor is there any good reason to resolve this conflict simply by stipulating that the more expensive property should be saved, rather than, for example, the more necessary property. Characterising necessity as an incomplete privilege, while technically possible in legal terms – my preference is to say that necessitous use remains a trespass but bars the remedy of ejection – otherwise provides no further argument or justification for its own recognition.

This is not a problem for criminal law, first, because statute expressly allows a defendant to destroy or damage another's property to protect their own, and second, because criminal law can exculpate in such circumstances while leaving the difficult question of who should bear the loss to tort law.

The rationale for necessity / duress of circumstances also means that, in both tort and crime, a defendant in necessity cannot act upon another's person. Once again, this is because such behaviour fails to respect the victim as a person, since it would only be using them as a means, a tool for self-protection.

There might be one exception in criminal law. Immanent in the case law is the following proposition. If two or more people are virtually certain to suffer death imminently and together, from the same cause, but one or more could be saved only by the killing of a particular person in that group, then such killing might be exculpated. This principle has its own distinctive rationale: if all life is otherwise going to be lost anyway, it is better to save at least some of that life. But once again, criminal law is concerned only with criminal culpability; there is nothing to suggest that such a killer would avoid liability in tort law.

The rationale for the criminal defence of duress by threats is different.

First, any person who seeks to avoid death or serious injury acts upon a vital impulse that is surely as constitutive of human nature as any other characteristic. But an impeccable motivation, though an important part of the story, does not give a free pass to any crime.

So, second, the defendant's position is morally strengthened by the fact that they too are a coerced victim of the duressor, no less than the third party they act upon. And the third-party victim is still protected and vindicated, because the criminal law continues to proscribe what the duressor does, and holds the duressor accountable for procuring the harm to the third party. (This latter point does not apply to duress of circumstances, which is why duress of circumstances needs to seek out a distinctive rationale.)

The same rationale might be given for a tortious defence of duress by threats. Although such a defence has not yet been recognised, it could be. As noted, tort does recognise the defence of necessity. It is substantively aligned with the criminal defence of duress of circumstances. This in turn is largely similar to the criminal defence of duress by threats. This suggests that tort law too could also recognise a defence of duress by threats, in similar terms to its defence of necessity. And even though duress by threats and duress of circumstances have different rationales in criminal law, those same rationales apply equally to support the respective defences in tort law.

In contract and crime, some of the cases purport to explain duress on the basis of an overborne will. Indeed, contract cases reference the discussion in criminal law. But ultimately this approach does not work. The will, whatever that might be, is not overborne, since it still has sufficient capacity to contract, or to commit a crime with the requisite *mens rea*. Rather, as noted, contractual duress is about policing coercion.

But that explanation does not work for criminal law. Coercion is a wrong by the coercer. A remedy might lie against them, which is the case in contract law, and in the tort of intimidation. But in criminal law, as with the tortious defences, we are concerned to justify how the defendant might escape liability for the harm they do in turn to an innocent third party. That is a different direction of inquiry. Hence a different rationale.

Another point of common debate in contract and crime is whether the duressee ought to resist the threats. But again, the structural differences between contract and crime point to opposite conclusions. In criminal law, the duressee avoids the threats by acting on an innocent third party. In those circumstances, some initial resistance to the threats might be expected. With contractual duress, the remedy lies only against the duressor themselves (or the person who has knowingly taken the benefit of another's duress). There seems no good reason in those circumstances why the duressor should be able to argue that the duressee should not have submitted to the threats which the duressor intended them to submit to.

Overall conclusions

Finally, let us stand back to consider this project in broader terms.

A common theme is the need for a threat or danger which is coercive and causative. Not every threat is causative: it might be ignored or dismissed. Even with those threats which do cause someone to change their behaviour, not all are coercive: the person threatened might acquiesce because they consider the demand inconsequential.

With the criminal and tortious defences, the defendant avoids the threat by acting on a third party. In these circumstances, the law sets a high standard for which threats it is prepared to countenance as furnishing a defence: usually serious threats to the person. With contractual duress and tortious intimidation, the complainant seeks a remedy against the duressor. It is a two-party scenario. As such, a broader range of threats is recognised (for example, including threats to breach a contract).

Coercion is a moral wrong for denying the complainant the dignity of an equal status, by depriving them of the (residual) freedom to choose their own goals, and of the exercise of their capacities in that regard. But we still need to distinguish unlawful coercion from legitimate if forceful persuasion.

In two-party cases, i.e. those which involve only the duressor and duressee, we do this in two ways.

First, if what the duressor does or threatens to do is itself unlawful, then they have transgressed a line which the law has already drawn elsewhere; they are indicted for leveraging activities which the law already proscribes. To this extent, two-party coercion also serves a law reinforcement function.

Second, with lawful act duress, the duressor acts maliciously, or knowingly victimises the duressee, adding further weight to the notion that the duressor is only using the duressee as a tool for self-gratification or a quick profit.

Three-party cases are different. This is where the duressee escapes the duress by acting upon a third-party victim. The fact that the duressee is coerced provides some sympathy for their position, but that alone cannot justify unburdening themselves at the expense of an innocent third party. Their position is enhanced by acknowledging that they act to avert such grave dangers as death or serious injury. This is not cowardice; the motivation to preserve life is fundamentally constitutive of human nature, and as such does not merit moral opprobrium. But the tipping point comes with two further arguments.

First, the duressee can act upon another's property by invoking a venerable theory of private property: a person's ability to privatise property and so exclude others is morally possible only by allowing for a proviso that entitles others to use that property in necessity; alternatively, property rights exist only to support, and so must yield to, personality rights.

Second, with duress by threats, the law does not abandon the third-party victim. Rather, the duressor will continue to attract criminal and tortious liability for what they have procured. The acts remain proscribed, thereby respecting and protecting the victim, and if carried out, the victim afterwards has the potential for vindication.

In short, threats can provide the duressee with a remedy against the duressor. Threats and circumstantial pressure can provide a defence when a duressee acts upon a third-party victim, as long as any rights that the third-party victim retains are otherwise capable of legal vindication.

Appendix

Draft criminal provisions

Duress by threats

Duress by threats is a defence in the following circumstances:

1 The defendant must reasonably believe that they have been threatened that, unless they capitulate to a demand to commit a crime, the defendant or another person for whom they reasonably feel responsible will suffer serious harm to the person.
2 The defendant must reasonably believe that the threat will be carried out.
3 The threat must coerce the defendant, and cause them to commit the crime.
4 It must be reasonable for the defendant to respond to the threat by committing the crime.
5 There must be no lawful alternative to committing the crime which the defendant reasonably should have taken.
6 When the threats are made by other criminals, the defence is not available if: the defendant has unlawfully associated with those other criminals, and the risk of being threatened was reasonably foreseeable; or the defendant has lawfully associated with those other criminals, and the risk of being threatened into committing crime was reasonably foreseeable.

Duress of circumstances

Duress of circumstances is a defence in the following circumstances:

1 The defendant must reasonably believe that they or another person for whom they reasonably feel responsible faces a danger of serious harm to the person.
2 The danger must be an emergency and not a continuous state of affairs.
3 The danger must coerce the defendant, and cause them to commit a crime.
4 It must be reasonable for the defendant to respond to the danger by committing the crime.
5 There must be no lawful alternative to committing the crime which the defendant reasonably should have taken.
6 If responding to any danger to another person, it must reasonably appear to the defendant that they are a suitable person to respond in the circumstances.

7 The defence is not available if: the defendant was engaged in an unlawful activity and the danger was reasonably foreseeable; or the defendant was engaged in a lawful activity, and the need to commit a crime in order to escape the danger was reasonably foreseeable.
8 The defence is not available when the defendant commits a crime against another's person.

Best interests intervention

Best interests is a defence when the defendant acts upon another's person or property in the following circumstances:

1 It must be necessary to act in order to preserve or advance the best interests of that other person.
2 It must not be possible to obtain that other person's consent. That other person must not previously have refused consent.
3 It must reasonably appear to the defendant that they are a suitable person to act in the circumstances.
4 The defendant must act with reasonable care.

Net saving of life

There is a defence to killing when a group of two or more people are virtually certain to suffer death imminently and together from the same cause, and only by killing one or more people in that group will any lives of people in that group be saved.

Bibliography

Aivazian, Trebilcock and Penny, 'The Law of Contract Modifications' (1984) 22 Osgoode Hall LJ 173

Akman, 'The Relationship between Economic Duress and Abuse of a Dominant Position Under Competition Law' [2014] LMCLQ 99

Alexander, 'Lesser Evils: A Closer Look at the Paradigmatic Justification' (2005) 24 Law & Phil 611

Alldridge, 'The Coherence of Defences' [1983] Crim LR 665

Alldridge, 'Developing the Defence of Duress' [1986] Crim LR 433

Allen, C K, 'Legal Morality and the *Ius Abutendi*' (1924) 40 LQR 164

Allen, M J, *Textbook on Criminal Law*, 13th edn (Oxford: Oxford University Press, 2015)

Allen and Cooper, *Elliott and Wood's Cases and Materials on Criminal Law*, 11th edn (London: Sweet & Maxwell, 2013)

Ames, 'How Far an Act May Be a Tort Because of the Wrongful Motive of the Actor' (1905) 18 Harv LR 411

Andrews, *Contract Law*, 2nd edn (Cambridge: Cambridge University Press, 2015)

Anonymous, 'The Burmah Oil Affair' (1965) 79 Harv LR 614

Aquinas, Summa Theologica

Arenson, 'The Paradox of Disallowing Duress as a Defence to Murder' (2014) 78 J Crim L 65

Ashworth, 'Commentary' [2008] Crim LR 138

Atiyah, 'Economic Duress and the Overborne Will' (1982) 98 LQR 197

Atiyah, 'Duress and the Overborne Will Again' (1983) 99 LQR 353

Atiyah, *Essays on Contract* (Oxford: Oxford University Press, 1986)

Bagaric and Arenson, *Criminal Laws in Australia*, 2nd edn (Melbourne: Oxford University Press, 2007)

Bagshaw, 'Can the Economic Torts Be Unified?' (1998) 18 OJLS 729

Bamforth, 'Unconscionability as a Vitiating Factor' [1995] LMCLQ 538

Bar-Gill and Ben-Shahar, 'The Law of Duress and the Economics of Credible Threats' (2004) 33 J Legal Studies 391

Barton, 'The Enforcement of Hard Bargains' (1987) 103 LQR 118

Bayles, 'Character, Purpose, and Criminal Responsibility' (1982) 1 Law & Phil 5

Beale, 'Inequality of Bargaining Power' (1986) 6 OJLS 123

Beatson, *The Use and Abuse of Unjust Enrichment* (Oxford: Clarendon Press, 1991)

Berger, 'Emotions and Veil of Voluntarism: The Loss of Judgment in Canadian Criminal Defences' (2006) 51 McGill LJ 99

Berman, 'The Evidentiary Theory of Blackmail: Taking Motives Seriously' (1998) 65 U Chicago LR 795

Berman, 'Justification and Excuse, Law and Morality' (2003) 53 Duke LJ 1

Berman, 'Lesser Evils and Justification: A Less Close Look' (2005) 24 Law & Phil 681

Bigwood, 'Coercion in Contract: The Theoretical Constructs of Duress' (1996) 46 U Toronto LJ 201

Bigwood, 'Undue Influence: Impaired Consent or Wicked Exploitation?' (1996) 16 OJLS 503

Bigwood, 'Economic Duress by (Threatened) Breach of Contract' (2001) 117 LQR 376

Bigwood, *Exploitative Contracts* (Oxford: Oxford University Press, 2004)

Bigwood, 'Contracts by Unfair Advantage: From Exploitation to Transactional Neglect' (2005) 25 OJLS 65

Bigwood, 'When Exegesis Becomes Excess' (2005) 21 J Contract L 208

Bigwood, 'Antipodean Reflections on the Canadian Unconscionability Doctrine' (2005) 84 Can Bar Rev 171

Bigwood, 'Four Questions on the Demise of Lawful Act Duress in New South Wales' (2008) 27(2) U Queensland LJ 41

Birks, *An Introduction to the Law of Restitution* (Oxford: Clarendon Press, 1989)

Birks, 'The Travails of Duress' [1990] LMCLQ 342

Birks and Chin, 'On the Nature of Undue Influence', in Beatson and Friedmann (eds), *Good Faith and Fault in Contract law* (Oxford: Clarendon Press, 1995)

Blackmail Symposium (1993) 141 U Penn LR 1565

Bohlander, 'In extremis – hijacked planes, "collateral damage" and the limits of criminal law' [2006] Crim LR 597

Bohlander, 'Of Shipwrecked Sailors, Unborn Children, Conjoined Twins and Hijacked Airplanes – Taking Human Life and the Defence of Necessity' (2006) 70 J Criminal L 147

Bohlen, 'Incomplete Privilege to Inflict Intentional Invasions of Interests of Property and Personality' (1926) 39 Harvard LR 307

Brudner, 'A Theory of Necessity' (1987) 7 OJLS 338

Burns, 'Tort Injury to Economic Interests: Some Facets of Legal Response' (1980) 58 Can Bar Rev 134

Burrows, *The Law of Restitution*, 3rd edn (Oxford: Oxford University Press, 2011)

Burrows, *A Restatement of the English Law of Contract* (Oxford: Oxford University Press, 2016)

Butler, 'Varieties of Malice and Corruption' in Rorty (ed), *The Many Faces of Evil* (London: Routledge, 2001)

Cane, '*Mens Rea* in Tort Law' (2000) 20 OJLS 533

Capper, 'Undue Influence and Unconscionability: A Rationalization' (1998) 114 LQR 479

Capper, 'The Unconscionable Bargain in the Common Law World' (2010) 126 LQR 403

Card, *Card, Cross & Jones, Criminal Law*, 21st edn (Oxford: Oxford University Press, 2014)

Cartwright, *Unequal Bargaining* (Oxford: Clarendon Press, 1991)

Carty, 'Joint Tortfeasance and Assistance Liability' (1999) 19 LS 489

Carty, *An Analysis of the Economic Torts*, 2nd edn (Oxford: Oxford University Press, 2010)

Carty, 'The Modern Functions of the Economic Torts: Reviewing the English, Canadian, Australian, and New Zealand Positions' (2015) 74 Cambridge LJ 261

Chan and Simester, 'Duress, Necessity: How Many Defences' (2005) 16 King's LJ 121

Chen-Wishart, 'The *O'Brien* Principle and Substantive Unfairness' (1997) 56 Cambridge LJ 60

Chen-Wishart, 'Undue Influence: Vindicating Relationships of Influence' (2006) 59 CLP 231

Chen-Wishart, 'The Nature of Vitiating Factors in Contract Law', in Klass, Letsas and Saprai (eds), *Philosophical Foundations of Contract Law* (Oxford: Oxford University Press, 2014)

Chen-Wishart, *Contract Law*, 5th edn (Oxford: Oxford University Press, 2015)
Chitty on Contracts, 32nd edn (London: Sweet & Maxwell, 2015)
Christie, 'The Defense of Necessity Considered from the Legal and Moral Points of View' (1999) 48 Duke LJ 975
Clarkson, 'Necessary Action: A New Defence' [2004] Crim LR 81
Clerk & Lindsell on Torts, 21st edn (London: Sweet & Maxwell, 2014)
Cohan, 'Private and Public Necessity and the Violation of Property Rights' (2007) 83 N Dakota LR 651
Cohen, *Self-ownership, Freedom, and Equality* (Cambridge: Cambridge University Press, 1995)
Coleman, *Risks and Wrongs* (New York: Oxford University Press, 2002)
Colvin, 'Exculpatory Defences in Criminal Law' (1990) 10 OJLS 381
Comte, 'The Continued Obscurity of Economic Duress' [2011] LMCLQ 333
Conaglen, 'Duress, Undue Influence, and Unconscionable Bargains – The Theoretical Mesh' (1999) 18 NZULR 509
Dalzell, 'Duress by Economic Pressure' (1942) 20 N Carolina LR 237, 341
Davies, *Accessory Liability* (Oxford: Hart, 2015)
Dawson, 'Economic Duress – An Essay in Perspective' (1947) 45 Michigan LR 253
Deakin and Randall, 'Rethinking the Economic Torts' (2009) 72 MLR 519
Deakin, Johnston and Markesinis, *Markesinis and Deakin's Tort Law*, 7th edn (Oxford: Oxford University Press, 2013)
Dennis, 'Duress, Murder and Criminal Responsibility' (1980) 96 LQR 208
Dennis, 'On Necessity as a Defence to Crime' (2009) 2 Crim Law & Phil 29
Diderot, Jacques the Fatalist and His Master (1796)
Dietrich, 'Lawful Coercive Threats and the Infliction of Harm' (2000) 8 Torts LJ 187
Dietrich, 'Accessorial Liability in the Law of Torts' (2011) 31 LS 231
Dressler, 'New Thoughts about the Concept of Justification in the Criminal Law' (1984) 32 UCLA LR 61
Dressler, 'Exegesis of the Law of Duress: Justifying the Excuse and Searching for Its Proper Limits' (1989) 62 S Cal LR 1331
Dressler, 'Reflections on *Dudley and Stephens* and Killing the Innocent', in Baker and Horder (eds), *The Sanctity of Life and the Criminal Law* (Cambridge: Cambridge University Press, 2013)
Duff, 'Choice, Character, and Criminal Liability' (1993) 12 Law & Phil 345
Duff, 'Rule-Violations and Wrongdoings', in Shute and Simester (eds), *Criminal Law Theory* (Oxford: Oxford University Press, 2002)
Duff, 'Rethinking Justifications' (2004) 39 Tulsa LR 829
Dupre, 'Human Dignity and the Withdrawal of Medical Treatment: A Missed Opportunity?' (2006) 6 EHRLR 678
Dworkin, *The Theory and Practice of Autonomy* (New York: Cambridge University Press, 1988)
Dyson (ed), *Unravelling Tort and Crime* (Cambridge: Cambridge University Press, 2014)
Dyson (ed), *Comparing Tort and Crime* (Cambridge: Cambridge University Press, 2015)
Edelman and Bant, *Unjust Enrichment in Australia* (Melbourne: Oxford University Press, 2006)
Edelman and Bant, *Unjust Enrichment*, 2nd edn (Oxford: Hart, 2016)
Edelman and Dyer, 'A Defence of Duress in the Law of Torts?', in Dyson, Goudkamp and Wilmot-Smith (eds), *Defences in Tort Law* (Oxford: Hart, 2015)
Elias and Ewing, 'Economic Torts and Labour Law: Old Principles in New Liabilities' [1982] Cambridge LJ 321

Elliott, 'Necessity, Duress and Self-defence' [1989] Crim LR 611

Elliott and Quinn, *Tort Law*, 10th edn (Harlow: Pearson, 2015)

Enonchong, Duress, Undue Influence, and Unconscionable Dealing (London: Sweet & Maxwell, 2012)

Epicurus, Letter to Menoeceus

Epstein, 'A Theory of Strict Liability' (1973) 2 J Leg Stud 151

Epstein, 'Defenses and Subsequent Pleas in a System of Strict Liability' (1974) 3 J Leg Stud 165

Feinberg, 'Voluntary Euthanasia and the Inalienable Right to Life' (1978) 7 Phil & Pub Aff 93

Feldman, 'Containment, Deprivation of Liberty and Breach of the Peace' [2009] Cambridge LJ 243

Finan and Ritson, 'Tortious Necessity: The Privileged Defence' (1992) 26 Akron LR 1

Fingarette, 'Victimization: A Legalist Analysis of Coercion, Deception, Undue Influence, and Excusable Prison Escape' (1985) 42 Wash & Lee LR 65

Finnis, 'Bland: Crossing the Rubicon?' (1993) 109 LQR 329

Finnis, 'Intention in Tort Law' in Owen (ed), *Philosophical Foundations of Tort Law* (Oxford: Clarendon Press, 1995)

Fletcher, 'Fairness and Utility in Tort Theory' (1972) 85 Harvard LR 537

Fletcher, *Rethinking Criminal Law* (New York: Little, Brown & Co, 1978)

Fletcher, 'The Search for Synthesis in Tort Theory' (1983) 2 Law & Phil 63

Freeman, 'Whose Life Is It Anyway?' (2001) 9 Medical LR 259

Fridman, 'Motive in the English Law of Nuisance' (1954) 40 Virginia LR 583

Fridman, 'Malice in the Law of Torts' (1958) 21 MLR 484

Fridman, *The Law of Torts in Canada* (Toronto: Carswell, 1990)

Friedmann, 'Restitution of Benefits Obtained Through the Appropriation of Property or the Commission of a Wrong' (1980) 80 Columbia LR 504

Gardner, J, 'Justifications and Reasons', in Simester and Smith (eds), *Harm and Culpability* (Oxford: Clarendon Press, 1996)

Gardner, S, 'Necessity's Newest Inventions' (1991) 11 OJLS 125

Gardner, S, 'The Gist of Excuses' (1998) 1 Buffalo Crim LR 575

Gardner, S, 'Direct Action and the Defence of Necessity' [2005] Crim LR 371

Geistfeld, 'Necessity and the Logic of Strict Liability' (2005) 5(2) Issues in Legal Scholarship

Giliker, 'A "New" Head of Damages: Damages for Mental Distress in the English Law of Torts' (2000) 20 LS 19

Giliker, *Tort*, 5th edn (London: Sweet & Maxwell, 2014)

Glazebrook, 'The Necessity Plea in English Criminal Law' (1972) 30 Cambridge LJ 87

Glover (ed), *Utilitarianism and Its Critics* (New York: Macmillan, 1990)

Goldberg and Zipursky, *Torts* (New York: Oxford University Press, 2010)

Goodhart, *Essays in Jurisprudence and the Common Law* (Cambridge: Cambridge University Press, 1931)

Gordley, 'Equality in Exchange' (1981) 69 California LR 1587

Gordley, 'Damages Under the Necessity Doctrine' (2005) 5(2) Issues in Legal Scholarship

Goudkamp, *Tort Law Defences* (Oxford: Hart, 2013)

Greenawalt, 'The Perplexing Borders of Justification and Excuse' (1984) 84 Columbia LR 1897

Gregor (trans and ed), *Immanuel Kant: Groundwork of the Metaphysics of Morals* (Cambridge: Cambridge University Press 1997)

Greig, 'Criminal Responsibility and the Concept of Evil' (1996) 3 Psychiatry, Psychology and Law 163

Gur-Ayre, 'Should the Criminal Law Distinguish Between Necessity as a Justification and Necessity as an Excuse?' (1986) 102 LQR 71

Gutteridge, 'Abuse of Rights' (1933) 5 CLJ 22

Hale, *The History of the Pleas of the Crown*, vol 1 (London: 1736)

Hall and Wigmore, 'Compensation for Property Destroyed to Stop the Spread of Conflagration' (1907) 1 Illinois LR 501

Halson, 'Opportunism, Economic Duress and Contract Modifications' (1991) 107 LQR 649

Hamson, 'A Further Note on *Rookes v Barnard*' [1964] Cambridge LJ 159

Harris, J, 'Human Beings, Persons and Conjoined Twins' (2001) 9 Medical LR 221

Hart, *Punishment and Responsibility* (Oxford: Oxford University Press, 2008)

Heath and Schneewind (eds), *Kant: Lectures on Ethics* (Cambridge: Cambridge University Press, 1997)

Hemming, *Criminal Law Guidebook: Queensland and Western Australia*, 2nd edn (Melbourne: Oxford University Press, 2015)

Herman, 'Mutual Aid and Respect for Persons', in Guyer (ed), *Kant's Groundwork of the Metaphysics of Morals: Critical Essays* (Lanham, MD: Rowman & Littlefield, 1998)

Hermida, *Criminal Law in Canada*, 2nd edn (Zuidpoolsingel, Netherlands: Wolters Kluwer, 2015)

Herring, *Criminal Law*, 8th edn (Basingstoke: Macmillan, 2013)

Herring, 'Escaping the Shackles at the End of Life' (2013) 21 Med LR 487

Herring, *Criminal Law*, 7th edn (Oxford: Oxford University Press, 2016)

Heuston, 'Judicial Prosopography' (1986) 102 LQR 90

Heuston and Buckley, *Salmond & Heuston, Law of Torts*, 21st edn (London: Sweet & Maxwell, 1996)

Heydon, 'The Defence of Justification in Cases of Intentionally Caused Economic Harm' (1970) 20 U Toronto LJ 139

Heydon, *Economic Torts* (London: Sweet & Maxwell, 1973)

Heydon, 'The Future of the Economic Torts' (1975) 12 U Western Australia LR 1

Hoffmann, '*Rookes v Barnard*' (1965) 81 LQR 116

Horder, 'Pleading Involuntary Lack of Capacity' (1993) 52 Cambridge LJ 298

Horder, 'Criminal Culpability: The Possibility of a General Theory' (1993) 12 Law & Phil 193

Horder, 'Occupying the Moral High Ground? The Law Commission on Duress' [1994] Crim LR 334

Horder, 'Self-Defence, Necessity and Duress: Understanding the Relationship' (1998) 11 Can J Law & Juris 143

Horder, *Excusing Crime* (Oxford: Oxford University Press, 2006)

Horder, *Asthworth's Principles of Criminal Law*, 8th edn (Oxford: Oxford University Press, 2016)

Hornle, 'Hijacked Planes: May They Be Shot Down?' (2007) 10 New Crim LR 582

Horsey and Rackley, *Tort Law*, 3rd edn (Oxford: Oxford University Press, 2013)

Howarth, 'Against *Lumley v Gye*' (2005) 68 MLR 195

Howarth et al., *Hepple and Matthew's Tort Law*, 7th edn (Oxford: Hart, 2015)

Howell, 'To Be Angry Is Not to Be Human, But to Be Fearful Is: Chewong Concepts of Human Nature', in Howell and Willis (eds), *Societies at Peace* (Routledge, 1989)

Husak, 'Justifications and the Criminal Liability of Accessories' (1989) 80 J Crim Law & Criminology 491

Husak, 'Conflict of Justifications' (1999) 18 Law & Phil 41

Husak, 'On the Supposed Priority of Justification to Excuse' (2005) 24 Law & Phil 557

Huxtable, 'Separation of Conjoined Twins: Where Next for English Law?' [2002] Crim LR 459

Ibbetson, 'Duress Revisited' (2005) 64 Cambridge LJ 530

Jackson, 'War Damage Act' (1965) 28 MLR 584

Jackson, *Criminal Law in Hong Kong* (Hong Kong: Hong Kong University Press, 2003)

Kadish, 'Excusing Crime' (1987) 75 Cal LR 257

Kant, *The Metaphysics of Morals* (Cambridge: Cambridge University Press, 1996)

Kant, *Groundwork of the Metaphysics of Morals* (Cambridge: Cambridge University Press, 2012)

Keating, 'Property Rights and Tortious Wrong in *Vincent v Lake Erie*' (2005) 5(2) Issues in Legal Scholarship

Keating et al., *Clarkson & Keating: Criminal Law*, 8th edn (London: Sweet & Maxwell, 2014)

Keeton, 'Conditional Fault in the Law of Torts' (1959) 72 Harvard LR 401

Keown, 'Restoring Moral and Intellectual Shape to the Law After Bland' (1997) 113 LQR 482

Keown, 'Restoring the Sanctity of Life and Replacing the Caricature: A Reply to David Price' (2006) 26 LS 109

Klar, 'The Defence of Private Necessity in Canadian Tort Law' (2005) 5(2) Issues in Legal Scholarship

Klepper, 'Torts of Necessity: A Moral Theory of Compensation' (1990) 9 Law & Phil 223

Klimchuk, 'Necessity and Restitution' (2001) 7 Legal Theory 59

Klimchuck, 'Property and Necessity', in Penner and Smith (eds), *Philosophical Foundations of Property Law* (Oxford, Oxford University Press, 2013)

Korsgaard, *Creating the Kingdom of Ends* (Cambridge: Cambridge University Press, 1996)

Lamond, 'Coercion, Threats and Blackmail', in Smith and Simester (eds), *Harm and Culpability* (Oxford: Oxford University Press, 1996)

Law Commission, *Murder, Manslaughter and Infanticide*, Law Com No 304 (2006)

Lee, 'Compromise and Coercion' [2012] LMCLQ 478

Lee, 'The Unlawful Means Tort in Canada' (2014) 130 LQR 559

Lenaerts, 'The General Principle of the Prohibition of Abuse of Rights' (2010) 18 European Review of Private Law 1121

Leverick, *Killing in Self-Defence* (Oxford: Oxford University Press, 2006)

Lewis, 'The Failure of the Defence Of Necessity as a Mechanism of Legal Change on Assisted Dying in the Common Law World', in Baker and Horder (eds), *The Sanctity of Life and the Criminal Law* (Cambridge: Cambridge University Press, 2013)

Liebermann and Syrquin, 'The Use and Abuse of Rights' (1983) 4 Journal of Economic Behaviour and Organization 25

Lippke, 'Chronic Temptation, Reasonable Firmness and the Criminal Law' (2014) 34 OJLS 75

Locke, *Two Treatises of Government*, Laslett (ed) (Cambridge: Cambridge University Press, 1988)

Loveless, '*R v GAC*: Battered Woman "Syndromization"' [2014] Crim LR 655

Lunney and Oliphant, *Tort Law*, 5th edn (Oxford: Oxford University Press, 2013)

Macdonald, 'Duress by Threatened Breach of Contract' [1989] JBL 460

McBride and Bagshaw, *Tort Law*, 5th edn (Harlow: Pearson, 2015)

McGee, 'Finding a Way Through the Ethical and Legal Maze: Withdrawal of Medical Treatment and Euthanasia' (2005) 13 Med LR 357

McKeand, 'Economic Duress – Wearing the Clothes of Unconscionable Conduct' (2001) 17 J Contract L 1

McKendrick, 'The Further Travails of Duress' in Burrows and Rodger (eds), *Mapping the Law: Essays in Memory of Peter Birks* (Oxford: Oxford University Press, 2006)
McKendrick, *Contract Law*, 11th edn (London: Palgrave, 2015)
McSherry and Naylor, *Australian Criminal Laws* (Melbourne: Oxford University Press, 2004)
Mead, 'Of Kettles, Cordons and Crowd Control' [2009] EHRLR 376
Michalowski, 'Sanctity of Life: Are Some Lives More Sacred than Others?' [2002] LS 377
Milgate, 'Duress and the Criminal Law: Another About Turn by the House of Lords' [1988] Cambridge LJ 61
Mill, *On Liberty* (Boston: Ticknor and Fields, 1859)
Mitchell, Mitchell and Watterson (eds), *Goff & Jones: The Law of Unjust Enrichment*, 9th edn (London: Sweet & Maxwell, 2016)
Moore, 'Causation and the Excuses' (1985) 73 Cal LR 1091
Morgan, *Great Debates in Contract Law*, 2nd edn (London: Palgrave, 2015)
Morse, 'Diminished Capacity', in Shute, Gardner and Horder (eds), *Action and Value in the Criminal Law* (Oxford: Clarendon Press, 1993)
Murphy, 'Understanding Intimidation' (2014) 77 MLR 33
Neyers, 'The Economic Torts as Corrective Justice' (2009) 17 Torts LJ 162
Neyers, 'Explaining the Inexplicable? Four Manifestations of Abuse of Rights in English Law', in Nolan and Robertson (eds), *Rights and Private Law* (Oxford: Hart, 2012)
Norrie, *Crime, Reason and History*, 3rd edn (Cambridge: Cambridge University Press, 2014)
Nozick, *Anarchy, State, and Utopia* (New York: Basic Books, 1974)
Oates, 'Life, Death and the Law' (2007) 36 Common Law World Review 1
Odgers, *Principles of Federal Criminal Law*, 3rd edn (Pyrmont NSW: Lawbook Co, 2015)
Ogilvie, 'Economic Duress: An Elegant and Practical Solution' [2011] JBL 229
O'Neill, 'Consistency in Action', in Guyer (ed), *Kant's Groundwork of the Metaphysics of Morals: Critical Essays* (Lanham, MD: Rowman & Littlefield, 1998)
Ong, 'Two Tripartite Economic Torts' [2008] JBL 723
Ormerod and Laird, *Smith and Hogan's Criminal Law*, 14th edn (Oxford: Oxford University Press, 2015)
Ost, 'Euthanasia and the Defence of Necessity: Advocating a More Appropriate Legal Response' [2005] Crim LR 355
Parry, 'The Virtue of Necessity: Reshaping Culpability and the Rule of Law' (1999) 36 Houston LR 397
Peel (ed), *Treitel, The Law of Contract*, 14th edn (London: Sweet & Maxwell, 2015)
Peel and Goudkamp, *Winfield and Jolowicz on Tort*, 19th edn (London: Sweet & Maxwell, 2014)
Perillo, 'Abuse of Rights: A Pervasive Legal Concept' (1995) 27 Pacific LJ 37
Perlman, 'Interference with Contract and Other Economic Expectancies: A Clash of Tort and Contract Doctrine' (1982) 49 U Chicago LR 61
Phang, 'Undue Influence Methodology, Sources and Linkages' [1995] JBL 552
Phillips, 'Protecting Those in a Disadvantageous Negotiating Position' (2010) 45 Wake Forest LR 837
Price, 'Fairly Bland: An Alternative View of a Supposed New "Death Ethic" and the BMA Guidelines' (2001) 21 LS 618
Price, 'What Shape to Euthanasia After Bland?' (2009) 125 LQR 142
Reath, 'Legislating the Moral Law' (1994) 28 Nous 435
Reed, 'Duress and Normative Moral Excuse', in Reed et al. (eds), *General Defences in Criminal Law* (Farnham: Ashgate, 2014)
Reid, 'The Doctrine of Abuse of Rights' (2004) Electronic Journal of Comparative Law

Robert and Cureton, 'Kant's Moral Philosophy' in Zalta (ed) *Stanford Encyclopedia of Philosophy* (Stanford, PA: Stanford University, 2016)
Robinson, 'Criminal Law Defenses: A Systematic Analysis' (1982) 82 Columbia LR 199
Rogers, 'Necessity, Private Defence and the Killing of Mary' [2001] Crim LR 515
Rousseau, The Social Contract (1762)
Sales, 'The Tort of Conspiracy and Civil Secondary Liability' [1990] Cambridge LJ 491
Sales and Stilitz, 'Intentional Infliction of Harm by Unlawful Means' (1999) 115 LQR 411
Sappideen and Vines (eds), *Fleming's* The Law of Torts, 10th edn (Pyrmont NSW: Thomson Reuters, 2011)
Schauer, 'Can Rights Be Abused?' (1981) 31 Philosophical Quarterly 225
Scheffler (ed), *Consequentialism and Its Critics* (Oxford: Oxford University Press, 1988)
Schopp, *Justification Defenses and Just Convictions* (Cambridge: Cambridge University Press, 1998)
Shaw, 'Sterilisation of Mentally Handicapped People' (1990) 53 MLR 91
Simester, 'On Justifications and Excuses', in Zedner and Roberts (eds), *Principles and Values in Criminal Law and Criminal Justice* (Oxford: Oxford University Press, 2012)
Simester et al., *Simester and Sullivan's Criminal Law: Theory and Doctrine*, 5th edn (Oxford: Hart, 2013)
Simon, 'Exploring the Intricacies of the Lesser Evils Defense' (2005) 24 Law & Phil 645
Simpson, 'Innovation in Nineteenth Century Contract Law' (1975) 91 LQR 247
Simpson, *Cannibalism and the Common Law* (London: Hambledon Press, 1994)
Sindone, 'The Doctrine of Economic Duress' (1996) 14 Australian Bar Rev 34 & 114
Smart and Williams, *Utilitarianism: For and Against* (Cambridge: Cambridge University Press, 1973)
Smith, J C, 'Civil Law Concepts in the Criminal Law' (1972) 31 Cambridge LJ 197
Smith, J C, *Justification and Excuse in the Criminal Law* (London: Stevens & Sons, 1989)
Smith, J C, 'Commentary' [1997] Crim LR 497
Smith, J C, 'Individual Capacities and Criminal Liability' (1998) 6 Medical LR 138
Smith, J C, 'Commentary' [2000] Crim LR 109
Smith, K J M, 'Must Heroes Behave Heroically?' [1989] Crim LR 622
Smith, K J M, 'Duress and Steadfastness: In Pursuit of the Unintelligible' [1999] Crim LR 363
Smith, S, 'In Defence of Substantive Unfairness' (1996) 112 LQR 138
Smith, S, 'Contracting Under Pressure: A Theory of Duress' (1997) 56 Cambridge LJ 343
Smith, S, *Contract Theory* (Oxford: Clarendon Press, 2004)
Spark, *Vitiation of Contracts* (Cambridge: Cambridge University Press, 2013)
Stark, 'Necessity and *Nicklinson*' [2013] Crim LR 949
Stephen, *Liberty, Equality, Fraternity* (London: Smith, Elder & Co, 1873)
Stephen, *A Digest of the Criminal Law* (London: Macmillan & Co, 1st edn 1877, 4th edn 1887)
Stephen, *A History of the Criminal Law of England*, vol 2 (London: Macmillan & Co, 1883)
Stevens, 'Why Do Agents Drop Out?' [2005] LMCLQ 101
Stevens, *Tort and Rights* (Oxford: Oxford University Press, 2007)
Stewart, 'Economic Duress – Legal Regulation of Commercial Pressure' (1984) 14 Melbourne U LR 410
Sugarman, 'The Necessity Defence and the Failure of Tort Theory' (2005) 5(2) Issues in Legal Scholarship
Sullivan, 'Making Excuses', in Simester and Smith (eds), *Harm and Culpability* (Oxford: Clarendon Press, 1996)

Sullivan, 'Is Criminal Law Possible?' (2001) 22 OJLS 747
Sussmann, 'The Defence of Private Necessity and the Problem of Compensation' (1967) 2 Ottawa LR 184
Swan and Adamski, *Canadian Contract Law*, 3rd edn (Markham, Ontario: LexisNexis, 2012)
Tadros, *Criminal Responsibility* (Oxford: Oxford University Press, 2007)
Taggart, Private Property and Abuse of Rights in Victorian England (Oxford: Oxford University Press, 2002)
Tamblyn, 'The Duty to Help the World's Poor' (2012) 23 King's Law Journal 312
Tamblyn, 'Lawful Act Conspiracy: Malice and Abuse of Rights' [2013] SJLS 158
Tamblyn, *Hong Kong Contract Law* (Hong Kong: Rights Press, 2014)
Tamblyn, 'Why Is Killing Morally Wrong?' (2014) 25 King's LJ 454
Tamblyn, 'Unjust Enrichment, Leapfrogging and a Defence of Entitlement' [2014] HKLJ 551
Tamblyn, 'Necessity and Murder' (2015) 79 Journal of Criminal Law 46
Tamblyn, 'Separating Rescission and Restitution' (2016) 33 J Contract Law 135
Teichman, *Pacifism and the Just War* (Oxford: Basil Blackwell, 1986)
Tettenborn, *Law of Restitution in England and Ireland*, 3rd edn (London: Cavendish, 2002)
Thal, 'The Inequality of Bargaining Power Doctrine' (1988) 8 OJLS 17
Thomson, 'Redrawing the Landscape of the Economic Wrongs' [2008] Edin LR 267
Tierney, *The Idea of Natural Rights* (Grand Rapids, MI: William B Eerdmans Publishing Co, 1997)
Tilbury, 'Money Remedies for Breach of Contract in Hong Kong', in Chen-Wishart and Ong (eds), *Studies in the Contract Laws of Asia* (Oxford: Oxford University Press, 2016)
Tiplady, 'The Judicial Control of Contractual Unfairness' (1983) 46 MLR 601
Trebilcock, 'The Doctrine of Inequality of Bargaining Power' (1976) 26 U Toronto LJ 359
Tur, 'Legislative Technique and Human Rights: The Sad Case of Assisted Suicide' [2003] Crim LR 3
Uniacke, *Permissible Killing* (Cambridge: Cambridge University Press, 1994)
Uniacke, 'Was Mary's Death Murder?' (2001) 9 Medical LR 208
Virgo, 'Demolishing the Pyramid – Presence of Basis and Risk-Taking in the Law of Unjust Enrichment', in Robertson and Tang (eds), *The Goals of Private Law* (Oxford: Hart, 2009)
Virgo, 'We Do This in the Criminal Law and That in the Law of Tort: A New Fusion Debate', in Pitel, Neyers and Chamberlain (eds), *Tort Law: Challenging Orthodoxy* (Oxford: Hart, 2013)
Virgo, *The Principles of the Law of Restitution*, 3rd edn (Oxford: Oxford University Press, 2015)
Virgo, 'Justifying Necessity as a Defence in Tort Law', in Dyson, Goudkamp and Wilmot-Smith (eds), *Defences in Tort Law* (Oxford: Hart, 2015)
Virgo and Buchanan, 'Duress and Mental Abnormality' [1999] Crim LR 517
von Hirsch and Jareborg, 'Gauging Criminal Harms: A Living Standard Analysis' (1991) 11 OJLS 1
Waddams, 'Unconscionability in Contracts' (1976) 39 MLR 369
Walters, 'Murder Under Duress and Judicial Decision-making in the House of Lords' (1988) 8 LS 61
Walton, 'Motive as an Element in Torts in the Common and in the Civil Law' (1908) 22 Harv LR 501
Wasik, 'Duress and Criminal Responsibility' [1977] Crim LR 453
Watt, 'Conjoined Twins: Separation as Mutilation' (2001) 9 Medical LR 237
Webb, *Reason and Restitution* (Oxford: Oxford University Press, 2016)
Wedderburn, 'Intimidation and the Right to Strike' (1964) 27 MLR 257

Weinrib, 'Two Conceptions of Remedies' in Rickett (ed), *Justifying Private Law Remedies* (Oxford: Hart, 2008)
Weinrib, *The Idea of Private Law* (Oxford: Oxford University Press, 2012)
Weir, 'Chaos or Cosmos? *Rookes, Stratford* and the Economic Torts' [1964] Cambridge LJ 225
Weir, *Economic Torts* (Oxford: Clarendon Press, 1997)
Westen and Mangiafico, 'The Criminal Defense of Duress: A Justification, Not an Excuse – And Why It Matters' (2003) 6 Buffalo Crim LR 833
Williams, 'The Defence of Necessity' (1953) 6 CLP 216
Williams, 'The Theory of Excuses' [1982] Crim LR 732
Wilson, 'Is Life Sacred?' (1995) 17 J Social Welfare and Family Law 131
Wilson, 'The Filtering Role of Crisis in the Constitution of Criminal Excuses' (2004) 17 Can J L & Juris 387
Wilson, 'The Structure of Criminal Defences' [2005] Crim LR 108
Wilson, *Criminal Law*, 5th edn (Harlow: Pearson, 2014)
Winder, 'Undue Influence and Coercion' (1939) 3 MLR 97
Witting, *Street on Torts*, 14th edn (Oxford: Oxford University Press, 2015)
Wood, 'Humanity as End in Itself', in Guyer (ed), *Kant's Groundwork of the Metaphysics of Morals: Critical Essays* (Lanham, MD: Rowman & Littlefield, 1998)
Woolf, 'Judicial Review: A Possible Programme for Reform' [1992] PL 221
Yeo, 'Necessity Under the Griffith Code and the Common Law' (1991) 15 Criminal LJ 17
Yeo, 'Killing in Defence of Property' [2000] New LJ 730
Yeo, 'Challenging Moral Involuntariness as a Principle of Fundamental Justice' (2002) 28 Queens LJ 335

Index

Note: see country main entries for references to that country.

For Product Safety Concerns and Information please contact our EU representative GPSR@taylorandfrancis.com Taylor & Francis Verlag GmbH, Kaufingerstraße 24, 80331 München, Germany